Please turn the page for more . . .

THE
NEW
VICTORIANS

THE
NEW
VICTORIANS

A YOUNG

WOMAN'S

CHALLENGE

TO THE OLD

FEMINIST

ORDER

RENE DENFELD

WARNER BOOKS

A Time Warner Company

Warner Books Edition
Copyright © 1995 by Rene Denfeld
All rights reserved.

Warner Books, Inc., 1271 Avenue of the Americas, New York, NY 10020

Visit our Web site at
http://pathfinder.com/twep

Ⓦ A Time Warner Company

Printed in the United States of America

First Trade Printing: November 1996

10 9 8 7 6 5 4 3 2 1

Library of Congress Cataloging-in-Publication Data
Denfeld, Rene.
        The new Victorians : a young woman's challenge to the old feminist order / Rene Denfeld
                p.   cm.
        Includes index.
        ISBN 0-446-67239-4
                1. Feminist theory—United States.   2. Feminism—United States.
I. Title.
HQ1190.5.U6D46   1996   94-27201
305.42′0973—dc20   CIP

Book design by Giorgetta Bell McRee
Cover design by Krystyna Skalski
Cover photograph by Scott Teitter

CONTENTS

ACKNOWLEDGMENTS

First, let me give my heartfelt thanks to all the young women, too numerous to name here, who were willing to talk to me openly and honestly about their feelings regarding feminism. I would especially like to thank Caryn Brooks, Julie Shaw, Samantha Levine, Anne Greenwood, Jim Scoville, Lauren Gwin, and Jenn Stout for sharing their friends with me. Susan Stanley generously shared writing know-how, and Bill Donahue provided fine research assistance.

Richard Pine is the agent writers dream about. His assistant Lori Andiman offered strong advice and, on one memorable evening, strong drinks. My editor Jamie Raab was always available and immeasurably supportive.

Katherine Dunn helped me constantly along the way—from concept to proposal to finish. Without her this book wouldn't have happened. She has been an invaluable friend.

My deep thanks to Bill Redden, who spent tireless hours reading proofs, debating points and making suggestions.

Finally, I want to thank my family for their support, and my mother, for teaching me what feminism means.

This book is dedicated to my sister, Nichole Appleton, in the hope that there will be a women's movement for her in the future.

INTRODUCTION

I was born a year after the National Organization for Women was created in 1966, and I was a small child while many of the battles for women's rights were being fought. Like most women of my generation, I can not remember the time when abortion was illegal. I can not remember a time—though my mother tells me it is true—when women were expected to go to college to snag a husband, not to earn a degree, when working women were confined to "pink-collar" jobs such as waitressing, when reliable birth control was unavailable, and when women were kept ignorant about their bodies and their sexuality. It was a time that translated into simple and devastating scenarios: a young woman denied birth control and dying from a back-alley abortion, a woman graduating from college, only to find the path of higher learning led directly to the typing pool, a ten-year-old schoolgirl wishing she could take shop class with the boys, only to be herded into home ec to make Jell-O and practice silverware arrangements. It was a time when, it is difficult to believe, sexism was not considered a problem or even recognized as a word in the public vocabulary.

We have it much better now than our mothers ever did. Abortion was legalized in 1973. There was the long fight to pass the ERA, which may have failed but which firmly planted the notion of equal rights in the public mind. There was the creation of NOW and the

Women's Equity Action League in the 1960s, and the battles they won against sex discrimination in the workplace and schools. There was the women's health movement, the publication of *Our Bodies, Ourselves*, the introduction of rape shield laws (which limit admissibility of a victim's sexual history), the founding of battered women's shelters, and the emergence of women in business, law, and politics. There were Betty Friedan, Gloria Steinem, Bella Abzug, Germaine Greer, Kate Millet, and many others. It was the second wave of feminism, and its impact on women's futures was profound.

For women of my generation, feminism is our birthright. While sexism may still permeate society, we know what it is to live without excessive confinement. We are the first generation to grow up expecting equal opportunity and equal education, as well as the freedom to express our sexuality. We are the first to assume what feminists had to force society to accept against its deeply ingrained prejudice: that we are the equals of any man. This belief may translate into the pursuit of a career or it may mean demanding respect for raising children—women of my generation believe in the right to choose.

Given, then, this huge debt we owe feminism, why do so many women my age refuse to join the women's movement? Why do we adamantly reject the feminist label?

While numerous polls show that American women of all ages overwhelmingly support feminist ideals, these polls also show that they largely avoid calling themselves feminists and in many ways have abandoned the movement—even though most feel there is still work to be done. A 1989 *Time*/CNN survey reported that a majority of women believed feminism had advanced women's rights but that only 33 percent considered themselves feminists. A whopping 76 percent polled said they paid little or no attention to the women's movement.[1] Another *Time* poll in 1992 found that while 57 percent of American women believed there was still a need for a strong women's movement, only 39 percent believed the movement at that time reflected the views of most women—and only 29 percent considered themselves feminists.[2] For younger women, even these numbers may be high. *In View*, a magazine for college students, conducted a survey in 1989 of over five hundred female undergraduates. While 90 percent agreed that sexism existed and 84 percent agreed women should have access to birth control, only 16 *percent* of women from my generation said they were feminists.[3]

This trend has not gone unnoticed by the women's movement or by the media. From the best-selling book *Backlash: The Undeclared War Against American Women* by Susan Faludi, to columnist Linda Ellerbee, to newspaper and magazine articles, the alienation of otherwise-feminist-thinking women from the movement has sparked debate.

The most fashionable argument for women's rejection of feminism is Susan Faludi's "backlash" theory. The basic idea behind the backlash concept—that various forces in culture are working to undermine feminism—has floated around the women's movement for nearly two decades ("Academia: Here Comes the Backlash," announced a September 1975 review of three books in *Ms.* magazine), but Faludi's modern rendition is the first time the idea has gained widespread credence. There is a likely explanation for its sudden currency. While numerous antifeminist articles and books appeared in the 1970s—many so Neanderthal that today's criticisms sound like compliments—the women's movement was healthy. Women were proud to call themselves feminists.

Today they are not.

"Seventy-two percent of young women say they don't consider themselves feminists. Why not?" posed the March 1990 issue of *Seventeen* magazine. The answer was quick in coming "Linda Ellerbee says it's because they don't know what it means, or what's at stake." The article by Ellerbee, a nationally syndicated columnist, was titled "The Feminist Mistake." In a patronizing and often vicious tone, Ellerbee tears into young women who would hesitate to call themselves feminists. "*Feminism*. There, I've said it. Try not to throw up. I know you don't like the word, but believe me, that's only because you've been misinformed about what it means. In fact, you've been misinformed about a lot of things." Ellerbee doesn't say where this misinformation is coming from. She says only that "somebody wants you to find feminism unattractive. And that somebody has been very busy."

Susan Faludi, however, makes it clear just who that somebody is. "The backlash's public agenda has been framed and promoted by men," Faludi writes in *Backlash*, ". . . men at the helm in the media, business, and politics." According to her book, such things as TV sitcoms (positive portrayals of nonworking mothers) and fashion (the revived popularity of lacy lingerie) are part of a devious male-orchestrated campaign to portray feminism as bad while extolling the virtues of hearth, home-cooked meals, and oppressive ideals of beauty.

The majority of women aren't buying this—in a 1989 *New York Times* poll, for instance, only 28 percent of the women queried believed that men were "trying to take away the gains made by women over the past 20 years"[4]—but Faludi has an explanation. "The force and furor of the backlash churn beneath the surface, largely invisible to the public eye," she writes. And though this conspiracy against feminism is so insidious that most women don't even know it's happening, its impact has been profound: "The backlash did manage to infiltrate the thoughts of women, broadcasting on these private channels its sound waves of shame and reproach."

Young women, supposedly, have tuned into Channel Backlash, and for that reason we hesitate to call ourselves feminists.

For feminist commentators such as Ellerbee and Faludi, blaming an amorphous and all-powerful cultural conspiracy for women's distaste for the feminist label is convenient as well as comforting. But it is wrong. For all the moronic depictions of women in popular culture, there are countless other role models—from Supreme Court Justice Ruth Bader Ginsburg to the rap group Salt n' Pepa—who portray independent women in a positive light. Besides, women of my generation are not stupid enough to take detergent commercials literally or to be led like sheep by hidden meanings in underwear fashions. Nor are we the brain-dead dupes of a nameless and yet very busy "somebody." If this was the case, then we would reject feminist *beliefs* as well as the feminist label—which we have not done.

As a 1986 survey of over ten thousand young adults by the U.S. Department of Education showed, both women and men of my generation wholeheartedly believe in women's rights. Of women and men who were attending high school six years prior to the survey (and were at the time of the survey working, raising families, and going to college), 98 percent of each sex believed "a woman should have exactly the same educational opportunities as a man," 90 percent of the men and 98 percent of the women agreed that "women should be paid the same money if they do the same work," and 91 percent of the men and 96 percent of the women believed that "women should be considered as seriously as men for jobs as executives or politicians."[5] And when it comes to staying home and raising the kids, both sexes say they would like the opportunity. A 1990 *Time* poll of young women and men eighteen to twenty-four found that 66 percent of the women and 48 percent of the men were interested in a full-time parenting job if given the option.[6] No one would have even thought to ask men this question in the early sixties.

That my generation has taken the women's movement to heart is illustrated by these numbers. We don't believe in sexual inequality, and we don't believe in confining ourselves—or one another—to traditional sex roles. Simply put, we are feminists—in action, if not name.

Then why do we shirk the label? "Feminism is a movement where women get more radical as they get older," was NOW president Patricia Ireland's evasive answer in the December 4, 1989, issue of *Time* magazine. If that's the case, then why do polls show that younger women hold stronger feminist beliefs than older generations? And why were more women of older generations involved in the movement during the 1970s, when they were young, instead of now, when they should be more radical?

The answer lies in the one pressing question that many commentators avoid examining: What exactly does today's women's movement stand for? Most appear to believe the movement hasn't changed since the early seventies. Faludi, for example, doesn't even mention the names of many of today's feminist leaders in *Backlash*, and she spends no time exploring the causes they espouse. Ellerbee, in a statement that is either disingenuous or naïve, simply writes, "Feminism means you believe in equality between men and women. Justice. Equal justice for all. *And that's all it means*."

If only it were true.

The fact is that feminism has changed—dramatically. While there are some feminists still in touch with most women's concerns, the movement for the most part has taken a radical change in direction. It has become bogged down in an extremist moral and spiritual crusade that has little to do with women's lives. It has climbed out on a limb of academic theory that is all but inaccessible to the uninitiated. It has lost contact with the ideas that sparked the second wave—individual empowerment and political activism—and has substituted a worldview that speaks to the very few, while alienating the many. For women of my generation, feminism has become as confining as what it pretends to combat.

There are, in essence, two different women's movements alive today. One is a cultural movement, reflected in women's magazines such as *Glamour* ("Your Ob-Gyn Checkup: Read This Before You Go" and "Supreme Court Justice Ruth Bader Ginsburg Talks About Women, Men and Work," from the October 1993 issue) and expressed in the independent actions of thousands of feminist-thinking women who fight for equality in their lives—such as Shannon Faulkner, the courageous young woman who battled for her right to attend the Citadel, an all-male military school, and Dallas Malloy, the fierce young female amateur boxer who fought in court for the right of women to fight in the ring. But this movement lives primarily in the hearts and minds of women: It isn't organized, and most of its members do not call themselves feminists. That's because that word refers to the *other* women's movement—the organized, ideological form of feminism represented by groups such as NOW, women's studies courses, and feminist leaders. It is this organized women's movement—which defines the feminist label—that is the focus of this book.

"Substitute the term 'feminism' for 'women's movement' in public-opinion polls and support plummets," writes Nina J. Easton in the February 2, 1992, *Los Angeles Times Magazine* article entitled "I'm Not a Feminist But . . ." "To many, the term *feminist* still evokes images of hairy-legged, humorless extremists who view men as the enemy. In an effort to combat those stereotypes, many feminist leaders have taken aim—at conservatives, at the media, at political leaders, at almost everyone but themselves. By lashing out, they have managed to underscore the militant image that alienated so many Middle American women in the first place."

Easton is right. The term *feminist* does evoke images of extremists, but this may be less a holdover of "hairy-legged" antifeminist perceptions from the 1970s than a message that something is seriously amiss today. In 1986, for example, 56 percent of American women considered themselves feminists—a number that was to drop to 29 percent by 1992.[7]

A young woman interested in joining the feminist movement is left in an odd position. Looking under "Feminism" in the phone book certainly won't take her far. Major organizations such as NOW offer little outreach, even on college campuses. Young women are far more likely to encounter organized feminism by taking an introductory women's studies course, attending rallies on campuses, picking up the latest issue of Ms. magazine, reading newspaper accounts, and browsing in the feminist literature section of bookstores.

The importance of women's studies classes, feminist literature, and local activist groups in shaping women's opinions of feminism cannot be overemphasized. They are not only intake mechanisms that define feminism for thousands of potential activists; they define it for the rest of the movement, as well. And this is where young women encounter a new feminist vanguard.

Widely recognized feminist leaders such as Betty Friedan, who in the late 1960s and early 1970s articulated the goals and the spirit of the movement, have been left by the roadside. Though Friedan is still active, her moderate stance, combined with her willingness to criticize certain aspects of current feminism, has caused her to be ostracized by the movement. When thousands marched in an April 1992 abortion rights rally in Washington, D.C., Friedan was conspicuously absent—because she hadn't been invited.[8] This slight reflects the depth of anti-Friedan sentiments in the movement. In *Backlash*, Faludi terms Friedan's 1981 book, *The Second Stage*, the "tantrums of a fallen leader" because the cofounder of NOW dared to criticize some leading feminist trends. Tellingly, Faludi neglects to name much of what Friedan found to criticize. These days, Friedan concentrates on issues facing older women. Her book on aging, *The Fountain of Age*, was published in 1993.

Other early feminist leaders also seem to be directing their energies toward older women. Germaine Greer's 1992 book, *The Change: Women, Aging and the Menopause*, examines cultural attitudes surrounding menopause, and Gloria Steinem's 1992 book, *Revolution from Within: A Book of Self-Esteem*, concentrates on inner health and spirituality—issues that women my age tend to see as secondary to economic and political inequality. This was demonstrated at a 1993 reading given by Steinem to promote the paperback edition of her book. The crowd was overwhelmingly white, in their late thirties and older, and decidedly middle-class to affluent. Women who are in the midst of the struggle to balance work, families, and relationships while barely avoiding poverty find Steinem's happy pursuit of her inner child disconcerting. Many women are more worried about caring for their actual children first.

While a few—particularly Steinem—have stayed in the media spotlight, feminist leaders of the seventies have passed the torch. Articulating the goals and spirit of the movement in their place are a new crop of feminist leaders. These feminists, to put it mildly, are of a much different school of thought from that of Friedan and others who are now considered too moderate.

There is Robin Morgan, a sixties activist who once called for a military-style training camp where women would learn how to use firearms, poisons, and bugging equipment ("I myself do not believe men as a class will cede their vast power for the mere asking," she wrote then[9]). Today she condemns sexual freedoms as antifeminist. Morgan, an author who carries great weight in the movement, retired as the editor of *Ms.* in 1993.

There is Catharine MacKinnon, a feminist lawyer and activist who questions whether consensual sex between women and men can even exist. "Compare victims' reports of rape with women's reports of sex. They look a lot alike," she expounds in *Toward a Feminist Theory of the State.* Yet MacKinnon often appears in the media as a feminist spokesperson—including TV talk shows such as *Today* and *Donahue*—and is considered a leader in both feminist circles and law. As a flattering October 6, 1991, cover story in the *New York Times Magazine* put it, MacKinnon is "the law's most prominent feminist legal theorist."

There is Andrea Dworkin, the antipornography activist, who writes, "Physically, the woman in intercourse is a space inhabited, a literal territory occupied literally: occupied even if there has been no resistance, no force; even if the occupied person said, yes please, yes hurry, yes more.[10] Dworkin's view that all sex is rape—and that all men are potential rapists—is considered gospel by many in the movement, cited reverently in many an article and book, and taught to women's studies students as mainstream feminism. Even Gloria Steinem recommends Dworkin heartily in *Revolution from Within.*

There are Mary Daly and other feminist spiritualists, who assert that feminists should practice religions based on female deities. These spiritualists have gained high visibility and influence on campuses and in women's organizations, and a trip through the feminist section of most bookstores will uncover dozens of books dedicated to their theology, from *The Language of the Goddess* by Marija Gimbutas to *Dreaming the Dark: Magic, Sex, and Politics* by a woman who calls herself Starhawk.

There is Susan Faludi, who attacks everyone from "improper" female movie producers to dissenting feminists as part of her theory of an all-encompassing backlash against womankind, and there is

Naomi Wolf. Wolf became a spokesperson for the movement with her best-selling 1991 book, *The Beauty Myth*. While that book echoed Faludi's theme that women are the hapless victims of men, Wolf dramatically changed her stance with her 1993 book, *Fire with Fire: The New Female Power and How It Will Change the 21st Century*, coming out strongly against what she terms "victim feminism" and preaching a more inclusive, empowering brand of equality-based feminism.

And there are a slew of other feminist leaders, from those who would have us believe heterosexuality is the root of all oppression (Adrienne Rich), to those who warn that meat-eating is a masculine evil (Carol Adams), to those who promote sexist stereotypes of women as the gentler sex (Carol Gilligan), to those who dismiss lobbying for legislation as virtually pointless (Patricia Ireland). All of these feminists, along with others who espouse equally, if not more, extremist positions, have gained powerful positions as theorists, spokespersons, and leaders in the movement.

Some women familiar with the feminism of the seventies might be under the impression that these activists and writers are simply the movement's radical segment. For women who are no longer active in the movement but still associate feminism with Friedan and Greer, they are. But for women who were children—or not even born— when Friedan published *The Feminine Mystique* in 1963, the early leaders of the second wave of feminism are often little more than footnotes. For us, the first encounter with feminist thought is likely to be the work of these so-called radicals—and no wonder. They have taken over the voice of feminism. "Only five years ago Dworkin and MacKinnon were leaders of a feminist fringe," wrote feminist author Wendy Kaminer for the October 1993 *Atlantic Monthly*. Today, however, "they're leaders in the feminist mainstream."

Kaminer is right. In the mid-eighties, activists such as Dworkin, though influential, were still considered part of the feminist fringe. But today, owing in part to an exclusion by the feminist vanguard of more moderate leaders, their voices dominate the movement. From campuses to local chapters of NOW, a woman encountering organized feminism will find that these activists are held up and even revered as leaders.

This is clear in introductory-level women's studies classes, one place that young women often go to learn about feminism. In collecting women's studies syllabi for this book, I was dismayed, but not surprised, to see how frequently Dworkin, MacKinnon, Daly, and Adrienne Rich are taught—often with little or nothing else offered to counter their views—and how rarely the courses dealt with such basic concerns as economic equality. And over and over again, I heard the stories: One woman told of being required to attend a speech by Andrea Dworkin for her women's studies class. Upset by that writer's virulent attack on men and sex, she tentatively questioned Dworkin's views in class, only to be bitterly condemned as antifeminist and accused of endorsing rape. Young women walk away from the organized women's movement thinking that feminism means agreeing with the extremist ideas espoused by these leaders and that disagreeing with them—no matter how much one supports equality—means you can't call yourself a feminist. They are told in no uncertain terms that only the organization's version of feminism is valid.

In the name of feminism, these extremists have embarked on a moral and spiritual crusade that would take us back to a time worse than our mother's day—back to the nineteenth-century values of sexual morality, spiritual purity, and political helplessness. Through a combination of influential voices and unquestioned causes, current feminism would create the very same morally pure yet helplessly martyred role that women suffered from a century ago.

From the mid-1800s to the early 1900s, women were held in place by an odd mixture of societal mores. The very virtues that the Victorians praised in a woman—moral refinement, chastity, sexlessness, and spiritual purity—were her damnation. Women were seen as paragons of virtue, and a woman's place was to offer spiritual guidance to men by providing a shining example. Contact with such sinful things as voting, free speech, sexual freedoms, and political power could only harm their delicate and lovingly pure nature. Instead, a woman's place was in the home and her voice in society was limited to issues of morality, such as condemning the evils of prostitution or drink.

It is said that Victorians placed women on a pedestal. They did—in fiction. In reality, this pedestal was a prison for the many middle-to upper-class women taught to revel in it: a dainty life indoors, a worship of illness, and an utter lack of recourse when abused by men. And this pedestal was a crushing weight to the lower-class working women who were most harmed by moral crusades such as those against prostitution, which were consistently used to take legal rights away from poor women. As the moral saviors of humanity, women were held to a much higher standard than men—and punished when they could not achieve it.

In pushing their varied causes, today's feminists promote a similar vision of womanhood. Discussing the dramatic redefinitions of rape by current feminists, journalist Stephanie Gutmann wrote for the July 1990 *Reason* magazine: "An almost Victorian denial of complicity—of woman's emotional stake in the sexual relationship—is a big feature of the date rape *oeuvre*. Man is entirely predatory; woman is entirely passive, a hapless victim, there by accident." Author Cathy Young, looking at similar sweeping definitions of sexual harassment, questioned this victim-centered view in the January 25, 1993, *New York Forum*: "This new, hypersensitive woman is remarkably similar to the Victorian lady fainting at any mention of sex. . . . Once upon a time, this view of women as dainty creatures with chaste ears was considered *anti-feminist*."

Today it is not—at least not by feminist leaders. Today's feminists *are* remarkably similar to Victorians in significant ways, and not only in their vision of sexuality. This is clear through an examination of several different causes and trends in today's movement that, if anything, are a complete reversal of the movement's progress during the seventies.

This is the New Victorianism. And this is why women of my generation are abandoning the women's movement.

One of the most powerful trends in New Victorianism is what can be called the feminist antiphallic campaign. Today's feminists have created an overarching theory that blames male sexuality for the world's woes. In short, they believe that heterosexual intercourse—as an inherently invasive and oppressive act—is the root cause of all oppression. This theory is espoused by such influential feminist writers as Adrienne Rich and Cheryl Clarke, taught to women's studies students, and promoted in organizations such as local chapters of NOW. It is behind much of the antimale sentiment in the movement, and at its logical end it calls for separatism—the cessation of all intercourse between women and men, whether social or sexual. By naming the "institution" of heterosexuality as oppressive, current feminists promote the Victorian view that relationships between the sexes are by nature unequal and will always remain so.

In light of the evils of heterosexual sex, a powerful school of feminist thought teaches that only lesbian relationships are acceptable for enlightened feminists. This topic is often shrouded in silence because feminist leaders consistently condemn as homophobic those who would discuss it. But it is true in groups such as NOW, and it is also true in women's studies literature and magazines. The June/July 1991 San Francisco NOW *Times* summed up this cause succinctly: "Embracing lesbianism, or lesbian-feminist theory, is pivotal to the feminist movement, which works to change society through the elimination of gender-defined roles . . . heterosexism and male supremacy reinforce one another in maintaining our oppression. Both must be eliminated for any woman to be free."

This antimale sentiment has led to what amounts to victim mythology, a set of beliefs that promote women as the helpless victims of masculine oppression. This bleak and uninviting—certainly not empowering—view of the sexes has crept into much feminist activism and theory. It is the basis of Faludi's thesis, when she names nearly every aspect of culture as part of an ambiguous yet devastatingly orchestrated war against women—a war in which men have consistently won and, since they are so conniving, will probably always win. And it has reached its apex in today's antirape movement.

Using a handful of extreme statistics from flawed surveys, today's feminists are pushing the idea that men are constantly out to rape women—and that women will constantly be raped. Sexual assault has been redefined to include whistling, touching, and sexual humor. "Other forms of sexual assault include . . . unwanted sexual comments, jokes, and gestures," declares just one among numerous college acquaintance rape pamphlets.[11] Even consensual sex has come to be considered rape, as it was in the nineteenth century. "Perhaps the wrong of rape has proven so difficult to articulate because the unquestionable starting point has been that rape is definable as distinct from intercourse," students attending "A History of Feminist Thought" at Duke University learn from an essay by Catharine MacKinnon, "when for women it is difficult to distinguish them under conditions of male dominance."[12]

Fitting hand in glove with this view is the feminist fight against pornography. Stamping out sexually oriented expression is considered a top priority for many of today's feminists. This goal is enthusiastically supported by leaders such as Robin Morgan and given mainstream credibility by others such as Gloria Steinem. It has become an issue for organizations such as NOW, and the fight extends to other countries, including England and Germany. Young women, particularly on campuses, are told that to be a good feminist they must support the censorship of all varieties of sexual material—from *Playboy* to even lesbian erotic literature—because such material will inevitably cause violence against women. By blaming sexual material for sexual violence, current feminists invoke the Victorian-era belief that sexuality is inherently evil and any display of it must be squashed.

The antiphallic campaign's attack on heterosexuality, victim mythology's sweeping redefinitions of rape, and the effort to censor sexual material combine to create a repressive sexual morality that judges women's personal lives according to strict Victorianesque standards. We are told what is proper for us to read, whom we can sleep with, and even when we are violated. While some aspects of current feminism have arisen out of a desire to apply a quick fix to complex problems—such as believing that banning sexual material will stop rape, though rape existed long before *Playboy*—at their heart these are simply recycled old morals that preach shame and repression. Introductory women's studies students at the University of Utah, for example, are told that enjoying sex is shameful: "Internalizing the devaluation of self is fundamental in being the screwed one, the slut, the whore, celebrating it, not rebelling one bit, female complicity does not even have the dignity or the insight of world-class misogyny. . . ."[13] Yes, it is the twentieth century, and the writer is feminist leader Andrea Dworkin. And it would seem that, once again, women who would dare enjoy sex are no more than complicit whores and sluts.

The feminist sexual-purity crusades would have appalled our mothers as they fought for liberation in the sixties and seventies. It appalls their daughters, as well.

But these are not the only causes in feminism to ape the moral order of the nineteenth century. A new focus on spiritual and moral purity has pervaded the feminist movement. Major feminist schools of thought extol an ideal of womanhood that rivals the best efforts of the Victorians to restrict our public role to nothing more than that of the shining example.

One of these is the growing feminist infatuation with goddess worship. Extrapolating freely from a few prehistoric artifacts, New Victorians have created a romanticized historical period where women not only ruled societies but were revered as deities. Ignoring all evidence that life at the time was not exactly Disneyland, feminists teach that these matriarchies were utopias. "Life was celebrated in all rituals, there were no blood sacrifices, or violence. Cultures were nurturing, non-violent, dependent upon each other and therefore respectful of each other's needs," asserts a NOW flyer entitled "Goddess cultural beliefs," which was handed out to women at a 1993 International Women's Day conference. "There were no weapons of violence, no fortifications surrounding goddess communities and no warfare." Only by returning to the worship of the goddess, this school of thought contends, can women find a spiritual balance and truly become feminists.

Goddess worship focuses on modern interpretations of witchcraft and magic, resulting in the popularity of all-women "covens," special magical ceremonies for different phases of the moon, casting spells, and chanting. Because it is often seen as just another form of New Age spirituality, many commentators offhandedly dismiss this religion. Yet young women encounter it constantly, from campuses, to feminist magazines, to major organizations. Young women attending women's studies courses are often assigned material by leading feminist spiritualist Mary Daly, whose creative use of language leads to convoluted prose such this example from *Gyn/Ecology: The Metaethics of Radical Feminism:* "This Spinster-Spooking is also re-calling/re-membering/re-claiming our Witches' power to cast spells, to charm, to overcome prestige with prestidigitation, to cast glamours, to employ occult grammar, to enthrall, to bewitch." This is a required text for students attending "The Roots of Feminism" at Harvard.

The emphasis on promoting matriarchal religious beliefs has led to the increasing popularity of a related feminist trend: feminism as a utopian vision. This vision places blame for all problems in the world—from violence to the shrinking ozone layer—on the "patriarchy," a sweeping view of culture that labels all male-created systems as evil. The key to women's liberation is said to lie in overthrowing these systems and substituting an ill-defined, feminist-inspired matriarchy. Given that such things as free markets, capitalism, democracy, education, all forms of hierarchy, meat-eating, and objective thinking have all been termed by current feminists as corrupt aspects of the patriarchal culture, this vision is absurdly unattainable. Yet it is has become a litmus test for young feminists—anyone who would work within the patriarchal system need not apply.

The feminist utopian vision is based on the belief that women are morally, ethically, and spiritually different from men—and, by extension, superior to them. From leading authors such as Carol Gilligan, who makes sweeping claims that women have a different "moral" voice from men, one that makes us less violent and more caring, to feminist commentators in the 1992 elections who were often far more critical of female candidates than male (a situation that analysts believe contributed to Geraldine Ferraro's defeat in New York's Democratic U.S. Senate primaries), this view permeates feminist thought. In pushing this vision, feminists have abandoned the idea that women and men should be treated equally, endorsing the Victorian view of women as the guardians of morality, alone responsible for making the world a more decent place.

Another component of the feminist moral pedestal is what can be termed the "passive voice." Following goddess worship and strictures against working within the "patriarchy," today's feminists have changed the focus from political reform to that of advocating an entirely passive means of enacting change. From NOW's refusal to work within the system to Steinem's claims that women should use meditation to gain equality, this ineffectiveness has infected feminist activism. Women joining feminist organizations often find more energy is directed toward sensitivity training, consciousness-raising, and group prayers than to pursing specific goals. The adoption of a cosmic feminist "transformative" philosophy has seen the movement diversified into many areas that have nothing to do with women's rights, such as "ecofeminism." And while widely accepted feminist literature easily identifies the enemy—from the backlash to the patriarchy—the all-powerful nature of the conspiracy we face leaves us no effective response. Instead, feminist writers offer us suggestions that tend to be vague, inner-directed, or just plain silly. "*Transformation* is necessary to save ourselves, sentient life on the planet, the biosphere itself," Robin Morgan writes in her 1989 book, *The Demon Lover: On the Sexuality of Terrorism.* "Transformation requires more than mere seeing; it requires all forms of perception, including remembering, imagining, intuiting, hallucinating, dreaming, and empathizing." If Morgan thinks that hallucinating and dreaming are going to help women, she must be practicing what she preaches.

But for all their inane vagueness, these feminist spiritual beliefs are ingrained in the places young women encounter feminism. At Indiana University at Bloomington, for example, students curious about the movement might sign up for "Women in Culture: Introduction to Women's Studies." They are assigned the work of feminist spiritualists

Starhawk and Merlin Stone. "Witchcraft as Goddess Religion" by Starhawk is popular in women's studies departments. "My own covens are based on the Faery Tradition, which goes back to the Little People of Stone Age Britain, but we believe in creating our own rituals, which reflect our needs and insights of today," she writes.

It's easy to treat this focus on hocus-pocus lightly, but it doesn't stop women of my generation from dismissing outright the feminist title. Together, Goddess worship with its ahistorical premise and New Age trappings; the feminist utopian vision, with its restriction of women to exacting moral roles; and the passive voice's promotion of inertia trumpeted as transformation have changed the feminist agenda from a pursuit for social equality to the preaching of an orthodoxy that alienates most young women. The message they give us is that feminism is no longer concerned with women's rights. Instead, feminism would have us accept a doctrine that dictates the most personal aspects of our lives—including religious, spiritual, and moral beliefs—while limiting our actions to ineffective romantic tripe.

From male bashing to goddess worship, each leading feminist cause today alienates women. Many heterosexual women—as well as gay— balk at the adoption of lesbianism as a purely political action, large numbers of liberal women are turned off by the campaign to censor sexual material, and many religious women find the conversation tactics of the feminist spiritualists appalling. All of these trends have distanced huge blocs of potential activists from the movement. Independently, each do enough damage to the movement.

Combined, they have almost killed feminism. It is their collective force that has redefined the meaning of feminism for women of all ages. And it is their sum total that has caused women of my generation to abandon the movement, leaving it without troops and without a future.

This is the danger of New Victorianism. This feminist promotion of repressive sexual morality and spiritual passivity promulgates the vision of an ideal woman, sexually pure and helpless yet somehow morally superior to men and all male-influenced institutions. The leading causes in feminism today are all morally driven. The influential voices are entirely passive, speaking always in the language of victim mythology or inner transformation.

And so the women's movement has come to duplicate Victorianism in all its repressive glory: the woman revered on the pedestal,

charged with keeping society's moral order yet politically powerless—
and perpetually martyred.

New Victorianism is not some sort of sinister conspiracy. Leading
feminists didn't sit down at a table and decide, cackling, to create a
movement geared toward promoting new versions of nineteenth-
century ideals. Each of these contributing causes—often born out of
different segments of the movement—gained popularity in the 1980s
due to several factors. The failure to pass the ERA left many feminists
burned out with regard to political activism and eager to find new
goals to take its place, something moral crusades against men,
pornography, and sex promised to do. The defeat also saw many
mainstream women abandon the movement, leaving extremists to
speak on behalf of feminism. This ensured that even more women
would reject the feminist label and the extremists would gain even
more power, driving more women away—a deadly cycle.

And each of these causes fostered the popularity of the others because they work together so well. The effort to censor sexual material, for example, fits perfectly with the utopian vision's claim of
female moral superiority. And the fact that this effort to ban offensive
pictures has yet to accomplish anything concrete is fully accepted
under the concept of the passive voice. There is no contradiction between "all sex is rape" theories and matriarchal teachings, since both
are based on the idea that men are inferior, morally demented predators. In fact, there is considerable crossover between feminist leaders
in all of these causes, from Mary Daly redefining rape to lesbian separatists promoting goddess worship.

What women of all ages want out of organized women's movement
is simple: They want it to champion political reforms and social
change that will address their needs and put them on an equal footing with men. In the 1989 *Time* poll, for example, 94 percent of the
women surveyed felt equal pay was a crucial issue, followed closely by
children's day care at 90 percent. Other high-ranking issues were
rape, maternity leave, job discrimination, abortion, and sexual freedom.

Asked to select the most important goal for the women's movement, these women chose "helping women balance work and family"
as number one. Second was "getting government funding for programs such as child care and maternity leave." In Betty Friedan's
words—as scribbled on a napkin in 1966 in a now-famous account—

women want feminism "to take the actions needed to bring women into the mainstream of American society, now, full equality for women, in fully equal partnership with men." It's been nearly thirty years since these words became the NOW statement of purpose, and the issues feminists identified then as stumbling blocks to full equality—child care, job opportunities, and reproductive rights—remain women's major concerns today.

For young women, these issues are crucial. We are much poorer than our mother's generation. In the December 1992 *Atlantic Monthly* article entitled "The New Generation Gap," authors Neil Howe and William Strauss report that over the past twenty years the poverty rate for young families has more than doubled and the median real income has fallen by one-third. In short, while older people have prospered, my generation has "fallen off a cliff." And while women age twenty-four to thirty-five now earn eighty cents for every dollar earned by men (up from sixty-nine cents in 1980), that eighty cents is harder to find as society comes to depend on a low-paid service economy.[14]

The result of this declining economic situation is that women of my generation are caught in a struggle to raise their children, complete college educations (if they are lucky), and find jobs while facing an often bleak and uncertain future. For us, a seemingly simple matter such as child care, health insurance, or access to birth control and abortion can decide that future.

There *are* feminist organizations that speak to women's actual concerns. The National Abortion Rights Action League remains an effective advocate for reproductive rights. Emily's List, a political fund-raising organization that finances women's campaigns, has seen its contributor list grow to 63,000 since 1985—donating $6.2 million to Democratic women running for office in 1992 alone. These organizations, among a few others, continue to advance women's rights and equality while remaining respectful of women's personal lives and choices.

But for young women—and many older women, as well—these organizations are not what represent the concept of feminism. This should not be surprising. NARAL's Campus Organizing Project—a national network for students organizing for abortion rights—did well in 1992, putting out a campus newsletter and forming coalitions among over four hundred pro-choice campus groups. But activism since Clinton's election is flagging, and on many campuses, NARAL is simply not highly visible. While Emily's List has gotten some media attention, its outreach is naturally aimed at those with the means to contribute.

And while NOW continues to devote some of its energy to political lobbying and funding campaigns for female politicians, the organization has been fragmented by New Victorianism. This is especially true on the local level, where young women are likely to encounter NOW in the form of chapter newspapers and community organizing. Reading a few issues of the Bend, Oregon, NOW newspaper, for example, could easily lead a woman to think that NOW stands for practicing modern witchcraft ("Halloween a holiday for witches other than traditional"), accepting goddess theories ("In Memory of Her: Honoring the goddess"), becoming a vegetarian ("What we eat will shape our environment"), and, of course, environmental causes ("Ancient Forest Adventures: Eco-feminism at its Best").

In almost every place young women encounter feminism, New Victorianism reigns. A married student may sign up for a women's studies class, only to be told that heterosexuality is oppressive. A politically liberal woman may attend an anti-sexual violence seminar, only to find the subject is really censoring free speech. A young Jewish woman may attend a local feminist organization meeting, only to find the night begins with a group prayer to invoke the goddess. A woman who couldn't afford college may pick up a feminist magazine, only to open the pages to article after article of obscure academic theory on subjects such as the "patriarchy" and "phallocentric" language. And, as happens so often, a young woman may meet with friends over coffee to discuss what they know and what they've heard concerning male students attacked in women's studies classes, organizations that promote strict ideologies, wacky theories that don't apply to their lives, and feminist activists they've met who, well, seem to hate men.

These are experiences that define feminism in personal and striking ways for women. They have far more impact than distant-sounding newspaper accounts about NARAL or inaccurate portrayals of feminism by commentators who seem stuck in the seventies.

And yet these experiences have been shrouded in silence. Using the cry of "backlash" whenever current feminist trends are criticized, New Victorians have effectively muzzled discussion within the movement—and, it would seem, outside the movement. While articles may appear on "The Year of the Woman," Hillary Rodham Clinton, or sexual harassment in the U.S. Senate, the mainstream press seldom looks critically at what is happening in the women's movement itself. Scant attention is paid to examining prominent causes, from redefinitions of rape to goddess worship. This silence does little to mitigate their growing power and much to perpetuate the continuing alienation of women from the movement. The message that women receive from feminist leaders and, by default, the mainstream media is that feminism is an all-or-nothing proposition. Either one accepts New Victorianism without question or one eschews the feminist title.

Most women's reaction—if one is to believe the polls—is clear. And if New Victorianism continues to flourish, the legacy it leaves behind will mirror the sad history of another women's movement. In the late nineteenth century, the suffragist movement became entangled in a spiritual- and sexual-purity crusade, with feminist leaders of the day speaking out against sexual freedoms, birth control, promiscuity, sexual literature, and the evils of male sexuality. Birth control, for example, was condemned because feminist leaders thought it would turn women into "prostitutes." The result was not only repressive social policies that served conservatives; by the late 1920s, the movement had alienated an entire generation of young women. The first wave of feminism soon died.

Unless we can reclaim feminism, this women's movement will die, too.

The success of the women's movement of the late 1960s and 1970s was due largely to the recognition that political, economic, reproductive, and sexual inequalities all needed to be addressed. As long as women were subjected to more restrictions than men based on the belief that women needed "protection," women's efforts to enter the workforce and politics would be difficult. As long as women were excluded from male systems, efforts to dismantle confining ideals of femininity would be nearly impossible. The second wave of feminism took a powerful step on behalf of all women when it declared that without equal treatment in both the public and private spheres—from education to reproduction—women were simply never going to gain true equality and parity in society.

But this movement also appears to be coming to a premature end—because feminism today, especially to women of my generation, has little in common with what it stood for in the sixties and seventies. In fact, it looks more like the feminism of the 1800s.

We must toss New Victorianism in the rubbish can and return to a movement that addresses women's concerns while respecting their personal lives and empowering their choices; a movement that prioritizes issues as women themselves prioritize them: child care, political parity, economic opportunity, abortion rights, and birth control; a movement that espouses the feminist ideal that our mothers taught us: that women can and should be equal and in full partnership with men, working together, both free from restraining sex roles—not tomorrow or the day after, but *now*.

We must return to a movement that, quite simply, represents the majority of women.

I was born in 1967, and I grew up believing fully in equality. I believe that I should earn equal pay. I believe I should have the same employment and educational opportunities as men. I believe in the right to abortion, and I believe that birth control should be accessible to all. I believe that all women and men should get paid family leave and that all families should have affordable child care and health insurance. I believe that women have a right to live free from discrimination, regardless of their sexual orientation. I believe that women have a right to bring rape charges without their personal histories being used against them. I believe that women have a right to work in environments free of sexual harassment and I believe that sex offenders should be severely punished. I believe in these rights, and many more.

And I believe all of these things are possible.

Throughout this book, you will hear voices from other women of my generation. These women come from a variety of backgrounds—from struggling young mothers, to students, to women in the workforce—but despite a tremendous diversity in their lives, all believe in women's rights. Yet they almost all refuse to call themselves feminists. I sought these women out in a variety of places, and I make no claim that I conducted anything even remotely resembling a scientific survey. But I do think that these women speak for many.

All of these women, as well as hundreds of thousands of others, *are* feminists. Women's rights are my generation's heritage and we've taken their promise to heart.

And now we need to take back feminism.

Part I

SEXUAL PURITY

Chapter 1

THE ANTIPHALLIC CAMPAIGN: MALE BASHING AND SEXUAL POLITICS

"The most alienating thing to me about the feminist movement is really the whole antimale thing—the way they are focusing on historical things that men have done more than any specific platform. . . . I get so frustrated by the whole male-slamming thing. My frustration came from being interested in the feminist movement, thinking about it, being supportive of it—and then figuring out that I don't feel like this. I don't hate all men. I don't think they're all bad. A friend of mine took a lot of women's studies classes; I think it was her minor. She told me once that she thought you had to be a lesbian or had to at least experience that to be a true feminist—which I thought was just really ridiculous. Ideally, it should be a moot point because nobody should care about what you do in the bedroom. Unfortunately, they do. I always wonder why."

—ELIZABETH EVERMAN, twenty-six,
administrative assistant in social services in Oregon

Elizabeth Everman, a slim young woman with the freckled pale skin and blue eyes of a natural redhead, relaxes in one of the worn couches in her living room while her son, age three, sleeps peacefully in the next room. Between their two low-income jobs, Elizabeth and her husband managed to buy a small home in a run-down neighborhood. With comfortable furniture buried under children's toys and homemade art decorating the walls, the house has a warm, friendly feeling. While Elizabeth wholeheartedly supports women's rights and equality, she only reluctantly considers herself a feminist. She explains that she dislikes any form of discrimination, including that against men or against women who choose to sleep with men. But based on her experiences with feminism—from women's studies classes to abortion-rights rallies—Elizabeth believes that this is exactly what the women's movement is pushing. "We need to quit making it a man/woman issue," she says before getting up to check on her son. Leaning over his bed, she forms a silhouette in the dim light: the clean line of cheekbone and eye, a faint glow of hair, a rounded arm reaching to tuck her son in. Thumb latched firmly in his mouth, he opens his eyes at his mother's voice and smiles sleepily at her. And somehow the look that passes between them makes the thought of gender discrimination absurdly repellent.

Elizabeth is not the only woman repulsed by discrimination masquerading under the name of feminism. Many women of all ages and walks of life choose not to call themselves feminists or participate in women's organizations because of feminist attacks on the male sex and the movement's dictates about the sexuality of its members. Yet the movement seldom acknowledges these women's objections. In the rare instances when these topics do arise, feminist leaders quickly dismiss women such as Elizabeth as antifeminists or denounce them as homophobes.

But the truth is that man hating and antiheterosexuality are firmly entrenched and loudly espoused in today's movement. Young women encountering feminism are confronted with male bashing and are made to feel they have to justify their sexual choices. This can even apply to lesbians if they don't toe the line by restricting themselves to proper feminist "egalitarian" sex. The women's movement seems preoccupied with what women do in the bedroom and with whom they do it.

The famous feminist phrase "the personal is political" has been taken to new extremes. Born out of the consciousness-raising movement of the early seventies, this phrase was originally used to illustrate how many things once considered women's "personal problems," such as reproductive choice, affect the quality of women's lives and should be considered political issues. Today, however, it has come to mean that virtually every aspect of a woman's personal life—including whom she sleeps with—is a political issue and a matter for feminist direction. For many feminists, there is no line drawn between the personal and the political, the private and the public. What we do in bed is seen as just as important, if not more, than how we vote.

In today's women's movement, the greatest problems facing women are not said to be political inequality, economic disadvantages, and the lack of child care or freely available abortion and birth control. The single problem is men. The entire system of oppression has been narrowed down to one simple root cause: heterosexuality. Instead of promoting women's rights, today's feminists are promoting man hating, separatism, and a stringent sexual morality. In fact, some respected feminist leaders—such as lawyer, author, and activist Catharine MacKinnon—have gone so far as to question the right to abortion because the option of ending a pregnancy may lead to more casual sex between women and men.

In the effort to blame male sexuality for sexual inequality, current feminists are eschewing political activism for an antimale crusade. This is what drives the current feminist promotion of male bashing and separatism.

"I think in my particular case, I wouldn't call myself a die-hard feminist, simply because of the exposure I had to feminism. I went to Emma Willard School, which was an all-girl boarding school in New York State. Oh, I'm supposed to say 'women's' boarding school [laughs]. Well, I was a girl back then. We pretty much had feminism in every aspect of every class, and guest lectures—the school is very closely affiliated with the National Organization for Women. And after a while, I just got the real hate-men feeling from the die-hard people in the movement—for example, people who say, 'You can set up your household structure so you never even have to see a man,' or 'You can go grocery shopping where there's only women working in the store and you can hire only female carpenters and plumbers.' I guess some women who have been severely abused need that. But I don't think that putting down the male gender, or the male sex per se, is any justification for what's been done to women in the past. Simply because, when you look at the role of gender in Western culture, it's not as if women haven't played a role. Women were the primary socializers of children, the educators—thereby reinforcing previous gender roles. And that's why I wouldn't really call myself a feminist, and that's why I'm kind of against feminism, the die-hard right-wing feminist viewpoint. Because I don't think they're looking at history with a fair viewpoint. And they're making the male sex out to be something far more than just a gender role."

—VICTORIA JACOBSON, twenty-three, graduate student from Connecticut

Victoria's experience with feminism is sad but far from unusual. Male bashing and advocating separatism, to the point of refusing to let a man step across your threshold, has become more and more common in today's women's movement. Young women encounter it constantly. And like Victoria, they walk away from the movement not only unwilling to call themselves feminists but feeling *opposed* to many aspects of current feminism. Alienated from the feminist label, many young women search for a different way to describe themselves, one that encompasses their support of equality and yet doesn't stand for such a reactionary, extremist standpoint. Victoria says she considers herself "an equalist." She believes in equal rights as well as respecting other people's individual choices and differences, including their personal relationships.

This is not a philosophy many current feminists would find valid.

"Men are the enemy," announced Louise Chernin, co-president of Seattle NOW, in a local television program on feminism. While Chernin wrote in the June 1993 Seattle NOW newsletter that this quote was "taken totally out of context" by the reporter, she didn't tell just what context she meant it in—except to complain that the program "did not offer much information about the depth and cause of our rage." But Chernin's apparent antimale bias is far from uncommon in the movement. In some cases, it is overt and amounts to reverse sexism. Women attending a public meeting for the New York Women's Action Coalition (a direct-action organization claiming eighteen hundred members that was formed in January 1992) find that men aren't allowed in the door. It doesn't matter whether they're husbands, reporters, or supporters—if they have a penis, they're not welcome. And in women's studies classes, male bashing is common. As an assistant women's studies professor confided in me, "Gender prejudiced attitudes about male students abound" in many classes, with male students subject to attack. One young woman, for example, tells of taking a women's studies class, only to find that the few men in the class were forced to sit in a circle and listen silently while the women "shared their feelings," a tactic that quickly blossomed into a vicious attack led by the professor, who denied the male students any chance to respond to accusations that they were rapists and oppressors. Other feminist professors, such as Mary Daly, refuse even to take questions from men when they lecture.

In other cases, antimale sentiments are subtler, captured in grossly overgeneralized negative statements about men. "Men generally do not take sex with children seriously. They are amused by it, wink by it and allow adult-child sex to continue through a complex of mores which applauds male sexual aggression," asserts feminist author Florence Rush in *The Best Kept Secret*, assigned in women's studies classes such as those at Portland State University.

It is hard to find anything positive said about men in today's women's movement. In the 1970s, through the emphasis on freedom from constrictive gender roles, much of the movement focused on enlightening and accepting men. In fact, they were often welcomed into the movement as partners. *Ms.* magazine, for example, published male writers such as Nat Hentoff, free-speech advocate and columnist for the *Village Voice*, and featured a plethora of articles on working out sexism in relationships and refuting stereotypes about both sexes. "We are beginning now to hear from men about their desires and hurts," wrote psychologist Carol Tavris in an article on sexuality in the April 1978 issue. "Women won't accept stereotypes about ourselves anymore, and we can't afford to hold on to those we have about men."

In today's *Ms.*, such an open attitude toward men is nowhere to be found. The work of male writers rarely appears, and few articles even acknowledge that women have relationships with men, much less that they work out sexism in relationships. Instead, stereotypes of men abound, portraying the most violent aberrations as the male norm. "Gang rape—like pornography—is pervasive, because it is a key feature of male bonding rituals within patriarchal societies," the September/October 1990 issue of *Ms.* announced.

Perhaps more than blatant male bashing, this complete lack of recognition that there are decent guys out there has given many women the perception that feminism stands for man hating. Whether through women's studies classes or feminist organizations such as NOW, women encountering feminism quickly learn the myriad ways that men oppress us and hurt us—and they encounter a ringing silence when it comes to the men who don't. In applying feminism to their lives, women see no allowance in the movement for their sons, husbands, brothers, lovers, and male friends. It is as if feminism says they can not exist.

But the truth is that women feel empathy for the men in their lives, men who often face similar economic troubles and personal problems. Feminist writer Gloria Watkins (with the lowercase pen name bell hooks) is one of the few current feminist leaders to note this. In *Feminist Theory from Margin to Center*, she writes that poor women, particularly women of color, ". . . have more in common with men of their race and/or class group than with bourgeois white women. They know the sufferings and hardships women face in their communities; they also know the sufferings and hardships men face and they have compassion for them." And another truth is that women of my generation are often friends with men—many of whom were raised by single mothers just as we were and who wholeheartedly believe in women's rights. Claims that these men are all gang rapists or laugh at child sexual abuse is not only ridiculous; it's insulting.

Faced with a choice between a feminism that requires them to view the men in their lives as inherently evil oppressors or opting out of the movement, many women choose the latter. "All the men in my life are wonderful people. Why would I want to pan them?" asks Elizabeth Dennis, a thirty-year-old from the state of Washington. "That's one thing that really irritates me [about feminism]: the man bashing. Because it's an excuse to vent your anger in a totally irresponsible way. In a sense, you're enfeebling yourself. You're saying, This man is to blame for my plight. No. We're all in this together. Pointing fingers makes us powerless—the victim. I think that man bashing is a total paradox. You're crying victim—the very thing you don't want to be."

Supporting the antimale bias in today's movement is feminist academic theory. Following the widely accepted characterization of society as a "patriarchy," today's feminists have created sweeping theories that effectively lump men together in one undifferentiated class. Patriarchy means "the rule of fathers," but in today's movement the term is used with reckless abandon and applied to every aspect of society that current feminists dislike. For author Sharon Doubiago, writing for the March/April 1992 *Ms.*, patriarchy "is the 'Oldest War,' the one that has to be waged on every human born—*Thou shalt commit psychic matricide*—because patriarchal civilization is the opposite of what comes naturally. It's Man's war against nature."

While definitions of the patriarchy may be vague, its membership roster is not. All men—regardless of class and cultural differences— are part of it. The perception of each individual man as a member of the evil patriarchy was captured at the 1992 National NOW convention, when women attending a seminar titled the "Problems of Male Violence" seemed aghast that it was moderated by men. Even though the men were sympathetic to feminism (one of them was the son of an ex-NOW president), some of the women turned on them, demanding to know why men rape. One member yelled, "Why do *you* feel the way *you* do about us?" as if the moderators themselves were actual rapists.

Yet for many of today's feminists, categorizing and judging men is considered acceptable. As members of the patriarchy, there is little to distinguish among individual men. But even if you discount personal influences in men's lives (such as parental influence) and just judge them by larger social constructs (class, education, etc.), it's hard to argue that most men share that much in common. An impoverished Catholic migrant farm worker, for example, won't share the same privileges or hold the same views as a wealthy Protestant business-man. Add in other cultural and individual differences among men and the link grows weaker.

But for feminists, there is one thing that ties all men together—no matter whether they're poor, rich, white, Asian, black, religious, or atheist—and current feminists have seized upon this one thing as the identifying patriarchal link, and thus, the wellspring of all oppression.

That, in short, is the penis.

While this may sound absurd—and is—leading feminists have de-veloped a theory that labels male sexuality and the practice of hetero-sexuality as the foundation of sexism and virtually all other forms of oppression. Feminist theorists have gone beyond blaming male-dictated law for sexual inequality and now blame what they term the "institution" of heterosexuality, or heterosexual sex. "I believe that we must explain how heterosexuality is central to our oppression," de-clared a paper presented at a 1981 London conference on sexual vio-lence, "and urge women to withdraw from heterosexual relations."[1]

A radical concept in the mid-seventies, this theory gained main-stream popularity in the eighties through women's studies, feminist literature, and conferences on sexual violence. Today it is entrenched as a major feminist tenet in the places young women encounter the movement—especially in women's studies classes. "I am suggesting that heterosexuality, like motherhood, needs to be recognized and studied as a *political institution*, . . ." writes feminist author Adrienne Rich in her immensely influential essay "Compulsory Heterosexuality and Lesbian Existence."[2] One of the most common assignments in women's studies classes—taught from the University of California at San Diego to Rutgers University in New Jersey—this essay stresses that heterosexuality is the "model for every other form of exploita-tion." Destroy this institution and you will destroy all oppression.

Young women attending an introductory-level women's studies class will in all likelihood be taught that they must adopt this view if they want to call themselves feminists.

The reason heterosexuality is seen as oppressive is because male sexuality is seen as oppressive. For example, students taking the introductory women's studies courses at UCLA are assigned the 1983 essay "More Power Than We Want: Masculine Sexuality and Violence" by Bruce Kokopeli and George Lakey, which states, "Masculine sexuality involves the oppression of women, competition among men, and homophobia (fear of homosexuality)."[3] Rather than viewing sexual violence as criminal acts by sick people, popular feminist theory defines rape as a "normal" part of male sexuality: "Rape is the end logic of masculine sexuality," this essay maintains. Even when rape does not occur and women in relationships don't feel oppressed, male sexuality is still negative—just more insidiously so. "Control through sexuality matters because it is flexible; it usually is mixed with love and dependency so that it becomes quite subtle," they declare.

Or, as students at Brandeis University in Waltham, Massachusetts, learn from Nancy Mairs's 1986 essay entitled "On Not Liking Sex," "Sex is not merely a political act; it is an act of war."[4]

For many of today's feminists, heterosexual sex *is* considered an act of war, one in which women are victimized whether they know it or not. Students at Rutgers University, Wesleyan University, and the University of New Hampshire, among many other schools, are assigned Cheryl Clarke's widely taught essay "Lesbianism: An Act of Resistance,"[5] which is recommended by the National Women's Studies Association (an organization founded in 1977 to promote feminist studies) in their list of suggested course syllabi. They are told that ". . . the institution of heterosexuality is a die-hard custom through which male-supremacist institutions insure their own perpetuity and control over us. *Women are kept, maintained, and contained through terror, violence, and the spray of semen* [emphasis added]."

Just how men supposedly control women through sex is made vividly clear by today's feminist leaders. "In practice, fucking is an act of possession—simultaneously an act of ownership, taking, force; it is conquering; it expresses in intimacy power over and against, body to body, person to thing," feminist spokesperson Andrea Dworkin writes in an essay assigned to students taking "Introduction to Women's Studies" at Tulane University. "Fucking requires that the male act on one who has less power and this valuation is so deep, so completely implicit in the act, that the one who is fucked is stigmatized. . . . In the male system, sex is the penis, the penis is sexual power, its use in fucking is manhood."[6]

Considered a radical by many outside the movement, Dworkin has generated controversy for her virulent antimale stance and outspoken view that heterosexual intercourse is actually an act of rape. Yet a young woman encountering organized feminism will find she is revered as a leader. Chapters from her book *Pornography: Men Possessing Women* are recommended by the National Women's Studies Association in their 1991 list of suggested course syllabi, and her work is taught as mainstream feminist theory in many women's studies courses. At MIT, for example, students attending "Introduction to Women's Studies" are assigned two chapters from *Pornography*. They learn that "The men who discuss sex say that there are two conflicting sides: those who believe only in reproductive sex versus those who believe in sex for pleasure not connected to reproduction. But there are not two sides: there is a continuum of phallic control." In Dworkin's view, this continuum of phallic control—exemplifying what she sees as a profound male hatred of women—can be found even in the most seemingly nonsexual places. The "epidemic of cesarean sections in this country," she asserts, "is a sexual, not medical, phenomenon. The doctors save the vagina—the birth canal of old— for the husband; they fuck the uterus directly, with a knife." Yes, the students are taught this in all seriousness: Dworkin's work is assigned under the section on "Violence Against Women."

It is true that some of these assigned works were originally published in the seventies and early eighties (Adrienne Rich's essay, for instance, was first published in 1980). In fact, an amazing amount of the material assigned to women's studies students today is ten or more years out of date. Reprinted in textbooks and handed out in photocopied packets, it is presented as feminist thought alongside more recent work. But the fact that some of this material is old doesn't mitigate that it's presented as *current* feminism. If anything, it points to just how exclusive and stagnant the movement has become, when new works are seen as unnecessary and dissent unacceptable.

It also illustrates just how far feminism has traveled from representing women's concerns, when what was once considered the ranting of radicals (Dworkin being a good example) is now considered the mainstream feminist position. In many women's studies classes, these writers not only appear with frightening regularity but little or nothing else is offered to counter their views. A young woman attending an introduction to women's studies at Wesleyan University will find one section of the course dedicated to "Unhinging Heterosexual Assumption," with Adrienne Rich's essay assigned along with two other works. Another young woman attending "Introduction to Feminism" at the State University of New York at Albany will spend part of the class on the "Lesbian Existence" by reading Cheryl Clarke's essay alongside lesbian-feminist writers Jo Whitehorse Cochran and Audre Lorde. The following week, she will learn all about "Romantic Ideas of Love/Heterosexism" by reading Andrea Dworkin and Adrienne Rich. It's no wonder that many young women who enter a women's studies course because of an interest in feminism become convinced that adopting the feminist label means adopting an extremist anti-male and antisex position.

It's also not surprising that in many women's studies classes, this wholesale condemnation of men and sex has seen many otherwise-feminist-thinking students rebel. As writer and Clark University professor Christina Hoff Sommers notes in an October 5, 1992, article from *The New Republic* on the 1992 National Women's Studies Association Conference: "Women's studies professors often describe their classrooms as being in 'crisis' because of 'rebellious students,' a situation that has been aggravated because, on so many campuses, women's studies courses are now mandatory." She continues: "Ordinarily, instructors facing persistent student protests would be moved to reconsider their own methods and arguments. But in the feminist classroom, opposition, counterargument, or complaints about methods serve primarily to convince the instructor that she is encountering backlash." Not surprisingly, the "White Male Student Hostility" workshop at the convention she attended was packed. Alan McEvoy, a professor at Wittenberg University in Ohio, offers an insight on this male "backlash" against feminism in an article on "Talking About Date Rape to Male Students" in the March 1992 *Education Digest*. "The problem is not that young males lack interest in considering the issue of sexual assault, but that they resent that, by virtue of their gender, they are treated categorically. They resent being automatically suspect, the implied premise that they constitute a generic enemy, the message that they are unworthy of the trust of their female peers." In other words, they resent being discriminated against.

The feminist condemnation of heterosexuality does nothing so much as echo Victorian times, when women were also told that sex automatically violated and defiled them. Sheila Jeffreys, a leading English feminist, perfectly illustrates just how regressive current feminism has become. In a 1990 essay, Jeffreys actually applauds some Victorian women's condemnation of sex. "I was enormously impressed by these feminists," she writes. ". . . at the end of the nineteenth century there were feminists who were prepared to challenge intercourse. They were prepared to say, for instance, that it was dangerous for women's health; that it led to unwanted pregnancies or *forced women to use forms of technology, contraception, that reduced them simply to objects for men's use.* . . . They felt sexual intercourse to be a *humiliating practice* because it showed men's dominance more obviously than anything else. They believed this practice should take place *only for the purposes of reproduction, maybe every three or four years* [emphasis added]."

According to Jeffreys, the fact that these Victorian women were later called "prudes and puritans" was simply a "backlash against feminists" by early sex reformers such as Havelock Ellis. Today, this backlash comes in the form of "sexual liberals." These sexual liberals have it all wrong. "We have got to understand that sexual response for women and orgasm for women is not necessarily pleasurable and positive," Jeffreys declares. "It can be a very real problem. It can be an accommodation of our oppression. It can be the eroticizing of our subordination."[7]

Not all feminists would agree with Jeffreys. But this is not something that would be apparent to a casual observer. Only a handful of feminists have been willing to challenge antiheterosexuality theory publicly—and in the places that young women encounter feminism, their works are widely ignored. In a rare critique of Adrienne Rich's essay, for instance, feminist writer Ann Ferguson wryly takes the antiphallic campaign to its ludicrous conclusion. "If compulsory heterosexuality is the problem, why bother to make alliances with straight women from minority and working-class communities around issues relating to sex and race discrimination at the workplace, cutbacks in Medicaid abortions, the lack of daycare centers, cutbacks in food stamps, and questions about nuclear power and the arms race? Just stop sleeping with men, withdraw from heterosexual practices, and the whole system of male dominance will collapse on its own!"[8] But Ferguson's critique is rarely assigned in women's studies classes—one exception is at Brandeis University—while Rich, Clarke, and Dworkin are staples.

Ferguson is not too far off—many feminist leaders do advocate abolishing heterosexual sex. As the Victorians attempted, they push for heterosexual chastity. "The heart of lesbian-feminist politics, let me repeat, is a recognition that heterosexuality as an institution and an ideology is a cornerstone of male supremacy," writes feminist activist Charlotte Bunch in her 1987 book, *Passionate Politics*, which is recommended by the National Women's Studies Association and assigned at many colleges, including the University of Richmond. "Therefore, women interested in destroying male supremacy, patriarchy, and capitalism must, equally with lesbians, fight heterosexual domination—or we will never end female oppression."

This has led to an increased movement for separatism, the cessation of sexual and social intercourse with men. In Dartmouth's introductory women's studies class, "Sex, Gender, and Society," for example, women's studies students are assigned Bunch's writings along with the 1983 essay "Some Reflections On Separatism and Power" by author Marilyn Frye.[9] Frye counts the ways women can be separatists. "The feminist separation can take many forms," she advises. "Breaking up or avoiding close relationships or working relationships; forbidding someone to enter your house; excluding someone from your company, or from your meeting . . ." Her list goes on.

Frye's argument for separatism is based on the idea that "heterosexuality, marriage and motherhood" are "the institutions which most obviously and individually maintain female accessibility to males, [and] form the core of antifeminist ideology. . . ." Frye's essay illustrates major problems with current feminist theory. It is true that marriage and motherhood have oppressed women—when divorce was unobtainable, birth control was unavailable and a woman's role was confined to the home. But many of today's feminists have taken this to mean that marriage and motherhood, as well as heterosexuality, are in themselves oppressive, no matter how many changes—such as the legalization of divorce, availability of birth control, and male involvement with parenting—have taken place to make them more egalitarian. And by naming these practices the "core of antifeminist ideology," feminists completely ignore the role that political inequality, economic disparity, and social mores play in maintaining sexism. Instead, they seem to place the blame for sexism squarely on the shoulders of married heterosexual mothers.

Women of my generation, thanks to earlier feminists, have choices. We can decide to marry or not, to bear children or not, and, thanks in large part to the sexual revolution, to take female lovers if we so chose.

But do current feminists really think that it's feasible for poor and working-class women to "avoid close relationships and working relationships" with men (in other words, divorce their husbands and quit their jobs) in order to chase after some separatist ideal? Where will they find jobs without male coworkers? How will they put food on the table and raise their children without work? What if they like their husbands and have male friends? Maybe some well-off feminists can afford to practice separatism, but for the majority of women, the suggestion is not only a joke but an insult to the economic and personal realities of their lives.

While not all feminists push separatism to the extent that Frye and other extremists take it—or to the extent that many women's studies courses do—the concept has gained adherents throughout the movement. An article on the dangers of heterosexuality by feminist writer Kay Leigh Hagan, entitled "Orchids in the Arctic: The Predicament of Women Who Love Men," in the November/December 1991 *Ms.*, recommends separatism as a practice "of limiting access of the oppressor to the oppressed." For heterosexual women unwilling to stop sleeping with men, Hagan advises that "one act of separatism is to require a man to wear a condom during intercourse—you are still very close but there is a boundary." Gloria Steinem believes that "some feminists books should be for women only[10]; students assigned Alison Jaggar's book *Feminist Politics and Human Nature* learn that "There is no doubt that women's liberation requires some kinds of separatism"; and groups such as WAC bar men from meetings. Many feminists argue that these forms of reverse sexism are perfectly acceptable because women need a space of their own in order to feel comfortable, and besides, everyone knows that men will just co-opt and destroy any group they're allowed to join.

It is duplicitous of today's feminists to say that they are fighting discrimination and then turn around and advocate it. And it is cheap to say that this discrimination is justified because it's directed toward men, who deserve a taste of their own medicine for being on top for so long. While few would maintain that men are now being oppressed as a class (particularly white middle- or upper-class men), that doesn't mean that they, any more than women, deserve to be judged solely on the basis of their gender.

Imagine the uproar if Gloria Steinem came out and said some

books should be for whites only, or if women's organizations didn't allow blacks to attend meetings because they thought blacks would co-opt the group. Imagine the outcry if feminist leaders came forward with sweeping statements that "Blacks are the enemy," "Minorities don't take child sexual abuse seriously," or "Gang rape is a key feature of bonding in Hispanic culture." Imagine the response if women's studies classes taught students that minorities are evil and then advocated that the path to freedom was segregation, including the refusal to hire minorities or allow any into your home. And imagine the upset if feminists announced that the root of the world's problems was actually mixed-race sex. All of these things would be condemned as racism.

And this is sexism—just what we are supposed to be fighting. For countless young women, the feminist movement doesn't only look hypocritical; it looks absurd.

"I think it [lesbian rights in feminism] should definitely be an issue, and I think that they should have just as many rights as anyone else . . . but it should not be a main focus, because the number of lesbians isn't more than the number of women who are straight."

—STEPHANIE, twenty, student in Massachusetts

Lesbian issues have come to dominate much feminist activism, and this is one reason why women see the movement as synonymous with the gay rights movement, if not even a strictly lesbian rights movement. Many women are put off by this focus not because they're homophobic but because the underlying agenda driving it has very little to do with promoting women's or even gay rights—and everything to do with promoting a new feminist sexual ideology.

The commonly accepted feminist wisdom is that discrimination against lesbians oppresses all women. NOW states, "Simply put, the threat of being called a lesbian keeps many women 'in their place.' . . . In order to secure the rights of all women, we must rid our society of the fears, prejudices and laws that prevent any woman from realizing her full human potential."[11] It sounds like a worthy cause, and it is. But many feminists have come to believe that fighting for lesbian rights should come before other feminist battles.

By arguing that there are fundamental differences between gay males and lesbians (because gay men are, after all, still men) that prevent the two from working together on homosexual rights, some lesbian feminists have taken another route. Instead of joining with gay activists, they have pushed their issues to the forefront of the feminist agenda. As Adrienne Rich writes, "To equate lesbian existence with male homosexuality because each is stigmatized is to deny and erase female reality once again." As proof that homosexuality in women differs from homosexuality in men, Rich cites "the prevalence of anonymous sex and the justification of pederasty among male homosexuals . . ."—as if all gay men are promiscuous and justify child molestation.[12]

It was in the early seventies that lesbian issues became firmly tied to the feminist cause. In a move that was to greatly impact the movement, NOW responded to the growing emphasis on radical lesbian feminism in 1969 and 1970 by ousting at least one lesbian activist from the organization. Exactly how far this infamous "lesbian purge" went is not clear. While current NOW president Patricia Ireland has stated that the incident was "greatly exaggerated by the pain that it caused,"[13] lesbian commentator Donna Minkowitz maintains that the then president Betty Friedan (who had come out against sexual politics being a focus of feminism) "systematically purged" a large, if unidentified, number of lesbians from the organization, including author Rita Mae Brown.[14] Brown had resigned, citing NOW's refusal to accept lesbians.[15]

Whether the incident was as Stalinistic as some believe, the results were long-lasting. Friedan, who stepped down from the presidency in 1970, has been ostracized from the movement to this day. Today's NOW officials are outspoken about their dislike of Friedan. "But Betty Friedan was homophobic then, she still is homophobic now, and she doesn't like NOW anymore, because we deal with lesbian issues too much," Susan Mackenzie, ex-state president for the Tennessee chapter of NOW, said in the March 24, 1992, issue of *The Advocate*. As the article summed up, "NOW organizers will probably continue to grimace at the mention of Friedan well into the next century, even longer than lesbians will." Friedan herself seems to grimace over the notion that, after twenty years, this is still an issue. She has long maintained that she could care less about what people do in the bedroom: She only cares about dividing the movement over any issue, including lesbianism, which motivated her vocal opposition to making lesbian issues a NOW priority in the seventies. "I have been pitted against the lesbians in NOW, and the lesbians have been pitted against me," Friedan told *Playboy* in September 1992. "When we allow that, we are playing into the hands of those who would diffuse our focus and our power. My biggest concern is polarizing women against one another."

After Friedan left, NOW changed its position. "All this time later, memories of the attempted purge of the 'Lavender Menace' by some NOW leaders and chapters remain painful," Patricia Ireland stated in the July/August 1992 issue of *Ms.* "But the overwhelming majority of the organization fought back in 1971 with a strong resolution clearly identifying lesbian rights as a feminist issue and a NOW issue."

Ireland is correct. NOW takes a very strong stand on lesbian issues. Since 1975, lesbian rights have been one of NOW's top four priority issues, along with passing the ERA, fighting racism, and protecting reproductive rights. A full-time lesbian rights staff position was established in 1979, and NOW organized their own lesbian conferences in 1984 and 1988. The organization increasingly spends more and more time and money on lesbian issues, from involvement in lesbian and gay rights parades to its support of National Coming Out Day.

NOW is not alone in devoting a great deal of time and resources to lesbian issues. In the fall of 1992, a rift opened up in the New York Women's Action Coalition over this subject. Some members of this direct-action feminist group were growing uncomfortable at the increasing amount of time spent on lesbian concerns—worrying that other issues were shortchanged and that the Lesbian Issues Caucus was receiving more than its fair share of funds (for events such as a Gay Pride parade). Conversely, the Lesbian Issues Caucus felt that these mutterings were the result of "lesbophobia."

After the subject came up several times in meetings, the caucus asked WAC members to write anonymously about lesbophobia. These comments were printed in a handout given to the members of the October 20, 1992, meeting, along with calls for discussion on the subject. This tactic—turning valid questions of just how much time and funding should go toward exclusively lesbian issues into lengthy inquisitions on whether members hate lesbians—is not uncommon in feminist groups.

Some WAC members challenged this. "I think we at WAC meetings spend a disproportionate amount of time on the 'Lesbophobic issue.' I agree it needs to be discussed, but we spend so much time on this, we cheat other issues and presentations," one member wrote anonymously. Another member agreed. "I find that most of the women's groups tend to be overtaken by lesbian women, and deserted by straight women. I personally quit NOW because of this situation. I fear that the common issues of *all* women are being ignored by most women's groups, in favor of concentrating effort and funds to address lesbian issues exclusively." Her sentiment seemed to be echoed throughout the packed meeting hall as the subject was discussed, with many women looking frustrated and a few walking out. "Not again!" one woman noted quietly to a friend before the two made a quick exit.

But feminism has made lesbian rights a major issue, and a major issue it shall remain. Peggy Norman, NOW's northwest regional director, expressed an oft-repeated sentiment in the March 24, 1992, issue of *The Advocate*. "Along with two other people," Norman stated, "I'm responsible for organizing a six-state region, and in some small areas they'll say 'In my community it's too controversial to organize on lesbian rights.' And that's homophobic. It's true that it's tough to do in a town that has 5,000 people and ten members. But I see it as my job to say, 'You can do something. You are required to work on all our issues . . .'"

Women's organizations often suffer from a lack of funds, and members are usually volunteers with little spare time. Small groups such as the one Norman cites, with ten members in a small town, are even worse off in terms of financial and time limitations. The reality is that a small group can usually afford to work on only a few issues at any given time, and by making lesbian issues a top priority, other needs inevitably get shortchanged. Perhaps it is homophobia that makes many women in feminist organizations—from WAC to NOW chapters—balk at spending a great deal of limited resources on lesbian issues. Or perhaps it is the question of just how much time and money should go to a concern that in all likelihood will not benefit or represent the majority of women in their community.

But in today's women's movement, this question is seldom raised. Any mention that women feel alienated by the priority given lesbian issues is grounds for attack. Take, for example, what happened after novelist Sally Quinn wrote an opinion piece for the January 19, 1992, *Washington Post* that characterized current feminism as out of touch with mainstream women. "Today the movement is more and more perceived as a fringe cause," wrote Quinn, "often with overtones of lesbianisms and man-hating." These words were enough to incite a wrathful counterattack from feminist leaders. "She's just been sailing along on the coattails of her husband [Benjamin Bradlee, former editor of the *Washington Post*]," Susan Faludi, author of *Backlash*, announced in the May 19, 1992, issue of the gay and lesbian magazine *The Advocate*. Considering Faludi's criticisms of the media for belittling women's intelligence, this seems hypocritical, as it did when she questioned whether Quinn had a right to voice her opinion: "Who is she to be commenting on feminism?" Faludi posed in the same interview. "Where has she been all these years during the struggle for woman's rights?" Faludi was not alone in her slights on Quinn's character and credentials. Gloria Steinem also weighed in, dismissing Quinn as "a water bug on the surface of life."

The uproar over Quinn's short opinion piece is a perfect example of how intolerant the movement is about even discussing the topic. Current feminists safely squash any discussion of these issues by raising the specter of lesbophobia, claiming they are, once again, being victimized—this time by homophobic women out to smear the movement. Even feminist commentators in the press use this ploy. In *The Advocate* piece lambasting Quinn's article, syndicated columnist Ellen Goodman said the reason "journalists call lesbianism a fringe issue and say it threatens the movement" is because of "homophobia" in the media. There are no doubt homophobic people in the media, just as there are in any other field. But it's a cheap shot to dismiss any reporting on the effects of the movement's lesbian emphasis by saying the writer is simply homophobic.

The issue should not be how many feminists are lesbian. (As one WAC member wrote sarcastically, "If someone is into split beaver—who cares! Not my business.") But current feminists think it's important. For example, Olga Vives, chair of NOW's national lesbian rights task force, stated in the March 24, 1992, issue of *The Advocate* that she estimates 40 percent of all NOW members are lesbian. Is it homophobia that makes women wonder just *how* NOW could possibly know what their members do in the bedroom or why they should even care?

Figures such as these are intended to make lesbianism visible and to help erase the stigma attached to the word. That is positive. But for many women, feminism should be concerned with representing all women—regardless of race, class, or sexual orientation—and the idea that any one group should be overrepresented is offensive. White women have always been overly represented in feminism, but no one would herald that as positive.

Without a doubt, some women harbor an irrational fear of homosexuals and many more grapple with a deep-seated discomfort over the topic. As a March 5, 1993, *New York Times*/CBS News poll showed, Americans hold contradictory positions on homosexuality. While 78 percent of adults surveyed believed that gays should have equal rights in job opportunities, more than half objected to their child being taught by a gay or lesbian elementary school teacher. And while more women than men believed that homosexuality is an acceptable alternative to heterosexuality (42 percent and 30 percent, respectively) and people under age forty-five were more supportive of gay rights, these numbers are still far too low. The rights of homosexuals must be fought for—and the women's movement is right to take a strong stand on behalf of equality for all. We need to push for the rights of gays to raise children, legally marry, and enjoy workplaces free of discrimination. We need to make it clear that discrimination against gays is not acceptable, whether in the military, the office, schools, or in a feminist group.

But there are critical flaws in the argument that lesbian issues should be given top priority among feminists. For one, many lesbian rights center on issues of gay discrimination, not gender discrimination—and the women's movement should be fighting gender discrimination first and foremost. And because their concerns tend to revolve around gay discrimination, many lesbian issues don't intersect with women's rights overall. For example, fighting for gay marriages benefits homosexuals, but fighting for equal job opportunities and health-care benefits *both* gay and straight women. Considering that feminist activism on lesbian issues concentrates more on visibility and community (such as coming-out days and lesbian-only gatherings) rather than on concrete legal changes such as same-sex marriage, it is questionable just how much this focus even advances gay rights.

This is not to say that women's organizations shouldn't stand against discrimination in all its forms, including homophobia, and it's not to say that lesbian rights don't have a place in the feminist agenda. But to make lesbian rights a major priority seems like a case of putting the cart before the horse—similar to arguing that gay rights should be the top priority of the NAACP because some blacks are gay.

If feminism is the struggle for *all* women's rights, then lesbian issues would have to come after efforts for such things as political parity, child care, and an end to job discrimination. In a movement for gender equality, whatever affects the most women *must* come first. Feminism needs to concentrate on reforms that affect women regardless of cultural, class, and sexual-orientation differences—issues such as sexual discrimination, equal opportunity, political parity, child care, sexual violence, accessible birth control, and abortion rights. Headway on these issues will improve life for nearly everyone, *including lesbians*.

But today's women's movement seems to ignore this reality. And the reason is simple. Many current leaders have moved beyond gay rights into an entirely different arena: the promotion of lesbianism as a political stand. In a nutshell, they believe that what women do in bed is of major concern to the movement—and, following the feminist theory condemning heterosexuality, only lesbian sex is considered acceptable. Young women hear this time and time again, from women's studies classes to women's organizations, and it is a major reason behind their alienation from feminism.

The personal is now intensely political in today's movement, and the chickens have come home to roost.

"I think that gays and lesbians have a right not to be discriminated against. But I've heard that there is something wrong with me because I am decidedly heterosexual. That because I like to get naked with men, I'm not a feminist."

—AUTUMN HARRISON, twenty-three,
student and bar worker in Oregon

For many of today's feminists, lesbianism is considered the key to liberation. "'The lesbian is the rage of all women condensed to the point of explosion,' read an early radical tract, and in the decade that followed *Roe v. Wade*, the mid-seventies through the mid-eighties, this seemed to be true," feminist Marcia Cohen writes in *The Sisterhood: The Inside Story of the Women's Movement and the Leaders Who Made it Happen*. "On many college campuses . . . [t]he implication in certain quarters was that feminism actually *meant* lesbian, and that the only way to become a true feminist was to be lesbian. Or to hate men." Cohen is right. From the mid-seventies onward, many college students were told that they must be lesbians in order to call themselves feminists. But she makes a mistake when she assumes that this trend miraculously disappeared by the late eighties.

It didn't. In fact, the feminist promotion of lesbianism is more prevalent today than it was in the mid-seventies through the eighties. From women's studies classes to organizations, women encountering feminism are frequently told they should become lesbian, an assertion that runs from the subtle to the blatant. "We may have much to learn from lesbian love and sex. As women loving women because they are women, lesbians point out that they are in a special position with regard to liberating female sexuality. . . . lesbian women contend that they are more able to discover and express authentic female sexuality than their heterosexual counterparts," states Sheila Ruth, editor of the textbook *Issues in Feminism: A First Course in Women's Studies* which is taught in many women's studies courses. It is common in introductory women's studies classes to devote part of the course entirely to lesbianism. In UCSC's "Introduction to Feminism" course for example, one section of the class is tellingly titled "On the Significance of the Lesbian Experience; the Meaning of Our Love for Women."

For many of today's feminists, lesbianism is far more than a sexual orientation or even a preference. It is, as students in many colleges learn, an "an ideological, political, and philosophical means of liberation of all women from heterosexual tyranny. . . ." This is according to an essay by feminist writer Cheryl Clarke in *This Bridge Called My Back*. Clarke argues that lesbianism is less a matter of sexuality than a political means to overthrow oppression. "I am trying to point out that lesbian-feminism," Clarke writes, "has the potential of reversing and transforming a major component in the system of women's oppression, viz. predatory heterosexuality."

Clarke is echoing a theory popular in feminism—that lesbianism is a transhistorical action that, regardless of time or situation, has always been political. "For the lesbian, her choice of lifestyle is not only a sexual act, it is a political act," declared the summer 1991 issue of Portland State University's *Lifestyle News*, distributed to students. Lesbianism is seen as a political act because it supposedly challenges the dominance inherent in heterosexuality. "Lesbians also threaten the dominant cultural system by presenting, or at least appearing to present, an alternative to the typical inequality of heterosexual relationships," states an essay on lesbianism by Rose Weitz in the widely assigned 1989 feminist textbook *Women: A Feminist Perspective*. Students learn that "It seems, then, that the fates of feminists and lesbians are inextricably intertwined."

In accordance with this theory, history has been rewritten to make every unmarried woman a lesbian engaged in a political revolt. As students attending introductory women's studies at Kansas State University read in Adrienne Rich's essay "Compulsory Heterosexuality," all "marriage resisters, spinsters, autonomous widows" throughout history qualify as part of a "lesbian continuum" because they didn't "collaborate" with men. From Christian women in the twelfth century who avoided associating with men in order to protect their virtue, to the "secret sororities" of an unnamed group of African women, to unmarried white intellectuals such as Emily Dickinson and divorced black writers such as Zora Neale Hurston, practically any woman from prehistoric times onward who didn't have sex with men qualifies as a member of Rich's "lesbian continuum." As she puts it, women such as these "resisted male tyranny."

This is ridiculous. Just as many nuns don't chose their vocation as a means of resisting male tyranny, many spinsters desperately wanted the "collaboration" of marriage. To insist these women and others, such as widows, were all part of a lesbian continuum pitted nobly against male dominance erases the dramatic differences between women's lives and the reality of their experiences—experiences that often included deeply missed husbands and the longing for loving relationships. Just because a woman was celibate doesn't necessarily mean she didn't want to have sex with men. In the Victorian age, having sex outside of marriage was considered unthinkable for "decent" women, and the spinster was resigned to a life of chastity whether she wanted it or not. In fact, it's silly to think that all lesbians see themselves as "resisting male tyranny." A lot of them just prefer women.

But this theory has been fundamental in crystallizing one of the key tenets of current feminism: that there is a distinct lesbian identity, one that operates regardless of class, culture, and time period. In her widely read 1988 book, *Homophobia: A Weapon of Sexism,* assigned to women's studies students at the University of Minnesota as well as many other colleges, author Suzanne Pharr writes, "To say that to be a lesbian is just a bedroom issue is to say that sexual identity is limited to sexual activity, which doesn't take into account all of the assumptions and behavior that go along with sexual identity."

Here current feminism embraces the very problem that gays are fighting: defining a person according to whom they sleep with. Simply by sleeping with women (or even by not sleeping with men), lesbians are said to have a certain identity, while active heterosexual women are said to be automatically homophobic and oppressed by the nature of *their* sexual lives. As Pharr suggests, "women will have to resist compulsory heterosexuality and risk its coercive and damaging force." Citing Adrienne Rich, Pharr goes on to say there is already "a tradition of resisting male domination" by women who don't sleep with men: spinsters, widows, and, of course, lesbians.

The irony here is that while many feminists claim heterosexuality and lesbianism are political rather than simply bedroom issues, they define both terms solely with regard to whom women sleep with. If only women who refuse to sleep with men are resisting male dominance, are we really trying to escape judging people according to what they do in the bedroom—or are we saying the end of sexism means all women become lesbians and all heterosexuals are condemned? There may well be general personality differences between lesbian and straight women, due to societal experiences. But to claim these differences result in two set identities blurs the tremendous differences that exist among us all, lesbian or straight. And while lesbianism can be construed as a threat to the political order—some conservatives would certainly argue it is—embracing this notion can be dangerous. It can have the effect of perpetuating discrimination and judging on the basis of sexual orientation ("those people") instead of fighting it by stressing that gays deserve equality not because they are different but because they are human.

Yet young women learning about feminism in women's studies courses often hear that lesbians are different—more enlightened and unique—from heterosexual women. "Because lesbians are oppressed by the ways in which society organizes sexuality into rigid roles, they are able to develop a unique consciousness as lesbian women," writes E. M. Ettore in "A New Look at Lesbianism,"[16] which is assigned to introductory-level women's studies students at the universities of Utah, Iowa, and Colorado at Boulder. This assumption—presented to many college students as mainstream feminism—goes largely unchallenged, though it is difficult to hold that those in same-sex relationships automatically develop a "unique consciousness" or erase role playing.

In fact, recent attention paid to battering in lesbian relationships by groups such as the Lesbian Battering Intervention Project of the Minnesota Coalition for Battered Women has shown that lesbian relationships are not exactly as uniquely egalitarian as many feminists would like to believe. According to Pam Elliott, coordinator of the project, violence in lesbian relationships probably occurs at a rate just a little lower than in heterosexual relationships. "We are still controversial," Elliott stated in the September/October 1990 issue of *Ms.* "We challenge the basic philosophy—that men are the only violent beings. We have to rethink and revaluate that philosophy. Violence is about people who need to use power and control." Obviously, not all lesbians are alike.

But because lesbianism is seen as a political identity, a great emphasis has been given to developing a separate lesbian culture, one that can easily be distinguished from heterosexuality. From "wimmin's" music to lesbian-only gatherings such as the Michigan Womyn's Music Festival, this cultural ideal often reflects the belief that, regardless of class, cultural, and personal differences, lesbians not only share the same perspectives but that they relate in the same ways.

An example of this comes from the 1990 essay "Dyke Methods," taught to students taking feminist theory at the University of Colorado at Boulder.[17] With lines such as "wimmin's space is defined partly by ways wimmin treat one another, the absence of conceptual/intellectual hegemony or, more broadly, serious respect for differences among wimmin, which is the point of the principle of nonpersuasion, is one of the characteristics of wimmin's space," it is often difficult to understand just what "dyke methods" author Joyce Trebilcot is espousing, but the gist of it seems to be a separatist community defined by a stereotypical view of women as sugar and spice and everything nice—or at least fundamentally different from men.

Trebilcot's convoluted prose is far from unusual in current lesbian-feminist theory, and it illustrates an ironic point. While lesbian-feminist theorists often claim they accept differences in women, their work is often so incomprehensible that it excludes all but the previously initiated. "The greatness of our differences signals the immensity/intensity of the Fire that will flame from our combined creative Fury," writes leading feminist Mary Daly in *Gyn/Ecology*, ". . . Lesbians/Spinsters find in our authentic likeness to each other the opportunity to exhibit and develop genuine differences. Rather than relying on stereotypic role relationships, Amazon friends/lovers/sisters cast our Selves into a creative variety of developing relationships with each other." Whatever it means, you can bet that many lesbians with "genuine differences" (such as a lack of education or perhaps even a distaste for calling themselves "Spinsters" and "Amazons") won't feel too welcome in Daly's supposedly accepting lesbian theory.

It is important to recognize that leading lesbian feminists do not speak for all lesbian women. "Being gay has never been an issue with me. I was always a civil rights person. That doesn't mean I've worn a banner or carried a sign. I've simply lived my life," a lesbian women was quoted as saying in a well-researched fall 1990 *Time* article titled "The Lesbians Next Door." As the article noted, "While a small, strident minority reject men altogether and advocate feminist separatism, most lesbians are fully integrated into mainstream American life." Katie Kent, a young woman writing for the 1992 book *Engaging Feminism: Students Speak Up and Speak Out*, responds against the notion that lesbian relationships are more egalitarian. "Of course, as a lesbian I am often tempted to accept this analysis," she writes, "and I do see it as a product of a specific moment in the women's movement. . . . However, there is just as much power floating around in lesbian relationships, whether acknowledged or not."

And not all lesbians agree with the current feminism promotion of lesbianism as an essentially political act. "Still, while lesbianism is certainly accepted in feminism, it's more as a political or intellectual concept," writes lesbian feminist Amber Hollibaugh in an essay pointing out that this focus has made discussing the sexual aspect of lesbianism almost heretical. "It seems feminism is the last rock of conservatism. It will not be sexualized. It's *prudish* in that way. Well, I won't give my sexuality up and I won't *not* be a feminist. . . . Sometimes, I don't know how to handle how angry I feel about feminism."[18]

For many younger lesbians, this desexualization of lesbianism is also alienating. In an article examining Madonna's status as a cultural heroine among younger lesbians for the March 26, 1991, issue of *The Advocate*, feminist author Alice Echols notes that lesbian women of my generation seem more comfortable in their sexuality than older women, and this may be leading them to reject feminist efforts to take the sex out of lesbianism. "It is no wonder that some younger dykes whose lesbianism is unambiguously about the pursuit of pleasure prefer to take the lust-affirming Madonna rather than the reprimanding Dworkin as their role model," she writes. This is true. Madonna has certainly been far more popular among young women— whether gay or straight—than any feminist activist today. This is not because we are all music-loving cretins more interested in dancing than gaining equality. It's because Madonna was one of the first female public figures ever to present ambition, power, strength, and sexuality rolled up into one empowering package. For too long, women in the public realm were prohibited from being both intelligent and sexual; one was either a sexless brain or a brainless bimbo. Madonna broke that rule, and it's no wonder that her driving ambition combined with frank sexuality has been far more appealing to young women than the repressive ideology of current feminism.

In insisting that women choose sexual partners for political reasons, the women's movement has tossed the baby out with the bathwater. It's difficult to argue for freedom of choice when you've named heterosexuality (which is certainly the choice of many women) as an agent of oppression to be avoided at all costs. In fact, saying that women should chose sex partners for political reasons is about as empowering as saying we should marry for money. It doesn't matter which gender we curl up with at night; women want sexual relationships based on personal attraction, commonality, desire, and—let's face it—lust. The day we choose our sex partners as political statements is the day when excitement, desire, intimacy, and love evaporate in our bedrooms, leaving only a cold act conducted for the coldest reasons.

It is difficult to argue that feminism can represent all women when leading activists make it clear that one must call oneself a lesbian to join the club. It is this assertion that has seen the movement tagged with the lesbian title. As feminist writer bell hooks notes in *Feminist Theory from Margin to Center,* "Large numbers of women see feminism as synonymous with lesbianism; their homophobia leads them to reject association with any group identified as pro-lesbian." What hooks neglects to question is just why women see feminism as synonymous with lesbianism in the first place; she doesn't ask whether the reason may be that, as heterosexuals, they've been told they aren't welcome in the movement. "What I'm reacting to so strongly here is the notion that a feminist must be a lesbian," writes student Miriam Shadis in *Engaging Feminism:* "Ultimately I find that elitist and degrading to my culturally constructed, socialized little self."

Women and men of my generation tend to be far more accepting of homosexuality than older generations. Many of us honestly don't care what people do in the bedroom; whether our friends are homosexual or straight isn't an issue. But the same sentiment that often makes us more accepting of homosexuality—that nobody has the right to dictate people's private lives—also serves to alienate us from today's women's movement. I want to make this point very clear: I believe it is reprehensible to discriminate on the basis of sexual orientation. I think archconservatives' attempts to dictate people's sexual lives is sick. The problem is *not* that some feminists are lesbians. The problem is that feminists, like the far right, are attempting to dictate what women do in the bedroom. They are telling young women they must be lesbians *in order* to be feminists.

Women of all ages often reject feminism not out of homophobia but because they refuse to accept a movement that tells them whom to sleep with—or how they sleep with someone.

The idea that heterosexual sex is the cornerstone of oppression but that lesbianism is liberating has seen the feminist movement today follow a strange circuitous path, arriving at promoting many traditional repressive sexual mores. From denouncing the sexual revolution (for promoting the institution of heterosexuality) even to attacking abortion rights (ditto), the focus on sexual politics in today's movement has seen many feminists perform an abrupt about-face, supporting positions the movement originally fought and mouthing lines that sound eerily reminiscent of Victorian-era sexual dictates.

An increasingly popular trend in feminism today is that of condemning the sexual revolution. Some feminists blame sexual liberation for creating rape and child sex abuse. As Diana Russell, a feminist writer and researcher, puts it in *The Secret Trauma: Incest in the Lives of Girls and Women*, the "so-called sexual revolution may have also contributed to the rise of child sexual abuse. Its nondiscriminating all-sex-is-okay philosophy appears to have resulted in a more accepting attitude in certain segments of the population toward adult-child sex." It is as if tolerant attitudes toward adult sexuality will inevitably lead to thinking sex with children is okay—making pedophilia and incest an expected extension of male sexuality that isn't properly restrained by traditional mores.

The major feminist criticism leveled at sexual liberation is that it has increased acceptance for heterosexual sex outside of committed relationships, which, of course, is said to oppress us. "In going into new sexual values we are really going back to the values women have always attached to sexuality, values that have been robbed from us, distorted and destroyed as we have been colonized through both sex-

ual violence and so-called sexual liberation. . . . Sexual values and
the positive, constructive experience of sex *must be based in intimacy*,"
asserts feminist Kathleen Barry in her influential book *Female Sexual
Slavery*, which is assigned to many women's studies students. The assumption here seems to be that the repressive sexual values (and lack
of birth control) prior to sexual liberation were actually based on
what women wanted. This argument sounds strikingly like Victorian
condemnations of sexual liberation. "[S]exual freedom, in the present
stage of its development, means greater slavery for the average woman who embraces it. . . ." a Victorian woman wrote in 1897 in response to a sexual liberation movement of the time, arguing that
women were too naïve to handle "indulgences" and invoking fears
that, once released, female sexual desire would turn women into degenerate sexual slaves. "So long has she been the tool and slave of
man, sexually, that she needs protection from herself. . . ."[19]

But many of today's feminists have become convinced that the traditional confining mores feminists originally fought—that sex must
be "based in intimacy," meaning only "sluts" have sex outside of true
love—*are* what women want, while more liberated views on sex are
patriarchal tools of oppression. As Robin Morgan put it in a Janu-
ary/February 1991 *Ms.* editorial, "If I had to name a single characteristic of patriarchy, it would be compartmentalization. . . . Sex
divorced from love."

"Until very recently, women weren't *allowed* to have sex with
someone they didn't love: It was considered unnatural, indecent, to
separate the act of sex from the desire to marry or at least have a romantic relationship with their sex partner," Dalma Heyn writes in a
May 1992 *Mademoiselle* article aptly titled "Anything but Lust,"
which discusses how repressive sexual mores hem women in through
guilt. As Heyn notes, women today are often told that to enjoy sex
simply for pleasure's sake is wrong: "only sluts seem to have just plain
sex. Real women always 'make love.'" The article ends like a gift of
empowerment. "If it brings you pleasure, just smile when you hear all
the judgements and know that you have no problem. No problem at
all." Compare this tolerant choice-giving attitude with that of today's
feminists and it shouldn't be surprising why more young women
would rather read *Mademoiselle* than *Ms.*

There is, of course, nothing wrong with having sex based in intimacy. Being intimate and relaxed with your partner usually makes sex
more emotionally fulfilling, playful, and exciting. But the feminist

message is not one of choice, but one of shame. "Sexual liberation has brought into the home many of the bizarre sexual activities that men have demanded of prostitutes," asserts leading feminist Kathleen Barry. Suddenly, a woman who might enjoy "bizarre" sex finds herself cast as no better than a prostitute. Barry doesn't explain what sexual practices she's referring to, but, like the Victorians, she seems to have a repugnance to anything but the most constrained sexual behavior. As one horrified Victorian wrote, in all seriousness, about a liberal book on sex: "Intercourse every night and morning and sometimes noon—with satisfaction to both parties—PRAISED. Handling the clitoris—advised. Intercourse in advanced years—hoped for—benefits recited. Intercourse in pregnancy—frequent—etc. Really, I can't remember in Forel or any other author—even the much quoted Martin Luther—anything approaching this . . ."[20]

Many feminists have turned their energies toward dictating the exact nature of a correct feminist's sexual life—heterosexual *or* lesbian. Any act that hints at dominance—no matter how consensual or loving—is said to mimic the violence inherent in heterosexuality. As students at UCLA read in Rosemarie Tong's 1989 textbook, *Feminist Thought*, as she quotes Audre Lorde, "'To degrade someone, even with that person's expressed consent, is to *endorse* the degradation of persons. It is to affirm that the abuse of persons is *acceptable*.'" And whatever current feminists find degrading is assumed to be degrading to everyone else. For this reason, any sex that falls outside of what Tong and others objectively describe as "vanilla" or "bambi" sex (side by side, no one on top or bottom, face-to-face contact at all times) is believed to reek of dominance.[21]

The feminist obsession with proper female sexuality extends to women's private thoughts, as well. "Sadistic and masochistic fantasies may be a part of our sexuality, but they are no more our freedom than the culture of misogyny and sexual violence that engendered them," writes feminist activist Dorchen Leidholdt.[22]

It hasn't always been this way. In the early 1970s, the sexual revolution became entwined with the women's movement and freedom from confining sexual mores became a rallying point. As long as women were expected to "save it" for marriage, and as long as birth control was restricted, it was held that sexual inequality would flourish. Germaine Greer's *The Female Eunuch*, published in 1970, joined Betty Friedan's *The Feminine Mystique* as a bible for the women's movement. Friedan wrote of releasing women from the prison of economic and political inequality, sending thousands of women—for the first time—into the workplace and into politics. Greer wrote of releasing women from the prison of repressive sexual morality—thus empowering women with her assertion that sex can be positive, pleasurable, and guilt-free. "The chief instrument in the deflection and perversion of female energy," Greer wrote, "is the denial of female sexuality for the substitution of femininity or sexlessness."

For the first time, women were told to have pride—not only in their intelligence and capabilities but in their bodies and in pleasure. We were told we could not only have great minds but great sex, as well. The Boston Women's Health Collective's *Our Bodies, Ourselves* hit the bookstores in 1971, receiving a joyous response for its frank talk about masturbation, sexual fantasies, and female health. "We are our bodies. Our book celebrates this simple fact." It did, and thousands of women celebrated with it. Feminist activists rallied to make birth control and the option of abortion available to all women. Ms. magazine, under the leadership of Gloria Steinem, ran article after article about the joy of female sexuality. "Alfred Kinsey and a squadron of sex researchers freed us from Victorianism's genital prison," Ms. announced in November 1976 in an issue dedicated to exploring sexuality.

Nowadays, the last thing current feminists would do is promote sexual freedom. In today's movement, the prison of Victorianism is preferable to the oppression inherent in unenlightened sex. Kinsey and other researchers are denounced for promoting rape and inequality. Ms. is chock-full of articles denouncing sexual freedoms. In the January/February 1991 issue of Ms., one article gives a glowing review to the English feminist writer Sheila Jeffreys, who claims sex experts such as Kinsey are actually part of an antifeminist conspiracy ("Sexologists have for a hundred years dedicated their lives to eliciting orgasms from women in order to prevent our liberation," she writes[23]), while another article denounces "sexual liberalism" for being antifeminist.

A woman who has shaped her perception of feminism on older feminist works such as Nancy Friday's *My Secret Garden* or Greer's *The Female Eunuch* will find herself in for a shock when she encounters the movement itself. Rarely do today's feminists even acknowledge these books exist. Instead, a young women attending a local NOW chapter meeting will be given handouts on rape that cite Diana Russell; a young woman taking an introduction to feminism class will be assigned writers such as Kathleen Barry, Andrea Dworkin, and others who all adamantly denounce sexual liberation. The only place a woman today is likely to find the tolerant views expressed in *My Secret Garden* is in women's sections in bookstores, where tattered old copies gather dust on forgotten shelves. With the exception of a few fringe works written primarily by lesbians (such as Susie Bright) and reprints of *Our Bodies, Ourselves*, there hasn't been a celebratory book on female sexuality written by a feminist since the mid-seventies.

Amazingly, some feminists leaders have even begun to question abortion rights because they are said to lead to increased heterosexual sex. This line of questioning stops just short of outright condemnation of the right to abortion. "In the context of a sexual critique of gender inequality, abortion promises to women sex with men on the same reproductive terms as men have sex with women," leading feminist Catharine MacKinnon writes. "So long as women do not control access to our sexuality, abortion facilitates women's heterosexual availability. In other words, under conditions of gender inequality, *sexual liberation in this sense does not free women; it frees male sexual aggression* [emphasis added]. The availability of abortion removes the one remaining legitimized reason that women have had for refusing sex besides the headache."[24]

Reading this, it's difficult to interpret MacKinnon's position as anything but *against* legalized abortion. Her argument that abortion "facilitates heterosexual availability" and "frees male sexual aggression" (presumably rapists won't assault us if they know we can't have abortions) mirrors Victorians of the late 1880s who condemned birth control on the grounds that it made "the woman into an instrument for the use of the man."[25] This view is echoed by Dorchen Leidholdt, who writes, "Sexually liberal men support abortion for women not because they want women to be able to control their bodies but because they know that unrestricted abortions heighten women's availability to men for sex."[26] Given this view, liberal men, from President Bill Clinton to our fathers, brothers, and husbands, support abortion rights not because they respect women's choices but because they want a piece of ass. If this is true, what's the solution? Outlaw abortion so women have a "legitimate" reason, in MacKinnon's words, to avoid sex?

Feminist critiques against abortion are taken to an even greater extreme by Sonia Johnson, a feminist activist who ran for President in 1984. Johnson believes that the passage of *Roe* v. *Wade* was actually a conspiracy hatched by men to derail the women's movement. She writes, "They knew precisely what to do when women began refusing to honor the old contract, and I am absolutely convinced that their move was conscious, plotted, and deliberate. . . . So the men let us have legalized abortion, and almost instantly the energy drained from the movement, like air from a punctured balloon." According to Johnson, *Roe* v. *Wade* "keeps us colonized, our bodies state property and our destinies in their hands, and it rivets our attention on them [men]." [27] As bizarre as this position sounds, during her campaign Johnson passed around a fund-raising letter signed by Gloria Steinem, Robin Morgan, Andrea Dworkin, and Mary Daly that asserted, "Only one candidate has had the courage to tell the truth . . . only one candidate has the radical vision to point us in another direction. Of course, we mean Sonia Johnson." [28] Of course.

All of this sounds like a sick joke, but it's true, and female college students attending women's studies classes often learn this is a feminist position. And some young women have accepted it. "Those women who are marching for pro-choice have a lot of nerve to call themselves feminists," a female student at New York University remarked following an abortion-rights rally. "By promoting abortions, these women are giving in to male dominancy." [29]

"Male bashing. Like I said, hairy armpits, no makeup, no lingerie—almost asexual, if that's the right word. Not sexual beings, because that would be 'objectification.' Wearing dumpy clothes, because if you were to wear a miniskirt or a skimpy top, you would be 'objectifying' yourself. . . . Just being really defensive toward men and maybe even going so far as not to have relations with men, sexual, romantic relationships. On the extreme end, feminists are lesbians."

　　　　—ESTHER PETTIBONE, twenty-five, welder from the state of
　　　　Washington, defining what young people see as feminism

Esther is not the only young woman today to be alienated by aspects of the antiphallic campaign. The perception that feminism stands for dumpy clothes, defensive attitudes toward men, and fitting into what Esther aptly terms an "asexual" stereotype didn't just materialize out of thin air. It's the result of leading feminist causes and trends—from the movement's condemnation of men, to attacks on sexual freedoms, to demands for politicized lesbianism and separatism.

Today's feminists have instituted a new set of confining rules for women, many of which smell suspiciously like the same repressive sexual mores that our mothers fought to escape. We are told that sex with men is dangerous and morally wrong, resulting not only in our own oppression and shame but the oppression of all women. We are told that lesbian relationships are the only form of acceptable sexuality, and while this might seem radical and liberating, it is, in fact, based on the same Victorianesque belief that male sexuality defiles the purity of unsullied womanhood. We are told that regardless of our orientation, the acceptance of sexuality we learned from the sexual revolution was a huge mistake and that the woman who pursues sexual freedoms cannot consider herself a feminist. We are even told that instead of freeing our choices, abortion rights actually free male aggression. We are told that all of these things are true—because men are evil—and that the decent woman recognizes this and avoids them at all cost.

By claiming that all men—whether black, white, rich, or poor—are inherently and equally responsible for oppression, and thus unredeemable as human beings, the women's movement comes off as grossly unsympathetic to the very women it is supposed to represent. Feminism has lost sight of something precious in many women's lives: love. A love that often includes men. According to many current feminists, this love is implausible, impossible—a lie. Yet it exists, regardless of sexism and inequality in society, and it will continue to exist, no matter how much feminists condemn it.

Other feminist leaders have condemned sex outside of what they deem proper relationships as wrong—an impossible, shaming standard that alienates women of all ages who believe their sex lives are their own business. Given a choice between the valuable relationships in their lives and dictates that require them to change their sexual partners and model their sex lives after feminist standards, many women will opt not to call themselves feminists.

In discounting the role that men play in women's lives, the women's movement today has made a serious mistake. As long as feminism stands for male bashing, mandated lesbian sexuality, separatism, and repressive sexual mores, countless women will turn their faces away from a movement that stands for hostility and discrimination.

Chapter 2

VICTIM MYTHOLOGY: RAPE AND THE FEMINIST AGENDA

"There's this whole victim thing going on. . . . I get tired of having women portrayed as being the victims of crime, or having a woman portrayed as continuously living her life in a victim role and being victimized. It seems to be everywhere, and I'm not just talking about women's studies classes. I feel like I'm terrible to say that—that I'm being cold. But you can't live your life with those kind of blinders on. You can't live your life in hate. Look, if a guy is driving drunk and runs me over and breaks my legs, I'm dealing with the fact I have broken legs. I have to go through the healing process. But there's a certain point in my life where I have to get over it. I can't live the rest of my life believing I have broken legs. It's crazy."
——AUTUMN HARRISON, twenty-three, student in Oregon

Dressed in flamboyant bright colors and laughing readily, Autumn Harrison is a striking young woman. Broad cheeks emphasize her ebony black eyes, and she carries her large frame with grace and confidence. Her hands—roughened from work in a tavern—cut through the air to emphasize her points. Autumn considers herself a feminist, but not as defined by current feminist leaders. Unlike them, Autumn does not consider herself a victim. While she believes that women who suffer at men's hands deserve support, she feels that the women's movement has gotten off the track by insisting that all women have been, or will be, physically and emotionally abused by men. This is why Autumn Harrison—who believes that women are the equals of any man and deserve equality at work and at home—pauses before saying that she considers herself a feminist. Today's women's movement would have her believe something she knows is not true: that she is doomed to be a victim.

Women today are constantly confronted with the dangers of being born female. Magazine articles, newspaper accounts, and feminist literature all report chilling statistics: that at least one in four women will be raped, that as many as one in four girls are victims of incest, and that nearly all men—if given the chance—would sexually force themselves on women. To be female today sounds like a terrifying proposition: Surrounded by a society of male predators, we are constantly in danger of being attacked by friends, lovers, husbands, and strangers. Many of these attacks are said to occur on dates, by men we trust. Others, we are told, will happen in the office, on the streets, in our homes.

Naturally, we are frightened. To protect ourselves we constrain our lives, viewing every relationship as if it were a dark alley filled with menacing shadows. It would be too easy, it seems, to become that one woman in four. "It's horrible thinking of yourself as vulnerable, that each time you walk out your door some violent HE may be waiting," writes Marcia Ann Gillespie, Ms. magazine's executive editor, in the September/October 1990 issue. "That the man you meet for dinner tonight may assume he has unlimited rights to the use of your body. That the man you know as warm, funny, and kind may one day turn around and slam his fist into your skull, throw you against a wall or down a flight of stairs. That your husband, lover, son, or brother may be a terrorist in waiting." Her fears seem backed up by the numbers. We are told that almost nine out of ten women will be assaulted or harassed.

But where do these terrifying statistics come from and what are they based on? Not from government figures or reliable studies, nor are they based on legal definitions of sexual assault. In fact, they come from just two surveys conducted by separate feminist researchers, Diana E. H. Russell and Mary P. Koss. Their surveys, as this chapter will illustrate, reveal scientific flaws. Russell and Koss have included everything from consensual sex to obscene phone calls in their figures on rape and sexual abuse. Their numbers have little to do with what most people call rape, and everything to do with a new feminist agenda.

By promoting these skewed studies, current feminists promote a new status for women: that of the victim. In their view, those women who have been sexually assaulted are not the only ones deeply traumatized. Joining them are women who have experienced wolf whistles, off-color jokes, glances from men, and even the most loving of sexual relationships. All these things, according to today's feminists, are forms of rape. "Rape, as we have defined it, is any sexual intimacy, whether by direct physical contact or not, that is forced on one person by another," assert Andrea Medea and Kathleen Thompson in *Against Rape*, which is assigned to students attending introductory women's studies courses at the State University of New York at Albany. Considered radical when published in the seventies, this tract joins many more current works presented as mainstream feminism to women today. As examples of rape, the book includes "whistles and comments" from men on the street, "familiar" pats from coworkers, and "the obnoxious drunk at the next table."

And this is far from just an American phenomenon—feminists in England and Canada, among other countries, also push extreme redefinitions of rape. As English feminist Liz Kelly explains in her 1988 book, *Surviving Sexual Violence*, "Sexual violence includes *any physical, visual, verbal or sexual act experienced by the woman or girl, at the time or later, as a threat, invasion or assault, that has the effect of hurting her or degrading her and/or takes away her ability to control intimate contact*." Just what does this mean? Kelly goes on to include "leering," "whistles," "sexual joking," "being touched by strangers on the streets," and "unexplained silent phone calls" as forms of sexual violence.

Rape is a brutal and ugly crime. The victims of sexual crimes deserve both legal help and community support for the trauma they've experienced. We need to confront the bitter reality that—according to the FBI—almost half of all reported rape cases (47 percent in 1990) are not cleared through arrest or other means.[1] As long as the arrest rate is this low, too many rapists stay free to rape again. We need to put pressure on law-enforcement agencies to catch and incarcerate rapists. We need to create and better fund police sexual-assault units, we need to increase sentences for rape, we need to institute more treatment programs for sex offenders in prisons, we need to improve the way rape victims are treated by the courts, and we need to help victims put their lives back together.

But few of today's feminists are pushing for these goals. "Programs and strategies to combat rape are not a priority on the federal, state or local level," former Congresswoman Elizabeth Holtzman stated in the May 1990 issue of McCall's. "It is a serious failure of political leadership." Part of this failure must rest on the shoulders of feminists, who should be putting pressure on politicians to make rape a priority—one of the functions of the movement has always been to offer viable strategies and programs on women's issues and then push to see they are implemented. For the most part, the women's movement gives little more than lip service to legislation and legal help for the real victims of crime. It is true that NOW supports the Violence Against Women Act (a bill that would increase funding for rape prevention and better fund sexual-assault prosecution), that feminist rape crisis centers often push for more government financing, and that activists in some cities train police in rape awareness. But in the places young women encounter feminism, these kinds of actions are given scant attention. Instead, while feminists focus heavily on victimization and assault, little discussion is paid to just what women can do to remedy the problem effectively.

That's because for many of today's feminists, lobbying efforts are viewed as a worthless Band-Aid for the deeper problem: men. To work with men, even on behalf of rape victims, is a betrayal of feminism. "While some feminists have demanded state recognition of and action against male sexual violence, the ensuing response often severely compromises feminist values," writes feminist Jill Radford, coeditor of the 1992 book Femicide: The Politics of Woman Killing. Why? Because some victim support programs "ensure these women will not reject men."

And that rejection will be assured only if women realize they are a powerless class of victims. By redefining rape to include a ludicrously broad range of experiences, many current feminists are trying to redefine what it means to be a woman. Rather than strong and self-reliant, today's feminists would portray women as weak and oppressed. Instead of being in control of our lives, they say we are at the mercy of a culture dominated by rapists. If consensual sex can count as rape, then most women are victims. If wolf whistles, glances, and jokes are sexual assaults, then many of us are raped on a near-daily basis. The chances are we cannot leave our homes without being attacked, and we cannot stay in our homes without experiencing rape from someone we thought we loved.

This is victim mythology. From rape redefinitions to feminist theory on the "patriarchy," victimization has become the subtext of the movement, the moral to be found in every feminist story. Together, these stories form a feminist mythology in which a singular female subject is created: woman as a helpless, violated, and oppressed victim. Victim mythology says that men will always be predators and women will always be their prey. It is a small place to live, a place that forgets strength, capability, trust, and hope. It is a place that tells women that there is really no way out. And it is a place that—instead of empowering women to change—teaches us paralyzing fear. Like other mythologies, victim mythology reduces the complexity of human interaction to grossly oversimplified mythical tales, a one-note song, where the message of the story becomes so important that fiction not only triumphs over fact but the realities of women's experiences are dismissed and derided when they conflict with the accepted female image.

And it is a mythology that harkens back to the mid to late 1800s and early 1900s, when women were also constantly portrayed as pure, dainty, and powerless. "The purity of women," wrote the author of *What Women Should Know* in 1873, "is the everlasting barrier against which the tides of man's sensual nature surge."[2] For Victorians, the purity of women was only a weak barrier against the surging tides of male "nature." In fact, they believed it was women's destiny to be victimized through sex—a burdensome obligation for married women and a fate worse than death for single women. As long as sex existed, rape was inevitable.

Feminist literature, women's studies classes, and women's organizations are pushing fear these days, not freedom—fear on campuses, fear in our homes, fear of our loved ones.

And the media is marching right along.

"When Is It Rape?" asked *Time* magazine in June 1991. After asserting that an estimated "one in four women" will be raped in her lifetime, *Time* didn't tell us where it got its chilling figure. The same one-in-four statistic appeared again in *Teen* magazine in November 1991, this time with the caveat that most of these victims will be between fifteen and twenty-four years old. And in Canada, it popped up in the November 11, 1991, *Maclean's*: "Of every four Canadian women, experts estimate, one will be sexually assaulted during her life."

Cosmopolitan tossed out the number as pure fact in a January 1992 article titled "Date Rape: When Intimacy Turns into Violence." Experts, according to the article, state that "One in four women will be raped in her lifetime." *Ms.* reported in September/October 1990: "At current rates, one woman in four will be sexually assaulted in her lifetime." And in the fall of 1992, *On the Issues*, a national feminist magazine, reported that up to 44 percent—close to one half—of all American women are victimized by rape or attempted rape.

Nowhere, it seems, are we safe. "One out of seven female students is a victim of rape," stated a *Glamour* article titled "Campus Rape" in September 1990. Furthermore, the article claimed that "one out of twelve male students will commit or attempt rape." *Good Housekeeping* warned the parents of female college students that "Rape has become increasingly common on college campuses across the country." How common? The magazine cited a figure of "one in six [women will be raped] within a one year period."

Rape appears to be impossible to avoid no matter what you do. Locking yourself up at home won't help. WARNING: SOMEONE YOU LOVE MAY BE DANGEROUS! announced a September 1990 headline in *Woman's Day*. The photo underneath showed a woman recoiling in fear from a man. "[Y]ou are most likely to be harmed by someone you know, perhaps even someone you love," the magazine intoned. The June 1991 *Time* reported a House committee's astonishing estimation that "1 in 7 married women will be raped by their spouses."

And in an April 1991 *Seventeen* magazine article on incest entitled "An Epidemic of Abuse," girls were warned that an estimated "one in five women in the U.S. is sexually abused by the time she is eighteen." Many of these assaults, the article concluded, will be committed by the girl's relatives. *Teen's* young readers were told in an October 1990 article that "one out of every four girls" is a victim of incest.

These numbers are horrifying. And they appear credible—after all, so many magazines and newspapers publish them. But they are not.

Many magazines and newspapers simply publish as straight facts the figures from press releases they receive about studies. Few check on who did the survey, how scientific it was, and how trustworthy the findings are. Once reported, these "statistics" are then repeated by other magazines and newspapers, which often have little idea where the numbers originally came from. In the case of the high rape and abuse numbers reported in the press, nearly all can be found in just two studies done by feminist researchers Diana Russell and Mary Koss.

While the media often reports on the slanted agendas of political pollsters, little has been written about surveys conducted by other special-interest groups. Results can vary widely depending on who is conducting a study and why. When the individual or group doing a particular study has a definite interest (including financial) in the subject, it is called advocacy research. As former pollster T. Keating Holland writes, "Don't be surprised when the Chocolate Ice Cream Council announces that chocolate is America's favorite ice cream flavor."[3] And don't be surprised if current feminists—who believe that there is an epidemic of rape—consistently find their opinions borne out by their statistics.

Jim Lynch, an associate professor at American University in Washington D.C., and an expert on research methodology, explains that this is his concern with feminist researchers. "I'm leery of the house [the individual or organization doing the study] effect, largely because the group that does it—a lot of people that study rape are advocates. They want more. They believe there's been an underestimate, and they want more," Lynch warns. "You don't want to say 'small earthquake in Chile, not many dead.' That's not going to catch the headlines." And it's the headlines that advocates want.

A survey's methods have a great effect on its results. The wording of questions, the choice of respondents, and the interpretation of their answers all influence the findings. In good surveys, care is taken to ensure neutral questions, to avoid leading the respondent, and to select a cross-section of people that represents the general population. Another rule of survey work is to use methods other researchers can repeat—and thus verify the findings. Advocates are notorious for playing fast and loose with these methods to produce the results they seek.

One of the two constantly cited studies on rape and sexual abuse was conducted in 1978 by feminist author and activist Diana E. H. Russell, whose findings hit the press in the early eighties. According to Russell—basing her study on face-to-face interviews conducted by volunteers with female subjects—rape has reached epidemic proportions.

Russell reports that one in four women—the number so frequently cited—are victims of rape. Adding in attempted rape, she reaches the amazing finding that 44 percent, or nearly one half, of all women are victimized by sexual attack. Russell also reports some shocking conclusions when she writes that approximately "one in every seven women who has ever been married" is raped by her husband (the figure which appeared in *Time*). And when the survey dug into child sexual abuse and incest, it unearthed a mother lode of abuse. Russell states that approximately one out of every six girls are sexually victimized by incestuous relatives. Adding in assault by nonfamily members, and using a broader definition, she concludes that 54 percent—or over one half—of all women are victims of childhood sexual abuse.

Using these high numbers, it's not surprising that Russell concludes that only 7.8 percent of American women will avoid being sexually assaulted in some fashion. This number has gained popularity in feminist literature, though it is seldom mentioned that Russell includes such things as obscene phone calls in her calculations.

Russell's survey is so unscientific, no researcher could ever hope to duplicate—let alone double-check—her startling results. One major problem is Russell's definitions of sexual assault.

In many states, rape is defined as penetration obtained through force, threat of force, or intentional incapacitation (such as drugging someone). In Russell's survey, however, many other kinds of experiences are termed assault. For instance, in her 54 percent figure for incestuous and extrafamilial sexual abuse, Russell includes such acts as "unwanted kisses and hugs." Trying to find victims who fit most state's legal definitions of sexual assault in Russell's survey is like trying to find Waldo in the popular children's books. Undoubtedly, hidden in these inflated numbers are victims of criminal assaults. But also hidden are an unknown number of women who may be surprised to learn that the uninvited hug they received from their grandfather when they were ten somehow qualifies them as incest victims.

Russell has written several books based on her survey—the first, *Rape in Marriage*, came out in 1982; it was followed by both *Sexual Exploitation* and *The Secret Trauma*. A professor emeritus of sociology at Mills College in Oakland, California, Russell coedited the 1992 book *Femicide: The Politics of Woman Killing* with Jill Radford. In 1993, she put together an anthology of feminist antiporn writings entitled *Making Violence Sexy: Feminist Views on Pornography*, in which she describes men looking at pictures of women's vaginas as "visual rapes."

In interviews with feminist magazines and newspapers, Russell often speaks of her activism in the feminist antipornography campaign. She was arrested in August 1990 on two counts of malicious mischief—for storming into stores in Bellingham, Washington, and tearing up copies of *Playboy* and other sexually explicit magazines. The charges were later dropped.

Russell is an advocate, and her work reflects the fact. Her study was originally designed to include two thousand interviews with women from San Francisco. Yet the number of interviews actually completed was only 930. This means over 50 percent of the interviews were not conducted. Standard criteria holds that at least 80 percent of the interviews for any given survey be completed. This is to avoid a lopsided result—if only people with an interest in a subject consent to be interviewed, then the findings can be biased.

But Russell claims that, despite her inability to complete half of her interviews, her sample still represents every woman in the United States. "It is indeed shocking," she writes in *Sexual Exploitation*, as she extrapolates to the lifetime likelihood of assault, "that 46 percent of American women are likely to be victims of attempted or completed rape at some time in their lives."

Furthermore, Russell conducted her survey in only one city. Dr. Gary Perlstein, a professor at Oregon's Portland State University, criminology expert, and author, says this is one of the primary problems with Russell's survey. "One of my great criticisms of her [Russell's] *Sexual Exploitation* book—though I use it in class, by the way—is the fact that her sample is drawn from one area of the country," he explains. "Several places in the book she says there is no reason to assume that the women of San Francisco are any different from anywhere else." He maintains that a study in one city may produce dramatically different results in another—for example, San Francisco has a higher crime rate than many other American cities. "She's trying to say that San Francisco is a typical example," Dr. Perlstein says. "No way. It's not."

But even if she had used a representational sample and had an acceptable refusal rate, this study would still disqualify itself. In order to get her results, Russell trained a crew of women to personally interview the female respondents in their homes. Exactly what this training entailed is unclear. In *Sexual Exploitation*, Russell writes that the "two week training" included "education about rape and incestuous abuse, as well as desensitization to sexual words . . ." If this training was, as Russell writes, to ensure that interviewers wouldn't prejudice their findings by acting judgmentally toward rape victims, then it is a positive method. In *Rape in Marriage*, however, Russell writes that a "key hypothesis of our study was that with high quality interviewing by women who had been sensitized to the issue of sexual assault, we would find that rape and other kinds of sexual assault are quite prevalent. . . ." In other words, her select group of trainees would come back with a lot of rape victims.

This is the hypothesis that helped create many of the extreme numbers later cited in so many reports. Her expectation that she would find rape "quite prevalent" apparently helped design Russell's methodology. For example, her trainees were told not to use the word *rape* itself. In *Rape in Marriage*, Russell states that this would have been "an unpromising approach." What was more promising was letting the interviewers seemingly question the respondents at random, using vague and potentially leading questions. "The interviewer's questions clearly greatly affected what the women said," Russell writes.

Yet rarely in her many books—i.e., *Sexual Exploitation*—does Russell state what those questions were, and even then she lists only three out of "many" pertaining to rape and attempted rape. Of these three, two come close to fitting the legal definition of rape—pertaining to the use or the threat of force. The other is dangerously ambiguous: "Have you ever had any kind of unwanted sexual experience with a stranger (etc.) [the same question was phrased for friends, dates, and husbands] because you were asleep, unconscious, drugged or in some other way helpless? IF YES: Did he (or any of them) either try or succeed in having any kind of sexual intercourse with you?"

There are many ways to interpret this question. A wife may remember a time her husband wakened her with fondling. Questioned further, she recalls she sleepily decided to make love. She would then qualify as a victim of rape. "My opinion is her definition of rape is too broad," says Dr. Perlstein.

Yet many who answered no to Russell's questions *still* seem to be classified as rape victims. In fact, she didn't even appear to follow her own loose criteria. In *Rape in Marriage*, for example, she quotes a respondent who denied her husband used physical force for sex. "No, when he sees I don't want to, he'll forget it. I have done it when I have not wanted to, to please him, but he won't force me. I say yes every now and then to please him." Russell frankly acknowledges that little in this woman's account sounds like assault. Yet she persists in classifying her a rape victim. "Whether her husband forced intercourse or other sexual acts, including manual penetration, is not entirely clear, but we interpreted what Mrs. Warren described as forced intercourse," Russell writes.

The reason Russell chose to classify this account of seemingly consensual sex as marital rape has nothing to do with legal definitions of assault. Mrs. Warren's words supposedly indicate that "feeling compelled to make oneself do certain sexual acts can be upsetting as being compelled by someone else." This is pure victim mythology: The woman doesn't think she was forced, but Russell knew better.

Russell's books on her survey are replete with instances such as this. Women who describe sexual incidents without any apparent force or threats are sometimes said to be in "denial." In one case, a woman responded to questions about "unwanted sex" with her husband by saying, "he has demanded it—as much as I may also make demands of him . . . I don't send out signals about sex. I was not sexually communicative and my husband wanted the full gamut of sex, like lots of foreplay. I really felt I didn't want to do this but I gave in to him. I think he wanted to satisfy me. . . ." Though the interviewer continually pushed for specifics, the woman gave no details of any incident which sounds like an actual assault. Yet Russell concludes this is another case of rape. The woman's description, she writes, "contains a great deal of self-blame and denial, and many excuses for her husband's sexual coercion." This is apparently why the respondent is "reluctant to confront" what happened to her. It appears that Russell's respondents often lie—that is, when it suits Russell's purposes.

Determining just exactly what Russell does classify as sexual assault is difficult. She claims she arrived at what she calls a "compromise" between feminist and legal definitions of rape—one that included oral sex as well as "forced digital penetration." But her accounts tell a different story, as do her study's findings on incest and sexual abuse. The scary numbers reported throughout the media—that at least one in six girls experience incest—are based on such vague and all-encompassing questions such as these:

- Before you turned 14, were you ever upset by anyone exposing their genitals?
- Before you turned 14, did anyone ever feel you, grab you, or kiss you in a way you felt was sexually threatening?
- Before you turned 14, did you have any (other) upsetting sexual experiences that you haven't mentioned yet?

Her definition of incestuous abuse was "any kind of exploitive sexual contact or attempted sexual contact, that occurred between relatives, no matter how distant the relationship, before the victim turned 18 years old." Included are cases of "contact with clothed breasts" and mutual sibling sex play. Under this definition, parents who touch their children's clothed chests (which is almost unavoidable when dressing and undressing them) could be incest perpetrators, as are brothers and sisters who caress one another (which is not necessarily considered abnormal at early ages).

As an example of abusive incest, Russell cites one respondent who told of a time her uncle touched her clothed chest—and the incident as Russell relates it could have been inadvertent. "He was just playing around . . . he put his hand on my breast. I was young and just laughed. We were so happy together. He just touched it a little." That the woman reported she was "not at all upset," Russell says, this just means that "denial is clearly operative in some cases."

Just how inclusive Russell was in her definition of incest and child sexual abuse is illustrated in her book *The Secret Trauma: Incest in the Lives of Girls and Women*. In a table titled "Incest Victimization Before 18 Years and Other Sexual and/or Violent Abuse," Russell includes such things as "upset on street by men's comments" and "respondent received an obscene phone call."

Accordingly, then, women who have experienced anything from obscene phone calls to being touched on the chest are victims of sexual abuse. This helps explain how 16 percent of the perpetrators of extrafamilial sexual abuse in her study are dates, boyfriends, and *husbands*. This is in perfect agreement with the current feminist portrayal of women as victims—if a touch on the chest from a husband can qualify as sexual abuse, then women aren't much more than overgrown children.

In Russell's study, rape, attempted rape, and sexual abuse are given sweeping new definitions. And whether a woman believes she was assaulted or whether she consented to and participated in a sexual act are incidental to Russell's findings.

The agenda of victim mythology behind Russell's study doesn't simply portray women who have experienced consensual sex as crime victims; it portrays what happened to the actual victims of sexual violence as really—at worst—no different from getting kissed on the cheek. This doesn't seem bizarre to Russell. "On a continuum of sexual behavior," she announces in *Rape in Marriage*, "much conventional sexual behavior is close to rape."

"As a general rule, a modest woman seldom desires any sexual gratification for herself. She submits to her husband's embraces, but principally to gratify him." This is from a widely read 1894 treatise on female sexuality by William Acton.[4] For this Victorian, Russell's belief that "much conventional sexual behavior is close to rape" would probably seem perfectly correct. Not only did Acton believe that women have a "natural repugnance" to sex, but he stated that women can only "counterfeit" sexual pleasure. Those who would have claimed otherwise were, to lift a phrase from Russell, simply in denial.

*   *   *

The second study behind the frightening rape statistics was conducted from 1984 to 1985. Titled "The Ms. Magazine Campus Project on Sexual Assault," this survey was conducted by Dr. Mary P. Koss, a professor at the University of Arizona. In 1987, Koss released her findings and the press gobbled them up. According to Koss, one in twelve male college students commit rape or attempt to commit rape, one in four will exhibit sexually aggressive behavior, and over one half of all women are "sexually victimized" after age fourteen. Of all the astounding figures she reached, one in particular got wide and immediate attention: One in four college women were said to be victims of rape or attempted rape.[5]

Koss's study was far more substantial and scientific than Russell's—her team interviewed just over six thousand students enrolled in colleges across the United States. Unlike Russell, Koss avoided personal interviews and instead gave written questionnaires. The seventy-one-page survey consisted of over three hundred questions. Koss took care to get a sample of students that reflected the average, trained her crew to be objective, and had a low refusal rate of under 2 percent.

Unfortunately, the survey has serious flaws—ambiguous questions and numbers that don't add up. Koss took the legal definition of rape and gave it a loose interpretation. "You simply can't make up a survey that's neutral," she frankly admits in *I Never Called It Rape: The Ms. Report on Recognizing, Fighting, and Surviving Date and Acquaintance Rape*, a book released in 1988. Koss is right: There is no perfectly neutral survey. But researchers can design questions that are clear and easily interpreted.

Koss did not. Out of three specific questions on rape, two clearly encompass the legal definition. The other, however, is confusing and misleading: "Have you had sexual intercourse when you didn't want to because a man gave you alcohol or drugs?" Koss insists her question was meant to uncover cases of rape when the victim was purposely incapacitated and unable to give consent. But the question could cover many other experiences. One possible scenario is exchanging sex for drugs, which may be ugly but is nonetheless consensual. Another incident that could be classified as rape is when a woman feels she has to have sex—and even initiates it—because a man bought her drinks. And still another is a woman having consensual sex she later regretted, because she was a little drunk at the time.

"There are all sorts of ways people could interpret that question," remarks Neil Gilbert, a professor at the University of California at Berkeley, who has written several critical articles on Koss's study. Gilbert points out that this question generated almost *half* of Koss's rape victims. "You can calculate the percent," he says. "I think it was forty percent of all the people [victimized by] rape or attempted rape.... She could have asked the question 'Did a guy get you so drunk that you didn't know what you were doing and had sex against your will?' Instead she asked it this way, and that's why a lot of people answered yes."

Koss responds that she was not trying to rope in consensual acts. "In my mind, if you have sex in exchange for drugs, that's a consensual thing," she says, adding that she would have phrased the question differently if she was trying to encompass acts of consensual sex or prostitution. Still, Koss recognizes that this "is the most controversial question in the survey." While she says that designing a question to uncover rape due to intentional incapacitation is very difficult—because a woman who is too drunk to consent might be too drunk to remember what happened—she admits there's no way of judging how women might have understood the question. "This is a battle that is unwinnable without doing more data collection to find out how people actually did interpret the question," she concedes.

But when it came to sexual coercion, Koss's questions grew even vaguer. Female students were asked, "Have you given in to sex play (fondling, kissing, or petting, but not intercourse) when you didn't want to because you were overwhelmed by a man's continual arguments and pressure?"

This question can also be interpreted in a variety of ways, from abusive relationships to miscommunication. The conventional script of pleading for sex is certainly pathetic, but it isn't a crime. If it were, then plenty of women could be considered sex offenders. But it was positive answers to questions like these that helped Koss arrive at her claim that 53.7 percent of her respondents were sexually victimized.

"Consider the following case," Gilbert wrote for the Spring 1991 issue of the magazine *The Public Interest.* "After having a drink, a young man and woman are sitting on a couch kissing in a tight embrace; she offers no objection, perhaps she even offers some encouragement. As he embraces her, with the thought of having intercourse in mind, the man touches the woman's genitals. She pushes his hand away and breaks out of the embrace. Although the man then stops and sheepishly apologizes, he has already committed a sexual act that involves alcohol, force, intent to penetrate, and lack of consent.

Many would say that the young man misbehaved. As Koss would have it, this encounter qualifies as attempted rape."

Compare Koss's figures with the number of reported rapes on campuses and a vast discrepancy appears. Actually, very few rapes are reported by college students. According to crime reports mandated by the federal government's Campus Security Act, less than one rape per campus was reported in 1990.[6] At Barnard College, with 2,200 students enrolled, for example, no rapes were reported in 1992. That same year at Columbia, out of approximately ten thousand female students, only two rapes were reported.[7] If Koss's calculations are correct—that the annual victimization rate (the percentage of women attacked per year) is 16.6 percent, or one in six—then we should be seeing hundreds, if not thousands, of cases of rape every year at each institution. For instance, at the University of Oregon where there are roughly eight thousand female students, according to Koss's figures at least *thirteen hundred* of them are attacked every year. But in 1990 and 1991, there were no reported rapes and in 1992 there was only one. And yet in this three-year span, by Koss's calculations, nearly four thousand women were supposedly attacked. Even assuming that only one in ten women reports rape (a suspect figure from Russell's study), we would expect to see several hundred cases of rape reported at the University of Oregon in this period, not just one. If you accept Koss, you would have to believe that only one in four thousand women was willing to report being assaulted, a ridiculous figure to swallow, given the wide range of rape counseling and legal services offered to female students today. Furthermore, if it's true that approximately one in six college women are being attacked every year, then even figuring in repeat victims, at least 50 percent of female students will have been sexually assaulted by the time they reach graduation—and for those daring enough to go all the way through master's programs, the rate would be close to 100 percent.

Confronted with this lack of reported rapes, many feminists simply argue that women are afraid to go to the police and campus security because of social stigmatization. It's hard to believe, however, that nationally less than one in several thousand female college students are willing to report what is a violent and reprehensible crime.

Part of the answer in this discrepancy may lie in another, less reported finding of the *Ms.* survey. The overwhelming majority of female students classified as rape victims didn't agree with the findings. In fact, only 27 percent of them believed their experience qualified as rape. Of the other 73 percent classified as rape victims, 49 percent labeled the experience "miscommunication," 14 percent said it was a "crime, but not rape," and 11 percent said they "don't feel victimized."[8] If these students didn't believe they had been raped, if in fact many didn't feel they'd even been victimized, then it is understandable that they did not report a crime they don't believe happened.

Another disturbing figure arising from Koss's study is that 42 *percent*—nearly half—of alleged rape victims had sex with their assailant again. In *I Never Called It Rape*, feminist author Robin Warshaw explains this finding. "Because the rape victim doesn't believe that what has happened to her is rape," Warshaw writes, "she sometimes decides to give her attacker another chance."

In a July 25, 1991, letter to the *Wall Street Journal*, Koss explains this figure with the theory that the women "lacked familiarity with what consensual intercourse should be like." This is insulting. How many female college students—even sexually inexperienced—are unable to tell the difference between consensual sex and rape? Women have long had to deal with conservatives insisting that the only proper sex is with their husband, beginning on their wedding night, and if they have any sex outside of marriage, they are only being used. Now Koss, in a feminist twist on *Father Knows Best*, insists that college women don't know the difference between consensual lovemaking and the vicious crime of rape because they lack familiarity with proper sex. The blaring message is that women are too stupid to decide for themselves, just as in Victorian times when women were believed to be so pure they couldn't understand sexual relations. "[T]he full force of sexual desire is seldom known to a virtuous woman," William Sanger wrote in 1858. "In other words, man is the *aggressive* animal, so far as sexual desire is involved."[9]

In the world of victim mythology, women can't win. Lost someplace in our apparently pea-sized brains is the knowledge we've been raped. It is up to today's feminists to bring us out of "denial." Not only are we raped when we don't know it but, like a bunch of dumb beasts, we blunder back to our attacker, asking for more. Our daintiness prohibits us from either fight or flight, and our naïveté prohibits us from knowing exactly what happens to our bodies. Hidden in Russell's and Koss's inflated statistics are women who haven't been assaulted—and lost in them is the woman who has.

Other rape studies get very little attention from the press, even though they show rape to be far less prevalent than Russell or Koss would have us think. The most complete crime study in the nation, from the federal Bureau of Justice, is one of these. Titled the National Crime Survey, this study is conducted every six months and consists of interviews with nearly 100,000 people. The NCS gathers statistics for both reported and unreported rape.

In 1991, the NCS reported that approximately one out of one thousand women were victimized by rape or attempted rape.[10] While this estimate includes unreported rapes, it is just an annual figure. Calculating the lifetime likelihood of rape and attempted rape, the NCS estimated in 1987 that roughly one out of every twelve women will be assaulted.[11]

Since about half of their numbers are for attempted rape, the chance of actual rape would be one out of twenty-four—or 4 percent of all women. According to the NCS, roughly half of these victims (not one in ten) report their experience to the police. These numbers are certainly frightening. Any single rape is cause for concern.

Yet both Koss and Russell attack the National Crime Survey as a deception. In *Femicide: The Politics of Woman Killing*, Russell quotes Koss as accusing the NCS of being "a cruel hoax that covers up rather than reveals women's risk of victimization." Koss defends this statement. "Well, I have been rather harsh on them," she says with a laugh. "But I am not the only one saying this. Diana Russell is saying this and there are several other people who have also made these observations. I think it's an extremely supportable point of view. The strongest evidence for it is the fact that the NCS changed their methodology for measuring rape last July [1992]." But Koss believes the new NCS questions "still aren't good enough."

The NCS asks respondents whether they've been the victim of a crime or assault. If a woman answers yes and says the assault was sexual, she's counted in the statistics. "In the National Crime Survey, each victim defines rape for herself. If she reports that she has been the victim of rape or attempted rape, she is not asked to explain what happened any further," the 1991 NCS report on "Female Victims of Violent Crime" asserts. One feminist criticism of the survey—and a deserved one—is that in the past the NCS didn't ask *specifically* about sexual assault. In 1992, the NCS changed its questions, as Koss notes, to probe more deeply for this crime.[12]

But even assuming that the old NCS missed some rape victims, it is still a fantastic leap from 4 percent, to 15.4 percent (Koss's numbers, remember, are for the number of young women who have *already* been raped, not lifetime likelihood), to 27 percent (Russell's estimate of lifetime likelihood) for actual rape. Figuring in attempted rape, the difference is 8 percent (NCS), to 27.5 percent (Koss), to 46 percent (Russell). If you were sitting in a room with a dozen women friends, then according to the NCS, it's likely one of them will be victimized by rape or attempted rape sometime during her life. According to Koss, three of them have already been attacked—and by a young age—and by Russell's count, five or six out of the twelve will be victims.

Other studies showing lower prevalence rates for sexual assault—from 2.6 percent for forcible rape (Breslau et al., 1991) to 7.3 percent for "any type of unwanted sexual activity" (Norris, 1992)—have been widely ignored in the press.[13] This may be less from a desire for sensationalism on the part of the media than from pure laziness. While these researchers tend to publish their findings quietly in academic journals, advocates inundate newspapers with easy-to-read, glossily produced press releases that make for quick news with little effort—essentially, prepackaged articles. For example, in April 1992, newspapers across the country received a beautifully produced brochure entitled "Rape in America: A Report to the Nation." Tucked inside a creamy white folder, complete with separate pie graphs and charts to accompany articles, this press release for a rape study by two crime victims advocate groups—the National Victim Center and the Crime Victims Research and Treatment Center—made national headlines. According to Dr. Dean Kilpatrick, director of the study, 12.6 percent of American women have been victimized by rape.[14] Professor Jim Lynch from American University comments on this study: "Now Kilpatrick does a nationally representative sample, uses better cues than the old NCS does. The problem with Kilpatrick is that he might have gone too far in the other direction, because he includes a lot of the very nebulous stuff—cues that could capture date rape stuff . . . Pestering, badgering, as opposed to knife at the throat or actual beating, or things like that that are clear, unambiguous heavy-duty felonies. Not to say that these acts don't merit attention, but that if you lump them together in an undifferentiated category, you are going to get a misleading sense of horrendous injury." He concludes that "the new questions from the NCS may strike a nice middle ground."

But for today's feminists, there is no middle ground. Creating the belief in an epidemic of rape is crucial to promoting victim mythology, and fear is an effective method. If women can be convinced that there is such an epidemic, then pushing the idea that all women are victims is made easier. Testifying in 1991 to a Senate Judiciary Committee hearing on rape, for instance, Mary Koss announced that "almost one in three women" is victimized by rape or attempted rape. Her proof was a mailed questionnaire sent to over 5,000 women in Cleveland, which concluded that 27.5 percent of women have been assaulted since their fourteenth birthday. Aside from the fact that 27.5 percent is closer to one in four than one in three, mailed questionnaires are not taken seriously by credible researchers. The major problem with a survey sent through the mail is that only people with an interest in the subject are likely to take the time to answer it and send it back—everyone else is probably going to toss it in the trash. As Kathryn Newcomer, a statistician at George Washington University commented on Koss's survey in the January 28, 1991, issue of *Insight* magazine, "When you have a mailed questionnaire, what you get back is what we call a volunteer sample, which means that it's not a probability sample in a mathematical way. . . . No one cares what the real numbers are, they just want to make political statements. Her [Koss's] study made a political statement. But is it generalizable to the general public? Absolutely not."

To question these politically motivated statistics is to court trouble. When Neil Gilbert published journal articles criticizing Russell's and Koss's studies, *Ms.* magazine castigated him as being part of a "conservative backlash,"[15] and he says he was shocked when outraged feminists bearing KILL GILBERT signs held a demonstration on his Berkeley campus. If women want to consider themselves feminists—or at least avoid being labeled antifeminist—they must not only accept these numbers without question; they must accept the entire agenda of victim mythology that created them.

"I think it [rape] is an aberration. I think the societal role is how it's dealt with after it happens—and why it's allowed to happen in the first place. Not that that particular person who did it is representative of every male in the country. I don't think that's true."

—ANNE MERKELSON, twenty-seven, production coordinator
for a publishing firm in California

But current feminists do think it's true that rapists are representative of nearly every male in the country. For example, the National Organization for Women asserts that not only is "one woman in every three" raped[16], but that sexual assault is "regarded as a cultural norm by society."[17] The New York City Women's Action Coalition also states that "One in three women will be a victim of sexual assault."[18] Clearly, if this many women are being attacked, then a shocking number of men must be incest perpetrators, sexual molesters, and rapists. An article in the August 1992 issue of the Bend, Oregon, *NOW News* makes this point clear: ". . . the undeniable fact [is] that if a man doesn't get sex when and where he wants it without force, he'll use force."

But it is on campus that young women encounter victim mythology in all its full-blown glory. Not only are they assaulted with extreme statistics, they are inundated with the entire redefinition of rape, which is the basis of much current feminism. From women's studies classes to date rape-prevention pamphlets to college rape-education programs, young women are constantly told that to be female is to be a victim, and to be a feminist they must embrace victim mythology.

In an introductory women's studies class at Indiana University at Bloomington, students learn they are assaulted with "rape language," "rape signs," and "stolen glances." These are concepts promoted in the book *Men on Rape* by male feminist author Timothy Beneke. According to Beneke, when a man looks directly at a woman in a sexual way, he has violated her. "One can peripherally notice a woman's attractiveness without denying her humanity," he says. As long as the glance stays properly averted, it's acceptable. But "[w]hen stealing glances becomes disrespectful and intrusive, when it makes women uncomfortable, it becomes one end of a continuum that includes (among other things) catcalls, street and office harassment, battery, and rape."

In a 1989 essay entitled "The Rape Culture," taught at the University of Arizona and recommended by the National Women's Studies Association, author Dianne F. Herman outlines the multitude of ways a woman is raped every day: "She knows also of the 'mini-rapes'—the pinch in the crowded bus, the wolf whistle from a passing car, the stare of a man looking at her bust during a conversation."[19] The idea that wolf whistles and stares are rape is also expressed in a 1983 essay by Barbara Sinclair Deckard entitled "Violence Against Women," which is taught in many women's studies courses, including those at Duke and Tulane universities. According to Deckard, ". . . women would frequently realize that their denial [about not experiencing rape] was not completely accurate. Almost all had been sexually harassed by men. Being shouted at and followed on the street, being pressured into bed through psychological warfare. . . ."[20]

In this psychological war, women are causalities without even realizing it. "For in our culture heterosexual love finds an erotic expression through male dominance and female submission," writes Susan Griffin, author of "Rape: The All-American Crime," an essay taught to women's studies students at the University of Iowa, MIT, and Dartmouth, among other schools. "[T]he basic elements of rape are involved in all heterosexual relationships," Griffin claims.[21]

Marilyn Frye, author of *The Politics of Reality*—assigned at Edgewood College in Madison, Wisconsin, and the University of Iowa, among others—outlines how women have been deceived about sex. Students who believe that "heterosexuality, marriage and motherhood are free choices" are making a serious mistake. Instead, Frye maintains, they are being tricked so subtly, they never realize it. They are pawns of the "plotting coercer" who succeeds "by manipulating the intended victim's perception and judgment through various kinds of influence and deception." Young women are taught that even in the most loving relationships, men are raping us through methods we cannot possibly understand.

Students at the University of Colorado at Boulder learn that "If present trends continue, however, it is estimated that one woman out of three in the United States will be forcibly raped in her lifetime." This is from their professor Alison Jaggar's book·*Feminist Politics and Human Nature*, and—not surprisingly—she offers no proof for this staggering figure. In fact, she goes further. "From the radical feminist perspective, indeed, most heterosexual relations are indistinguishable from rape. The reality of the coercion involved is concealed, however, often even from the participants themselves, by the patriarchal mystification of romantic love," she writes. Jaggar, a socialist feminist, at least qualifies this statement as coming from a radical feminist perspective. Much assigned reading presents such sentiments as straight fact.

"It is difficult to avoid the conclusion that penetration itself is known to be a violation . . ." writes Catharine MacKinnon in an essay entitled "Feminism, Marxism, Method, and the State."[22] MacKinnon's essay, which is taught in many women's studies programs, including those at Duke and UCLA, gets right to the nitty-gritty of the current feminist definition of rape: If it involves a penis, it qualifies. "Instead of asking, what is the violation of rape, what if we ask, what is the non-violation of intercourse? To tell what is wrong with rape, explain what is right about sex," MacKinnon poses.

In the current feminist promotion of victim mythology, there is never anything "right" about sex. It is not only dirty and dangerous; it is inextricably linked to death. At Tulane University, MIT, the University of Utah, and other schools, young women attending women's studies are assigned work by feminist leader Andrea Dworkin, who writes, "The power of sex, in male terms, is also funereal. Death permeates it. The male erotic trinity—sex, violence, and death—reigns supreme."[23]

Linking sex and death is nothing new. "In some exceptional cases, indeed, feeling has been sacrificed to duty," wrote the Victorian William Acton in 1894, "and the wife has endured, with all the selfmartyrdom of womanhood, what was almost worst than death."[24] For some of today's feminists, these words about sex must ring remarkably true. It is a fate almost worse than death.

Even those women students who avoid classes on feminism are still beaten over the head with victim mythology. Relying on Russell's and Koss's skewed studies, many campus groups and women's centers push fear and victimization through brochures, fact sheets and date rape education programs. "Acquaintance Rape: Is Dating Dangerous?" asks a pamphlet published by the American College Health Association. Given to students at colleges across the country, this glossy little brochure features a smiling couple happily dancing on the cover— the photo broken into sections like shattered glass.

According to its text, dating is dangerous, because "one in four" women are sexually assaulted, mostly by dates and acquaintances. These figures are cited again on a bright yellow information sheet available to students at Harvard. "Acquaintance Rape: Some Statistics" trumpets in heavy underlined letters that "1 in 4 women are survivors of rape or attempted rape."

"Sexual aggression," according to a UCLA brochure, "can range from forced sexual intercourse to any unwanted touching, and even verbal abuse." It furthermore warns that an "estimated 1 in 3 women will be the victim of an attempted or completed rape during her lifetime." "When Sex Becomes a Crime: Date and Acquaintance Rape," a pamphlet published by Indiana State University at Terre Haute tells students that 90 *percent* of women in a survey—which isn't named— "had experienced at least one sexually aggressive incident during a date." And at Humboldt State University, students are given a brochure on "understanding and preventing acquaintance rape," which blares, "ONE IN THREE WOMEN IN THE UNITED STATES WILL BECOME A VICTIM OF SEXUAL ASSAULT IN HER LIFETIME." No citation is given for this number, but the recommended reading list in the back is telling; Susan Griffin, Robin Warshaw's *I Never Called It Rape*, based on Koss's study, Timothy Beneke's diatribe against "stolen glances," and the feminist antiporn book *Take Back the Night*, featuring Russell and Dworkin, are included.

These examples go on and on, often citing the one-in-four statistic, which in one case is dredged up (at the University of Oregon) to represent the number of women not only raped but subjected to severe and regular beatings. No citation is given for this shocking figure.

"Nowhere in the country are we safe. Even on the public highways, the situation has become so serious . . . [that] the fragile and helpless women, innocent of any wrong" fears for her security. These are the words of an American Victorian woman, and the "situation" she refers to was considered quite grave in the early 1900s, resulting in widespread hysteria.

It was the racist belief that oversexed black men were roaming the streets, intent upon raping every single white woman in the South.[25]

"This is something I was just dealing with recently. I was in this situation with sexual pressure from a man, and not wanting to give in. But my body's saying I want to, so why shouldn't I? And then thinking that I didn't want to yet, but his pressure leading up to my giving in anyway. In the end, I felt resentful and angry at him. And then I thought, Wait a second. I'm turning myself into a victim by doing this. I was saying it was all under his control. And I have to take responsibility for my own power. That's one thing in our culture we have to learn how to do. It's so ingrained to be docile and go along. Then I started thinking, If this is culturally ingrained in me as a woman, what about him? I told him about it, how it made me feel. And he felt like shit. . . . it turns into this big rapist/victim thing. But it's really about unlearning bad behaviors."

—MIMI PETTIBONE, twenty-seven, belly dancer
in the state of Washington

Many women have had an experience like Mimi's, where they feel mixed emotions about having sex but consent nonetheless. To call this rape, as Mimi notes, turns women into victims. It says such encounters are completely under the man's control, when, in fact they are not—when the woman could say no and have that no respected, when she could just get up and walk away. And Mimi is right. We do have a responsibility to say no if we don't want sex. Experiences such as hers aren't rape, but they aren't positive, either. Turning them into what Mimi terms a "big rapist/victim thing" doesn't help either sex unlearn negative social behaviors. It only reinforces the Victorian notion of women as helpless victims and men as sexual predators. This is exactly the opposite of what the feminist fight against rape started out espousing.

When concern over rape exploded during the women's movement of the mid-1970s, the focus was on action. Hundreds of rape crisis centers opened around the country (now over four thousand), new laws were adopted which prohibited dragging up a victim's sexual history in court, legislation was overhauled, and activists worked in conjunction with law-enforcement agencies in improving police training. Feminism can take credit for immense changes in the legal system, social services, and popular culture. For the first time, rape was seen as a crime that did not have to be hidden by the victim out of fear she would be condemned. It was through the feminist activism of this time that society learned that rape victims do not "ask for it," that women should not be grilled about their private lives in court, and that husbands can indeed be guilty of raping wives.

Susan Brownmiller's landmark book, *Against Our Will: Men, Women and Rape,* published in 1975, was one of the first works to proclaim that rapists act not out of sexual desire but out of aggression and the desire for power. "The popularity of the belief that a woman seduces or 'cock-teases' a man into rape" she wrote, ". . . is part of the smokescreen that men throw up to obscure their actions." Another of Brownmiller's conclusions was that women become "indoctrinated into a victim mentality." Part of this mentality, which Brownmiller cites Viennese psychoanalyst Helen Deutsch as exemplifying, is believing the old-fashioned assertation that intercourse is "an essentially painful encounter for an essentially passive woman."

But that old-fashioned mentality is exactly what today's feminist activists are promoting. But redefining rape in such broad terms, current feminist leaders have found themselves pushing a repressive antisex morality. Intercourse is once again seen as an essentially painful encounter and women are once again seen as the essentially passive recipients of these encounters. As young feminist Katie Roiphe writes in her 1993 book, *The Morning After: Sex, Fear, and Feminism on Campus,* the image "that emerges from feminist preoccupation with rape and sexual harassment is that of women as victims. . . . This image of a delicate woman bears a striking resemblance to that fifties ideal my mother and the other women of her generation fought so hard to get away from. They didn't like her passivity, her wide-eyed innocence." Instead of fighting victim mentality, current feminists are trying to sell it. In this, they are much like the Victorians, who used the vision of women as sexless and helpless dainties to reinforce confining notions of female purity.

While radical feminist authors have been redefining rape for years, it has only been in the past decade that these theories have been accepted by mainstream feminism, taught in women's studies classes, and trumpeted in feminist magazines and organizational literature. In her 1992 book, *The Word of a Woman: Feminist Dispatches 1968–1992*, former Ms. editor Robin Morgan reprints a seventies essay on rape and pornography. As Morgan would have it, even when women say yes it can still be rape. "*I claim that rape exists any time sexual intercourse occurs when it has not been initiated by the woman, out of her own genuine affection and desire*," she writes.

In this case, if the man initiates sex, it is rape. If a woman has sex without "affection"—or perhaps love—it is also rape. If a woman isn't feeling particularly desirous yet still decides to have sex, it is rape. So, according to Morgan, rape is not a crime of assault or even a question of consent. It is a crime of women having sex that doesn't meet Morgan's moral criteria. "[I]t need not be a knife-blade against the throat; it's in his body language, his threat of sulking, his clenched or trembling hands, his self-deprecating humor or angry put down or silent self-pity at being rejected," Morgan writes. "How many millions of times have women had sex 'willingly' with men they didn't want to have sex with? Even men they loved? . . . It must be clear that, under this definition, most of the decently married bedrooms across America are settings for nightly rape."

When Morgan first wrote these words, she was considered a radical feminist. Much of her writing dealt with subjects such as demanding the release of Valerie Solanos, the woman who shot and wounded artist Andy Warhol and fronted a group called the Society for Cutting Up Men, or SCUM. Morgan made her points about man-hating clear. "I feel that 'man-hating' is an honorable and viable *political* act," she wrote.[26]

Now Morgan is considered a mainstream feminist, until recently heading a magazine that supposedly represents the women's movement. Her sweeping definition of rape doesn't seem to have changed since the seventies. In fact, in her 1992 introduction to the essay quoted above, she only reiterated her stand. Her theories have been accepted. And following the focus on sexual violence generated by

Russell's and Koss's studies, it's views like hers that are often the first thing women hear when they encounter feminism today.

"In a situation where you know the man and he forces sex on you, it's still rape. It's important that the courts are beginning to acknowledge that and people are starting to be educated on that. But at the same time, I think the idea of it [current feminist theory on rape] presents women as powerless, as if they have no control, and if they want sex, there's something wrong with that. The whole idea of date rape assumes women never want sex."
    —ANNE CUNNINGHAM, twenty-four, salesperson from New York

Anne puts her finger on why victim mythology disturbs many young women. Running like a dark stream through current feminist thought is the assumption that women never want sex, that not only are we helpless innocents but if we should fail to live up to this image of chaste, sexless victims, there is something wrong with *us*.

At Dartmouth College, students sit down for a movie as part of their Sexual Awareness and Abuse Program. The movie is "Rethinking Rape," and it is shown not only in college rape-education seminars but in many introduction to women's studies classes, including those at Duke and SUNY Plattsburgh. Cheaply made, the film opens with scratchy seventies music. "One in three women will be raped in their lifetime!" the commentator announces. The number hangs there, unattributed, offered as unquestionable fact. In this film—shown to thousands of students—men alone are not responsible for rape. Women are to blame, too: "When you laugh at a sexist joke at a party, you are giving someone in that room permission to rape," the film states. In that case, the blame for rape lies on women's shoulders as well as men's. If we would only use clean language and faint at dirty words, rape would stop.

Another example of this attitude comes from the University of Minnesota. One section of the "Introduction to Women's Studies" course devoted to sexual assault opens with the movie *Rape Culture*, another popular educational film shown at many colleges. In this movie, even women's private thoughts are said to be linked to rape. "Sure, women can have rape fantasies," an activist proclaims, "but it's very unhealthy" and, furthermore, an "extension" of rape itself. Feminist author Mary Daly is featured redefining rape as the "sometimes subtle but equally devastating mind rapes that happen all the time."

The film then changes scenes, leaving students wondering just what a "mind rape" is and how it can compare to physical assault.

But the question is indirectly answered in the movie: If a rape fantasy can promote assault, then what people think is just as dangerous as what they do. If we want to see rape stopped, we must be pure in thought and body. "Why do some women participate in wet T-shirt contests or allow beer to be poured on their breasts? Why do they sometimes participate in their own victimization and thus help support an inhospitable atmosphere on campus?" asks a brochure from the Association of American Colleges titled "Peer Harassment: Hassles for Women on Campus" that is given to many female college students. This "colluding," as it is called, includes such things as laughing at sexist jokes. The brochure goes on to state that women who "inadvertently or knowingly participate in their own victimization or that of others help perpetuate a climate conducive to peer harassment." In other words, *bad girls cause rape*. If good feminists want to stop sexual violence, they had better chastise women who laugh at sexual jokes, participate in wet T-shirt contests, or act sexual in public. In this brochure's "Dos and Don'ts" recommendations to students, women are not only told they shouldn't "participate in wet T-shirt contests, 'nude olympics' " and "other demeaning activities" but they should refuse to condone such forms of "collusion" by other women. Women who do these things are a direct threat to the purity and chastity of women. They are a direct threat to feminism—just as in Victorian times, when "fallen" women were ostracized lest they taint decent, chaste "ladies."

"If you dress in a 'sexy' manner and flirt," warns an American College Health Association brochure on acquaintance rape, "some men may assume you want to have sex." While this pamphlet acknowledges that this "does not make your dress or behavior wrong," it also promotes the belief that men rape out of sexual need, not because of aggression or desire for power—and that women who wear short skirts are asking for it. Or, as Victorian Sylvanus Stall argued in his 1897 book, *What a Young Man Ought to Know*, the male body is "like a cage that encloses a beast, an angel and a devil, and no young man can afford to arouse the beast."[27] When sexy clothing leads to rape, then young women really are just arousing the uncontrollable "beast" inside men.

Other college pamphlets also offer advice to young women who want to avoid the likely chance of being raped. "What Can You Do?" asks a handout on acquaintance rape from Humboldt State University's women's center. Reading this, it seems there's not much women can do to prevent rape. They should realize "there are a thousand different ways someone can force you to 'comply.'" They can, for instance, "gain your trust and then verbally confuse you." Such sentiments echo Victorian times, when young women were also treated as naïve, confused children easily misled by cunning men.

"When you are on a date, it can be difficult to determine when a 'normal' encounter is leading to a potentially problematic situation," states one brochure from UCLA. Another pamphlet, however, from the American College Health Association, gives clues. If you are on a date, a rapist will follow a "common pattern" that leads to assault. "First there is an intrusion into a woman's physical and/or psychological space (e.g. a hand on her shoulder or thigh) testing her response . . . this behavior is often subtle."

Avoiding Rape On and Off Campus, written by Carol Andrews-Pritchard, gives other pointers to identifying "potential" rapists. If a date "ignores your space boundaries by being too close or placing his hand on your thigh" or "asks personal questions" he's displaying characteristics—according to Pritchard—that are "frequently" exhibited by rapists. Just in case women might question how a man who asks personal questions is necessarily a rapist, Pritchard states that rapists "may appear to be great guys," but when "they find a vulnerable victim, their personalities change."

This same Jekyll and Hyde syndrome is promoted in a bright blue brochure from Eastern Illinois University. For help in "Recognizing Potential Date Rapists," women are told that "men may exhibit behaviors which could indicate tendencies to be date rapists." They may:

- act bored
- not listen to their dates
- call dates by endearing names when the relationships are only casual

If something as harmless as touching a woman's shoulder or calling her an endearing name signifies an oncoming assault, then the best advice for women must be to simply avoid men. As a Harvard University "Date Rape Prevention Strategies" information sheet advises in bold type: "Beware of vulnerable situations such as being alone together in bedrooms or secluded areas." This conveys that such behavior may lead to sex, and sex is dangerous.

Many feminists and crime-prevention specialists argue that suggestions such as these are necessary. Teaching women how to avoid assault is a good idea, and some of these brochures offer worthwhile suggestions, from watching your alcohol intake on dates to learning self-defense. But these valuable precautionary ideas are overshadowed by the current feminist agenda. A curious omission develops in these brochures and educational sheets: Rarely is it acknowledged that women might *want* to have sex. In victim mythology, the idea alone is an affront. The assumption is that they don't.

"[S]it not with another in a place that is too narrow; read not out of the same book; let not your eagerness to see anything induce you to place your head close to another person's." This is the Victorian answer to the problem of maintaining the chastity of women in a world full of oversexed male predators. The 1860 book it is from is titled, not surprisingly, *The Young Lady's Friend*.[28]

There is nothing new or radical in this current feminist portrayal of men and women. It is simply a new twist on an old favorite: men as wicked demons with sex on the brain, women as defenseless, chaste innocents in need of protection. And the media has gone for this view whole hog. In a nostalgic tone, the September 1989 *Good Housekeeping* recalls the days of "a different, gentler campus life in which men and women lived in separate dorms and adhered to curfews." " 'Does he make suggestive remarks or tell off-color jokes just to make you uncomfortable?' " the September 4, 1992, issue of *Woman's Day* quotes a University of Florida rape prevention director. Watch out girls, " 'Those are red flags. Sexual assault may be ahead.' " A January 1992 *Cosmo* article concludes that the "old-fashioned advice moms have been giving daughters for generations" is the best policy for dating: "Don't allow yourself to be alone with him."

Even otherwise feminist-thinking magazines have fallen for this antifeminist view. In a May 1992 article on date rape, *Glamour* offers "a few cautions about going out with men and getting physical with them." Women are advised to watch for assault clues, such as men who buy them drinks: "Men *try* to get women drunk; it's the means to a very specific end." But above all, *Glamour* makes it clear that hanky-panky is a good way to get raped. "Should you be kissing, hugging and/or touching when you start feeling uncomfortable, his mind is likely to have fogged over somewhat," the article declares. A sexually aroused man is uncontrollable; "A man in heat is, well, a man in heat," or, as Victorian writers put it, a beast.

Should anyone miss the message that delicate, sexually restrained, and traditionally well-mannered nice girls won't get raped—and that bad girls will—an April 1992 *Mademoiselle* article makes it clear. Activities such as "teasing," "barhopping," and "allowing alcohol to color one's behavior," we are informed, are acts of "moral turpitude." In fact, it seems that the best idea is just to turn back the clock to the nineteenth century. "Indeed, some people who work with sexual assault victims say that violence may be increasing as the advances made by women in society trigger a backlash," an article titled "The Spectre of Male Violence: A Backlash Against Assertive Women" in the March 5, 1990, issue of the Canadian magazine *Maclean's* announced. Talk about blaming the victim.

Those who remember Germaine Greer might think that feminists would be up in arms over articles such as these. But from the current feminist front, there is only silence. It is the silence of assent. In fact, the idea that women's equality has generated more sexual violence (by placing women at greater risk) has gained popularity throughout the women's movement. "We see this escalation of violence against females as part of a male backlash against feminism," Diana Russell and Jane Caputi wrote in a September/October 1990 article for *Ms.* that identifies everything from "forced heterosexuality" to "cosmetic surgery" as part of a conspiratorial "reign of sexist terror comparable in magnitude, intensity, and intent to the persecution, torture, and annihilation of women as witches from the 14th to 17th centuries in Europe."

Undoubtedly, victim mythology is appealing to many women. In a time when AIDS and venereal diseases are cause for concern, when women are still taught to have mixed feelings about sex and when college students are facing important and difficult decisions about their own sexuality, a theory that paints all men as rapists and all women as helpless victims can gain converts. It's a simple answer to confusing questions. And let's be honest. Seeing ourselves as victims is often far easier than taking responsibility for those aspects of our lives we can control, whether by telling a guy who leers at us to bug off instead of feeling helplessly violated or by acknowledging that even if we regret it the next day, consensual sex is still consensual sex—and that if we aren't threatened or incapacitated, we must take responsibility for our own decisions. A victim status based on an ideal of chaste womanhood can be deeply appealing, not only because it dismisses the responsibility of the power we do have but because it fits into comforting societal views of femininity: fragility, sexlessness, and helplessness are often still rewarded, while frank sexuality is condemned. The woman who says, "He talked me into it" after having consensual sex is still seen as a good girl. The young woman who says, "I invited him up to my place; we got naked and had a blast" is often still deemed a slut.

But accepting victim mythology is not without a price. To accept feminist redefinitions of rape, women must accept that even when they say yes, feminists will say no. They have to accept that men cannot be trusted. And they have to accept that, from the bedroom to the boardroom, equality with men means a greater likelihood of assault. Since male glances and jokes are assaultive, working with men will only encourage rape. Since women's rights have caused a "backlash" of violence, fighting on behalf of equal pay and job advancement in a man's world will only increase the occurrence of rape. Since heterosexual sex is a violation, fighting for better birth control and national day-care programs will only promote the practice of assault, taking place, as Robin Morgan insists, in bedrooms across America that are "settings for nightly rape." This twisted logic is one reason why young women, and women of all ages, reject today's women's movement. We have been told that feminism no longer stands for equality; it stands for things that once were considered the antithesis of feminism: helplessness, hysteria, paralyzing fear, sexual repression, and, finally, retreat.

"Once it did feel powerful to be part of the movement, to declare that all things were possible to she who dared, to cast off the limits of the past that defined us as weak, dependent, passive, in need of protection, unable to speak for ourselves, childlike," *San Jose Mercury News* editor Joanne Jacobs noted in a 1993 column on how victim mythology has changed feminism. "Women share experiences as women and have aspirations as individuals that may be restricted because we're women," writes Jacobs. "We need to be feminists. But not victims."[29]

Current feminists say they are trying to help rape victims. But are they? If the women's movement wants to reduce the occurrence of rape, it would put pressure on law-enforcement agencies to catch, convict, incarcerate, and, if possible, treat rapists. If our country spent a fraction of the time and money on fighting rape that has gone into fighting drugs, immense changes would occur. If current feminists were interested in enhancing public sympathy for the victims of sexual assault, they would show it as it is: brutal, ugly, vicious, and traumatic. They would not trivialize rape by lumping it together with consensual sex or unwanted grandfatherly hugs. "If you start calling anything rape, then it takes away from the real rape where you are walking down the street and you are completely physically overtaken and there is nothing you can do about it," Esther Pettibone, a twenty-five-year-old welder from the state of Washington, comments with regard to rape redefinitions. "Then you'll tell someone you got raped and it'll be like, oh well, she got her butt touched. Big deal."

Today's feminists are using the word *rape*—and the fear it invokes—to promote their agenda of victim mythology. It is a method used by many advocacy groups. Anti-abortionists parade photos of bloody fetuses in an effort to outlaw abortion even in the case of rape and incest. Anyone disagreeing is decried with shouts of "babykillers." Current feminists use the word *rape* to push the Victorian vision of women as helpless victims and then label anyone who questions this repressive view "antifeminist."

It is an effective method for pushing victim mythology, but it doesn't help rape victims. In fact, it does them great harm. Their experiences, lost in numbers that include consensual sex, are trivialized. What happened to them—and continues to happen to women day after day—has become a tool to be used by current feminists. It is in their names that today's feminists push what they truly want: the institution of a new morality, a morality that echoes the repressive, confining mores of old. A morality that makes women, in Germaine Greer's words, "sexless." It is under the guise of fighting rape that current feminists are actually fighting sexual freedom. And in the name of rape victims, they have established one of their first priorities: the destruction and censorship of sexual words and ideas.

This is the feminist antipornography struggle. And this is their answer to the reprehensible crime of rape.

Chapter 3

DIRTY PICTURES: THE FEMINIST FIGHT AGAINST PORNOGRAPHY

"There're these two women; they stand on Fifty-seventh Street. They hold up these signs with disgusting pictures of women being gagged and tied up in these horrible positions. They've been around for six or seven years, and they just stand there and scream. They're really, really obnoxious. Then finally one day, I stopped and talked to one of them, and she was the most conservative person I ever spoke to in my life. She was saying really offensive things. . . . That's like the only kind of [feminist] organization I've seen around New York, and those two women just drive me crazy. . . . I guess I get caught up in the censorship thing. I think I feel more strongly, identify more, with not having art censored. That's something I care about a lot. It's hard to draw a line for me in that situation. I wish it wasn't."

—SARA, twenty-four, social worker and student in New York

Curled up on the couch in her spotless New York apartment, Sara speaks in soft tones. The sunlight catches her short blond hair and a tabby purrs incessantly under her hand. Dressed in a loose-fitting green shirt and leggings, she is fine-boned, with tapering wrists and translucent skin. Sara has always considered herself a feminist. But faced with the feminist fight against pornography, Sara hesitates. Speaking carefully, she explains that the issue confuses her. On one hand, she finds some pornography degrading. On the other, she doesn't

approve of censorship—or the extremism of the activists she encounters. And from her work with sex offenders, she knows that to blame
pornography for rape "doesn't help anything," as she says. Yet Sara
also knows that to be a feminist today one must support the censorship of sexual material. And so when she says that she doesn't agree,
her voice trails off, leaving a note of apology hanging in the bright,
clear room.

The feminist fight against dirty pictures goes far beyond the actions
of the two feminists Sara sees screaming on New York street corners.
This battle has generated countless books, magazine articles, essays,
college seminars, slide shows, rallies, and marches. It has spawned numerous organizations—from Women Against Pornography to Feminists Fighting Pornography—and has become a major focus in
women's studies classes. Not only the United States but Britain,
Canada, and Germany also boast strong antipornography crusades. In
fact, the feminist battle against porn has created a new set of feminist
leaders, activists who have dedicated themselves solely to this campaign and work on little—or nothing—else.

Virtually every segment of today's women's movement has become
embroiled in this issue. "If I had to do it in a percentage," says supporter Robin Morgan, "I would say 85% to 90% of the feminist
movement is involved in one way or another in the feminist campaign against pornography." Feminist organizations have fallen in line
as well. NOW, for instance, has thrown its weight behind this cause.
In 1984, it passed a resolution to fight pornography. In 1990, ex-
president Molly Yard appointed a NOW National Committee on
Pornography.[1] In 1991, the organization even proposed launching a
national campaign against sexually explicit material, which failed
when porn actresses showed up and told NOW to butt out of their
lives.[2] Eleanor Smeal, president of the Fund for the Feminist Majority, has also endorsed this cause, joining hands with Andrea Dworkin,
Catharine MacKinnon, Dorchen Leidholdt, and other activists at a
March 1993 antiporn conference held at the University of Chicago.[3]
Even feminists who once advocated freedom from sexual guilt and
empowered women with the idea that sexuality should be based on
choice now whistle a completely different tune. "It cannot be too
often or too clearly said that all our commercial pornography is sadomasochistic and degrades the individuals depicted in it . . . ," Ger-

maine Greer writes in her 1991 book, *The Change*. "The sex inspired by it is just not worth having, it is fundamentally destructive."

Feminist legislation that could censor even the softest erotica has been proposed in several American cities, including Bellingham, Washington, and Indianapolis, Indiana, as well as in Great Britain and Ireland. Sweeping definitions of porn taken from this feminist ordinance were adopted in a 1992 Canadian obscenity ruling and have been used to censor lesbian and gay literature in that country. Simply condemning sexual material is not enough for many current feminists. They want it banned.

For countless women such as Sara, the feminist fight against dirty pictures raises troubling questions. Does pornography actually cause rape? Who gets to define pornography? Does literature count? Is there a difference between porn and erotica? And should feminists, of all people, try to restrict the right to free speech? Overwhelmingly, women of all ages wonder whether campaigning against sexual material isn't just a tremendous drain of energy—energy that could be directed toward issues such as child care and reproductive rights. But for many current feminist leaders, these doubts are unacceptable. The feminist fight against dirty pictures is one of the leading causes in the women's movement today. And to question it is heresy.

On a balmy fall evening, students at Reed College in Portland, Oregon, chat as they file into the auditorium to watch a slide show on pornography. Members of a feminist organization called Stopping Violence Against Women hand out information sheets trumpeting the title "Pornography Is Violence Against Women." After being told that one-third of all women in the United States will be raped and that pornography is to blame, the slide show begins.

Within minutes, the students are gasping at grainy black-and-white bondage photos—nude and partially nude women muzzled and bound with ropes. The shock of S&M paves the way for slides of *Penthouse* centerfolds and, amazingly, makeup advertisements. The speaker ties these images together and says they all promote rape. The students are told that women are bound up, raped, and hacked to pieces in the production of pornography. (Although not a single slide depicts actual violence against women—the only example of a rape scene is narrated from the pages of a cheap paperback.) The slide show concludes with this clincher: If we want to stop rape, we need to get rid of sexual material—all of it.

This is the theory behind the current feminist crusade against porn: Sexual images cause sexual violence. To support this theory, activists cite their own evidence—the flawed rape studies of Diana Russell and Mary Koss. This epidemic of rape, feminists say, proves that pornography makes men assault women. If there wasn't pornography, rape would rarely occur. Voilà, the cure.

Leading researchers in the field—including Dr. Edward Donnerstein, a professor at the University of California at Santa Barbara, Dr. Daniel Linz, also of the University of California, and Dr. Steven Penrod, from the University of Wisconsin—have concluded there is no identifiable link between sexual material and rape. History also discounts the idea (rape was prevalent before mass-market pornography). But these points are dismissed. When consensual sex can be rape, as it is defined in Koss's and Russell's studies, then any depiction of sex can also be an assault.

"*Playboy*, in both text and pictures, promotes rape. *Playboy*, especially in its cartoons, promotes both rape and child sexual abuse," feminists Catharine MacKinnon and Andrea Dworkin declare in their 1988 book, *Pornography and Civil Rights*. As they put it, "The women in *Playboy* are presented in postures of submission and sexual servility. Constant access to the throat, the anus, and the vagina is the purpose of the ways in which women are posed. . . . Underlying of all *Playboy*'s pictorials is the basic theme of all pornography: that all women are whores by nature, born wanting to be sexually accessible to all men at all times." The key phrase is "sexually accessible." Running through Dworkin's and MacKinnon's work is the theme that women who would be sexually accessible, who would welcome—or even pursue—sexual encounters are, and always will be, whores. You would think you were reading Victorian condemnations of female sexuality as the root of all evil, not so-called feminist literature. As a Victorian novelist wrote, even "as woman is supremely virtuous, when once fallen, the vilest of her sex."[4]

In fact, the women's movement today has found itself repeating history—nineteenth-century history. "But I warn you, with yet more solemn emphasis, against EVIL BOOKS and EVIL PICTURES," expounded an American Victorian preacher in a widely read sermon. "This black-lettered literature . . . hatches in the young mind broods of salicious thoughts."[5] It was this attitude that lead to the passage of the Comstock bill (nicknamed after the moral crusader Anthony Comstock) in 1873—which fiercely censored sexual material, including birth-control information, on the grounds that it promoted "lascivious" behavior and led youths to act out plots of seduction and violence.[6]

Now feminists want to outlaw porn—on the very same grounds as the Victorians. It inflames male desire, leads to rape, and displays female sexuality, thus degrading women. It is always under the guise of protecting women that extremists try to ban erotic expression. Current antiporn feminists are no exception.

In battling dirty pictures, feminists have found themselves sharing ideals with those other modern Victorians, the religious right. Religious zealots are notorious for trying to censor material they dislike. In fact, feminist literature such as *Our Bodies, Ourselves* has often been the subject of their attacks, and, according to Betty Friedan, *The Feminine Mystique* was suppressed as pornographic. It doesn't seem to disturb or surprise feminist activists to find themselves agreeing with the same ultraconservatives who have tried to censor feminist literature.

And it shouldn't. They've been working together.

"I think the entire pornographic movement is really stupid. The fact that it's aligned with the right wing—it's just really hard to imagine being aligned with that. Plus, I don't buy into arguments that pornography perpetuates violence against women, or that it is [in itself] an act of violence against women. I just don't see it."

—SARA MANAUGH, twenty-three, student in California

"An unusual coalition of radical feminists and conservative women politicians in Minneapolis and Indianapolis is leading a novel campaign against pornography," the *New York Times* reported on June 10, 1984. At that time, feminist lawyer Catharine MacKinnon was in Indianapolis, Indiana, pushing an antiporn ordinance she had written with activist Andrea Dworkin. But while MacKinnon and Dworkin claim their legislation is inspired by feminism, feminists kept a low profile throughout the Indianapolis proceedings.

Instead, MacKinnon was bedding down with the far right. To sell censorship, she worked with a cast of religious extremists and other conservatives. The councilwoman who introduced MacKinnon's bill—and helped her promote it—is Beulah Coughenour, a self-proclaimed "conservative Republican" who led the successful "Stop

ERA" campaign in Indiana and opposes abortion as well as laws allowing the prosecution of marital rape.[7]

That the two women worked closely together is no secret. "Philosophically we are not in the same ballpark," Coughenour says of MacKinnon. "But we saw eye to eye on this particular item and we were able to work together." Coughenour, who speaks clearly and frankly, doesn't believe that there is anything odd about feminists siding with conservatives. "I think we learned a lot within the past few years. We don't let one point of view on one subject alienate us from working with one another," she says.

Indianapolis is a conservative city—run at the time MacKinnon was there by an overwhelmingly Republican city council—that has a long history of church-based activism against porn. When MacKinnon proposed her ordinance, two of the city council members belonged to Citizens for Decency Through Law. A leader of this religious group explained to Donald Alexander Downs, author of *The New Politics of Pornography*, that "Satan is still Prince of this world. . . . I believe a Christian has the obligation and duty to battle pornography and other sins, no matter what it is."

David McGrath, a Republican councilman at the time, told Downs that MacKinnon was seen as an ultraconservative while she was in town. In fact, Downs writes, "Two influential Republican council members in Indianapolis told me that they did not know that Mac-Kinnon was a radical feminist. To them, her ordinance was simply a new method to restrict sexual material."

In an interview, ex-council member McGrath confirms this was indeed the case. He adds that because of the nature of the bill, it wasn't difficult to see McKinnon as a right-winger. "This ordinance was kind of like saying, well, we don't care about First Amendment rights. We are going to be the ultimate conservatives," he says.

MacKinnon's censorship bill won in a council meeting packed with over three hundred religious fundamentalists. All twenty-four Republicans on the council voted for it, while five Democrats voted against it. That the conservatives loved this bill shouldn't be surprising. MacKinnon promised them, if "it works, it will make pornography no longer available," writes Downs.

It would do that by allowing lawsuits for "trafficking in pornography," "forcing pornography on a person" (such as displaying it in a bookstore), and for "coercion into pornography performance." While the trafficking clause is outright censorship, the coercion clause is most troubling for its legal precedent. Even if the woman in question signed a contract, accepted payment for posing in porn, and showed no resistance, the bill says that these conditions fail to prove that she consented to be a porn model.

In essence, this clause claims even when women agree to pose for porn, they can't possibly mean it. Because, according to MacKinnon and other feminists, women are raised under such an overbearing sys-- tem of male dominance that we are incapable of giving knowledge-able consent. This concept reduces us to the status of children in the eyes of the law.[8]

MacKinnon and Dworkin's legislation censors a lot more than so-called hard-core porn. In the Indianapolis version, pornography was defined in sweeping, ambiguous terms, such as women "presented in scenarios of degradation, injury, abasement, torture, shown as filthy or inferior." Just what qualifies as "degrading" or "filthy" is a matter of interpretation. For some religious extremists, any drawing of female genitalia (such as in a sex-education textbook) is degrading. For others, all lesbian erotica is filthy. Under this ordinance, selling any material that fits this broad definition can be cause for a lawsuit. By pushing her law, MacKinnon was handing the power to censor on a silver platter to antifeminist conservatives.

MacKinnon's ordinance was eventually overthrown by a U.S. district court on the grounds that it would violate free speech. This decision was upheld by Judge Frank Easterbrook of the U.S. Court of Appeals in Chicago. "This is thought control," Easterbrook wrote scathingly. "It establishes an 'approved' view of women, of how they may react to sexual encounters, of how the sexes may relate to each other." In other words, the ordinance was nothing more than an attempt to legislate morality—a morality that is far more repressive to women than it is to men.

"It was one of the biggest mistakes we ever made," says McGrath, who seems to regret the day MacKinnon stepped into town. The city spent $200,000 passing and then defending (to no avail) her unconstitutional ordinance.[9] "We ended up with a lot of egg on our face," McGrath says.

And this is far from the only case of feminists forming alliances with the right wing to push censorship. Both MacKinnon and Dworkin—as well as Diana Russell and other prominent activists—took part in the 1985 Meese Commission on Pornography. Led by Edwin Meese, Ronald Reagan's attorney general, to study "the prob-

lem of pornography," the membership list of this commission read
like a circus program of archconservatives. It included James Dobson,
founder of Focus on the Family (a Christian group dedicated to maintaining "traditional values"), Dr. Park Elliot Dietz, a psychiatrist who
believes that young men who masturbate to images of deviant behavior develop criminal aberrations, and Father Bruce Ritter, a Catholic
priest who once condemned Dr. Ruth Westheimer for advocating orgasms in premarital sex—and was later accused of sexually molesting
young boys.[10]

It should come as no surprise that the Meese Commission concluded—largely on the basis of what they termed "common sense"—
that pornography degrades women and might lead to rape.
Ambiguous definitions and moral conclusions based on personal "experience" are replete in the commission's final report. Several scientists who were cited in the final report immediately repudiated it,
saying their work was misrepresented and misused.[11]

That current feminists played a big role in this conservative commission is undeniable. In fact, Andrea Dworkin's speech was quoted
at length in the final report.[12] Henry Hudson glowingly cited her in
his personal statement, in which he denounced pornography for promoting sodomy, "fornication," and distorting "the moral sensitivity of
women." James Dobson also thanked Dworkin for her input, before
going on to write that pornography (which he defines as including
rock music and television shows) leads to sexual "perversions," homosexuality, broken families, and an "addiction" to sex.

Along with MacKinnon—who told the commissioners that
women who defend pornography aren't real feminists—other well-
known activists to take part in the proceedings were researcher Diana
Russell, who used her rape study to imply that pornography leads to
sexual violence. Professor Mary P. Koss's survey was also cited in the
final report. The extremely conservative commission ate this up.
While the Meese Commission admitted that evidence is "sketchy,"
current feminists provided them with more than enough ammo to say
that porn (which remained ill-defined) causes rape and so should be
suppressed. It was perfect fodder for conservatives: They could advocate censorship in the name of feminism. And feminists applauded
their "findings." A July 9, 1986, NOW news release on the Meese
Commission baldly asserted: "NOW believes pornography violates
the civil rights of women and children. NOW supports the findings

of the Attorney General's Commission on Pornography that pornography harms women and children."

Alliances between archconservatives and feminists continue. They united to push a 1992 U.S. Senate bill titled "The Pornography Victims' Compensation Act," modeled after MacKinnon and Dworkin's ordinance. The supporters of this bill included Republican senators Strom Thurmond and Orrin Hatch—both with hideous track records on women's rights—as well as Morality in Media, a religious group that believes "titillating ads in the U.S. mails" are responsible for promoting "promiscuity."[13]

Joining hands with these right-wingers was Page Mellish, president of Feminists Fighting Pornography. Mellish, who lobbied in support of the legislation, wasn't bothered by the alliance. In a letter asking senators to pass the bill, Mellish proudly hailed her group as one among a "diverse coalition [that] includes some of the nation's largest feminist [and] conservative" organizations. And in a March 9, 1992, article in *The New Republic* on the legislation, Mellish claimed the support of "the majority of grass-roots NOW members."

Patricia Ireland, president of NOW, didn't disagree. She called this piece of conservative legislation "empowering" for women and congratulated the sponsor, Republican senator Mitch McConnell, for "doing a great service." When it came to taking a public stand, however, NOW waffled and would neither endorse nor condemn the legislation.[14] The bill was trashed as unconstitutional and never passed.

But nothing better illustrates the potentially antifeminist results of bedding down with the right to censor porn than what happened in Canada in 1992. A man named Butler, convicted under Canada's sweeping criminal code for renting out pornographic videos, appealed on the grounds that it violated the free-speech provisions of the fairly recently enacted charter of Rights and Freedoms. Enter Catharine MacKinnon. Together with the powerful feminist group Woman's Legal Education and Action Fund, MacKinnon argued that Butler's right to free speech was secondary to women's right to equality. As long as porn is available, they maintained, a climate that fostered sexual violence was created. The conservative Canadian Supreme Court bought this argument and handed down a ruling—now termed the Butler decision—upholding the criminal code over the charter's free-speech provisions and further allowing that "degrading" porn should be censored, borrowing freely from MacKinnon and Dworkin's vague definitions.[15] The May/June 1992, issue of Ms. happily termed this a "stunning victory" against sexual violence.

One of the first things to go was an issue of Bad Attitudes, a magazine published for and by lesbians. The magazine contained a short story fantasy of a lesbian rape scene. This qualifies as degrading porn under MacKinnon's ordinance. And so does a long list of other gay and lesbian publications, which have been banned since the ruling. And so do hundreds of books that have been detained or seized at the border by Canadian customs officials, including Andrea Dworkin's book Pornography: Men Possessing Women. That Dworkin's antiporn manifesto would be detained shouldn't be surprising—it's replete with sexually explicit details of pornography. Bookstores devoted to gay and lesbian works have borne the brunt of the ruling. The gay and lesbian bookstore that carried Bad Attitudes, for instance, was convicted of obscenity as defined under the Butler decision and fined. As Thelma McCormack, a professor of sociology at York University in Toronto notes, since the Butler decision, "there's no doubt that they've been going after gay and lesbian publications."[16]

Seeing feminists working with the right wing is enough to alienate, or at least confuse, young women. Today's feminists are friendly with groups that worked against the ERA, fight hard to outlaw abortion, want to restrict birth control, and try to censor feminist literature. Yet leading activists—under the banner of women's rights—are giving these antifeminists the most explicit kind of approval: political alliance.

For feminists to work with their enemies is a grievous mistake. Do they think that giving the religious right the power to censor material will benefit women? Of course it won't. Conservatives would censor all material they dislike—including gay and lesbian literature, abortion and birth-control information, and scary ideas (such as Andrea Dworkin's). If we allow the religious right to determine what we read, perhaps Playboy will go away—but not until The Joy of Sex and Our Bodies, Ourselves are long gone.

But this apparently doesn't concern many of today's feminists. The eradication of sexually explicit material has become a holy crusade; a battle to be won at any cost, even at the expense of women's rights. Antiporn activists spend little time on other feminist causes, from equal pay and job opportunities to child care and abortion rights. Many, such as Dworkin, seem to direct all of their energies to this campaign. Young women hearing Andrea Dworkin lecture at their college on stopping violence against women, for example, will hear very little—if anything—outside of condemnations of pornography and heterosexual sex. The truth is, the only reason many of these activists are called feminists is because they've taken the title for themselves.

"I understand that when I look at pornography, I can see the feminist side that the women are totally degraded. It doesn't turn me on, and I understand that. But at the same time, I guess it really clashes with the censorship issue. I'm not sure how much would be banned and who would draw the line. And if they ban pornography in magazines, would they ban it in books? Literature, like Henry Miller? Would we be banning books again?"
—SARA, twenty-five, student in Louisiana

The answer to Sara's question is yes. In a letter to the May 3, 1992, *New York Times Book Review*, Andrea Dworkin recalls her first experience with what she terms "dirty books." These were Henry Miller's *Tropic of Cancer* and D. H. Lawrence's *Lady Chatterley's Lover*.

Her statement reflects a serious flaw in the feminist fight against porn: Whatever activists find personally upsetting must go. One of the most widely accepted definitions of porn in feminist circles comes from Catharine MacKinnon. "We define pornography as the graphic sexually explicit subordination of women through pictures or words that also includes women dehumanized as sexual objects, things, or commodities . . . in postures of sexual submission or servility or display; reduced to body parts, . . ." she writes in her 1987 book, *Feminism Unmodified*—which is assigned reading for women's studies students at the University of Kentucky and other institutions. These terms are highly ambiguous. Do written erotica or explicit romance novels make women "sexual objects"? Is a nude woman photographed reclining on a sofa in a position of "sexual submission"? And what exactly is meant by "reduced to body parts"? Would a birth-control pamphlet with a drawing of a vagina count?

For leading feminists, it doesn't seem to matter whether sexual material is gentle or crude, straight or gay, soft or hard. In a June 1984 interview with the feminist newspaper *Off Our Backs*, MacKinnon said that lesbian literature, if it fit her sweeping definitions, "would not be exempt" from action under her ordinance. Looking at the situation in Canada, we can see this is true. In fact, MacKinnon asserts that she doesn't know of *any* sexually explicit material that isn't degrading and worthy of action. In an August 1992 interview with *Ladies' Home Journal*, MacKinnon stated: "Theoretically, there should be sexually explicit materials that are egalitarian. But I don't know of any that are." And in *Pornography: Men Possessing Women*, Dworkin makes her position on material designed for the woman's market clear: ". . . erotica is simply high-class pornography."

The biggest problem in defining porn is that the very language we use to talk about sex is far from concise or neutral. Words like *degrading, exploitive*, and *filthy* are extremely vague terms that mean little without a moral context—which, in our culture, has historically been antifeminist and antisex. By relying on such ambiguous and morally colored terms, current feminists often find themselves sounding more like antisex fundamentalists than the fundamentalists themselves. In her 1993 book, *Making Violence Sexy*, for example, Diana Russell defines porn as "*material that combines sex and/or the exposure of genitals with abuse or degradation in a manner that appears to endorse, condone, or encourage such behavior.*" At first this sounds like a definition of hard-core porn, but the fact that Russell has been arrested for tearing up *Playboy* magazines in stores implies that her definition goes much further. This is made clear when Russell attempts to clarify her vague terms and ends up including everything but the kitchen sink as pornography. She didn't use the term *sexually explicit* in her definition, she explains, because she wanted to embrace what she calls the "long-standing feminist tradition" of including such things as "record covers, jokes, ads, and billboards" as porn. In this wide range of material, she writes that *abusive* refers to "demeaning," "derogatory," and "contemptuous" sexual conduct—but just what these terms mean is unexplained. "Degrading" material, she says, refers to sexual conduct that is "humiliating, insulting, disrespectful." Finally getting down to some concrete examples, Russell defines *degrading* as women "eager to engage in whatever sex acts a man wants" and men ejaculating on a women's face. Let's be frank. Playing the love slave or having a man ejaculate on her face may not be every woman's cup of tea, but to say that such behavior is automatically "degrading" to women is a sentiment straight from the prudish Victorian era. Is there something humiliating about being eager to please a lover, something degrading in male ejaculate? The question is not whether we all have to agree on what we find personally distasteful. The question is whether the women's movement should be declaring a static, confining sexual moral code—one that decrees that certain acts *always* degrade *all* women—and then using that morality as a yardstick to judge what we have the right to read.

Some feminists have taken pornography definitions even further. Twiss Butler, a NOW staff member responsible for analyzing sex discrimination in pornography, health insurance, and the media, claims that a nude photo of then-pregnant actress Demi Moore that appeared on the August 1991 cover of *Vanity Fair* magazine is, amazingly, "the pornography of pregnancy." Butler explains how this discreetly posed and nonsexual photo is obscene. "It was an absolute emblem that a woman has been invaded by a man and colonized," she says.

In the feminist definition of porn, it seems that anything that acknowledges women have sex—from lesbian erotica to pictures of pregnant women—is considered evil.[17] Probably the ultimate irony in this is just how many of their own works qualify. Several of Andrea Dworkin's books, for example, are extremely pornographic. Take this excerpt from her 1980 short story collection, *The New Womans Broken Heart*: "her lover fingered her cunt slowly, dispassionately . . . then her lover mounted her and the second man mounted him from behind. then her lover fucked her and the second man fucked him. This double man on top of her, heaving, the weight of that cock inside her driven by this double weight, this two headed, two assed man on top of her, like a mountain, volcanic, erupting, on and on, fucking and fucking . . ." Of course, Dworkin would probably deny this piece of fiction is pornography. Her explicit, highly imaginative depictions of violent and degrading sex are supposedly written for the "right" reason, to educate the rest of us about just how horrible men can be. But context can be a shaky foundation to erect law upon.

"No language is too strong," wrote Victorian author John Morely in 1866, "to condemn the mixed vileness and childishness of depicting the spurious passion of a putrescent imagination, the unnamed lusts of sated wantons." Morely was attacking what Victorians considered the most morally defaming and destructive social evil: pornography. Of course, porn at that time meant romantic poems and explicit etchings—in fact, any material that admitted people have sex. According to Morely, these things are simply "the most awful influx the world ever saw of furious provocatives to unbridled sensuality and riotous animalism."[18]

Current feminists concur.

*   *   *

This is how the feminist theory on pornography works: Men have a natural propensity to rape. Sexual material incites the hidden rapist inside every man—it is the fuse that explodes the powder keg. As Diana Russell puts it, pornography "undermines men's inhibitions."[19] It does so by portraying women in an "objectified," or primarily sexual, light. Men, being stupid, see a picture of a woman being sexual and assume that's all women are good for. They subsequently objectify all women as sex outlets, and their already-frail inhibitions against committing rape decline. Thus, pornography taps into a deep-seated violent element in men that is otherwise manageable. Without pornography, today's feminists assert, many rapists simply would not commit their crimes. In fact, the idea wouldn't even cross their minds. They would be perfectly normal, loving men—if it wasn't for sexual images.

But scientists and researchers who study both rapists and pornography have concluded that this theory just doesn't wash. Dr. Nicholas Groth, director of a sex-offender program in Connecticut and author of Men Who Rape, writes, "Although a rapist, like anyone else, might find some pornography stimulating, it is not sexual arousal but the arousal of anger or fear that leads to rape. Pornography does not cause rape; banning it will not stop rape. In fact, some studies have shown that rapists are generally exposed to less pornography than normal males." According to Groth, men who rape do so because of aggression and the desire to dominate. He believes that blaming pornography perpetuates the myth that rape is an act of sexual desire, and this shifts "the responsibility from the offender to something outside of him. That is what the offender himself does. He projects the responsibility of his own behavior on external objects like liquor, drugs, the dress and behavior of his victims and the like—anywhere but where it really belongs."

All of us are socialized: through our families, our schools, our friends, the media, television, literature, religion—you name it. Not a single aspect of our culture, including pornography, is devoid of possible influence. But the role that pornography plays in "creating" rapists is probably minor, if not negligible. Studies on rapists show that, rather than viewing pornography, the common links among them are beliefs that women are secondary (as with men raised in a family in which women were excluded from decision making), views that legitimize violence toward women (thinking that a woman alone in a bar is "asking for it"), and feelings of powerlessness and lack of control (such as having been abused in childhood or raised in an authoritarian family). These familial and social influences seem to combine in a deadly combination of hostility toward women and permission to act upon it. Many rapists tell of fantasizing about hurting women during childhood and early teen years—ages when few are exposed to pornography. One rapist in a study, for example, said his fantasizing about rape started young, after having been severely abused by a series of foster mothers. "[T]hese women would beat me unmercifully and very early I became obsessed with getting even. For as long as I can remember my fantasies related to hurting women."[20] But these early influences should not diminish the responsibility rapists have for their actions. As Dr. Groth points out, rapists love to blame anybody or anything but themselves—while they are fully aware that rape is wrong and society views it as a horrendous crime that calls for punishment.

Many feminists, however, argue a direct cause-and-effect relationship between porn and rape: that men literally view pornography, get all excited, and then go rape a woman.

Dr. Edward Donnerstein, coauthor of the 1987 book *The Question of Pornography: Research Findings and Policy Implications*, is considered one of the leading researchers in the field of laboratory research on pornography. Feminists often cite Donnerstein as a supporter. He testified in Indianapolis during the proceedings for MacKinnon and Dworkin's ordinance and he appeared before the Meese Commission (where he argued that more research was needed). Donnerstein even went on *Donahue* in 1984 with MacKinnon and Dworkin, where he told the talk-show host that pornography fosters "aggression against women."[21]

But now the social scientist has some serious doubts. "Since that time, the research has really shown some new things, and I have to respond to that," he says. According to Donnerstein, recent studies have shown that when you remove the sexual aspect from violent images, the effects (increased willingness to aggress) remain the same. If there is a causal relationship—and we should be very careful when extrapolating from the laboratory to real life[22]—it would seem to be violence, as in slasher films, not sexuality.

"Violence is really the key component in all its domains," Donnerstein says, explaining that studies have shown that rapists will become sexually aroused at completely *nonsexual* violent images. And

Donnerstein points out that men are far more likely to see violence on television than in *Playboy*. "If you're looking for violence against women, you don't have to go much further than representations in the mainstream media," he says.

In fact, Donnerstein questions the whole concept of "degrading" pornography causing harm—mostly because the term means different things to different people. He notes that the Meese Commission, which concluded degrading porn is harmful, relied upon studies that used material rated PG. "You look at some of those studies closely and you'll find they used material from television shows," he says. "The issue is, images that objectify and stereotype women are found throughout the media." Donnerstein is right. From perfume ads to mainstream movies, few forms of media present women (or men) as multifaceted beings; people are simplified and objectified all the time.

But for current feminists, nonsexual objectification of women isn't deemed as dangerous. Diana Russell explains that this is because "men's viewing of pornography frequently culminates in orgasm, [thus] the lessons of pornography are learned much faster and more tenaciously than when they view nonpornographic media."[23] This entirely unproven notion—that orgasm in men leaves them vulnerable to evil influence—comes straight from the Victorian era. At that time, sexual literature was condemned for "exciting the animal feelings and weakening the judgement." Once excited and then weakened, the masturbator was susceptible to "false and imperfect ideas of human nature."[24]

Other scientists who have extensively researched pornography, such as Steven Penrod and Daniel Linz, have also concluded that sexual material does not cause rape.[25] Marcia Pally's 1991 *Sense and Censorship: The Vanity of Bonfires*, published by the Freedom to Read Foundation, is a comprehensive analysis of scientific findings.

In an interview in her New York apartment, Pally—an articulate feminist and free-speech activist whose energetic gestures are a perfect match for her athletic frame and tousled hair—talks knowledgeably about porn research. "The data on violent pornography seems to be this," she says. "First of all, it's the violent element, not the sexual element. If you separate those elements you get no change [in aggression] with the depiction of sexual material in the laboratory."

In fact, Pally says that research has shown that anything that gets people's adrenaline levels up will increase aggression in the laboratory. "If you raise the adrenaline of subjects in the lab, from anything at all, including an exercise bicycle, you'll find that when subjects are asked to aggress, they will be more aggressive," she explains. "You would then have to conclude that the key to stopping violence in this country is to ban exercise bicycles." Pally pauses and laughs, then adds, "or Jane Fonda."

Because most sexual material appears to be harmless, Donnerstein and other scientists don't support legislation designed to suppress it. In a September 1990 article in the *Chronicle of Higher Education*, Donnerstein and fellow scientist Daniel Linz denounced Senate bill 1521, the Victims' Compensation Act, stating: "Very little is accomplished for the victims of violence by singling out pornography."

Yet many current feminists still push the "porn causes violence" spiel. The theory has a tenacious position in the women's movement. In 1985, the National NOW Conference resolved that: "pornography promotes sexual assault and is used increasingly and commonly in battery and in rape." Educational films on sexual assault shown to college women, such as *Rethinking Rape*, baldly state that pornography makes men rape. So do a wealth of women's studies literature and rape pamphlets. Students attending women's studies classes at Duke University, for example, are given a brochure from the Center for Women Policy Studies that is entitled "Campus Gang Rape: Party Games?" It asserts that "[p]ornography on campus may be another factor relating to fraternity party rapes." Although the pamphlet admits it is actually "difficult" to prove a direct link, that doesn't stop it from implying there is one.

Those interested in joining the movement to stop violence against women will often find that stopping pornography is the only form of activism offered. In New York City, for instance, an announcement in the January 1993 *Learning Alliance* suggests women concerned about rape come to a "Violence in the Lives of Women" workshop. Those attending this feminist seminar on sexual violence will find it moderated by Dorchen Leidholdt, cofounder of Women Against Pornography. Her speakers include two other members of Women Against Pornography, as well as John Stoltenberg, founder of Men against Pornography and the author of *Refusing to Be a Man*—a touching account of how Mr. Stoltenberg has risen above the burden of being born a "child-with-a-penis."[26]

Young women in Seattle, Washington, who join their NOW chapter's "Ending Violence Against Women" task force to fight rape find the focus is actually on eradicating sexual literature, advertisements, and movies. The chapter's actions in 1993 included lobbying against "erotic" and "pornographic" computer software, a letter-writing campaign against ads that "glamorize and trivialize violence, thus sanctioning and perpetuating real-world violence" (including ads portraying naked women), and organizing a rally against a campus model-search visit by *Playboy*. The May 1993 Seattle NOW newsletter termed this rally against *Playboy* a "tremendous success," crediting the signs activists made illustrating "the destructiveness of pornography." When the topic of rape comes up in the women's movement, porn is soon to follow.

As proof that sexual material makes men rape, current feminists rely on faulty evidence. One frequently touted source is Diana Russell's 1978 rape survey, in which her interviewers asked women, "Have you ever been upset by anyone trying to get you to do what they'd seen in pornographic pictures, movies, or books?" According to Russell, 10 percent of her respondents answered yes. In *Rape in Marriage*, she quotes some of their statements. "He tried to get me to stand and dance naked" is one. Other responses—which Russell says proves that pornography is dangerous—are from women claiming they've been asked to engage in oral sex. Russell states this is "assaultive behavior." It's not clear whether she believes asking for oral sex is assaultive or the practice itself. Of her entire sample, 1.6 percent (fifteen respondents) suffered what Russell believed was a pornography-related rape or attempted rape. Since a whopping 44 percent of her respondents were classified as victims, this tiny percentage would actually show porn is a minor factor in causing rape.

An interesting point here, as even Russell points out, is that numerous statistics show that up to and over 50 percent of rape and wife-battering incidents are committed by men who are drinking heavily at the time.[27] In fact, Russell found that between 20 and 25 percent of marital rapes in her survey involved alcohol—and she didn't even specifically ask respondents about this factor. Yet, despite the fact that this number far exceeds her own statistics for pornography-linked rapes, Russell hesitates to say that alcohol *causes* rape, because heaving drinking may be symptomatic of a disturbed personality, not the reason for it, and plenty of men who drink *don't* rape. One never hears feminists arguing that prohibition would stop rape, but by their own logic they should work to outlaw beer instead of beer commercials.

Without scientific evidence, antiporn feminists fall back on suspect anecdotal evidence, such as the statements of serial killer Ted
Bundy. The day before he was executed in Florida, Bundy told James
Dobson (of the conservative group Focus on the Family) that pornography made him stalk and murder women. Actually, when Bundy was
arrested in 1978, police didn't find porn in his car—they found advertisements for cheerleading camps.[28] There is absolutely no reason
to believe that Bundy, who had exhausted all appeals, wasn't making
a last-ditch effort to escape his fate by shifting the blame for his actions. But for some of today's feminists, Bundy became an unlikely
ally. "We owe a lot to Ted Bundy," Page Mellish of Feminists Fighting
Pornography said to *The New Republic*. Try saying that to the families
of the women he killed.

To believe the rationalizations of psychopathic serial killers is absurd. Clearly, Bundy was a sick man, but he alone was responsible for
his crimes. As Marcia Pally notes, "Look at who gets off the hook.
First it was the Devil that made them do it, now it's Miss Jones."[29]

*"I don't really think it should be an issue. The women who are in porno-
graphic films, I think, for the most part, have chosen that way of living to
make money. If a woman is abducted, tied down and forced to do it, then
yes, her rights have been violated. But if she went over there and said,
hey, I need a job and I want to pose nude, and do this, that and the other
thing, with other women or men, whatever, those are choices she's
made. . . . Personally, I do think they're degrading to women. But the
women are in there voluntarily. It is their choice."*
—DIANA MESSIER, thirty-two, marketing manager in Massachusetts

But it's not a free choice according to current feminists. Many of today's antiporn leaders are adamant that women do not, and can not,
consent to be in porn. In slide shows and feminist literature, young
women are frequently told that porn is the record of actual violent
rapes, physical mutilation, torture, and murder of women. Even in
the cases where this is obviously untrue, activists assert that women
should not be allowed to pose in porn because their images violate
the pure, sexless nature of women. In fact, following the feminist redefinition of rape, some feminists believe that even the softest erotica
is, in itself, another form of sexual assault.

"'Hard' pornography does not confine itself to binding women but displays scenes of mutilation; breasts are sliced off, throats bleed, and genitals are penetrated with broken glass," states the feminist text-book *Women's Realities, Women's Choices*, put out by the Hunter College Women's Studies Collective and assigned to students at Indiana University at Bloomington. Telling students that snuff (sex murder) and mutilation scenes are common in pornography is an effective method of winning converts. Many young women have seen few, if any, porn films, or hard-core material.

This idea has been accepted as conventional feminist wisdom. In *The Beauty Myth*, author Naomi Wolf writes, "Pornography world-wide, according to researchers, is becoming increasingly violent." Her footnoted source? Andrea Dworkin. This assertion pops up again in *Backlash* when Susan Faludi offhandedly claims that there has been a "rise in pornography that depicts extreme violence against women." In her footnotes, Faludi cites the Meese Commission, which reported that violent depictions in pornography (it is important to recognize this includes simulated and suggested violence) had increased since the 1970s.

Dr. Donnerstein, among other scientists, disputes this claim. "The available data might suggest that there has actually been a decline in violent images within mainstream publications such as *Playboy*," Donnerstein asserts, "and that comparisons of X-rated materials with other depictions suggest there is in fact far more violence in the *non-pornographic* fare."[30]

In fact, finding violent pornography today can be difficult. I found this to be the case after hearing allegations from a feminist group that a local adult-film store carried snuff films, which, of course, are illegal. After several visits to the store and hours of X-rated film footage later (I tried to pick the most disgusting-sounding ones available), I not only couldn't find a snuff film; I couldn't find any depictions of sexual violence. I certainly didn't find any material portraying women having their breasts cut off or with their throats bleeding; such material would be evidence of a crime, not pornography. My entirely unscientific sampling of porn mostly uncovered a bunch of badly dubbed tapes of sex, with a heavy emphasis on oral sex for both men and women; few of the films were tastefully done and actually erotic. In fact, many of the examples of violent porn—such as mock rape scenes—that feminists use in slide shows are now unavailable in stores and difficult to obtain. This shouldn't be surprising to the women who watch X-rated videos. A 1991 survey of video stores and distributors by *Adult Video News* found that couples rent 29 percent of all porn films, and women alone rent 15 percent. While these numbers may be suspect—given the source—thousands can still attest that the worst aspect of most porn movies are their utterly boring plots.

But even if porn consists of nothing worse than consensual acts between bad actors, and doesn't spur men to rape, current feminists still insist it's evil. "Much recent feminist opposition to pornography has focused on the fact that, whether or not causal connections between it and acts of sexual violence can be proven, it constitutes a form of sexual violence itself," writes English feminist Liz Kelly.[31]

"We can be said to be breeding a nation of whores," asserts activist Judith Bat-Ada in an interview for the 1980 feminist antiporn book *Take Back the Night*. Bat-Ada, who compares Hugh Hefner to Hitler and claims that *Playboy*—through "carefully planned" cartoons—is creating child sexual abuse, takes the feminist line in this book. In reality, she is anything but a feminist. Bat-Ada is, in fact, Judith Reisman, an archconservative who took part in the Meese Commission.[32] Reisman appeared in a homophobic video used in a campaign sponsored by a right-wing group to pass an Oregon law that would equate homosexuality to pedophilia. She is devoutly antihomosexuality as well as antiporn. This fact, however, doesn't seem to trouble some current feminists. In June 1990, NOW defended Reisman's work for the Meese Commission.[33] And at the State University of New York at Albany, Bat-Ada's essay claiming that porn is breeding a nation of whores is assigned to students as part of the "Introduction to Feminisms . . ." course—in order to teach them the "feminist" position on pornography.

This shouldn't be terribly surprising. By claiming that depictions of women's bodies are in and of themselves degrading as well as inciting men to rape, today's antiporn feminists have found themselves sharing not only political goals with the ultraright but sexual mores. "Pornography emphasizes sensation without feeling," wrote Audre Lorde in "Uses of the Erotic," an essay taught to students at Colorado State University, in Fort Collins, as well as in many other women's studies classes. To enjoy sensation without the proper emotion is to "allow ourselves to be reduced to the pornographic, the abused, and the absurd."[34]

With few exceptions, women's studies courses push antiporn ideology with a vengeance. Many classes require students to attend special lectures and slide shows on pornography as well as devote sections of the class to the topic. The National Women's Studies Association recommends antiporn work repeatedly in their 1991 suggested syllabi. In fact, in one of their recommended syllabi, students are assigned two antiporn essays under the topic of "Sexual violence" before they even get to the section titled "Pornography"—where they read four more essays—*and* they watch the film *Not a Love Story*.

Not a Love Story, a feminist antiporn documentary, is shown to many female students, including those taking women's studies at Kansas State University and the University of Indiana at Bloomington. The film features several feminist leaders, including Kathleen Barry, Susan Griffin, and Robin Morgan. Morgan discusses sexual practices she finds repugnant: "superficial sex, kinky sex, appurtenances, and toys," which she claims numbs "normal human sensuality." In a triumph of repressive morality, Morgan implies that what many people do in the privacy of their bedrooms is not only her business but requires her sanctimonious advice on what is "normal" and what is not. Ironically, *Not a Love Story* was initially banned from public showing in Ontario, Canada. The Ontario Censorship Board apparently thought it might give people dirty ideas.

"This big uproar happened last year [at Penn State]. . . . There's this competing newspaper on campus, which is sort of the right-wing newspaper, which tries to compete with the daily newspaper, which is a little more left-wing. And so they bad-mouthed this woman columnist, and I guess had this suggestive cartoon of her. The women's group on campus got irate about it. Some representatives of it ended up taking copies of this competing newspaper and burning them. Personally, I was really pissed off by it, because I do not condone censorship by any means. . . . I'm very much against censorship, but at the same time I'm very much against pornography. It's really hard to draw the line. If people want to do one thing, they should be allowed, but at the same time it's hurting other people. So it's hard."

—KIMI EISELE, twenty-two, student in Pennsylvania

Many women, like Kimi, do not approve of pornography. But they also do not condone censorship. It *is* hard to draw the line between material we find personally distasteful and the right of others to free expression. For women of my generation in particular, who grew up better informed about their bodies and birth control thanks to the protected speech of feminists in the seventies, this line is even more difficult. The specter of censorship raises immediate and strong fears among young women. Open public discussion about many issues— lesbian sexuality is a good example—seem too fragile and new to chance such a threat. And young women know that where a slippery slope exists, it is to be found in efforts to ban literature. They see it in their lives: feminist activists who one day espouse outlawing porn on the grounds it causes rape and the next are more than willing to burn newspapers for running cartoons they dislike.

But in the effort to impose a feminist morality, women's concerns about freedom of speech have been tossed out the window. "Free speech is being used to protect the violence," asserts Eleanor Smeal, president of the Fund for the Feminist Majority.[35] In her essay "Violence Against Women," which is assigned at Duke and Tulane universities, Barbara Sinclair Deckard advises ominously "In the short run, there may not be an answer short of breaching the First Amendment."

The feminist argument for breaching the First Amendment is best summed up by Catharine MacKinnon in her 1993 book, *Only Words*. This is how MacKinnon's reasoning works. From pinups to depictions of seemingly consensual sex, there is only one message of porn: "'get her,' pointing at all women. . . . This message is addressed directly to the penis, delivered through an erection, and taken out on women in the real world." Since all porn embodies this message, men who view it "experience this *being done* by watching it *being done*." They are partaking in rape as surely as a rapist does, and they will inevitably (and MacKinnon is adamant on this point) feel compelled to act this out. In other words, porn is like saying "kill" to a trained attack dog—it is an action with intent to harm, not an issue of free speech. The First Amendment doesn't protect the right to say "kill" to an attack dog, because it is an act intended to cause physical harm, but it does protect the right to publish a picture of a German shepherd in *Dog Lover* magazine or to write the sentence "Attack dogs are good," because these express ideas. Just as you would be held liable for saying "kill" to a trained attack dog, MacKinnon argues, sexual material should be considered a command. It should not be protected under the First Amendment. There are several assumptions here: that there is only one message of sexual material ("get her"), that once men hear this supposed order, they are incapable of refusing it, and that the key to eradicating actions we don't like is eradicating speech about those actions.

Imagine this: I am discussing Malcolm X. In a grand generalization, I declare that rather than expressing a multitude of ideas that people might interpret differently, accept, or reject, there is only one message from Malcolm X: "Get whitey." I further argue that "this is addressed directly to black people's brains, delivered through emotions, and taken out on whites in the real world." Every black, I assert, who reads Malcolm X "experiences this *being done* by reading about it *being done*." They are partaking of murdering whites just as surely as real murderers, and (I am adamant on this point) every one of them will inevitably feel compelled to act this out. Thus, reading Malcolm X is the same as saying "kill" to a trained attack dog—it is an act tantamount to white people's death, not an issue of free speech. It should not be protected as political dissent by the First Amendment. His words are a premeditated criminal act inciting blacks to revolution and murder.

Sure, this argument is absurd. But MacKinnon's argument is just as absurd. While some might argue that political dissent, no matter how offensive, has redeeming value and pornography does not, that's a matter of personal judgment. The First Amendment protects bad hotel paintings as well as fine art. The lines dividing porn and political speech are murky at best—sexually explicit work has played a profound historical role in expressing and shaping political thought. *Our Bodies, Ourselves* was sexually explicit, but it was also a form of political speech that inspired women to demand social change. We do have rights and freedoms, and they are not confined to materials expressing only noble thoughts and feelings, the most mannerly political debate, and the highest forms of rarefied social intercourse. Our rights also include so-called unredeeming material, from the mundane to the base: stupid TV sitcoms, silly magazine articles, bad movies, meaningless popular music, and pictures of consensual sexual intercourse. The notion that speech is acceptable only when it promotes a higher political and moral vision is the old fascist view of art, not democracy. And the idea that imposing a static vision is progressive is a contradiction in terms: Without fresh ideas and open debate, there is no change.

But for many feminists, censorship of ideas and expression has become quite acceptable—even when the victims are other feminists. Joan Nestle is a lesbian feminist who has long been active in the women's movement and cofounded the respected Lesbian Herstory Archives in 1972. Yet according to the August 1989 *Progressive*, Women Against Pornography now pickets her speeches and calls for censorship of her writings. Her crime? Nestle writes graphic descriptions of lesbian sex. "If I wrote about flowers," Nestle remarked to *Progressive*, "if I used metaphors, it would be okay. But I couldn't."

And at the University of Michigan, where MacKinnon teaches, an art exhibit was yanked because it upset some feminists. The November 13, 1992, *New York Times* reported that the exhibit on prostitution (which included a video clip of porn star Veronica Vera testifying against antiporn legislation) had the misfortune of being shown at the same time MacKinnon and Dworkin were holding a conference against pornography at the school. A few of their guests—including John Stoltenberg—apparently found this video upsetting and raised enough of a ruckus to get the entire exhibit removed. MacKinnon supported this act of art censorship. Responding to the controversy, she even turned the issue around, claiming, "My real view, so far as this pertains to me, is that this is a witchhunt by First Amendment fundamentalists who are persecuting and blacklisting dissidents like Andrea Dworkin and myself as art censors."

But who is blacklisting whom in the feminist community? In an action that demonstrates how quick she is to suppress what she disagrees with, Andrea Dworkin orchestrated a campaign to blacklist and intimidate Carol Downer, who is considered a folk hero in the woman's health movement. According to the October 26, 1992 *New York Observer*, Dworkin was given an advance copy of a feminist book on abortion titled *A Woman's Book of Choices*, written by Downer and Rebecca Chalker. While other feminists wrote flattering blurbs for the back cover, Dworkin took offense at one section (it described how women faked rape before abortion was legal) and promptly started making phone calls. Before long, feminist bookstores across the country were threatening to boycott the book. In fact, according to a letter written to the publisher by a feminist leader close to Dworkin, Dworkin was suggesting that *she* be the one to rewrite the offending section. Dworkin refused even to talk to Downer, who complained that she "spread poison around the country. We're facing whispers and half-truths everywhere we go." Dworkin won the battle for censorship. The publisher, afraid of boycotts, had the section rewritten.

The women's movement's response to this ugly action was . . . nothing. From NOW, not a whisper. At an October 20, 1992, Women's

Action Coalition meeting, a few outraged women suggested the group write a letter to Dworkin, saying her actions were unacceptable. This idea was shot down because it might "censor" Dworkin. Yet the Women's Action Coalition has written several letters to magazines (such as *Rolling Stone*), pressuring them to drop advertisements the group finds sexist. Apparently, censorship means different things when applied to different people.

The truth is, women's organizations were silent about Dworkin's actions because a key belief of current feminism is that feminist leaders must not be questioned. If it had been conservative Senator Jesse Helms trying to censor the same book, women's organizations would have screamed bloody murder. Since it was a feminist, the response was mute consent.

It's true that not all feminists agree with what current leaders are doing. But it's also true that when it comes to doing anything about it, many just sit on their hands. In the effort to avoid controversy and protect their feminist label, many women refuse to deal head-on with the issue. As a result, antiporn activists are given free reign to censor with impunity.

Some feminists, however, refuse to shut up. Betty Friedan, Erica Jong, and Jamaica Kincaid all belong to Feminists for Free Expression, a nonprofit organization started in the winter of 1991 to fight The Pornography Victims' Compensation Act—also, interestingly, known as the Bundy bill. Joining them was the California branch of NOW. The National Coalition Against Censorship created a group, which includes Marylin Fitterman (ex-president of New York State NOW) and Betty Friedan, to oppose feminist antiporn activism. There is the Feminists Against Censorship Task Force (FACT), which was primarily active in the mid-eighties, opposing the Meese Commission, but has geared up since feminists' efforts to censor sexual material increased. And there are several feminist writers, such as Carol S. Vance and Ellen Willis, who have written critically on the cause.[36]

These feminists have come out forcefully against the antiporn crusade. In return, they have been roundly condemned. "The Black movement has Uncle Toms and Oreo cookies. The labor movement has scabs. The woman's movement has FACT," Catharine MacKinnon writes in an essay in *The Sexual Liberals and the Attack on Feminism.*

"Are our new censors attempting, under the guise of feminism, to reinforce our culture's age-old tradition of paternalism—of treating women like infants?" Karen DeCrow, a former President of NOW, asked in the May 1985 issue of *Penthouse*. "Sexuality for women has been distorted and suppressed. How ironic that women themselves would want to add to this. The time is long overdue to be rid of the myth that if one believes in equality between the sexes, one is against erotic literature. Being a feminist means you are against sexism, not against sex."

DeCrow feels the feminist fight against porn is dangerous because it detracts from political activism and diverts the movement's emphasis toward sex. Other feminists agree. "I think it is an appalling throwback for women to be caught up in the antiporn movement," says Marcia Pally, a member of Feminists for Free Expression. Pally doesn't mince her words. "What it says is that women in pictures of sex, naked, having sex with each other, with men, in groups, whatever—that those women are degraded. Now, this strikes me as extremely bizarre. In order to think that, you have to think that sex degrades women," Pally points out. "That's traditional male sexism. And here you find a segment of the women's movement repeating it in the name of women. I think these women have collapsed completely into the ideology of their oppressors."

Without free speech, the women's movement wouldn't exist. And if feminism continues to promote censorship—to the point of working with those who want women forced back into the kitchen—it's possible that feminism won't exist in the future. "We have a responsibility to spread the word that numerous and serious feminists oppose such censorship on the grounds that such suppression is harmful to women," Leanne Katz, director of the National Coalition Against Censorship, told a June 1987 workshop on censorship. "It is a serious mistake to underestimate the short-term and long-term effect of the antipornography feminists. . . . Significant numbers of well-meaning people, especially women, have been persuaded that even lukewarm support for feminist principles requires support for restrictions on pornography," she stated.

Katz is right. Many women today believe that being a feminist means supporting the censorship of sexual material. "Those that debate antiporn feminists should be prepared for very hostile rhetoric," she concluded, "such as accusations that they are pimping for pornographers."

And there has been some very hostile rhetoric. Robin Morgan, for example, denounces anticensorship feminists as sick and perverted. "And surely such women can realize that what they, in their *piteously twisted sexuality* [emphasis added], are upholding has nothing, nothing to do with the feminist vision of freedom," she states in her 1984 book, *The Anatomy of Freedom*. In a personal interview, however, Morgan took a more conciliatory tone, allowing that the "minority" of feminists opposing the antiporn campaign may be "good women who only have the most sincere concerns." Be that as it may, under her stewardship of *Ms.* magazine, the debate was decidedly closed.

Women who work in pornography are also coming forward. Candida Royalle, a former porn actress and a member of Feminists for Free Expression, now runs her own adult-video production company, Femme Distribution. Royalle's popular X-rated videos, such as *Christine's Secret*, are designed to appeal to women and couples; they feature extensive foreplay and drawn-out erotic lovemaking. Speaking firmly of her experience as an actress in porn films, Royalle takes to task the feminist assertion that the women involved in porn are all rape victims. "I was never forced or coerced to do *anything*," she says.

In fact, Royalle questions whom antiporn feminists are trying to protect. "They couldn't have cared less about whether we were victims or not," she says, speaking of her years in front of the camera. "In fact, they never *spoke* to us. They would never *know* if we were victims. They had no idea what was going on. When we tried to tell them, they didn't want to hear it. They simply didn't want to hear it—and that's why they despise me. They don't want to hear that I was never forced into doing anything. They don't want to hear that *I made the choice to do this*." According to Royalle, if the women's movement wants to do something positive about porn, it should concentrate on improving women's economic status so they have more options, instead of pushing porn actresses even further underground.

Yet when interviewed for an October 18, 1992, *48 Hours* television program on the subject of pornography, Norma Ramos, legal counsel to Women Against Pornography, claimed that Royalle's films are no different from the most disgusting sexist porn produced by men. Ramos dismisses Royalle as "a pimp."

For all the impact they've had on women of my generation, however, feminists who oppose the antiporn campaign might as well be whispering down an empty well. Few young women encountering feminism are aware that anticensorship feminists even exist.

"If you say, Yes, I like pornography, then you are buying into a system that in very many cases is oppressive or promotes violence against women. But

*if you say that you are against it, then you're buying into a position that
says any kind of public display of sexuality is by definition oppressive.
Which is something I think we should be fighting against. . . . I'm not closing my eyes to the fact that there are women who are forced to perform in
these films, to be involved in sex trade—maybe not by someone holding a
gun to their head, but just by economics. They might choose to be in, but
it's not as if they're choosing between being in porn movies or going to Harvard. But I don't think that a woman who enjoys her sexuality, enjoys having sex with men, is an exhibitionist or whatever should be condemned by
other women and told she is not a feminist, not a proper feminist."*
—SHANNON KOKOSKA, twenty-three, student in Pennsylvania

For many young women such as Shannon, the message of the feminist
fight against porn—that any public display of sexuality is automatically
oppressive—is deeply disturbing. They feel that such a puritanical attitude is something the women's movement should be fighting, not promoting. Young women don't believe the women's movement should
attack women who express their sexuality and call them antifeminists—or, as Shannon puts it so succinctly, not "proper" feminists.

As Shannon notes, women in porn are often there because of their
economic situation. Yet antiporn activists seldom raise the economic
issue. In the fierce attempt to outlaw porn, current feminists have
avoided examining why women work in the porn field or whether
improving education and job opportunities might change these wom-
en's lives. For feminist leaders, this kind of action might have a terrible result—what if the women in porn were given more options and
still chose to take their clothes off in front of the camera? Pornography wouldn't go away, and erotic literature certainly wouldn't go
away. And that's what these feminist leaders really want: the eradication and destruction of all sexual material.

By forgoing political and economic activism, current feminists
have created a campaign that smacks of classism. Many of the feminist activists working against porn are middle-income and well-
educated women. The subjects of their attacks (porn actresses and
nude models) are predominantly lower-income and less-educated
people—and usually not boasting choice jobs at magazines or universities. It must be recognized that many women freely choose to enter
the porn field. And some of their choices are no doubt influenced by
the fact that it pays more than flipping hamburgers.

But the antiporn activists don't seem interested in helping lower-class women—try telling an impoverished mother on welfare that out-lawing *Playboy* is the answer to her troubles. And try telling a porn actress that it's better to starve on the minimum wage than it is to pose for pictures that middle-class women find immoral. Lost in the rarefied world of academia and backed with cushy jobs, these feminists forget that women can't feed their children on censorship. But that's not their concern. They could care less about economic and political activism. From their intellectual towers, they have seen the enemy: sex.

The feminist fight against dirty pictures isn't motivated by the de-sire to help the women in pornography. It isn't motivated by the de-sire—as they claim—to prevent rape. It's motivated by the belief that sex violates women. "The image of women in pornography is ex-tremely negative and demeaning," writes Deckard.[37] Here is the crux of the feminist antiporn fight: If a public depiction of sex is vile and degrading, then what is the act in private? "The thrusting is persis-tent invasion. She is opened up, split down the center," writes Dworkin.[38] Sexual material is evil because it *publicly* reveals the de-grading, demeaning nature of sex in *private*.

Just as in Victorian times (when respectable ladies condemned un-respectable lower-class strumpets), a select group of middle-class women have bestowed upon themselves the title of saviors of female virtue. And just as Victorian ladies blamed prostitutes for their hus-bands' faithlessness, today's feminists implicitly blame the women in pornography for the most reprehensible crime: rape. For example, Jennifer Lyn Beegle, cofounder of Miami University's Students Orga-nizing Against Pornography (their effort to cleanse society of dirty books is aptly translated into the acronym SOAP), wrote a vicious letter to the Spring 1993 issue of the feminist magazine *On the Issues*, condemning ex-porn star turned performance artist Annie Sprinkle. Sprinkle, who espouses female sexual pleasure through a performance that includes nudity, had been interviewed earlier by the magazine. According to Beegle, Sprinkle "helped to create" the rape problem. It's unfortunate, she writes, that "Sprinkle never once sees the obvi-ous connection between her life as a porn star" and the fact that women have to work in rape crisis centers. Or, as a porn actress said on a 48 *Hours* program in regard to feminists, "They want to blame *us*."

Many feminists maintain that they would rather "save" porn ac-tresses than blame them. But this sentiment changes quickly to con-demnation when the women refuse to be rescued. Like the fallen woman of Victorian times, who faced complete ostracization and punishment if she refused to act contrite, the porn actress who rejects the role of a sullied maiden in need of salvation then becomes the enemy. Should porn actresses claim they were forced into it, were traumatized and defiled, broken and victimized, they would be subjects of patronizing sympathy from feminists. But if they refuse to portray themselves as victims, these same feminists would deride them as suffering from "false consciousness" or brand them as accomplices to rape. "In talking to reactionary feminists," porn actress and feminist Nina Hartley writes, "it becomes clear that they view me, and others of my ilk, as brainwashed, deluded, woefully misled or out-and-out lying about our experiences. Their blatant lack of respect for the voices and experiences of other women would be laughable if it were not so insulting."[39]

This elitist attitude toward women involved in porn is prevalent throughout the movement, causing some feminists to treat any woman with a "questionable" life as a pariah. Take what happened to a twenty-eight-year-old woman named Ivory. In an essay for *Blue Stocking*, a feminist newspaper, Ivory writes about her experience calling the Los Angeles NOW chapter in response to a help-wanted advertisement. At first, the NOW coordinator was enthusiastic and wanted her to come for an interview. But when Ivory mentioned she worked as a nude model for a local college's art class, the reception turned cold. "All of a sudden," Ivory writes, "she said, 'I'm sorry, but we can't take you after all.'" Ivory asked her why not. The coordinator said, "Because NOW is against pornography. It would ruin our image to hire someone like you." Ivory pointed out that she had only posed nude for an art class, not for *Playboy*, and asked whether there were any other job openings at NOW. The coordinator grudgingly allowed, "You can work as a volunteer when our supervisor isn't in. But, we can't pay you. And we can't condone your lifestyle." Ivory writes that she responded, "So much for condoning the rights of all women to have jobs and representation from NOW," and hung up.

After the initial shock wore off, Ivory writes, her upset turned to outrage—outrage that NOW would accuse her of working in porn when in fact she did not; outrage that the organization would espouse to help such women but refuse to hire them; outrage that feminism would show such little respect for women's choices. And Ivory didn't even pose sexually: She simply revealed her body in an art class. For many current feminists, that alone is an unpardonable sin. That alone makes a woman so tainted that to be associated with her would ruin feminism's "image," so low and disgusting that to even allow her to work for free was unthinkable unless she did so at times when the decent, pure ladies of NOW weren't around to be sullied by her mere presence.[40]

The women in porn are real, live, breathing human beings. They are revealing things in public that have been hidden, out of shame, for centuries: Here is a *Playboy* model revealing her breasts. Here is a *Hustler* model explicitly revealing her genitalia. Here is a woman in one of Royalle's films moaning as a man gives her oral sex. Here is Nina Hartley with a man between her legs, a close-up shot of him entering her. Here is Annie Sprinkle, ex-porn star, standing on stage in her art performance dressed only in corset and robe, showing the audience a diagram of the female reproductive system. Here is a photo from the lesbian porn magazine, *On Our Backs*, of two softly rounded women lying naked like spoons, their legs sweetly entangled: One is turning her head backward for her lover's kiss, her eyes closed, searching with a blind hand across her lover's thigh.

These depictions do bother many women. They can make us feel odd, ill at ease, even if we seek them out. We hear a little voice inside of us that says, Those are real women doing that in public. How can they? Aren't they ashamed? How can they think men will *respect* them? How can they respect *themselves*?

Current feminists want us to accept that voice without question. They say, Yes, those women should be ashamed: They have all been victimized, forced into it—no woman would do such dirty, degrading things of her own volition. They say, Don't listen to the porn actresses who come forward to say it was their choice, because feminism means listening only to women who say the "right" things—the rest are either in denial or "pimps." They say that it's true that men don't respect women who reveal their bodies. In fact, they disrespect them so much, it makes them disrespect all women. They say, These women promote rape. And nothing could be more reprehensible than that. Nothing else could make a woman more of a traitor to her own sex than to condone and promote rape.

But we need to question this voice. We need to ask if it isn't a remnant of the repressive antisex morality that has been used by religious conservatives against women for centuries. The echo of a confining morality that taught us our genitalia is disgusting and shameful, that our revealed bodies defile our personhood, that there is only one kind of sex a decent woman can have: in the dark, under the covers, with her husband, for the purpose of reproduction. And the woman who defies these rules is no more than a slut, a whore by nature, undeserving of respect. This repressive sexual morality lingers today, exemplified in mainstream movies such as *Basic Instinct* and *Fatal Attraction*, where women who want and enjoy sex are invariably portrayed as evil, conniving bitches who destroy everything they touch. We must question why today's feminists, through the crusade against sexual material, would want to perpetuate this antifeminist crap. We must ask why the women's movement has bought into an ideology of oppression.

For many women of my generation, the feminist fight against porn is distressing. "I don't know what the problem is," a young woman from California says over coffee, glancing at me as if she expects rebuke. "I read pornography—what the heck, I like it. I don't get this feminist thing." My own mother tells me how much the 1971 feminist book *Our Bodies, Ourselves* changed her life—before she read it, she had never seen an explicit drawing of a vagina, hadn't read a frank discussion about masturbation, and hadn't heard that sexual pleasure can be empowering, joyful, fun, loving, and *female*. It affected her greatly, and thus affected me. I grew up with that book on the bookshelf. I learned that other women masturbated and had sexual fantasies. I looked forward to having sex. I read: "We can excite each other with erotic pictures, by sharing our fantasies, with the stimulation of a vibrator. Use your imagination. The possibilities are endless." It sounded wonderful, this part of being female.

It still does.

"I think the whole thing about pornography is that it's not the pornography that's bad. It's the attitude that surrounds the whole sexuality issue. I think it's natural for people to want to look at people doing things. People are just interested—like whoa, what's going on here? And you watch it for five minutes and then you get kind of bored. It's just something that you see. And it can be erotic if it's done really well. I've seen some scenes that are erotic. So what's wrong with that? . . . If you have a violent personality, that's why you rape. If someone sees a beautiful lovemaking scene, why would it make somebody rape? It's just easier to say, Censor all the pornography and all the problems will be gone. Total denial. Something bugs me about the censorship thing. Even though I think there's a lot of really horrible pornography out there, something bothers me about looking at that as a solution—looking at me veiling up as a solution."

—ELIZABETH DENNIS, thirty, belly dancer,
from the state of Washington

Elizabeth, an attractive woman with touches of early gray in her dark hair and the assured moves of a dancer, knows all about the feminist antiporn crusade: She's been attacked by feminists in her community for taking up belly dancing. For Elizabeth, this ended her willingness to label herself a feminist. She looks at belly dancing as a celebration of female power and sexuality, a sensuous, artistic dance. And so when Elizabeth considers the women's movement today, she talks about the repressive antisex nature of current feminism—a movement that would take something so natural and beautiful as a woman's body and turn it into something so fraught with danger, rape, violence, and fear. Because for her, as for many young women, there is nothing wrong with female sexuality, nothing wrong with sexual material, nothing wrong with depictions of lovemaking. Elizabeth refuses a feminist label that says there is, a label that looks upon her and other women as the danger, demanding they veil themselves.

In the feminist fight against pornography, the women's movement has come full circle, preaching censorship under the banner of refined feminine morality. In the Victorian age, "evil pictures" were censored because they were reputed to incite the hidden lust that lies inside of every man, leading to "riotous animalism"—and thus destroying the image of women as chaste, pure, and sexless. It was in the name of women that Victorians kept sex a secret and condemned "sated wantons." And it was in the name of women that they used this fear of sex to deny women birth control as well as social and political opportunities. It was a method used to oppress women, and it worked.

And now current feminists, in the name of women, want to make sex a secret once again. They want us to believe that exposure of our bodies degrades us, defiles us, and incites male lust; they want to censor expression of our sexuality because, once again, we are truly the sated wantons, the whores by nature who are to blame for rape. They want us to, in Elizabeth's chilling phrase, "veil" ourselves once more—in silence and in shame.

Part II

THE MORAL
PEDESTAL

Chapter 4

THE GODDESS WITHIN: THE NEW FEMINIST RELIGION

"This is one reason I don't want to get involved in feminism. It seems more like New Age religion than political stuff anymore. I don't like people telling me what to believe spiritually. Spirituality is a very private matter for me."

—ANNE O'DONNELL, twenty-nine, mother and businesswoman in Oregon

On a clear, windy day, small groups of women talk quietly among themselves outside a West Coast convention center. It's March 7, 1993—International Women's Day—and local feminist activists have organized an all-day conference with speakers, information tables, food, music, and other entertainment. Articles about the event have promised that over fifty feminist organizations will be present, as well as local and out-of-town activists hosting a variety of seminars on everything from domestic violence to "womyn's words." Like similar events across the country, this International Women's Day Celebration has been billed as the perfect opportunity for women curious about feminism to learn about the women's movement.

I am with my friend Anne, a young mother who adamantly supports women's rights and yet refuses to label herself a feminist. Tall, with a shock of long burgundy-black hair and a strong angular face,

Anne is wearing her customary bright red lipstick. She's the kind of person so visually striking that both women and men do a double take. After paying our suggested donation, we enter the cavernous hall and slowly wind our way through two floors of booths and tables. The attendance appears slim. The majority of women have gathered in the eating section on the main floor, where a few food booths offer vegetarian fare to be consumed on rickety plastic tables. Downstairs, a lesbian choir sings gustily to a room that seems populated more by activists at tables than by conference attendees.

The first thing we notice is how many of the tables seem dedicated to spiritual subjects. From the moment we alight from the escalators to the minute we step out the doors, we pass table after table arranged with colorful assortments of goddess statuettes, crystals, feathered Native American pipes, rich wood sculptures, necklaces bearing little pagan charms, and other New Age and spiritual apparatus. Flimsy paperback books on the "goddess" are offered for sale alongside mystifying hand-painted sticks and small stone bowls. There are calendars that feature different goddesses for each month and ritual books on modern witchcraft. The price tags on many items carry sums calculated to bust the budget. Scattered here and there—looking almost lost in the midst of all these spiritual gewgaws—are information tables for formal women's organizations. One of the largest tables is for an antiporn group. Finally, near the back of the room, we happen upon the local chapter of NOW.

Anne stops curiously at the NOW table and picks up a flyer. With a puzzled look, she hands me the sheet. It is a printed comparison of "goddess cultural beliefs" with the evil nature of "male-god cultural beliefs." The goddess section seems to be about prehistoric cultures, though no dates or time frames are given. According to the local NOW chapter, goddess cultural beliefs in the past had created a paradise. For example:

- There were no weapons of violence, no fortifications surrounding goddess communities and no warfare.
- The earth was, and is, the goddess' body. The earth is a living, breathing entity, and all life forms are sacred.
- Women controlled the religious, social, political and legal institutions, which were all focused on community improvements and equitable distribution of wealth and work.
- Every woman was required to work as a priestess for varying

amounts of time each year, and men were on all-important community councils, though women were given the highest honors.

- Women were free to change sexual mates, bear or not bear children, without social guilt or belittling stigmas attached to their actions.
- People were closely connected to nature, its cycles, power and beauty.

It sounds like a feminist Disneyland. And other NOW information turns out to be even more glowing about goddess worship, both in the past and present. Arranged neatly alongside the flyer was an array of the chapter's newspapers, with nearly every issue featuring articles praising goddess worship as an important feminist cause. The November 1992 NOW newspaper claimed that: "The modern Wicca [witchcraft] is feminist in theory. Feminist, meaning that all of us have those feminine qualities which create life and love in each other. Every single one of us is part of the Goddess and celebrate her in each other."

Many of the articles glowingly recommended feminist witchcraft, or wicca. "The Witchcraft of today, as before, encourages spirituality and diversity," asserted an October 1992 article on Halloween as "a day for witches."

I scan the rest of the information table and find only a few pamphlets on subjects other than goddess worship and witchcraft—these are from national NOW and deal with abortion rights and lesbian issues. The woman at the table talks quickly and excitedly with a conference attendee: The subject is ecology and healing the earth. I think of a "women's ritual" advertised in that month's issue of the local NOW paper. NOW members were asked to bring a handful of seeds—representing their hopes and dreams—to an event honoring "the goddess." The ritual was to act as a rite of passage to a better, if vague, future. As we leave the table, Anne snorts derisively, telling me in soft, sure terms just how alienating she finds this feminist focus on spirituality.

Later, we head outside for a breath of fresh air. The sun is shining and the air is fresh and clean; we smile at the reprieve from winter and decide to chuck the rest of the conference for a late lunch. "Now, tell me something," Anne asks, suddenly intense. "Just what does any of that goddess stuff have to do with feminism? With things like my daughter, her education, health insurance, child care?" She turns her winter-paled face and dark hair toward the sun and then gently toward me. "Correct me if I'm wrong, but just what does it have to do with women's rights?"

The truth is, nothing. But this fact hasn't stopped the goddess trend from becoming one of the fastest-growing segments of the women's movement.

This feminist promotion of goddess worship and its sister, feminist witchcraft, is one of the most visible, vibrant, and screwy trends surfacing in the modern women's movement.

Dozens of feminist books have been published in the past few years on goddess worship. Feminist magazines and newspapers such as *Ms.* and *Sojourner: The Women's Forum* regularly praise the virtues of this religion, while a recent crop of spiritual magazines such as *Sage-Woman* and *Crone Chronicles* are devoted solely to the cause. In women's organizations, goddess worship is gaining wide acceptance as a feminist issue—especially on the local level, where adherents will call upon the goddess in meetings and use updated witchcraft rituals as forms of political and social activism.

The religion is thriving in Canada, England, Germany, South Africa, Argentina, and other countries, according to Diane Stein, editor of the 1991 book *The Goddess Celebrates*. But it appears to be most popular in its birthplace, the United States. Followers estimate the movement involves anywhere from 100,000 to 500,000 women in the United States, but figures are impossible to establish.[1]

The feminist promotion of goddess religion goes back to the early seventies, when critiques of organized religions—notably Mary Daly's influential 1973 book, *Beyond God the Father*—pioneered the feminist spirituality movement. Despite unease on the part of many politically oriented feminists—who fear such an emphasis is alienating to religious women and is a narcotic on activism—feminist writers began experimenting with the notion of a female-centered deity; hence, the goddess.

In the late seventies, following a spate of feminist works proclaiming to have uncovered proof of peaceful prehistoric "goddess cultures," the worship started gaining serious momentum in the movement. This feminist rendition of Stone Age goddess cultures is disputed by archaeologists, but many feminists have latched onto these theories not only for an idealized history but as an argument for spiritual conversion. As Merlin Stone, author of the highly influential 1976 book *When God Was a Woman*, writes today, "I have had the joy not only of contributing to the very beginnings of Goddess reclamation and to the women's spirituality movement but also observing and participating in the rapid and widespread expansion of this knowledge."[2]

Throughout the eighties, this expansion of feminist goddess religion was bolstered by a wealth of popular literature from Jungian and New Age perspectives. Oversimplified Jungian archetypes—which often perpetuate sexist stereotypes of "feminine" and "masculine" traits—became the backbone of feminist books promoting goddess worship, reaching best-selling status in the 1992 book *Women Who Run with the Wolves*.[3] Meanwhile, many New Agers such as Lynn Andrews, author of several imaginative books, including *Medicine Woman*, appropriated goddess theory for mass consumption. The growing debate among feminist theologians over male bias in traditional faiths served to add fuel to the fire.

The result of these trends saw the term *goddess* become a household word—even *Megatrends for Women*, a book on the major trends of the day and their effect upon women, devotes a chapter to "The Goddess Reawakening." And in many households, this term is intrinsically tied to the feminist label—for good reason. The promotion of goddess worship is approached with near-evangelical zeal by many feminists. These leaders feel that theirs is the only empowering religion for women, and they're out to convert.

For young women, goddess worship is prevalent in the places they encounter feminist theory, from bookstores to coffee shops to grassroots activist groups. But it is on campuses that this religion gets pushed with a vengeance. "Women's studies have brought about a great resurgence. Both women and men have found empowerment through the Goddess," claims Laurie Cabot, self-styled "high priestess" and author of *Powers of the Witch*."[4] No wonder. Some women's studies programs seem to teach students that if they want to consider themselves feminists, they had better kneel at the altar of the goddess. At Tulane, SUNY Plattsburgh, George Washington University, Dartmouth, and other campuses, for example, students attending introductory women's studies courses are assigned Carol P. Christ's minor classic, "Why Women Need the Goddess: Phenomenological, Psychological, and Political Reflections," which might be best described as a religious tract. And students attending introductory women's studies courses at the University of New Hampshire not only read several essays on goddess religion and watch a heavy-handed video entitled "Goddess Remembered"—on supposed prehistoric goddess cultures—but actually end the semester with a "closing ritual." Heaven knows how they are graded on that.

Goddess religion has been given approval by feminist theorists, including, of course, women's studies professors. "After attending the morning session Louise and I visited the Exhibition Hall. There, dozens of booths offered women's studies books and paraphernalia. Witchcraft and goddess worship supplies were in aisle one," feminist writer Christina Hoff Sommers wrote after attending the 1992 Women's Studies Association conference. "Last year, at a meeting of Women's Studies Directors, everyone joined hands to form a 'healing circle.' They also assumed the postures of trees experiencing rootedness and tranquility."[5] While not all women's studies programs are influenced by the Women's Studies Association—internal bickering has seen the conference's attendance drop substantially—the group still serves as a barometer for much of what is being taught to students about feminism.[6]

Rituals such as healing circles and imitating trees has led many to regard goddess worship as merely a goofy trend. But it is far from a benign or simply amusing fad. It has contributed substantially to the alienation of women from the movement. Christian, Jewish, and other religious women often find the common assertion that they are being victimized by their churches insulting, and they balk at converting to a new religion. Atheistic and agnostic women often find this emphasis on spirituality deeply distressing.

As the authors of *Megatrends for Women* found, "The constant litany of *strictly* 'feminine' traits espoused in some Goddess books is enough to nauseate many thinking women." The religion is based on theory that reeks of old fashioned sexist stereotypes. Women, again, are held to be the gentler, nurturing, compassionate and clearly unassertive sex.

This vision of women as spiritually superior—and spiritually pure—has led to devastating inertia. Political and economic activism is suddenly portrayed as quite unnecessary, even distasteful. Instead, goddess adherents are convinced that witchcraft rituals of chanting, burning sage, sending spells, and channeling Aphrodite will effectively advance women's rights.

And so feminism today has taken a distressing step away off the path to equality onto a detour down a yellow brick road. Feminist leaders are now telling women to perform the modern equivalent of the Sioux Indian Ghost Dance, to spend our energies frantically calling upon a mythical golden age in an effort to create a dreamlike future—because such rituals are better suited to our superior nature than fighting directly with men for our rights. This ideal of feminine spiritual purity was used effectively against women in the Victorian era; they were told that, for the more spiritual sex, prayer was the only appropriate means of improving the world. Then, as now, it's striking that the more ineffective an action, the more it's said to reflect "female" values.

Meanwhile, millions of women—young and old—have to cope with unequal pay, lack of affordable child care, nonexistent job opportunities, and raising families without health insurance. Countless more face unavailable birth control and abortion, sexual harassment in the workplace, or no workplace at all. And many face the trauma of rape and domestic violence under a judicial system that too often slaps offenders lightly on the wrist. Goddess worship does absolutely nothing for these women.

Yet they, and many others, are often told that to be a proper feminist one must convert to goddess religion and practice modern witchcraft. Feminism is now an ideological contract, complete with religious deities, doctrine, and even a set program for worship and rituals. There's no warranty on this contract and no guarantee, because none of these spiritual beliefs even hints at doing something to better women's lives.

The question is not whether goddess followers are entitled to worship what they please—of course they are. The question is whether feminism should be synonymous with a religious doctrine. Undoubtedly, goddess religion is spiritually satisfying to many women; it is often rich in ritual, creative, and exuberant. But there is a tremendous difference between belief and proselytizing. For many women like my friend Anne, spirituality is a private matter. Confronted with a feminist label that requires conversion to a religion—and demands they partake in rituals and worship—many women decline to sign on the dotted line.

The feminist infatuation with goddess worship is bolstered by a controversial rendition of prehistoric cultures. According to numerous feminist writers—including Marija Gimbutas, Riane Eisler, Marilyn French, and Merlin Stone—Europe, from roughly 25,000 B.C. to 3000

B.C., was home to a continent-wide "Goddess" religion.[7] Women were supposedly worshiped for their reproductive abilities, societies were peaceful, egalitarian, nonsexist, and people lived in an understanding harmony with nature and one another.

As many feminists would have it, it was a magical, wonderful time: the true Garden of Eden. Leading feminist spiritualist Miriam Simos, who goes by the pen name, Starhawk, captures this fanciful view when she asserts that goddess worship gave its followers amazing powers. "[S]ome among the clans were gifted, could 'call' the herds to a cliffside or a pit, where a few beasts, in willing sacrifice, would let themselves be trapped. These gifted shamans could attune themselves to the spirits of the herds, and in doing so they became aware of the pulsating rhythm that infuses all life, the dance of the double spiral."[8]

The time periods of this reputed Eden are the Upper Paleolithic (the Old Stone Age, before agriculture), the Neolithic (the New Stone Age, with the development of agriculture and later, copper), and some of the early Bronze Age (the advent of bronze tools, trade, and social stratification). They are prehistoric, meaning that written language had not been invented—or, in the case of the Linear A script from the Mediterranean Sea's Minoan Cretes, has yet to be deciphered.

The Upper Paleolithic peoples—also known as the Cro-Magnons— were migratory hunters and foragers who lived in caves and rude huts, using the simplest of stone tools. Following these hunter-gatherers came the Neolithic peoples, who settled into stable farming communities and created increasingly sophisticated tools and pottery. The latter part of this period is also referred to as the Copper Age. An example of a European Neolithic man from the Copper Age is the Iceman, a remarkably preserved 5,300-year-old corpse found frozen in an Austrian glacier. Dressed in furs and a woven grass cape, carrying stone and copper tools, and sporting teeth worn from a diet of gritty bread, the Iceman has given prehistorians important insights into what many consider cavemen.[9] Many feminists place the height of goddess religion during this man's time.

After these Stone Age periods came the Bronze Age, when trading and the use of metals created thriving cities and a distinct ruling class. According to popular feminist theory, the Minoan Cretes of the Bronze Age worshiped a goddess.

Despite the incredible time span of thousands of years and the profound transitions from foraging to farming, from stone tools to bronze, and from crude huts to organized cities, these prehistoric cultures are said to have followed a continent-wide goddess religion. Presumably because of the gender of the deity, they lived idyllic lives—that is, until male-god religion ruined everything.

The saga of the goddess has a villain, and naturally that villain is male. Sometime around 4400 B.C., tribes of patriarchal male-god-worshiping brutes known as Kurgans are believed to have staged a series of violent invasions into peaceful matriarchal Europe. Within a few thousand years, they conquered most of the goddess-worshiping communities. As some feminists have it, these Kurgans—out of spite—then destroyed crucial evidence that goddess cultures ever existed.

By roughly A.D. 500, according to author Merlin Stone, the last vestiges of goddess religions were wiped out.[10] This vicious Kurgan conquest was to change the world forever. Marija Gimbutas, the creator of the Kurgan theory, goes so far as to claim that this conquest "eventually led to such people as Stalin and Hitler."[11] But many archaeologists and historians find the Kurgan theory suspect.[12] Geoffrey Ashe, author of *Dawn Behind the Dawn: A Search for the Earthly Paradise*, persuasively argues that the idea of a patriarchal—or any other—invasion at the time is highly unlikely, especially considering that no evidence of the supposed invaders appears in the very areas they are said to have conquered.

Still, this dramatic story of paradise destroyed has gained great favor in feminist circles. "Archeological remains from about ten thousand years ago reflect goddess-worshiping communities living in egalitarian harmony and material well-being," asserts Marilyn French in her 1992 book, *The War Against Women*. "War may have begun about ten thousand years ago, but not until about the fourth millennium BCE did men begin to build what became patriarchy—male supremacy backed by force. . . . For women, it has been downhill ever since."

Because there aren't any written records to prove the existence of goddess cultures—or their supposed conquest by patriarchal meanies—feminists have to rely almost entirely on speculative interpretations of archaeological remains to uphold their theories. Many also employ the controversial method of interpreting myth as literal history. For example, Patricia Reis, author of *Through the Goddess*, claims that Greek goddess myths actually stemmed from goddess cultures thousands of years before. And others fall back on the Jungian notion of a collective memory that links the individual with the long-lost past.

The most-oft-cited pieces of physical evidence used to support the existence of goddess cultures are the famous Venus figurines. Probably the best-known of these is the Venus of Willendorf, a stone figure from the Upper Paleolithic period. Like others of its kind—some molded quickly from clay, others carved from soft stone or ivory—this is a tiny figurine of a woman who would be called obese by today's standards. All of the emphasis is on her tremendous breasts, hips, belly, and bulbous behind. Her legs are no more than token nubs, and her face is featureless. Over sixty Venuses come from the caves and crude huts of the Paleolithic period; hundreds more from the Neolithic period, where they are found in abandoned homes and the Stone Age equivalent of garbage dumps.

According to leading feminists, these figurines represent a "Great Goddess" that was worshiped for millennia. "In the beginning, the feminine principle was seen as the fundamental cosmic force. All ancient peoples believed that the world was created by a female deity," writes feminist spiritualist Judy Chicago. "Woman's creative power was embodied in a multitude of female figurines that emphasized Her breasts, belly, hips, and vagina. . . . they attest to a time when women not only were venerated, but actually had social and political power."[13]

But evidence contradicts the theory that these figurines represent a female deity, let alone attest to women's status. One problem is that the abundantly fleshed female figurines are actually a minority of all found statuettes—most are sexless and many are *male*. "Of the many hundreds of carved figures so far discovered throughout Europe," writes Richard Leakey in *The Making of Mankind*, "some can be identified as female, although most of these have natural rather than exaggerated proportions, some are clearly male, but most are, to our eyes at least, sexless."

This fact, however, is seldom mentioned by feminist goddess theorists. For example, pictures of the famous Laussel carving (a ripely rounded woman holding a horn in one hand) adorn many feminist books on the goddess. Yet the authors tellingly neglect to mention that the same rock shelter that produced this stone "goddess" also produced a figure of a man. He is wearing what appears to be a belt and is gesturing as if throwing a spear, and for all we know, he may symbolize a coequal "god."[14]

There is also the problem of interpreting figurines from completely disparate times and cultures as having the same meaning and usage. In our societies, things can change greatly in just a few years—and feminist theorists are lightly dismissing millennia in their interpretations. A crude clay figurine found in a Cro-Magnon cave next to a pile of gnawed bison bones in one part of Europe does not necessarily represent the same thing as a beautifully carved stone statue found in a Copper Age home on the other side of the continent. Thousands of years, hundreds of miles, and incredible cultural changes separate the two, and it's a serious stretch to claim they meant the same things to their creators. In fact, there is a period of *ten thousand years* between the Paleolithic period and the Neolithic period in which no female figurines appear at all—making the idea of a continuous religion based on their use highly unlikely.[15] As Leakey concludes: "The idea of a continent-wide cult of the mother-god, symbolized by the bulbous 'Venuses,' appears to have been greatly overstated."

There are many possible explanations for the Venus figurines. In her 1989 book, *Women in Prehistory*, anthropologist Margaret Ehrenberg lists several. She notes that mortality rates were high in these times, and so the importance of reproduction must have been tremendous. The figurines could have represented "sympathetic magic," or models of unborn children and adults. Sympathetic magic is common in many cultures. For instance, among the Zuni of North America, a woman who wishes to conceive carries a small model of a child or a model of that child as an adult. When she conceives, she discards the fetish. It is possible that Stone Age people also used their figurines—especially the sexless ones that may represent children— in a similar manner. Another possible explanation is that they were children's toys. This is less odd than it sounds. That the figurines include both human sexes as well as animals, were often quickly created from cheap material such as clay and soft stone, and then apparently thrown away suggests that they may have been used as children's playthings. But, as Ehrenberg warns, it's unlikely that all the figurines had the same use. Some may have represented spirits or deities; others might have been used as sympathetic magic, sorcery tools, or toys. We simply have no way of knowing.

While these Venus figurines are the most frequently cited proof, feminist writers present other evidence to uphold their theory.

The leading—and by far most credible—feminist researcher on the subject was Marija Gimbutas, a professor of archaeology at the University of California at Los Angeles and author of several immensely popular books, including *The Language of the Goddess* and *The Civilization of the Goddess*. Gimbutas, who passed away in February of 1993, provided the backbone of the current feminist promotion of goddess worship, and she often presented a strong case for the existence of prehistoric goddess religions. In her books, she gave example after example of prehistoric art—and from the Venus figurines to designs on pottery and masks, all are said to denote various aspects of the "Goddess." For those without a formal education in archaeology, Gimbutas's work is often impressive and her books are gorgeously produced and lavishly illustrated.

But other archaeologists believe there are crucial flaws in Gimbutas's scholarship. Archaeologist William Barnett is one skeptic. In an interview in his office at the Interdepartmental Laboratories of the Museum of Natural History in New York City, Barnett keeps one ear eagerly posted toward the phone—his wife is due to go into labor at any minute—and talks knowledgeably about Gimbutas's work. Barnett makes it clear that he believes Gimbutas has made a "very positive contribution" by questioning traditionally sexist assumptions of prehistoric societies. But he says that "she gets carried away in a few points, and I think that really detracts from some important points she makes." He pauses, then adds, "Then again, I think she just kind of lets her imagination run wild."

This is obvious in Gimbutas's creative stretching in the interpretation of the meaning of ancient artifacts. Spiral designs, for instance, are found throughout the prehistoric world, from cave paintings to pottery. As Gimbutas would have it, these designs represent aspects of the "Goddess," rather than decorative tradition or other symbolism. "It's really difficult either to prove or disprove this," Barnett comments. "Because even if you can find constant associations of, say, a spiral in one place at 5000 B.C. and then another place at 2000 B.C, that's *three thousand years*. Reasonably, it's very difficult to expect that that symbol had exactly the same connotation in the two different places at two different times." And, as Barnett points out, spirals and other designs appear in modern graffiti as well, though few would argue that inner-city teenagers are using subway cars to honor the goddess.

At other times, Gimbutas makes what can only be characterized as absurd claims. In her 1989 *The Language of the Goddess*, for example, she suggests that the depiction of bulls in prehistoric art actually represent—of all things—female fertility. Her evidence for this claim is a picture taken from a medical textbook: The shape of a bull's head and horns resembles a woman's uterus and fallopian tubes. This must mean, Gimbutas declares, that prehistoric cultures painted and sculpted bull's heads to signify reproductive organs.

This doesn't wash. As Barnett points out, fallopian tubes "are barely visible upon dissection and have little cognitive connection to birth outside the realm of modern medicine."[16] In other words, it's very unlikely that prehistoric people even knew that women had fallopian tubes—which are incredibly tiny—much less knew that the tubes transport microscopic eggs to the uterus or that children are the result of sperm reaching the eggs. Gimbutas herself claimed in an earlier book that there's no evidence that Neolithic people understood the concept of biological conception.[17]

It's important to realize that interpretations of prehistoric artifacts will always be tainted with cultural bias. In the past, this has meant some blatantly sexist assumptions, especially from Victorian archaeologists—such as the once-common claim that the Venus figurines were Stone Age pornography. Today, it can mean equally biased assumptions from feminists who seem intent to prove that God was once a woman—and still is. Gimbutas's agenda is made clear in *The Language of the Goddess*, when she claims that ". . . now we find the Goddess reemerging from the forests and mountains, bringing us hope for the future, returning us to our most ancient human roots." Such an agenda disturbs many archaeologists, who would prefer to keep their science a bit more objective and a lot less religiously and politically motivated.[18]

The question of whether a Stone Age goddess religion existed is not easily resolved. Female deities may well have been worshiped in some forms, whether alongside male deities or even as a singular goddess that was worshiped above all else. Then again, maybe not. For most of the archaeological community, the jury is still out on goddess cultures. "I would even be so bold as to propose that there are no appropriate modern analogies for what was going on in 5000 B.C.," Barnett says, "because we can't say for certain that there's anything in the present that can be used to model that." These cultures might have been so radically different from ours that to interpret artifacts according to our ideas of religion—such as the notion that deities have to be either male or female instead of, say, animal or wind spirits—is a big mistake.

But for many in the women's movement, the subject is closed. Not only are feminist spiritual leaders quite certain that for thousands of years Europe worshiped a goddess, they are adamant that their cultures were virtual paradises, nurturing, nonviolent, nature-loving, and reverent toward *all* women. In *The Language of the Goddess*, Gimbutas claims that these cultures didn't fortify their villages or make violent weapons. As she puts it, it was "an age free of strife."

This vision of a golden age is crucial to the promotion of goddess worship by feminists: Put women in charge and the world will exist in peaceful harmony. But credible archaeologists beg to differ with this idealized past. "There *are* fortified sites there," says David Anthony, an assistant professor of anthropology at Hartwick College in Oneonta, New York, and an expert on many of the archaeological digs Gimbutas bases her work on. "For instance, in northeastern Bulgaria, most of the sites there—and these are some of the most spectacular old European sites from which many of the female figurines have come—were fortified from the very beginning." Anthony explains that these are "tell" sites, meaning that villages were built on top of one another over time. The fortifications go back throughout Neolithic villages. "They're fairly massive fortifications, with three rows of palisade walls," he says, along with wooden gates and a ditch outside the walls. "Which," he adds, "implies chronic inner-village warfare."

Violence was not unknown to these peoples. "You also find in these settlements mace heads," Anthony says in crisp professional tones. "A mace is a round stone object, still used as a symbol of royal power. . . . Essentially, a mace is an anti-personnel weapon. Axes can be used for something else; a mace is there specifically to crush skulls with . . . it's an anti-personnel weapon that represents a glorification of warfare and violence." There are also indications of human sacrifice in these cultures, including, as Anthony says, "infant burials under house floors." While archaeologists aren't sure why these peoples buried babies under their homes, Anthony speculates they may have been sacrificed as "foundation deposits." In fact, in her 1982 book, *The Goddesses and Gods of Old Europe*, Gimbutas herself notes that human sacrifice probably occurred. This seems distinctly at odds with a vision of an egalitarian age "free of strife."

From the hunter-gatherers of the Paleolithic period to the Neolithic farmers, prehistoric life was probably not as bad as the description "poor, nasty, brutish, and short" given by the seventeenth century philosopher Thomas Hobbes. But it certainly wasn't a paradise. Few lived past the age of forty. People faced starvation over long winters and in times of drought, women in particular faced the dangers of childbirth without modern medicines, and children often died from disease. And apparently, many faced warfare and death by skull-crushing maces, along with the chance of ending life as a sacrifice.

Although some adherents claim that they are not trying to paint goddess cultures as utopias, their warm and fuzzy portraits of these times—and their omission of the more unsavory details—suggest that they are. "This is not to say that these were ideal societies or utopias," writes Riane Eisler. "But, unlike our societies, they were *not* warlike. They were *not* societies where women were subordinate to men."[19]

But just what status women enjoyed in these cultures is open to question. To decipher status, archaeologists usually look at cemeteries. For example, if the graves of men contain more valuables than the graves of women, then it's likely that men were deemed more important. But the majority of Neolithic people didn't have cemeteries at all. Corpses were placed in mass tombs and sometimes the bones were later scattered. There is one area with cemeteries—and the richest graves in which the sex of the corpse could be determined belong to men, not women. "Because we're lacking cemeteries for big parts of southeastern Europe," says Anthony, "it's hard to tell if women had high status across the whole region."

The more advanced civilization of the Minoan Cretes is a good example of just how feminists determined women's status from archaeological remains. "In Crete, for the last time in recorded history, a spirit of harmony between women and men as joyful and equal participants in life appears to pervade," writes Riane Eisler in *The Chalice and the Blade*.

This idea is largely based on artifacts uncovered in the *palace* of the time. The Minoan castle frescoes often depict women in what may be religious ceremonies; they are being waited on hand and foot by what appear to be slaves and men bearing gifts. There is also the famous Snake Goddess sculpture—of a woman in what seems to be an extremely tight corset, with snakes on her arms. These artifacts undoubtedly say something about the lives of the women of the time—the ruling class of women, that is. Perhaps the royal women of Crete were revered, but that in no way speaks to the status of all women of their culture. To say that it does is similar to arguing that the best way to understand the lives of American women is to watch reruns of *Lifestyles of the Rich and Famous*.

Not all feminists accept such romantic theories about past matriarchies. "Let's be blunt," stated a critical article by writers Jean Napoli and Donaleen Saul in the July/August 1991 issue of *New Directions for Women*. "What the proponents of this interpretation of human history are really saying is that men are responsible for the horrific state of our planet and that if women had continued their rule, life would go in peace and harmony."[20] Sherrian Lea, a student at MIT and a self-described pagan interviewed in the May 1992 issue of *Boston* magazine, captures many young women's feelings on the feminist golden age: "I've had enough sociology and anthropology to know solid theory from bushwah."

In what Mary Lefkowtiz, a professor at Wellesley College, has termed "another exciting and unlearned shopping spree in the great mall of the world's traditions,"[21] goddess worshipers have patched their religion together from a disparate and often outlandish mishmash of sources. New Age practices such as channeling, Jungian theory on intuition and gender differences, ancient and modern paganism complete with pentagrams and hexes, shamanism, herbal healing, and pick-and-choose appropriations of Native American, ancient Greek, Australian Aboriginal, and even Buddhist teachings—all backed by popular feminist theory decrying "patriarchal" religion—form the goddess religion. Add in a healthy dose of creative imagination and it all becomes clear as mud.

From feminist leaders channeling goddesses to articles in feminist magazines, however, there are some basic tenets to feminist goddess worship.

The first and foremost belief is in a female deity. Worship of this deity is at the same time polytheistic and monotheistic. It is polytheistic in the sense that many different goddesses culled from mythology—from the Egyptian goddess Isis to the Greek goddess Aphrodite—are named in ritual. But in the end, it is far more monotheistic, in that these deities are often seen as different manifestations of one female entity. The entity is sometimes referred to as Gaia (the Greek word for earth), but most often as the Great Goddess. She is decidedly omnipresent. "The Goddess is not separate from the world—She *is* the world, and all things in it: moon, sun, earth, star, stone, seed, flowing river, wind, wave, leaf and branch, bud and blossom, fang and claw, woman and man," writes Starhawk in her book *The Spiral Dance*, excerpts of which are taught to students at Indiana University at Bloomington. Students learn that while men are part of and "contained" in the goddess, women *are* the goddess. We should, as Starhawk writes, be "inspired to see ourselves as divine."

Just what makes women divine is clear in goddess literature. All the traditional "female" traits are paraded out: compassion, nurturing, connection with the earth, ecological consciousness, and especially that old bugaboo, female intuition. "Another trait closely associated with the Feminine is that of intuition, which has inspired both admiring awe and negative criticism," writes Merlin Stone.[22]

Feminist leader Mary Daly calls this female intuition "metamemory," when women go "spiraling into the past, carrying vision forward."[23] Appallingly, this dizzying notion of female intuition stems directly from Victorian times, when English philosopher Herbert Spencer proposed that women inherited special intuitive powers through evolution, in order to compensate for being the weaker sex. Spencer called this "the natural language of feeling," and he used it to argue that the irrational nature of intuition leaves women unable to cope with the rigors of education and the workforce.[24] Like Spencer, goddess feminists do not base their ideas of female intuition—or, for that matter, any other supposed gender differences—on any even faintly scientific evidence. They don't have to: They just have a feeling.

For goddess feminists, the belief in "feminine" intuition and other ultrasensitive traits are necessary to promote the idea that women are inherently the better sex. This superiority isn't due to women's traditional roles or societal conditioning, we are told, but is literally a biological imprinting. The seat of this power lies pretty much, well, in our seats. "Woman's power comes automatically by virtue of our femaleness, our natural and personal acquaintance with blood—menstrual blood," claims the Fall 1992 issue of the spiritual magazine *SageWoman*. The reason? The passage of blood from the vagina helps women "transcend linear time and pass into a heightened state of shamanic awareness, establishing an ongoing deep connection with cycles." Or, as Victorian James Burnett put it nearly a century earlier, ". . . the damsel throws away every month a vast amount of fluid power in the order of Nature. Let us call this *pelvic power*."[25]

Our mere existence—or rather, the existence of our reproductive organs—is said to be holy. "Because of women's unique position as menstruants, birthgivers, and those who have traditionally cared for the young and the dying, women's connection to the body, nature, and this world has been obvious," students at Old Dominion University read in Carol Christ's "Why Women Need the Goddess." According to Christ, in goddess religion, "The female body is viewed as the *direct incarnation* [emphasis added] of waxing and waning, life and death, cycles in the universe."

The belief in pelvic power has seen menstruation, menopause, and birth become the primary focuses of goddess rituals. "There is power in the blood of wimmin. There is power in the blood that transforms us" is offered as a ritual chant in the 1991 book *The Goddess Celebrates*. An article in *SageWoman* suggests that women make vulva prints ("smear your blood around your vulva; press a piece of white paper against you. Sacred art!"), along with wearing red and meditating as powerful rituals during their periods. And author Christ relates another feminist menstrual rite. "They raised power by placing their hands on each other's bellies and chanting together. Finally, they marked each other's faces with rich, dark menstrual blood saying 'This is the blood that promises renewal. This is the blood that promises sustenance. This is the blood that promises life.' From hidden dirty secret to the life power of the Goddess, women's blood has come full circle."

From the hidden dirty secret that signified our status as breeders to the feminist "life power of the Goddess," women's blood has definitely come full circle—landing once again right where we started: our only legacy and only claim to power.

Theories and rituals such as these may help ease the shame that many women have been taught regarding menstruation. But they also harken directly back to the days when women were defined solely by their reproductive systems. "The Uterus, it must be remembered, is the *controlling* organ in the female body, being the most excitable of all, and so intimately connected, by the ramifications of its numerous nerves, with every other part," wrote one Victorian doctor. For the Victorians, the belief that women's reproductive systems exercised "gigantic power and influence" over the "animal economy of woman" was the basis for arguing that everything from higher education to masturbation would simply drain important energy away from female pelvic power.[26]

By putting all of women's eggs—literally—in one basket, feminist goddess worship does the same thing. Our uteruses reign above our intellects, independence, ambitions, religious and personal beliefs, and especially our individuality. All class and cultural differences between women are conveniently erased under this school of thought, and all of the important contributions that women make to society outside of childbirth are suddenly portrayed as secondary—if they're even acknowledged at all.

In the end, goddess religion places women's identity right where traditional sexism does: our genitalia.

One of the most popular ways of practicing the goddess religion is feminist witchcraft, or wicca. As the January/February 1993 *Ms.* announced, "Witchcraft is about wholeness, about celebrating one's intimacy with the Goddess and the earth, who are one and the same."

Margot Adler, a leader of this revival of superstition and author of *Drawing down the Moon*, explains that witchcraft "has many forms, ranging from those that are indistinguishable from feminist Goddess spirituality, to those that revive other forms of Western European Paganism, where the male and female deities coexist, usually hailing from the British Isles and Northern Europe."[27]

The idea that they are reviving an ancient religion—one that once saw "millions" persecuted—has lent feminist witchcraft adherents a distinct air of martyrdom. Elinor Gadon, author of *The Once and Future Goddess*, claims an estimated 9 million people, mostly women, were tortured and put to death for practicing "the way of the Goddess." This claim is echoed in Gloria Steinem's *Revolution from Within*, when Steinam quotes *Ms.* magazine cofounder Letty Cottin Pogrebin, who also cites this 9 million figure. This claim is treated with skepticism by many. Monsignor William B. Smith, a professor of moral theology at St. Joseph's Seminary of the Archdiocese of New York, told the May 9, 1992, *New York Daily News* that while he doesn't dispute the persecution of supposed witches, he notes there just weren't enough people in the countries of pre-industrial Europe at the time to support such estimated slaughter. "Somebody should check their medication," he added sardonically.

While traditional "witches" recognize a male god (a consort to the Goddess, called the "horned God"), others preferring a more separatist angle of goddess worship practice reinvented forms. "Within the two streams of Goddess-worship—the feminist and the Wiccan—are further distinctions," writes Rusty Unger for the June 4, 1990,

New York magazine. "Some Wiccan covens are open to visitors, some closed. Some are heterosexual, some are feminist, others are lesbian-separatist. Some followers worship in the nude. Feminist Goddess groups, or circles, vary, too—with those in the Dianic tradition emphasizing the Greek-goddess archetypes in their rituals and others focusing on herbal healing. The latter call themselves Green Witches or Wise Women. Still others concentrate on Native American teachings and deities."

For most observers, however, lines dividing goddess worship and feminist witchcraft are not clearly drawn. Feminist spiritual leaders such as Starhawk freely mix many traditions, including Dianic, Native American, and pagan into their rituals. Feminist literature gives directions for goddess rituals that include drawing pentagrams, chanting, burning incense, channeling, and invoking Greek and Egyptian goddesses.

Amusingly, followers of goddess worship often shade those details of myth that contradict their philosophy. Carol Christ, for instance, rejects that Persephone was raped, claiming that this is a "patriarchal addition" to the tale.[28] Merlin Stone claims that the legend that Athena was born from the head of Zeus is an "Indo-European" misrepresentation. Some insist that Athena was actually the goddess of intuition and omit such unsavory details as her penchant for eating meat.[29]

And others have been accused of simply lying for profit. Lynn Andrews, a best-selling author who writes allegedly "true story" accounts of her experiences with a mysterious worldwide female shamanistic society called the Sisterhood of the Shields, has been denounced by Aboriginal and Native American women as more sham than shaman. According to the July 2, 1993, *Sydney Morning Herald*, an Australian Aboriginal women's group derided Andrews's account of a ceremonial initiation in *Crystal Woman: The Sisters of the Dreamtime* as "laughable." Andrews describes a ceremonial gathering of women in an unspecified area of central Australia and says her naked body was smeared with bandicoot grease; central Australian Aborigines point out they haven't seen a bandicoot (a marsupial animal) in their land for thirty years, no one had seen or heard of Andrews visiting, and she even got the name of their language wrong (she calls it "Koori," which refers to aboriginal people in Victoria, not central Australia). It turns out, according to paper trails, Andrews was in the country for a mere two weeks. In the United States and Canada, North American Indians have been angered at Andrews, as well. Manitoba Cree Indians claim the rites portrayed in *Medicine Woman*, such as Andrews being told to strip naked before a council of Cree elders (she seems to get naked an awful lot in her books) are unheard of and that the names of her supposed mentors, Agnes Whistling Elk and Ruby Plenty Chiefs, are no more Cree than Koori is the language of the central Aborigines. And the Ontario Mohawk newspaper *Akwesasne Notes* has denounced Andrews as one of several "plastic" medicine women and men who charge "gullible white people" for their services. Yet Andrews, possibly because her books help pay for her Beverly Hills home and macrobiotic cook, continues to maintain her stories are true, even if she refuses to divulge exact locations or proof the "Sisterhood" exists. Her next book will be based on her "true" experiences in Tibet and Nepal.

In feminist goddess worship, nearly anything goes—as long as it's based on the divine and pelvic-powered feminine, and as long as it involves one of the more powerful forces in today's women's movement: the belief in magic. "There is a certain way that magic works: it is, in a sense, a technology," Starhawk writes in an essay for the 1990 book *Reweaving the World*.

It is this belief in the "technology" of magic that underlies goddess and witchcraft rituals. And it is this trust in magic that has many feminist leaders of this cause convinced that goddess religion is far more than simple spirituality. It is, in fact, considered *fundamental* to feminist political activism. "This is a model for Female Politics, 1990s (recalling that brief but fine feminist holism of the 1960s): no justifiable separation between 'being spiritual' and 'being political,'" claims a July/August 1990 article in *Ms.* by leading goddess feminist Barbara Mor. "No choice between personal well-being and global change. One signifies/necessitates the other, and She will kick shit if necessary. *Anything less is a lie* [emphasis added]."

What is apparently a lie to many feminists today is the belief that activism has any validity without a conversion to goddess worship.

"There remains a large schism between the so-called political feminists and spiritual feminists," acknowledges Zsuzsanna Budapest, author of highly popular books such as *The Holy Book of Women's Mysteries*. But, she claims, this is not the fault of spiritual feminists. She writes, "It is an imaginary difference that exists mostly in the minds of political feminists; the spiritualists know that politics and spirituality go hand in hand, historically reinforcing each other."[30]

Just what form does this marriage between goddess spirituality and political activism take? Budapest gives several examples of "activism" for spiritual feminists. At demonstrations for abortion rights, she suggests "Ask women to bring instruments of any kind, rattles, drums or clicking stones," and make an "image of the Great Goddess from papier-mache." Once prepared, the demonstrators might want to try this chant: "Tremble, tremble, the witches have returned!"

Similar magic is proposed for antiporn marches. Budapest tells of one march in front of porn shops, in which "candles gave it all a religious glow; the Goddess gave it all a divine integrity that anger alone could not have mastered." The demonstrators chanted, "Lovely Goddess of the night, I pray to you with all my might. Let the hatred against women, Ebb, Ebb, Ebb, then die." The use of candles and religious doggerel give such actions a purity spin that echoes Victorian times, when women took similar actions against sexual material. The Women's Christian Temperance Union, for example, established a Department for the Suppression of Impure Literature in 1883. Their "divine integrity" actions saw the removal of a painting of a nude from a Cincinnati restaurant.[31]

Starhawk's account of her work against the Diablo nuclear power plant in California is the perfect example of what is considered a "successful" feminist goddess political action. Her "affinity" group of witches took part in an organized blockade of the plant, but their action had little to do with any actual blockading.

Starhawk and friends dressed in dark clothing and hiked through the woods to a ridge above the power plant. "We gather in a circle on the ridge," she writes. "Some of us have brought offerings—I leave an abalone shell on the hillside. The ritual is loose and wild. Dark falls, and as we feel our power and our anger rise, we break from the circle, line up on the ridge, shine our flashlights down on the plant, and scream. We yell out curses. We want them to know that we are here, shining our flashlights down, to draw their searchlights playing over the hills. We are banging on pots and pans, pointing our anger like a spear."[32]

The result of this flashlight ritual? Starhawk claims that new problems were discovered at the plant, which led eventually to it being shut down (it soon reopened). There's not much doubt in her mind that this was divine intervention brought about by her actions. "So the blockade succeeded—not by physically stopping the workers, but by changing the reality, the consciousness, of the society in which the plant exists," she writes.

In another work, Starhawk takes credit for the withdrawal of Cruise and Pershing missiles in Europe.[33]

While all this hocus-pocus sounds like rantings of a lunatic fringe, it is often presented to young women as mainstream feminism. At the University of Utah, for example, Mary Daly's *Gyn/Ecology: The Metaethics of Radical Feminism* is assigned to introductory women's studies classes. According to Daly, a vague concept called "Goddess murder" has been one of the tenets of "patriarchy." In order to overcome this, women need to invoke the "goddess within." This is done through Daly's idea of "journeying," a form of magical "exorcism."

Students are taught—in all seriousness—: "The Background into which feminist journeying spins is the wild realm of Hags and Crones. It is Hag-ocracy. The demons who attempt to block the gateways to the deep spaces of this realm often take ghostly/ghastly forms, comparable to noxious gases not noticeable by ordinary sense perception." Whew. Nearly all of Daly's books are written in this style. She earns rave reviews in the feminist press (as one claimed, "Mary Daly has written a bible!") and has been heralded as one of the most brilliant theorists in the women's movement today.[34]

This promotion of magical thinking in place of more difficult political activism has seen goddess worship gain favor outside of women's studies classes—from local chapters of NOW to women's centers. Students at Humboldt State University, for example, can pick up a copy of *Matrix*, a magazine put out by the university's women's center. The spring 1993 issue, decorated throughout with hand-drawn Venus figurines, features several references and articles on goddess worship, including one titled "Meeting the Goddess Again for the First Time." Students are told that a good way to honor the goddess is to "perform rituals at their altars" on days such as Halloween (termed "The Witches' New Year"). These rituals can "be as simple as relaxing before the altar to light candles and burn incense or as complex as casting a circle and chanting songs."

Following their belief in magic, these feminists feel quite assured that even if it seems as if they're not accomplishing anything, they in fact are. As Apara Borrowes-Toabe, who teaches a workshop on goddess religion where students chant and burn sage in Massachusetts, told *Megatrends for Women,* "This is still very much feminism, but it's not so angry. It's power without the anger."

And it's activity without any impact.

"I'm a Catholic woman. I've chosen to stay in a church that's sexist, because I believe that there's room for reform, and the only kind of reform that can be effective is reform from within. I have a lot of friends who have left the church altogether and have gone to other denominations or have decided that there is no organized religion that's willing to hear women's voices. But for me, I was brought up Catholic, and it's not something I'm willing to leave behind. Although the Pope's newest encyclical letter is pretty depressing, I still feel that there has to be change within the church. . . . My general philosophy in life is not to walk out of situations like that. To me, that's agreeing with the way the status quo is. And I just can't do that kind of thing. I've got to figure out how my voice can be heard in those kinds of situations."

—JANE, twenty-seven, public-relations coordinator
for a nonprofit educational organization in New York

Jane is only one of countless women who identify themselves not only as Catholic but as deeply committed to women's rights. She says she considers herself a feminist, defining the term as a person who believes in equality between women and men.

In April of 1993, over two thousand women gathered in Albuquerque, New Mexico, to discuss issues facing women and the Catholic Church. It was the third national Women-Church conference, organized by thirty-five Catholic feminist groups. More than thirty varieties of morning services were offered—including an Indian pipe ceremony, a Holocaust remembrance, a Quaker meeting, and a goddess ritual complete with drumming, shaking plastic egg rattles, and chanting to ancient Greek goddesses.

The only thing missing was an actual Catholic Mass celebrated by a male priest. A proposal to include a traditional Mass to make mainstream Catholic women more comfortable had been shot down by the conference planners. The conference's closing ritual made it clear which deities were being honored. Organizers called upon "the deity whom some call Goddess, some call Mother God, some call Christa, some call Jesus, Spirit, Holy One." This emphasis on alternative religions left some of the attendees—who are committed to their own churches—put off. The Reverend Kay Huggins told the April 16, 1993, *New York Times* that she felt the conference "didn't include me as a white, heterosexual, Protestant pastoral woman dedicated to the organized church." And another woman pastor remarked that she was "really uncomfortable with the pagan elements."[35] For its part, the Catholic Church doesn't look too kindly upon these kinds of religious services. In July of 1993, the Pope condemned Catholic feminists pursuing "nature worship" and paganism.[36]

Goddess worship in feminism today is at the heart of a growing debate among religious feminists. While many women in organized religions—from Catholics to Episcopalians—are fighting to reform their institutions, other feminists believe that these religions are inherently sexist and utterly hopeless.[37] And while conferences such as Women-Church are only one aspect of a much larger movement in religious feminism—one that some see as the radical fringe—they capture this battle over reform versus rejection in traditional churches. As the title of the *Times* article on the conference put it, "Catholic Feminists Ask, Can We Remain Catholic?"

The answer, according to many feminists, is no. Sheila Ruth, editor of the textbook *Issues in Feminism*, sums up their arguments. "Many feminists question whether a reformed, non-sexist portrayal of the Judeo-Christian religions is possible. . . . Feminists ask whether women can or should relate to a religion that worships male gods and ideals in male language, demeans women's full humanity, and prohibits the full exercise of women's potentials."

Feminists have an easy solution to the historical cultural sexism in many organized religions. Change the gender of the deity. As Carol Christ writes in her essay "Why Women Need the Goddess" in *Womanspirit Rising: A Feminist Reader in Religion*, a male God creates "moods" and "motivations" that "keep women in a state of psychological dependence on men and male authority, while at the same time legitimating the *political* and *social* authority of father and sons in the institutions of society." On the other hand, a female deity symbol would affirm women's potential.

But for many traditionally religious feminists, the gender of the deity is not really the issue. "Catholic feminists are not interested in simply changing the gender of God to goddess," Rosemary Radford Ruether, a feminist Catholic theologian and a prominent voice on the subject, wrote in the September 18, 1993, *National Catholic Reporter*. "They are concerned to affirm that God is beyond gender, literally neither male nor female, and can be spoken of in metaphors drawn from both male and female experiences and images. This is what the Bible does when it makes extended metaphors of God as a female-personified Wisdom. Catholic feminists do not reject traditional Christology because Jesus was a male."

Ruether is right. The majority of Catholic women, though displeased with some aspects of the Catholic Church, seem to have no interest in changing their faith. For example, according to a June 22, 1992, *Time*/CNN poll, an overwhelming 81 percent of Catholic women disagreed with the Catholic Church, believing that practicing birth control is not morally wrong; 59 percent believed that women should be allowed to be priests; and 75 percent believed that divorced Catholics should be allowed to remarry and remain Catholics. But at the same time, these women seem largely content with their faith—64 percent surveyed were satisfied with the Catholic Church's overall treatment of women, 80 percent were happy with their bishop, and 90 percent were similarly content with the Pope.

The role that organized religions have played, and continue to play, in perpetuating sexism is certainly a matter for feminist concern. But examinations of religion need to be balanced with a healthy respect for women's spiritual lives—and this is something today's feminists fail to do. When Mary Daly asserts that for women to strive to be ordained as Catholic priests "would be like black people wanting to be members of the KKK," it's no wonder many Catholic feminists feel there is no place for them in the movement.[38]

With the assertion that all male-God religions are inherently oppressive to women, current feminists dismiss the complex, diverse, and often contradictory ways that individuals approach their faiths. Just as many Catholic women are comfortable believing both in abortion rights and their antiabortion Pope (only 13 percent of American Catholics believe abortion should be illegal under all circumstances[39]), women from all religions interact with their faiths in individual ways, finding balance between their spiritual and political beliefs. Although these contradictions should demean women involved in organized religions, they simply illustrate that women can't be pigeonholed on the basis of what church they attend or the gender of the deity they worship.

Women who recognize a male God are not all victimized by their beliefs. As Ruether points out, many women use their deities as metaphors—in Jesus Christ, for instance, many women find a love for humanity, kindness, and sympathy. They don't conceive of their deity as literally male, nor does it dominate their psychology and make them believe that oppression against women is acceptable.

Yet that is exactly what feminist theory on male-God religions claims. It says that women in organized religions are no more than dumb sheep, blindly following where religious leaders direct them, inanely bleating whatever they are told, easily brainwashed into accepting ideologies that victimize them, incapable of any independent thought, and devoid of any individual differences. They have been misled by false gods, while feminists alone recognize the true religion. It is the spiritual duty of the women's movement to save these poor misguided sheep and bring them into the fold.

It's no wonder that women of all ages and backgrounds from traditional faiths find current feminism deeply insulting. In an article on current feminism for the January 1992 *Commonweal*, David R. Carlin, Jr., noted: "Women who prefer the religion found in churches and synagogues might be drawn to feminism as a political program; but they recoil from feminism as a mode of salvation." And so do many women with no strong religious affiliation, finding the feminist flight into fancy a waste of effort that draws energy away from reforms that would address real-world concerns.

For much of the women's movement, however, feminism is not an engine of reform, but a mode of salvation: not just the religious salvation of goddess worship but the social and political salvation of a strict orthodoxy—one that tells women how to conduct every aspect of their lives, from their diet (vegetarianism) to their role in the workplace and politics (virtuous example, not equal partner).

This is the utopian vision. Following popular feminist theory that pits women against men in every arena, and feminist spirituality that names women as the inherently superior peace-making sex, today's women's movement has embarked on a campaign to preach ideology instead of equal rights.

Feminism, as feminine virtue was in the Victorian period, has been deemed the salvation—not only for ourselves but for the world at large.

OVERTHROWING THE PATRIARCHY: THE FEMINIST UTOPIAN VISION

"I think that a lot of the feminist movement—when you look at it, there're a lot of people who look at things negatively. They think that there's a whole conspiracy, that people are really banding together to keep us down. And I really don't agree with that. I think that people won't do things unless they see there's a good reason for it. I can see where they [current feminists] are coming from, but more and more I think that it's not a conspiracy—because it's not that simple. If it was a conspiracy, it would be very easy to overthrow; it would be like, okay, we'll just find the people who started this and get it replaced. But it's just much more complex. . . . Humans aren't that simple. Even within us, there's not one side of me against another side of me; there're many sides of me. If I looked at it that simply, I wouldn't be able to know myself at all. I wouldn't be able to get anywhere with anything. I think that maybe that's part of the problem. . . . For me, it's much more natural to look at individuals. When it starts getting blanket, I think that's also why I'm not involved. I can't look at things that broadly. It just doesn't work for me."
—ANNE MERKELSON, twenty-seven, production coordinator for a California publishing firm

Sitting outside a small California restaurant on a balmy summer night, Anne Merkelson—a young woman with soft brown hair tied back into a casual ponytail, clear tanned skin, and intelligent hazel eyes—

expresses reservations about today's women's movement. There's no question that Anne is a feminist: She greets questions about equal pay, abortion rights, and political representation with a baffled "Of course!" But there are aspects of current feminism that she can't stomach. One of these is the mainstream feminist theory condemning *all* of society, from politics to pop culture, as an oppressive "patriarchy"— and all women as the helpless victims of that male-controlled system.

For Anne, such a simplified view of the world comes off like an implausible conspiracy theory. She feels that in their rush to find an all-encompassing common enemy, feminists negate the contributions women have made to society and dismiss as illusionary the power women do hold. Anne believes that by scapegoating an ill-defined patriarchy for every conceivable problem, feminists ignore the complexities of individuals and culture. This, she notes, doesn't help anyone get anyplace. Watching people pass on the sidewalk, she tried to sum up her feelings. "If you think it's a conspiracy, what happens when you talk to someone involved on the other side and you find that, oh my god, they're human? And they're complex? But wait a minute—I thought you just subscribe to this theory . . . You start out very simply because you're angry and you need something to lash out against. And then you have to move on."

Feminists have found something to lash out against, and that's the patriarchy. But instead of venting frustration and then moving to change things, they have sunk into the miasma of their own theory. They have created a straw man to condemn. And they have created an equally false ideal to exalt.

Standing opposed to the all-powerful patriarchy is the feminist matriarchy, a vision of a utopia that promises a world of peace and plenty. To justify this simple view of good versus evil, feminist theorists and leaders are pushing the idea of gender differences—that men and women are vastly and fundamentally different. Backed by bad science and echoing the sexist stereotypes of the Victorian era, this trend in feminism threatens to undo many hard-won victories and plunge the movement into a vain quest for an unattainable goal.

Anne is not alone in her feelings about popular feminist theory. Many young women encountering feminism today can't be blamed if they feel they've entered a den of conspiracy nuts. Attend women's organization meetings or pass by a rally, take a women's studies course, or pick up a feminist book and it is nearly impossible to avoid the "patriarchy."

Though seldom defined, this all-encompassing system is blamed for all of the world's troubles; it is the amorphous force that works behind the scenes to oppress women and to undermine feminism; it is so overwhelming and insidious that nearly every aspect of society embodies its evil. Our language, government, entertainment, education, you name it—everything is patriarchal; and for that reason, the enemy of women.

Feminist scholarship on the patriarchy may not have originated as a conspiracy theory, but to many women it certainly sounds like one today. By claiming that nearly every aspect of culture is controlled exclusively by men, current feminists implicitly portray our world as one great spiderweb of interconnected plots, all threads held by a faceless enemy whose sole goal is to oppress women.

"We *all*, regrettably, live in a patriarchal culture," asserts Robin Morgan.[1] Like many other feminists, Morgan uses the term without bothering to explain it. In the women's movement, the "patriarchy" is condemned so frequently that its existence has become accepted as a fundamental, unquestionable truth. Yet by applying the term to all of culture—from fashion magazines, to politics, even to objective thinking—the current feminist definition of patriarchy includes more than what can be found in any dictionary.

The anthropological definition of patriarchy is a social organization marked by male supremacy, in which women are completely dependent on men (such as being forbidden to inherit property or vote) and descent is reckoned only through the male line. A patriarchy is a society that is literally ruled by men, particularly fathers. A matriarchy is a society ruled by women, particularly mothers.

Some feminists recognize that the gulf between their use of the word *patriarchy* and the dictionary definition can be baffling. "Such a circumstance can be confusing unless it is realized that feminists can use the terms *patriarchy* and *matriarchy* in various ways. Depending on context, the terms may be scientific . . . political, philosophic, or even poetic," writes Sheila Ruth, editor of the widely taught women's studies textbook *Issues in Feminism*. "Thus feminists frequently use *patriarchy* to denote a culture whose driving ethos is an embodiment of masculist ideals and practices. Feminists argue that we in contemporary Western culture inhabit a patriarchy, both in the anthropological and in the political, feminist sense. Patriarchy, then, has determined almost entirely the nature and quality of our society, its values and priorities, the place and image of women within it, and the relation between the sexes."

Assertions that our society is patriarchal in the anthropological sense—Ruth explains it as "a society in which formal power over public decision and policy-making is held by adult men"—are hyperbole. Perhaps no one told feminists that women won the vote and now hold political office. Similarly absurd is University of Colorado professor Alison Jaggar's definition of patriarchy as grounded in "men's control of procreation," as if birth control doesn't exist and all pregnancies are forced.[2] Obviously, the lack of legal and accessible birth-control methods and abortion was a major cause of inequality in the past, but today many women can choose when to conceive. Parroting the "all sex is rape" school of thought, however, some feminists believe that pregnancy under the "patriarchy" is always forced—a colonization—whether women realize it or not.[3]

But it is Sheila Ruth's other definition of patriarchy—a society shaped and driven by an embodiment of masculine ideals and practices—that comes closest to common feminist usage. The beauty of this definition is that feminists don't have to rely on actual political or economic indicators of power. All they need to do is slap the label of "masculine ideals" onto society, and voilà, it's a patriarchy. "All of us, women and men throughout the world, live under patriarchal structures," writes Marilyn French in her 1985 book, *Beyond Power*. "This means we learn to speak languages formed and weighted by patriarchal values, that the culture we absorb is pervaded by patriarchal images and ideas, and that we learn to approach problems—and indeed living itself—in 'masculine' modes."

But just what are these masculine ideals that make everything, from the way we speak to how we think, patriarchal? In the textbook *Issues in Feminism*, they include "aggressiveness," "courage," "perseverance and endurance," "individuality," "self-reliance," "autonomy," and "competence and rationality." Other feminists name similar values, all revolving around independence and separation from other people, emotions, and the earth. These ideals are also often called "androcentric" (male-centered) and "phallocentric" (penis-centered), further cementing the notion that they are intrinsically male. While labeling perservance and competence as negative may sound extreme—and is—this example is no exception from the feminist norm. In many introductory-level women's studies courses, from the University of Iowa to the University of Utah, *Issues in Feminism* is assigned as a text to teach students what feminism means. At the University of Virginia, for example, it is the required textbook, and students spend several weeks studying the chapters on the "patriarchy," with nothing else on the syllabus offered to counter its views.

Patriarchal theory is popular because of its simple assertion that since men held political and economic power in the past, cultural ideals must be masculine. The question is, of course, just why feminists think that these ideals are necessarily masculine instead of human. What's to say that if women had the power for centuries, they wouldn't have instituted exactly the same value system?

The answer to this question is simple. Current feminists have rejected specific ideals, and, reinforced by their belief in prehistoric goddess cultures in which women's rule created paradises, they are quite convinced that the ideals they spurn were created solely by men in order to oppress women. These ideals—even those that seem admirable—are seen as negative because they are believed to spawn hierarchy, or "power-over" practices, which instill in people an acceptance of oppression of others and of the earth. For example, the ideals of perservance and competence are held to lead to competition, which means that one person wins over another, leading to oppression someplace down the line.

This slippery-slope reasoning is why it has become common in feminist circles to denounce hierarchy. These condemnations go far beyond the rigid structures many think of as classic hierarchies—the military, for example—to include anything that uses "power-over." Our entire educational system has been denounced as patriarchal because administrators hold power over teachers and teachers hold power over students. Our workplaces are considered patriarchal because bosses hold power over employees. Capitalism, of course, is a key offender because one class holds power over another, technology is patriarchal because it uses power over nature, and killing animals for food is patriarchal because it uses power over different species.[4]

In fact, condemnations of hierarchy extend even to our thoughts. Rationality and objectivity are often rejected by feminist theorists because these methods value one ideal (scientific fact) over another (superstition, magic, or emotion). In women's studies classes, one of the hottest trends today is to denounce objective thinking on the basis that it is "androcratic." Women's studies professors actually tell students to forget rationality and fact and base their opinions on emotions and experience.[5]

All of this talk about masculine ideals, hierarchies, androcratic this, and phallocentric that can be very confusing to women encountering feminist theory—especially in women's studies classes and feminist literature, where such lingo is used with wild abandon but seldom backed up by any coherent reasoning. A woman trying to unravel just *how* feminist theory applies to her out of this snarled mess of vague terms is easily daunted.

Take Gloria Steinem's version of patriarchal theory in *Revolution from Within*. "In societies shaped by patriarchy and racial divisions, the prevailing paradigm comes in three parts. The first is the either/or way of thinking that divides almost everything in two . . . dominant and passive, intellect and emotion, mind and body, winner and loser, good and evil . . ." she writes. "The more unequal this genderized dyad became, the more it turned into the next part of the paradigm: linear thinking. Rating and grading people, the notion that all accomplishment lies in defeating others, even a linear view of abstractions like time and history—all these things were organized by the same paradigm. Since a straight line was too simplistic to be practical for most human interactions, however, it split into the third and last part of the paradigm: hierarchy . . . from a 'male-headed' household to corporate structures in which all authority flows from the top; from hierarchical classrooms to religions in which God's will is interpreted by a pope or ayatollah."

Minus the five-dollar words, this is what Steinem seems to be saying: In a "patriarchal" society such as ours, culture is shaped by certain patterns or forces. The first one of these is dualism, or either/or thinking. This somehow fosters linear thinking, or the belief that one thing follows another, as in time. This, for no clear reason, creates hierarchies. From "classrooms" to " 'male-headed' households" (ironically, not female-headed ones), these "power-over" structures form the patriarchy, which then shapes society. So what exactly *is* a patriarchy? Well, it's the *thing* that creates these forces, the first is dualism, which creates linear thought, which leads to . . . and back to square one. You get the picture.

This type of circular reasoning is the basis of feminist theory on the so-called patriarchy. Starting with the unquestioned assumption is that our culture *is* patriarchal, feminist theorists then set out to prove it. Since women obviously do have economic and political power (from the consumer dollar to the ballot box), leading theorists have decided that the values *underlying* our social structures must be patriarchal. Why are they patriarchal? Because men control them. How do men control? By imposing "masculine" values. What makes them masculine? Because they're hierarchical. What makes them hierarchical? Because they're based on linear thinking. Why are they based on linear thinking? Because they come from dualism. Where does dualism come from? From a society shaped by patriarchy. Just what makes it a patriarchy? Because men control it. How do they do that? By imposing masculine values, you dimwit. This is the philosophical equivalent to a clogged toilet bowl, with terms like *masculine ethos, dualism, hierarchies, paradigms, and dyads* swirling in a meaningless whirlpool with no beginning and no end. And while feminist theorists may gather around and proudly point to their wealth of scholarship, others might see an unpleasant mess threatening to flood the bathroom and dash for the plunger.

Obviously, we live in a system that has been historically biased against women, and often still is—which is why we need a women's movement. Clearly, many injustices such as racism and sexism impinge upon people's rights—which is why they should be fought. And feminists are correct when they criticize the negative results of a lopsided emphasis on competition, aggression, and other "cold" ideals in our culture, rather than on cooperation, caring, tolerance, and other humanist ideals. A little humanity would go a long way to solving problems from poverty to prejudice that hurt so many.

But mainstream feminist theory vastly oversimplifies these problems and their causes. All hierarchies are not equally evil. As even Steinem admits, hierarchy is necessary for problems requiring quick action, such as surgery or fire fighting. It is also necessary for parenting: Try to manage small children near a busy street and then claim all "power-over" is oppressive. Dualism, linear thinking, and hierarchies are fundamental to our communities and our conceptualizations of the world. It is nearly impossible to do anything, from prosecuting rapists to running a day-care center, without them. A good illustration of this is feminist theory itself, which in the attempt to condemn dualistic, linear, and hierarchical concepts ends up relying on them: Good versus evil; one thing leads to another; our ideal is superior to your ideal and so should be instituted.

The truth is, feminist theory on the patriarchy is often little more than a shallow justification for feminists to condemn those aspects of society they dislike. Just as Steinem denounces male-headed households but not female-headed ones, other feminists pick and choose what's patriarchal and what's not: academia but not women's studies programs, pornography but not feminist antisex writings, racism but not lesbian separatism, Catholicism but not goddess religion, Phyllis Schlafly but not Andrea Dworkin.

While not all feminists buy into the extremes of antihierarchical thought, few question the constant vituperations against the "patriarchy" heard so often in today's women's movement. Patriarchal theory, even when not named as such, is the underpinning of best-selling books such as Susan Faludi's *Backlash:* and Naomi Wolf's *The Beauty Myth*, which blame everything from political conservatism to liposuctions on a sweeping "backlash" orchestrated by mysterious, amorphous, and yet deadly male forces. It is the drive behind most women's studies programs—as feminist writer Karen Lehrman notes, the majority of "women's studies professors seem to adhere to the following principles in formulating classes: women were and are oppressed; oppression is endemic to our patriarchal social system; men, capitalism, and Western values are responsible for women's problems."[6] It is the basis for much feminist scholarship and it is the refrain heard from feminist magazines and conference podiums.

Patriarchal theory appeals to many feminists because it takes the onus off women when it comes to problems such as racism, sexism, and violence—although from female Ku Klux Klan members to abusive mothers, women have done their share to add to these ills. It is also appealing because it acts as a rallying cry, allowing feminists to condemn a common enemy while ignoring class and cultural differences among women. By asserting that all women are oppressed under the patriarchy, feminists often implicitly dismiss the experiences of minority, poor, and working-class women: A single mother on welfare and Gloria Steinem are portrayed as having more in common than not.

What makes this ironic is that oppression is defined solely from the viewpoint of current feminist leaders, who tend to be well-educated, affluent white women enjoying careers as authors, speakers, and tenured professors. For instance, in *The Beauty Myth*, a 1991 book detailing how there is a "backlash" against women via beauty standards, Yale graduate Naomi Wolf likens the beauty methods of upper-middle-class women to the medieval torture instrument known as the iron maiden, a spike-lined body-shaped casket in which victims suffered slow, agonizing deaths. When women who exemplify the American dream and the fruits of feminism—educated in the finest universities, getting paid for the careers of their choice, well-respected, and enjoying all the freedoms and comforts life has to offer—write books comparing their lives to medieval torture, it's not surprising that many lower-income women don't find much in common with the movement.[7]

Wolf, however, in a radical departure from *The Beauty Myth*, comes to the conclusion in her 1993 book, *Fire with Fire*, that the feminist emphasis on victimization is profoundly alienating to many women.

"Women are fed up with the reminders of their own oppression," she declares. "We are moved far more effectively by appeals to our strength, resourcefulness, and sense of responsibility." But Wolf skirts the issue of how her previous book contributed to this obsession with oppression, and she falls into the very trap she accuses others of falling into when she refers to society as patriarchal and women's progress as "minute inroads."

Patriarchal theory is also a handy excuse feminists can pull out of a hat when confronted with the alienation of women from the movement. It's not our fault; it's the "patriarchy," engaged in another clever plot against feminism—one Susan Faludi defines as "encoded and internalized, diffuse and chameleonic." Just what does she mean? Who knows? But it's nice to have an all-purpose scapegoat no one can define.

But it comes at a heavy price. Patriarchal theory is, above all, pure victim mythology. Naming all society as patriarchal promotes a view of women as powerless victims in every aspect of their lives. The Catholic Church and many corporations are ruled by men; they are patriarchal. Our political system, which now has women senators, governors, and mayors—not to mention a large female voting population—is not. Our language, which is often taught to children by women, is not. Our social values, which, even when sexist, are maintained by women as well as men, are not. Our press, which can now boast that 46 percent of all editors and reporters are women, is not.[8]

To argue otherwise erases women's contributions to history, and in doing so, it erases any notion of our present power and worth. While feminists claim to be recapturing women's history (popularly called "herstory"), the very nature of patriarchal theory says women's roles in history are irrelevant—because their acts fall under the umbrella of the all-encompassing patriarchy and are therefore without true merit. This is the irony of mainstream feminist theory. With the exception of the mythical age of the goddess, women have supposedly had no input in creating our culture: We live outside of history and thus outside of the world. But from political activists such as Jane Addams, the suffragist who won a Nobel Peace Prize for her work on behalf of the poor, to Harriet Beecher Stowe, author of the famous cry against racism, *Uncle Tom's Cabin*, to the millions of women throughout history who have taught children how to speak and think, took action, and took office—from Margaret Sanger to Margaret Thatcher—women *have* shaped society.

And their contributions have been important and relevant. As feminist historian Gerda Lerner reasonably argued over a decade ago in

The Majority Finds Its Past, basing a feminist view of history entirely on women's "inferior status and oppressive restraints" makes it appear "either that women were largely passive or that, at the most, they reacted to male pressures or the restraints of patriarchal society. Such inquiry fails to elicit the *positive and essential* [emphasis added] way in which women have functioned in history." One reason it has been difficult for feminists to acknowledge these essential contributions is because doing so would require acknowledging that women have often perpetuated sexism. In the Victorian era, for example, some of the most vocal opponents to suffragism were women. The mistake made by feminists is judging these women from our standpoint, instead of placing them in a historical context and according them the place they deserve in history regardless of their position on feminist issues. Instead, feminists try to dismiss their actions as irrelevant by claiming they were pawns of the patriarchy. This may absolve women in history of responsibility for their actions, but it also denies them the respect society accords to men, who are judged by their individual merits, ofttimes regardless of the historic environment they were born into. By relegating all women—both in the past or present—who disagree with current feminism to the role of unenlightened victims, today's feminists don't have to accept them as equals. This makes it easy to dismiss their opinions as well as to avoid honest debate within the movement.

While some activists continue to pursue equality—as in endorsing female political candidates—in many of the places young women encounter the movement, they are told such reform is simply buying into the patriarchy. Students taking "Introduction to Women's Studies" at the University of New Hampshire, for example, find the section on "Visions for the Future" confined to work taking only the most radical stance. They begin with feminist Pat Parker's essay entitled "Revolution: It's Not Neat or Pretty or Quick," which claims the women's movement has been co-opted by "media pigs and agents of this insidious imperialist system"; Parker argues for a violent revolution. From there they read two poems by black feminist radicals and Audre Lorde's classic essay "The Master's Tools Will Never Dismantle the Master's House," which asserts that feminists must not use "male" methods to fight the patriarchy. That wraps up the week dedicated to feminist visions for the future. Far from being a brief foray into delirium, this extremism simply mirrors the rest of the course—the section on spirituality focuses on Mary Daly and Carol Christ—and almost lost among dozens of radical works by the likes of Cheryl Clarke, bell hooks, Susan Griffin, Shulamith Firestone (a diatribe claiming "men can't love"), and Adrienne Rich are only a handful of more moderate works, such as the NOW bill of rights. A young woman who takes this class will likely walk away believing that being a feminist means being a fanatical kook.

The feminist war against the patriarchy sends a loud, clear message to women: Every door, every road, every path to power is tainted. Men made the world, every inch of it, and men control the world, down to the last concept and practice, the thoughts in our heads, even our language. For millennia, women have been completely manipulated by negative male ideals. If we accept this view, we must see ourselves as helpless puppets.

And if we refuse to accept this view, feminists make it clear we are simply victims again—this time of false consciousness. As Susan Faludi stated in the March 9, 1992, issue of *Time*, "sometimes it's very hard to know what one thinks under the pressure of the backlash, to sort out what's *you* [sic] thinking and what's the internalized message about what you're supposed to think." If you don't agree with current feminists about the enemy, that's only another sign that he exists. "[P]atriarchy is as invisible as spiritual or non-material reality," claims an article in the December 1992 feminist magazine *At the Crossroads*. "However, both patriarchy and non-material reality exist, you just have to change your consciousness to become aware of them."

Overthrowing this all-encompassing patriarchy is fundamental to today's women's movement. As long as our society embodies hierarchical "masculine" ideals, no gains in equality will change it from an oppressive system. What is needed is a complete transformation of society—anything less is a waste of time. To do so, we need a glorious revival of what Sheila Ruth refers to as "what historically has been taken to be the female principle, or the rule of feminist ideals."

These "feminist" ideals, however, look suspiciously like a newly washed Victorian-era corset dragged out of the trash a century after it was thrown away. Much feminist literature lists as its ideals such traits as pacifism, interdependence, irrational and intuitive "feeling," nurturing, and a repugnance for all things faintly hierarchical, especially power. If the world were only run according to these principles rather than masculine principles, the basic theory goes, we would find ourselves back in the Garden of Eden. There wouldn't be any sleazy politicians, because the hierarchical political system would be abolished. There wouldn't be any class or religious differences, because capitalism, class structures, and traditional faiths would disappear. All things would live in harmonious interconnection, with no greater value assigned to person, animal, or tree—except for men, who presumably would live on reservations.

Here we are presented with the feminist utopia. Sometimes referred to as "cultural" feminism, this utopian vision has gained adherents from many different schools of feminist thought, from the liberal to the radical. It can be found in books as diverse as Steinem's *Revolution from Within* and Riane Eisler's *The Chalice and the Blade*, it is espoused by leaders such as Robin Morgan, and it is the drive behind the movement's foray into issues such as environmentalism and animal rights. A perfect example of the utopian vision at work is Suzanne Gordon's 1990 *Prisoners of Men's Dreams: Striking Out for a New Feminine Future*. Gordon argues that by embracing a "masculinized corruption of feminist ideals" and placing women in a competitive workforce, unenlightened feminists who promote equal opportunity have helped cause a widespread "societal crisis in caring." Unlike women who believe they can and should compete in society ("female clones"), true feminists should embrace Gordon's vague "transformative vision"—a modern Victorian rendition of women's role as gentle caretakers shepherding the family and culture into greener pastures. If this sounds like a ring-wing tract denouncing feminism for destroying family values, it's because it certainly reads like one.

It seems odd that feminists would condemn what their own movement fought to gain, but according to proponents of the utopian vision, women never wanted equal opportunity in the first place. "We were not in a battle with men to live imitation men's lives," syndicated columnist Anna Quindlen told a 1993 feminist conference at Barnard College. "We knew that we could reshape institutions, structures, power struggles, even world events. Not just so women could participate, but so that our ways of working, dealing, negotiating, living would be vastly improved by the special gifts that we bring to the table." While this idea may be appealing—it's nice to think you're special—it places even more burden on working women, who now must transform the world as well as bring in the paycheck. If they don't agree, why, they should just consider themselves "imitation men." And as even Susan Faludi notes, special might sound better, but it can also mean handicapped.

The notion of a "feminine" future based on an ideal of women as saviors—alongside the ominous warning that if we don't fulfill our duties of caretakers, society will self-destruct into a crisis of uncaring—is nothing new. "On you, ladies, depends, in a most important degree, the destiny of our country," stated Victorian minister Jonathan Stearns. "Yours is to determine, whether the beautiful order of society . . . shall continue as it has been, to be the source of blessings to the world. . . . And be assured, ladies, if the hedges and borders of the social garden should be broken up, the lovely vine, which now twines itself so gracefully upon the trellis, and bears such rich clusters, will be the first to fall and be trodden under foot."[10]

The feminist utopia is also seen as a garden, literally, with women tending the vegetables all day while happy children scamper underfoot—and while men live in separate preserves, properly complacent about their secondary status. This notion is illustrated in an article in the December 1992 issue of the feminist magazine *At the Crossroads*. "All of the patriarchal institutions—medicine, religion, government, academia, science—are set up to deny female power and deny females access to their powers." The answer to this problem? The writer gives her fantasy rendition of prehistoric cultures ruled by women, complete with "matriarchal clans" composed of women and children that would only welcome men at times if they were "cooperative." Women controlled everything, men had no rights, and because of this, everyone lived in peaceful harmony with all creation. And that is the way it should be today. "This is my vision of the past and the future," the writer asserts. The vision is one widely shared in feminism.

The key to the garden gate is the belief that men have ruined everything, but women, through their special attributes, can solve the world's problems. Ironically, this belief extolls the ideals of femininity that earlier feminists fought so hard to escape. "The future of humankind," asserts Elsa Gidlow in an essay assigned to students attending an introduction to women's studies course at the University of New Hampshire, "may depend on acceptance of the gentler, womanly qualities as a key to survival on this miraculously evolved and evolving Earth."[11] Or, as a leading Victorian writer put it when he claimed that in his every book he portrayed "women as the teacher, the natural and therefore divine guide, purifier, inspirer of the man."[12]

Joyce McCarl Nielsen sums up the agenda driving the utopian vision in her objective work *Sex and Gender in Society*: "In a very real sense, then, feminist-inspired utopias celebrate what we usually think of as traditionally female tasks and traits: nurturance, expressiveness, support for personal growth and development, a link with the land or earth."

While nurturance and support for personal growth are worthy

human ideals, their lopsided application to women in the Victorian era didn't lead to a bright future. In fact, they were used as powerful arguments against suffragism. Women's "nurturance" meant that early feminists were wrong to take women away from their babies and put them into the political arena, women's "expressiveness" supported arguments that women were too hysterical and irrational for politics, and women's "support for personal growth" meant the suffragists should just give up and go home, where they obviously were better suited to caretake their families, not society. To give women equal rights, in the words of an American senator in 1866, would only destroy their "milder, gentler nature, which not only makes them shrink from, but disqualifies them for the turmoil and battle of public life. They have a higher and a holier mission."[13]

What is interesting about this feminist revival of feminine ideals is the unquestioned assumption that while our entire society, including our language and social values, is a male-controlled "patriarchy," somehow traditional ideals of womanhood are exempt from its taint. Thus, while men created traditionally "male" values, such as competition, they did not create traditionally "female" values, such as sensitivity or empathy. But feminists seem to avoid addressing just how sexist ideals of "gentler, womanly qualities" can reflect "true" womanhood if men have created everything, including our ideas of gender.

The popularity of the utopian vision has been bolstered by several feminist trends—including condemnations of individual liberties in favor of the collective good, feminist theory heralding women's "difference," and the idea that women's private acts are of greater importance than their public actions. But it owes its birth largely to patriarchal theory and goddess religion. In the patriarchy, feminists have an all-purpose enemy, and in goddess worship, they have found the easy answer to that enemy: Bring back the golden matriarchal age.

Overwhelmingly, the utopian vision reeks of separatism, not necessarily lesbian separatism—although utopianism has been fervently adopted by many lesbian-feminist theorists—but a cultural separatism, the modern-day version of the nunnery, where women create a culture separate from men. As feminist scholar Hester Eisenstein describes in *Contemporary Feminist Thought*, by the early eighties, feminists as diverse as Betty Friedan and Mary Daly found themselves arriving at similar conclusions: The structures of power are intrinsically evil, and so the good feminist rejects them. In the *Second Stage*, Friedan criticizes feminism for delivering women into "the militaristic, materialistic bowels of late capitalist American imperialism," while Daly continues to advocate that women turn their backs on reform for an inner voyage into la-la land. "The salvation of women, . . ." writes Eisenstein, "lay in the creation of another, private realm, where the values associated with women could be safely nurtured. Daly and Friedan, in different ways, had created parallel versions of a retreat to the separate sphere of women."

By viewing the world as a gender-specific battle between the forces of darkness and light—the bad and all-powerful "masculine" versus the good and yet constantly oppressed "feminine"—today's women's movement promotes gender polarities and a biologically determined view of the sexes. As the corrupt heart of the patriarchy, the masculine ethos is beyond redemption. As the shining hope of the utopian world to come, the female ideal is the savior.

And these ideals are translated into biology, and thus set in stone. The genders are presented as irrevocably different. Equality and partnership between the sexes can never exist. For the utopian vision to become reality, Woman must triumph over Man. "For some ecofeminists and other members of the woman-is-better school," feminist psychologist Carol Tavris writes in her dissenting 1992 book, *The Mismeasure of Woman: Why Women Are Not the Better Sex, the Inferior Sex, or the Opposite Sex*, "this dream, and visions of how to achieve it, rest on the most basic male-female dichotomy: that men are the warlike, dominating, aggressive, planet-destroying sex and women are the peacemaking, emphatic, nonaggressive, planet-saving sex."

" 'Women are born innately nurturing, and men are born to be cold.' Ugh! Once again, I disagree with that. Because everything they [current feminists] are saying is a universality, and you have to question, is it really? The only way you can do that is by looking at ethnographic examples. And if you can find one example—you need only one example—to say that's not a universality, then their theory is untrue. To say that all women are one way is a terrible misconception. And it's terribly misleading to those women who are reading it and believing it, because they respect the movement."
—VICTORIA JACOBSON, twenty-three, student from Connecticut

Asked what she thinks about feminist theory on gender difference, Victoria, a graduate student in anthropology from the East Coast, doesn't hesitate. It's nonsense, she says. But the idea that women are innately nurturing and men innately cold has gained an incredible amount of credence in the women's movement, and young women are likely to encounter it constantly, whether in college or through feminist magazines and literature. For many, such an oversimplified view of the sexes and society is ridiculous. Any anthropologist will note that there are cultures in which men are the primary nurturers, which, as Victoria says, immediately disproves feminist theory. And many young women find such universalities dangerously misleading. They don't like the idea of anybody, whether current feminists or archconservatives, promoting such sexist stereotypes. Young women today want women and men to form equal partnerships in work and family, not to be driven apart and forced into confining gender roles.

Feminists in the sixties and seventies argued that outside of anatomy, the gender differences assigned to women and women are socialized, not biological. In Simone de Beauvoir's famous words, "One isn't born a woman, one becomes a woman." From girls being taught to play with dolls to boys being told that only sissies cry, social factors shape what people consider "natural" for the genders. People, of course, are not just passive recipients of socialization, automatically accepting whatever they're told. Both women and men are capable of independent thought, and they interact with their environment in individual fashions. But in many ways, we *are* taught what is considered appropriate behavior.

In the late seventies through eighties, however, academic feminist theory took a sharp turn. Instead of critically examining the role of socialization, many feminists became enamored with reclaiming and validating traditional feminine ideals. A glut of literature poured forth, asserting not only that women are immensely different from men—more nurturing, caring, and "intuitive"—but that we should exalt this supposed difference.[14]

Some writers, such as Carol Gilligan, author of the highly influential 1982 book *In a Different Voice*, ignore individual, class, and cultural differences to assert that women as a group develop a profoundly different moral reasoning than do men, one that makes us less hierarchical and more nurturing. This different "voice" is believed to be so deeply embedded in us that it shapes our every action. Other leading feminists, such as sociologist Alice Rossi, argue that women are far more caring, while men are more emotionally removed, and they conclude that these differences are bioevolutionary—biologically imprinted before we are born and then shaped by society. According to

Rossi, this makes a coequal approach to parenting not only unrealistic but potentially harmful to mothers and children.[15]

To a certain extent, feminist theory on gender difference was a response to the common complaint that the movement was trying to "make women into men" by teaching that we should give up babies for careers and dresses for power suits. But what was lost in the fervor to validate traditional feminine traits was the fact that this complaint often arose from a desire to escape the confining roles of both femininity and masculinity, not to reiterate them. Women want options and choices— whether to pursue a career or raise children—and they resent being told by anyone, including feminists, what kind of life they should lead.

While most feminist theorists do not use strict biological determinism to explain gender differences, they do not offer any concise explanation for them either, preferring to spend their time expounding on and then applauding women's so-called different nature. Gilligan, for example, opens her book by stating that gender differences "arise in a social context where factors of social status and power combine with reproductive biology," presumably meaning they're both environmental and genetic. But the rest of her book is devoted to sweeping statements (such as "women perceive and construe social reality differently from men" and "the major transitions in women's lives would seem to involve changes in the understanding and activities of care") that come off as deterministic. There is little acknowledgment that, having grown up after the birth of feminism, younger women often have dramatically different views on gender than older women do, and that other cultural, social, and religious differences all add up to make women incredibly diverse.

By ignoring these differences and presenting all women as alike— right down to how we perceive reality—Gilligan implicitly dismisses social factors and ends up presenting supposed gender differences as immutable. Women who don't fit her sweeping generalizations are left feeling like aberrations instead of variations. (The idea that the major transitions of women's lives involve "activities of care," for example, might be true for some stay-at-home mothers whose lives consist of caretaking children and others, but for many women, major life transitions also include career changes, getting laid off from work, moving cross-country for a job or school, and other completely non-care-related activities.) To arrive at her conclusions, Gilligan asked small and unrepresentative samples of children and young adults—primarily upper-class whites, such as Harvard undergraduates—questions on morality and then interpreted their remarks as consistent with her own ideas. She then concluded that males think in hierarchical terms, while females think more in collective terms—ones that embody an "ethic of care." But anyone else reading these vague and similar transcripts (if you cross out the respondents names, gender is often impossible to decipher) could easily come to completely opposite conclusions.[16]

Gilligan's work illustrates one of the fatal flaws in difference feminism: Evidence and reasoning tends to come from an exclusively upper-class white perspective. For instance, Sara Ruddick, author of *Maternal Thinking*, argues that mothering turns women into sensitive, caring pacifists. However, as feminist writer Katha Pollitt notes in a critique of difference feminism published in the September/October 1993 *Utne Reader*, from the widespread acceptance of spanking children in the United States to genital mutilation in Africa, evidence suggests otherwise. Who hasn't seen a mother screaming threats at her children in grocery stores or known of women who neglect or belittle their children? If mothering makes women antiwar, pacifistic, and sensitive to helping others, how do we explain the countless mothers who send their sons off to war, condemn welfare mothers, fight against busing programs, applaud punitive policies against the poor, or support the death penalty? Ruddick dismisses such realities as exceptions. But, Pollitt points out, when you subtract all these exceptions, "you are left with a rather small group of people, women like Ruddick herself, enlightened, up-to-date, educated, upper-middle-class liberals." The ideal of the peaceful mother, writes Pollitt, is simply another version "of the separate-spheres ideology of the Victorians," when women ruled the home and men ruled the world.

Other difference feminists also promote a modern version of the Victorian separate spheres. In her 1990 best-seller, *You Just Don't Understand*, feminist linguist Deborah Tannen espouses that women and men have vastly different ways of communicating—women using language to create intimacy, consensus, and community, while men use it as part of their hierarchical struggle for power. These supposed different gender dialects, according to Tannen, illustrate how women approach life as a "network of connections" in which they "struggle to preserve intimacy," while men see life as a "contest" to "preserve their independence" and "achieve and maintain the upper hand." Tannen does make it explicitly clear that she believes these supposed different views are the result of socialization and not biology. And she also makes it clear that both views are "equally valid," going to great effort to warn her readers not to interpret one as better than the other.

But Tannen's caveats are contradicted by her own work. By painting a stereotypical picture of women as sweet and unassertive and men as calloused and cold, Tannen ends up playing on a highly value-ridden theme: girls as sugar and spice and everything nice and boys as everything bad. In her discussion of grade-school children, for example, Tannen portrays boys as rough-and-tumble little dictators who boss one another around and fight over who is in charge. On the other hand, girls are said to play intimate, egalitarian games such as house; they "don't give orders," preferring suggestions, and they "don't grab center stage—they don't want it—so they don't challenge each other directly." Perhaps this sugary portrayal of girls was true for those raised in the fifties . . . or those living today in some mythical pocket of Norman Rockwell America, but in the city grade schools I went to, girls were just as bossy as the boys (saying, "Gimme that!" or "My turn!" as they scrabbled over art supplies or played dodgeball), loved to grab center stage (saying, "Look at me!" as they hung upside down from the monkey bars or clowned for attention), and would often challenge one another directly, verbally *and* physically—even when it came to fistfights, which were not rare.

All women can tell plenty of stories about aggressive, competitive behavior in other women, from the viciousness of high school cliques to political back-stabbing in the workplace. These stories suggest that rather than "negotiations for closeness," much female communication is indeed just as hierarchical and power-hungry as men's. Sometimes it may be expressed in a traditionally feminine way—veiled and sugar-coated—but it has everything to do with gaining the upper hand. From the blunt weapon of honesty to the power of tears, women can use seemingly egalitarian and caring communications as tools for manipulation and hurt. The opposite can be said of men: Sometimes the most seemingly brute communication (telling one another, "Let's kick some ass" before a weekend softball game) can be intended to foster a sense of community and consensus.

This is not to dispute that there are some differences in how women and men communicate, particularly for generations raised in the era of *Father Knows Best.* But Tannen's examination of these differences runs only ankle-deep. She seems to buy into simplistic public perceptions of the sexes (men never want to talk about their feelings; women always do) and then makes the giant leap of assuming that these ways of communication show how people actually see the world. There is no mention, for instance, of the many ways men express intimacy to women, from secret words of love in bed to affection lavished on daughters. There is no acknowledgment that sometimes people find it easier to pretend their lives fit popular stereotypes than to expose intensely private, complex, or embarrassing truths in public.

From Gilligan to Ruddick to Tannen, the feminist vision of women's "difference" is based more in fancy than in fact. In their quest to reclaim the positive aspects of traditional femininity, feminists ignore and dismiss the many unpleasant ways women don't fit this ideal. My most painful memories of childhood, for example, were the racist attacks my younger brother (I come from a mixed family) and I received, for some reason predominantly from girls and women. "Who's your daddy?" the girls in grade school chanted in a threatening circle as we walked home. Hurt and enraged beyond measure, I fought back with tears in my eyes. Much of my childhood later felt comprised of standing woodenly in a haze of anger as the aspirin-faced woman at the corner store would call my brother "boy" and falsely accuse him of shoplifting; as the mothers of the neighborhood spoke to us with voices dripping with contempt; as a little old lady in the supermarket pinched my youngest siblings' cheeks and said, "My, what cute pickaninnies." This was not in the Deep South; it was in a supposedly liberal West Coast city. I don't believe girls at school and the women of the neighborhood were operating under a female "ethic of care," welcoming us into their loving "network of connections," "negotiating closeness" with us, and communicating intimacy, egalitarianism, and a sense of community. They were communicating hate. But difference feminists rarely even broach the issue of racism, classism, or other forms of prejudice in women. To read their work, one would have to assume that women do not hold such repugnant beliefs and do not communicate such hostile ideas.

It is precisely this unrealistic romantic vision of women that has seen difference feminism become so popular in feminism. Appropriated by a large and enthusiastic chunk of the women's movement with a cry of Hallelujah! Women *are* naturally the better sex—and always will be—women's "difference" became the emblem of the eighties and early nineties, the subject of feminist conferences, and one of the most popular subjects in women's studies classes. It was also eagerly adopted by many women running for office. "We speak in a different voice," Senator Barbara Mikulski told the 1992 Democratic National Convention when she introduced several female candidates.[17] Gilligan was named Woman of the Year in the January 1984 issue of Ms., and her work received enough academic and mainstream attention to merit a cover story in the January 7, 1990, *New York Times Magazine*. And Tannen, who saw her best-selling thesis blossom into article after article portraying women as gentle lambs in need of special chivalry in communication, even found herself giving a little consciousness-raising session to the Senate in the wake of several sexual harassment scandals.

Throughout the eighties, this women-are-better campaign was bolstered by the revival of traditional ideas of femininity through the focus on rape and porn (women are naturally chaste and pure) and goddess religion (women have special magic powers derived from fertility). The feminist vision of women was now complete—superior in all realms of social behavior, sexuality, spirituality, morality, and ethics.

By the late eighties, the focus on difference had feminists chanting age-old sexist stereotypes like a mantra. An article on environmental issues in the September/October 1991 issue of Ms., for example, claims that a lack of objectivity in women isn't only natural but desirable. "And if women have a single truly philosophical contribution to make, I believe it is to render the lack of traditional proof an irrelevant argument in environmental matters. . . ."

Maybe it's patriarchal, but shouldn't we ask just what evidence supports these claims of gender differences?

Clearly there are anatomical differences between the sexes. Women bear children, and men tend to be a bit larger and have hairier butts. But all questions of inherent *behavioral* differences boil down to our brains and the influence of hormones on this organ. The truth is, as Carol Tavris writes in *The Mismeasure of Woman*, "There is no persuasive evidence that women are naturally or even actually more pacifistic, empathic, or earth-loving than men."

A few feminists try to cite scientific evidence for their theories. Robin Morgan jumps on a tidbit of proof. "She studies the accumulating research in the neurosciences about sex and gender differences; hormonal impact, chromosomal differentiation, brain lateralization," Morgan writes in a mystifying third person voice in her 1989 book, *The Demon Lover*. "She is amused by the finding that the *corpus callosum*, which communicates information between the two hemispheres of the brain, is larger and bulkier in female brains than in male brains, implying a greater 'ease and frequency in communication' between right and left brain in females than in males."

Interestingly, this "corpus callosum" finding also pops up in work by Christian fundamentalists. In *The Language of Love*, published by the fundamentalist group Focus on the Family, the authors use the corpus callosum theory to argue that since women "spend the majority of their days and nights camped out on the right side of the brain [which] harbors the center for feelings," traditional sex roles are clearly natural for the genders.[18]

But in a well-researched article for the April 1993 *Glamour*, "The Search for His and Her Brains," award-winning journalist Le Anne Schreiber investigated the evidence behind brain-difference theories, which rest on the corpus callosum study cited not only by feminists such as Morgan but throughout the media. What she found was an amazing distortion of the facts.

As Schreiber reports: In 1982, researchers autopsing the brains of nine males and five females found differences in the shape of the tail end of the corpus callosum—nerve fibers that link the right and left brain hemispheres. These differences were assumed to be caused by a wash of testosterone affecting males in utero, and the findings hit magazines such as *Science* as proof that men are better at performing specialized tasks and more proficient at math, while women are more communicative, though more inept at math. Feminists such as Morgan took this report as straight fact—at least the part about women being more communicative. Christian fundamentalists also appropriated the parts of the theory they found useful.

But the truth is that the corpus callosum theory is no more than a few unproven assumptions held together by a little imaginative spit and glue—all balanced precariously on top of a finding that has since shown itself to be quite shaky. For one, scientists aren't sure just how the corpus callosum works, let alone what is has to do with math ability or communication. As one expert told Schreiber, there is "absolutely no way at this point that they can make a connection between any difference in brain structure and any particular behavior pattern or any particular aptitude." Second, there is no clinical support for the notion that alleged brain differences are caused by testosterone levels in the womb. In fact, there's no proof that such an influx of the hormone occurs at all. And the third and most damaging fact is that several studies since have shown that size and shape differences in corpus callosums can be greater in members of the *same* sex than *between* the sexes—which tosses the whole theory in the garbage can of bad science, where it belongs.[19]

Other feminist and mainstream notions of gender differences— such as claiming that the hormone testosterone makes men more aggressive—are also quite questionable. "The idea that male hormones make men more competitive, better at sports, go-getters in the business world, and ready to fight to defend their honor and family certainly captures the popular imagination," Dr. Anne Fausto-Sterling writes in her exhaustive 1985 account of biological research, *Myths of Gender: Biological Theories about Women and Men.* "Could it be there is scientific evidence to substantiate such claims?"

In short, the answer is no. Examining the very few studies (six in all) on testosterone and aggression in men, Fausto-Sterling concludes there is "no reliable correlation" between the two. Testosterone is only one part of a complex interacting system of hormones that both women and men share, and this system is affected by social factors. In one study on testosterone and women, for instance, professional women had slightly higher concentrations of the hormone than did housewives. Lest archconservatives believe this shows the nasty effects that working has on women, housewives report higher levels of stress (probably from dealing with the kids), and stress, from surgery to threat of violence, *reduces* testosterone levels. Many who want to believe that testosterone causes violence point to studies done on male rats. These have shown a link between intermale aggression and testosterone—provided the rats are placed in stressful overcrowded cages and sometimes given electrical shocks, because otherwise they won't fight. As Fausto-Sterling points out, extrapolating from studies done on rats in unnatural environments to human interaction in real life is unreasonable. Besides, rats don't represent all animals; studies on gerbils and hamsters have shown the females are just as aggressive as the males.

Our hormones interact with environmental influences in complex ways. The situation is the chicken versus the egg, and we might never know which comes first. While our hormonal levels affect our sex drives, for example, how much sex we have affects our hormonal levels.[20] While growth hormones account for men being taller, some studies have suggested that these hormones are stimulated by exercise—and teenage boys have historically been, and still are, encouraged to be far more active than teenage girls.[21] Research such as this opens up exciting questions about how much our socialized gender roles have influenced our biology, and thus, perpetuate themselves. How have historically shaming mores against women enjoying sexual activity—including masturbation—affected women's sex drives? How have past strictures against women exercising vigorously affected size differences between the sexes?

Some scientists examining these questions have come to surprising conclusions. "Clearly there are inborn sex differences," writes Ruth Hubbard, a professor of biology emerita at Harvard and author of *The Politics of Women's Biology*. "Most babies are born either with ovaries and a uterus, vagina, and clitoris or with testicles and a penis. . . . Each of us is also born with our specific, unique inheritance, with Aunt Mary's nose and Grandpa John's dimpled chin." But outside of that, "[s]ociety defines the sex-appropriate behavior to which each of us learns to conform, and our behavior affects our bones, muscles, sense organs, nerves, brain, lungs, circulation, everything. In this way society constructs us as biologically, as well as socially, gendered people. It does not give us a vagina or a penis, but it helps give us the muscles, gait, body language, and nervous responses that we associate with people who are born with one or the other."

Gait is a good example of this construction. When we think of women's gait, we see a particular style of walking: a slight swing to the hips, shorter steps, arms held close to the side—traits labeled as feminine. In the Victorian era, it was believed that the width of a woman's pelvis . . . "render[s] even walking difficult."[22] But the incredible gains of women in athletics have shown us that rather than being programmed into us in the womb, most, if not all, gait differences are the result of social factors, starting when we're toddlers: placed in dresses instead of pants, taught to be sedentary while boys run footraces, raised to wear high heels and confining skirts and to mimic the sashay we see so often on television and in real life. Just as constantly wearing high heels can mangle your feet, all these factors affect our muscles and joints, and in this way they can make us walk differently. If these social differences disappeared tomorrow, it's unlikely there would be any discernible difference between men and women's style of walking. That is one way society constructs gender differences.

And that is why it is a big mistake to assume that any traits women might have—from gait, to pacifism, to communication, to hairstyles—are inherent. Feminists might as well argue that poor people are born with a taste for Kmart clothes and fast food, or, even more offensively, that blacks are born programmed to speak a certain dialect and the Japanese are genetically programmed to work hard. Those kinds of disgusting assertions would rightly be condemned by feminists, but somehow their application to women has been endorsed.

Despite the utter lack of proof, assumptions of gender differences have not only become feminist tenets but also the media myth of the nineties. From *Time* magazine to the Discovery Channel, the idea that women and men are cast into behavioral molds before they even leave the womb and are then driven like mindless sheep by hormones has gained an amazing amount of credence.[23] In fact, it's interesting that the explosion of feminist theory on difference happened at the same time—the early eighties—that the pendulum of scientific interest swung toward brain differences. Both interests seemed to flower after the widely reported corpus callosum theory.

In many ways, this excited rush to find proof for gender differences echoes the findings of Victorian scientists in the mid-1800s, when they went looking for proof that blacks were subhumans and arrived at some highly questionable "evidence" that blacks have smaller brains and are thus childlike. These scientists sold their idea to a society eager to have its racist beliefs confirmed by supposedly objective, unassailable science.[24] As Dr. Ruth Hubbard notes of today's emphasis on gender difference in brain research, "It is well to be suspicious when 'objective science' confirms long-standing prejudices."[25]

Just as it's possible that some percentage of both women and men are genetically programmed to be homosexually oriented, it *is* possible that it will one day be proven that the sexes have some inherent differences outside of the anatomically obvious. Yet any possible differences must be weighed against the similarities among all of us. Feminist scholar Catharine Stimpson criticized her colleagues' promotions of difference in *Women's Studies in the United States*: "Similarities between men and women are greater than their differences. To emphasize difference over similarity polarizes human nature and reinforces sexual duality as a basis for society."

Stimpson is right. The feminist emphasis on difference divides the sexes and reinforces traditional sex roles. As Naomi Wolf writes in *Fire with Fire*, the movement interpreted difference feminism "not as *descriptions* of women's behavior, but as *prescriptions* for it. . . ."

But even feminist leaders who once argued that people should be judged on the basis of merit, not genitalia, have picked up the party line on difference. "Some feminists still do not understand that true equality is not possible unless those differences between men and women are affirmed," Betty Friedan writes in her 1982 *The Second Stage*, "and until values based on female sensitivities to life begin to be voiced in every discipline and profession, from architecture to economics, where, until recently, all concepts and standards were defined by men." Friedan doesn't offer any proof that women are more sensitive to life. Nor does she explain just what male "concepts" are and how they differ from "female" ones. Yet the disturbing idea that imposing sexist stereotypes will somehow lead to "true equality" has become perversely popular in feminism today.

The feminist declaration of difference may not be based on science—most, like Friedan, don't even bother making a factual case—but that hasn't stopped it from becoming very powerful, and very dangerous.

Popular notions of biology can influence lawmaking and public policy. For example, some rapists have gotten lighter sentences by agreeing to take female hormones to lower their testosterone levels—as if the natural function of testosterone causes men to rape and therefore the ones who don't are simply hormone-deficient.[26] Such biologically determined "he couldn't help it; it was his hormones" sentencing not only absolves criminals of responsibility (and leaves one to envision a future where rapists get off scot-free by citing feminist works claiming that men are naturally more aggressive) but also sets a public standard by which women and men are judged differently *throughout* society on the basis of their gender.

This has the potential to wreak havoc on arguments for equal opportunity. When feminists proclaim that there are profound and irreconcilable differences between women and men, then the goal of equality in education and the workplace becomes harder to reach. Conservatives, for example, can latch onto difference theory and use it to argue that women's differences mean that girls shouldn't be encouraged to enter fields requiring mathematical skill, such as the sciences; that women clearly are unsuitable for any work requiring aggression, such as the military and police; and that pay discrimination is acceptable because men are obviously better at some jobs. This can bar women from high-paying jobs and condone sex discrimination. After all, who wants to retain a "sensitive" and "nurturing" criminal-defense attorney?

And this, in the end, is what the declarations of gender difference—feminist and conservative alike—accomplish: proscribing women's role in society. And this is what this debate boils down to in the public sphere: money. "Jobs and education—that's what it's really all about," writes Fausto-Sterling on questions of difference, ". . . about whether boys and girls should attend separate schools, about job and career choices, and, as always, about money—how much employers will have to pay to whom."

But this problem doesn't seem to faze current feminists. In the headlong rush to prove feminine moral superiority, economic equality has fallen by the wayside. Many of today's feminists leaders couldn't give a fig about women being shut out of high-paying corporate jobs. As part of the war against the patriarchy and the pursuit of the utopian vision, these jobs have been condemned as part of masculine hierarchical structures—which decent feminists should flee, not join.

Women seeking support from feminism for their attempts to get ahead in their career and financial lives find that, as the better sex, they shouldn't even bother trying.

"You have to make some real concrete changes in terms of economic situations, health care, and all these issues that will really affect the way people live before you start concentrating on the way words are used to define things. I know they go hand in hand, but I do think more women would be involved and concerned if they really thought it was going to impact their lives. I think that it's true that a lot of women see the feminist movement as too theoretical and really don't know how it's going to affect them. And so they stay uninvolved."

—ANNE CUNNINGHAM, twenty-four, salesperson in New York

Anne's point is a good one. Many women do see the feminist movement as too theoretical. From theory on the patriarchy, to "phallocentric" language, to difference feminism, it is often difficult to see how feminist theory is going to impact their lives. And so they stay uninvolved.

But for many feminists, theory is what the movement is all about. "Women need to know (and are increasingly prevented from finding out)," bell hooks lovingly quotes feminist Carol Ehrlich in *Feminist Theory from Margin to Center*—which is assigned in many women's studies classes—"that feminism is *not* about dressing for success, or becoming a corporate executive, or gaining elective office . . . it is most emphatically *not* about becoming a police detective or CIA agent or marine corps general."

If feminism isn't about economic and political power or equality, then what is it about? The common view is summed up by Charlotte Bunch in a 1983 book; feminism "is an entire world view or gestalt, not just a laundry list of 'women's issues.' "[27]

The feminist world view is a simple one. The public spheres—politics and the workforce—are believed to be patriarchal, embodying ideals that are immoral and oppressive. To work in those areas on a laundry list of women's issues, or to adopt those ideals and become a corporate executive or hold political office, only corrupts female nature. Instead, true feminism means trying to transform the world into a feminine image. But traditional femininity has always resided in the private sphere, the home—and this seems to be where some feminists argue we return. After all, if you close off routes to parity in the workforce, politics, and popular culture, what is left? By returning to the private sphere and exalting traditional notions of femininity and inherent gender differences, feminists tell us, we will transform society into a utopia.

This is what was promised to women in the Victorian era. Told that public power would only corrupt her pure nature, the Victorian woman was advised that *real* power resided in the home, where a woman could act as a beacon of morality while remaining safe from the sullying influence of men. Only by retreating from the public sphere, she was assured, would she ever arrive at ruling with sweet order. Of course, it was a lie.

"Once again, women are defined by their family roles," dissenting feminist Katha Pollitt wrote on difference feminism in her article reprinted in the September/October 1993 *Utne Reader*. "Child-raising is seen as women's glory and joy and opportunity for self-transcendence, while Dad naps on the couch. Women who do not fit the stereotype are castigated as unfeminine—nurses nurture, doctors do not—and domestic labor is romanticized and sold to women as a badge of moral worth." Current feminists have, ironically, gone full circle, romanticizing the so-called female traits that have been used to confine us in the past, and by extension castigating those women who fail to meet these standards. "It is as though women don't really believe they are entitled to full citizenship unless they can make a special claim to virtue," Pollitt writes. "Why isn't being human enough?"

Women of all ages find this return to Victorian-era ideals of femininity confusing, but it's particularly upsetting to women of my generation. Many of us work—we don't have much choice there—and we have to balance our jobs and a devastating economic situation (roughly one in five members of my generation lives below the poverty line[28]) with our desire to raise a family. This is the real-life question many of us face: Can I afford to have children? To say that only women can be "sensitive to life," caring, and nurturing isn't only a slap in the face to the many dedicated fathers out there; it implicitly condones dumping all family responsibilities on women's shoulders. Not only are men let off the hook when it comes to child rearing but our so-called patriarchal society is also relieved of any obligation to assist.

Instead, the message is that the responsibility to carry the full burden of child rearing is the woman's, along with the often unacknowl-edged need to bring in a paycheck. In this way, today's feminists send young women a very confusing message. We are expected to refuse to work within the so-called patriarchal systems that would help us gain a better economic footing, and yet we are also expected to fulfill our role as family nurturer—and it takes cash to feed, nurture, clothe, and in many ways love children. Either way, women my age can't win. If we excel in the competitive workplace, we are considered patriarchal collaborators, or what Suzanne Gordon calls "female clones." If we fol-low feminist dictums and don't compete in the workplace—or if we are forced by economics into dead-end jobs and poverty—we can't af-ford to have children, and feminists, ironically, inform us we are ne-glecting our true calling, and thus we are failures again. And if we do stay home and raise the kids in a traditional heterosexual two-parent family, we often feel there isn't a place for us in the movement.

Working in a pizza restaurant years ago (most of my adult life, I've worked in service jobs, from tossing pizza to bartending), I remember talking with a female coworker who had taken a women's studies course and learned all about women's "different voice." We were working full speed in a kitchen the size of a dime, where it was about a hundred degrees; the ovens were blasting heat and we were covered with flour and were sweating grease. The conversation turned to the ludicrous: My coworker laughingly wondered whether her different voice was the one she used to yell at the waiters with, or was it the one she used in bed, and was it true that women made better pizzas? We were laughing, but there was a desperate note to our hilarity. Talking about women's supposed moral superiority and sensitivity while slapping pizza sauce on dough and making five bucks an hour for it—no benefits, no parental leave, no insurance—not only seemed irrelevant, it also illustrated the stark chasm between feminist theory and real life. The least pressing of my coworker's concerns were supposed gender differences. The men we worked with were per-fectly fine people. The reality was a bit more mundane and a lot more depressing: When you can't afford to have a family, superior nurturing ability is a moot point.

For many women *and* men of my generation, true equality means a future where both sexes can afford to spend time with children, where women are valued just as much as men in the workforce, and where men take just as much responsibility in child rearing, wipe just as many dirty bottoms, and give just as many hugs—and *neither* sex is deemed more intelligent, sensitive, caring, rational, or irrational than the other. We don't want to be the better sex. Victorian French feminist Maria Deraismes put it so well over a century ago: "Of all women's enemies, I tell you the worst are those who insist that woman is an angel. To say that woman is an angel is to impose on her . . . all duties, and to reserve for oneself all rights. . . . I decline the honor of being an angel. No one has the right to force me to be both dupe and victim."[29]

Women going about their lives today know that things are more complex than feminists paint them. Our workplaces may not be beds of roses, but that's not necessarily because they're corrupted by evil masculine ideas. No one ever promised us that equality meant paradise. Our culture may sometimes abound with negative images of women, but that doesn't mean there's an insidious "backlash" being orchestrated against feminism; it just means that sexism is still alive and the women's movement has more work to do. There is plenty of headway to be made for equal opportunity and equal representation, but that doesn't mean that all men are oppressors and all women are saviors. There is no conspiracy operating behind closed doors. There is only a society comprised of individuals, a society that has changed a great deal in twenty years and can change some more. As Anne Merkelson—the woman whose words opened this chapter—believes, patriarchal theory only makes sense until you meet the enemy. And then you find out that he is just as complex, multifaceted, and often contradictory as you—and just as human.

But none of this seems to matter to many leading feminists. The utopian vision has become so entrenched that few feminists seem willing to step back and ask whether they truly represent women's immediate concerns. Instead, many feminists seem to be backpedaling as fast as they can. After fighting so hard to see that women of my generation have the opportunity and right to equality in education, the workplace, and politics, feminists now appear to want to take it all back.

Utopia literally means "no place." My use of this word in this chapter has been intentional. By rejecting present society—from political systems to higher education—current feminists have abandoned the fight for equality. By dreaming of an improbable future ruled by age-old notions of femininity, they have refuted the freedom from gender roles. And by promoting their vision, they have closed off every single effective method of activism in the movement.

They are, literally, going no place.

THE PASSIVE VOICE:
INERTIA INSTEAD OF ACTION

"It's kind of removed from our generation, because I think we weren't around when it was just starting and it was a real empowering organization. I think that with my circle of friends, male and female, feminism is just kind of considered the norm—women are given just as much respect as men."
——MICHELLE NORDHOUGHEN, twenty-seven, program instructor for a residence home for mentally retarded adults in Minnesota

"I haven't noticed anything going on. And maybe if I had, I would have gotten involved in it. If I don't hear about it, I don't do it."
——KATE MOISE, twenty-nine, teacher in Louisiana, speaking about the lack of feminist activism in her area

There is a reason Kate Moise hasn't noticed anything going on and Michelle Nordhoughen sees feminism as removed from our generation. Today's women's movement has grown passive. Ask a number of women what feminists are doing in their area and many of them will draw a blank. To the uninvolved, it's obvious that feminists are upset about something—with leaders loudly denouncing the patriarchy, heterosexuality, pop culture, and other supposed forms of female oppression—but it is not clear just what they are *doing* in terms of concrete activism on specific issues.

In July 1992, when feminists for the first time in over a decade saw a chance to help elect a sympathetic administration, they blew their chance to get in on the action. The National Organization for Women, declaring—in president Patricia Ireland's words—that "parties are irrelevant," boycotted the Democratic National Convention in New York.[1] Instead of earning gratitude when the Democrats could have used all the help they could get, NOW simply exposed *itself* as irrelevant. While the national NOW was boycotting the convention, the New York city chapter of the organization spent its efforts on a political nonevent: a rally denouncing "violence against women," organized by antiporn leader Dorchen Leidholdt and featuring Andrea Dworkin as a speaker.[2] Later in Houston, when the Republicans at their convention were declaring a "cultural war" on feminism as well as other antifamily evils, the feminists—in this case members of the New York–based Women's Action Coalition—were busy entertaining themselves with a slide show. According to the July 20, 1993, *Village Voice*, it was a very nice slide show, but it was held miles from the Astrodome, where the Republican delegates were safely ensconced, and wound up being little more than a forty-thousand-dollar sermon to the converted. None of these actions—or nonactions—had the slightest effect on national politics.

While these are only a few incidents, they illustrate the paralysis and ineffectiveness of today's movement. When major gains for women are made, it is more likely that they are the result of trends outside the movement than of activism inside. "The Year of the Woman," for example, didn't happen because of the movement; it happened *to* the movement. With a few exceptions, it was the result of women independently deciding to run for office and the mainstream media trumpeting their campaigns, not a preplanned effort on the part of feminist organizations to find, fund, and promote female politicians. Once feminists noticed how many women were running for office, some did dedicate energy crusading for them. But their activism was largely reactive, not proactive.

Such passivity is self-inflicted, as feminist leaders usher their movement into a soft, muffled Victorian twilight, where women retreat from the daylight world of public involvement to the roles of outsider, moral leader—and martyr. The feminist voice is no longer vibrant and invigorating. Instead, it has become extreme, distracted, fragmented, and overwhelmingly passive.

This is the result of several trends that promote inertia, fragmentation, and divisiveness. Taken together, they have seen much of the movement frozen outside of the public spheres, preaching passivity over effective action.

One of these trends is the feminist outsider stance. Consistent with the utopian vision's condemnation of so-called patriarchal systems, many women's organizations and feminist leaders have posed themselves as radical outsiders, taking only those actions that confirm this ideal—such as NOW's boycott of the Democratic National Convention. This kind of protest activism may come off as strong and combative, but its effect is passivity: It accomplishes little in the way of concrete change. And yet the extremist outsider stance is presented as the only acceptable feminist position. This self-induced inertia parading under the banner of radical action is one reason why so many women refuse to call themselves feminists. We know it's not getting any real work done.

Pity those women who *do* try to get some work done. Inspired by the women-are-better trend that permeates the movement, current feminists have embarked on a purity campaign, demanding that women in politics and business live up to the highest feminist ideals. Women with power who don't toe the feminist line on every conceivable issue have been subject to vicious attacks from feminist leaders. This was illustrated in the 1992 New York primary race for the U.S. Senate, when Geraldine Ferraro and Elizabeth Holtzman faced off. The fight turned nasty when Holtzman, a maverick feminist politician, dared to run negative ads against Ferraro.[3] This move spurred feminist leaders to denounce Holtzman to the press. "Women are promising to do it differently and do it better," Ms. cofounder Letty Cottin Pogrebin told the August 27, 1992, *New York Times*. "With her sleazy campaign, Liz Holtzman has betrayed that promise." Former Representative Bella Abzug chimed in with the claim that Holtzman was using "antifeminist standards." The uproar against Holtzman seemed to taint both women's campaigns. Neither won the election. A man did.

And from Gloria Steinem's explorations of her inner child ("Wild Child," as Steinem calls her) to new forms of consciousness-raising, a trend toward self-examination plays a major role in the creation of a passive voice. Instead of effective activism, feminists have adopted "transformation" as a model for change. The idea is that if women "transform" themselves, the world will follow. Hence, utopia. This cosmic view has led to the diversification of the movement into many areas that have little conceivably to do with women's rights. Transformation is passivity masquerading as activism.

Along with the antiphallic campaign, the promotion of victim mythology, and the crusade against porn, these trends have turned the feminist focus away from a fight for equality to a flight into an ineffective moral ideology. Instead of a clear, uncompromising voice insisting on our rights, the feminist voice has become a passive whisper, repeating to itself its own irrelevant sermons—a voice that fewer and fewer women want to hear.

Debates over whether to reject existing society or to attempt to integrate women into established systems (capitalism, for example) have raged within the movement since its inception. But from the late sixties through the early eighties, these debates were tempered by the need for a united front to fight for abortion rights and the Equal Rights Amendment. When the ERA failed, however, the blame was placed on our political system, and many feminists became convinced that political reform can't work. The condemnation of reform created one of the more bizarre aspects of the movement today: an almost-complete refusal to acknowledge the incredible gains—from legalized abortion to women in high political office—made by the women's movement. To read most feminist literature, organization newsletters, and comments by feminist leaders in the press, one would think that things are worse, not better, than in the fifties and sixties.

By the mid-eighties, dictates against working inside the system were firmly entrenched in much of mainstream feminism. The effect since has been devastating to the strength of the women's movement.

Take, for example, the National Organization for Women. To much of the general public, it is considered to represent mainstream feminism. This perception is part of the reason women refuse to call themselves feminists: Many women who support equality feel that if NOW stands for feminism, they'll pass. NOW offers a perfect illustration of just how far feminism has traveled from representing the majority of women, and just how deadly the outsider stance can be to effecting progress.

In NOW, the long-debated position of outsider was confirmed in 1985 when then president Judy Goldsmith was ousted from office. Her crime? Seen as too moderate because of her emphasis on lobbying and coalition building, Goldsmith had dinner with Democratic presidential nominee Walter Mondale and encouraged him to select Geraldine Ferraro for his running mate. He did, and Ferraro became the first woman ever to run for vice president. It was one of NOW's greatest political achievements, but other bigwigs in the organization didn't think so. In a divisive and ugly election—one the *New York Times* termed "a palace coup"—Goldsmith was replaced by Eleanor Smeal, who had served as NOW's president from 1977 to 1982 and espoused a radical, outsider approach. "NOW is about being on the outside and shaking the foundations of the ruling class," one insider said regarding Goldsmith's role in the Ferraro/Mondale affair. "Judy misunderstood the role of the organization."[4] Or maybe she mistakenly thought she was working to fulfill the NOW mandate that vows to take the actions needed to "bring women into full participation in the mainstream of American society."

With her loss, NOW left its inclusive, equality-oriented mandate behind. Since the Goldsmith incident, the group has increasingly veered off center onto a separatist sidetrack, busily applauding themselves as heroic outsiders the entire time. Under Smeal, NOW retreated from lobbying to focus on street demonstrations and other forms of protest politics, a combative outsider stance they've kept to this day.[5] Today, Smeal heads the Fund for the Feminist Majority (a nonmembership funding organization that works closely with NOW on many issues) and is a vocal proponent of the antiporn cause.

Current NOW president Patricia Ireland—who ran Smeal's campaign against the unfortunate Goldsmith[6]—hasn't broken rank with the policy of protest politics. If anything, she has taken her organization further afield, dismissing legislative strategy as pointless and heralding a 1991 resolution in which, for the first time in its history, NOW called for civil disobedience.[7] In order to kick off this civil-disobedience strategy, Ireland managed to get herself arrested at a small demonstration against the Supreme Court's Casey ruling (a June 1992 decision upholding Pennsylvania's state-mandated twenty-four-hour waiting period for abortion). Joining Ireland in the police van was Smeal, who also deliberately got herself arrested. Though the press chose largely to ignore this protest action, NOW claimed the arrests were a "major step in a historic battle to reclaim women's lives"—just how is not clear—and Ireland has since repeated the meaningless gesture.[8]

NOW idealizes itself as a subversive force shaking the foundations of the ruling class, but all it is really doing is rattling its own cage.

And this cage is of their own making. NOW may blame hostile Republican administrations for their group's ineffectiveness since the mid-eighties, but this excuse doesn't float. Times of opposition can solidify and increase organizational power and activism: With a clearly defined enemy, groups often have an easier time soliciting donations and enrolling members.

The truth is, NOW's extremist stance has alienated the public, destroyed their political credibility, and seen the group come to promote little more than passivity. As syndicated columnist Julianne Malveaux notes, "The organization is perceived as part of the feminist fringe and has a membership roster of less than 300,000."[9] Compare NOW with the National Rifle Association—which boasts a membership of over 3 million—and it becomes obvious that NOW's roll of 270,000 is shockingly low. It's even more baffling when you consider that women's rights have far more popular appeal than defending the sale of semiautomatic weapons. There are over 129 million women in the United States, and, according to polls, the majority of them favor equal opportunity.[10] That NOW can only muster a paltry 270,000 members out of all these women (not to mention the millions of men who support equality) isn't a reflection of societal sexism; it's a reflection of just how far NOW has moved from representing the mainstream. "The fact that half the population of the United States is female and that only 250,000 are members of NOW," one woman wrote in a March 22, 1992, letter to the *New York Times*, "is hardly an affirmation of its leadership."

And while NOW once helped put a woman on the ballot for vice president, their current approach has seen their political clout slip precipitously. Their refusal to work inside the system—and accept the compromises this sometimes entails—has given the group the reputation of a toothless tiger in Washington: all roar with no bite. Insiders say NOW is famous for slitting their own throats over legislation (rather than bend on any points, they'll see a bill fail[11]) and, even more deadly in the political arena, for a reputation for turning against politicians who can't keep up with their incessant and often completely unmeetable demands.

Take Bill Clinton. Prior to his election, Clinton promised to overturn several of the antiabortion legacies of Reagan and Bush, including rescinding the gag rule at federally funded health clinics. He also promised to appoint women to cabinet positions and make health care a priority. And Clinton kept those promises.

But before he was even inaugurated, NOW was attacking him for not naming enough women to cabinet positions, even though it was far too early to judge. Clinton's response—labeling his critics "bean counters"—was certainly not met with a wave of outrage from offended women.[12] Even Patricia Ireland admits that these unrealistic and premature criticisms of Clinton alienated some of NOW's members. "We started hearing from our constituency," Ireland told the July 1993 NOW convention. "They were saying: 'Give the guy a chance. He's made some good appointments. Aren't you ever satisfied?' " Pausing, Ireland answered her own question: "No!"[13] She wasn't being apologetic. She was obviously proud she had lost touch with her constituents.

Given their stance against working inside the system, just what exactly does NOW do? With a scattered agenda reaching from environmental issues to lesbian rights, the group often seems to be trying to be all things to all feminists. In many ways, this attempt to be inclusive has created exactly the opposite effect: They are fragmented into so many areas that while they may pass reams of commendable-sounding resolutions, what they actually accomplish is another story. NOW does deserve recognition for some inside-the-Beltway tactics they still manage to take despite their avowed outsider stance. Their PAC does good work funding female candidates, and the NOW Legal and Education Defense Fund pursues equality through the courts. But some have criticized NOW for being more window dressing than representing effective action on many important issues.

Efia Nwanganza, who ran unsuccessfully against Ireland in 1993 for NOW's presidency, claims that the current leaders of the group have reduced women's struggles for economic survival to photo opportunities and fund-raising events.[14] She also questioned whether Patricia Ireland's annual paycheck of about $140,000 isn't a little excessive for an organization whose average member earns $25,000.[15] It is quite an increase from 1985, when Goldsmith as NOW's president made $55,000.[16]

Just how far NOW has moved away from representing women's immediate concerns is demonstrated by their new "feminist" political party, the 21st Century party. Conceived in 1989 as the brainchild of Eleanor Smeal and midwifed by NOW, which resolved in 1992 to help fund its creation, the 21st Century party was a response to the belief that the Democratic party no longer represents women's concerns. Instead, while NARAL and other women's groups played key roles in the Democratic National Convention, NOW boycotted the Democrats in favor of the 21st Century party's founding convention. Democratic and even pro-choice Republican women politicians were understandably angered by this divisive move, noting that it is nearly impossible for third-party candidates to win, and upset that NOW would want to split the women's vote by directing energy into a ploy that might well be self-defeating.[17]

But for NOW, it was the politics of screw you. "I don't want to play with the boys anymore," Ireland told the March 1, 1992, *New York*

Times, sounding more like a petulant separatist than the president of an organization supposedly devoted to putting women in the mainstream of society. "There is total gridlock in Washington. Our entire government is an obstacle. Fie on both their houses."

Just what does this third party offer us that the "boys" can't? According to an October 1992 *National NOW Times* article titled "21st Century Party Drafts Bold Political Agenda," party workshops included a bevy of worthy-sounding but often vague principles, such as "Restoring a Sustainable Environment," "Rising Above Violence," and "Respecting the World." One idea is that the party will call for "constitutional guarantees" against all forms of discrimination. Another is calling for rights to everything from a clean environment to freedom from all violence, including wars.

While a political party based on women's rights has an appeal, this wide-ranging utopian platform has little to do with actual equality. There is no reason why environmental and antiwar causes should be considered exclusively women's issues. By placing them under the banner of feminism, NOW only ensures more women will see the feminist label as belonging to an ideologically correct fringe group rather than to a movement concerned with equal opportunity for *all* women, regardless of their political differences. And, as the December 4, 1989, *Time* magazine noted, "NOW's call last summer for a third political party that would represent women's concerns seemed laughable to young women who do not want to isolate themselves by gender, but prefer to work *with* men."

The party also sounds politically naïve. What kinds of laws will make people "respect the world"? Do NOW officials really think that voters will elect candidates who would refuse to send our country to war, no matter what the threat? Does the organization really believe that money and energy should go to a third party instead of supporting Democratic or even Republican women who might stand a chance of winning?

These questions may be answered soon. Party officials say they hope to have a presidential candidate on the ballot in 1996.[18]

Another example of the flight of feminism from the mainstream is the fate of *Ms.* magazine. Originally launched as a supplement to the 1971 year-end issue of *New York* magazine, the first official issue of *Ms.* sold 300,000 copies in ten days. Colorful, filled with advertising, and boasting some of the best journalists of the day, for years *Ms.* magazine was considered *the* voice of mainstream feminism. Its tone was empowering, exciting, even fun, with articles that addressed women's interests and concerns, from child care ("The Great American Child-Care Disgrace,"), to social activism ("How to Make Trouble: Getting Rid of Sexism in Schools"), to young women ("What It's Like to Be Me: Young Women Speak for Themselves"). From getting equal pay to having good sex, Ms. covered it all.

But as it entered the eighties, Ms. became stuck in a rut—repeating the same old lines and rehashing the same old oppressions—and this inability to change with the times, constructively criticize the movement, or address new concerns showed in a loss of readers and advertisers. After changing hands several times and being briefly suspended from publication in 1989, Ms. was resurrected by Robin Morgan and Gloria Steinem. Today this once-inclusive mainstream magazine is a truly fringe publication, catering only to the most ideologically pure feminists. Considering itself too high-minded for advertising, it's printed on flat stock, heavy with type and often obtuse with academic feminist jargon. The journalists have been replaced by writers such as Andrea Dworkin and Adrienne Rich. The articles are often extremist (Catharine MacKinnon's July/August 1993 cover story on pornography), baffling to the uninitiated (special sections include "inner space" and "ecofeminism"), and usually devoid of dissent or even factual reporting (the January/February 1993 cover story was titled "Believe it! Cult Ritual Abuse Exists"; the article was written under an alias, shady on detail and frankly unbelievable).

Journalist Peggy Orenstein wrote in the November/December 1990 issue of *Mother Jones* that both Steinem and Morgan no longer seem concerned with reaching "younger, more casually feminist women" as the magazine did in the seventies. Pressuring Morgan as to why, the editor told her: "Reaching you women of whatever age is one function. But another and, quite frankly, more basic one is to speak to our own constituency, which has been ignored by everybody." Even, it appears, at the cost of alienating many potential activists from the movement. As Anne Cunningham, a twenty-four-year-old salesperson from New York, says of Ms., "It's almost like the pc handbook. The feminist handbook. It tells you, if you are a feminist, you should be this, do this; don't change your name if you get married; it's preferable if you're a lesbian. Everything it approaches, it approaches with a patent perspective, so that you know what they're going to say. . . . They're always patting themselves on the back: Here's a young feminist; we're showcasing her. And often it's just the daughters of the old-school feminists. I don't think that's very effective, because it's not bringing people into the movement."

The sad histories of both NOW and Ms. should not cloud the fact that there are organizations that continue to work effectively for equality and to place women into the mainstream. There is the National Women's Political Caucus, a multipartisan organization founded in 1971 that recruits, trains, and funds pro-abortion rights women for public office. At their 1993 convention, for example, the group hosted a variety of workshops on issues including campaign financing, child care, health policy, and—hallelujah—a forum for young women just getting started in politics. Harriett Woods, president of the NWPC, is distinctly pragmatic about the methods and goals of her organization, freely admitting that she doesn't expect all female politicians to espouse the full feminist agenda. "In the long run, if women are ever going to be the majority (in public office)," she told one reporter, "they won't be women we agree with 100 percent."[19] There is also Emily's List, another political fund-raising group for female politicians, and the National Abortion Rights Action League, which lobbies to protect and advance reproductive rights, including the availability of RU 486. By focusing on priority issues, these organizations have steered clear of the many extremist and irrelevant causes of current feminism, keeping themselves on track to fight for women's rights. It's important that we do not dismiss their valuable contributions to equality just because so much of the feminist movement has gone astray.

But the idea that feminists shouldn't work within the system has been taken by many within the movement as gospel. Many of the newer feminist organizations, such as the Women's Action Coalition (WAC) and the Women's Health Action Mobilization (WHAM), were founded on this principle. New York city's WAC is famous for staging noisy, exuberant actions ("WAC attacks")—including a drum corps and eye-catching banners—on issues from child support to rape, while WHAM is best known for its head-on confrontations with the anti-abortion group Operation Rescue. While rallies and protests are definitely media savvy and great for releasing energy, it's questionable if they can effect concrete change. The National Women's Political Caucus, for example, decided not to cosponsor the April 1992 abortion-rights march on Washington organized by NOW because they believe that marches are largely a waste of time and money. "For what it would cost us to participate in this march," their spokeswoman Pat Reilly stated in the February 3, 1992, *Time* magazine, "we can elect several women."

Happening across a WAC counterdemonstration against a paltry group of anti-abortionists in the fall of 1992 in New York City, I asked a young woman watching from the crowd what she thought of the protest. Shrugging, she watched a group of activists taunt the anti-abortionists by shaking enormous plastic penises in their faces. She then told me she thought it was kind of funny but mostly "pointless." For many women of my generation, civil disobedience and protest activism often do seem pointless: more of a feel-good nostalgic return to the sixties than an effective means to gain and exercise power.

Women once had to stand outside in the rain yelling for their rights because they were forbidden a place inside government or the workplace. Now that we have a foot in the door, going back outside seems like admitting defeat in a battle we are winning. Why should NOW, for instance, boycott the Democratic National Convention after all the work the movement did to see that women have a strong voice in the party? In Victorian times, women's groups also took outsider-based actions. Members of the English suffragist organization the Women's Social and Political Union, for example, held huge demonstrations, deliberately courted arrest, and then went on hunger strikes in prison. Without the vote, economic influence, or self-sufficient means to power, protest activism was one of their few options. Women had to work outside the system because they *were* outside the system. But that's not our only option now—and to advocate it as such only throws the efforts of earlier feminists out the window.

While demonstrations, marches, and radical tactics can give the immediate impression of activity, their effect is at heart one of passivity. Insisting that women take their concerns to the street ignores the available and effective recourses of funding candidates, introducing legislation through sympathetic lawmakers, running for office, or the myriad other avenues the women's movement has won. Current feminists, essentially, are saying that women are powerless. No amount of yelling, chanting, or waving plastic penises erases this passive impotence. Rather than representing the mainstream and working effectively for equality, outsider politics only cements paralysis by promoting a view of feminists as shrill fringe radicals incapable of actually accomplishing progress.

From WAC attacks to the president of NOW getting herself thrown in jail, the current feminist emphasis on outsider-based politics alienates potential political supporters. Many people are put off by the reduction of complex emotional issues—such as parental notification for minors seeking abortions—to bumper-sticker slogans and meaningless placards (EVERY EJACULATION DOES NOT DESERVE A NAME and ABORT PATRIARCHY were two from a San Francisco march). Difficult issues need discussion, not placards dictating a simpleminded position. Many women resent being placed in the enemy camp because they have mixed feelings and can't take such a hard-line approach.

Others find this extremism damaging to the very causes they care about. Sarah Beck, a twenty-four-year-old woman working in a medical firm, was active in her college's pro-abortion rights group, Penn Students for Choice. But she tells how put off she was by another campus organization, which used confrontational tactics. "They kind of harassed people and they were very vocal [in their activist role] with the pro-choice movement, in what I thought was a detrimental way," Sarah says. "I just think it's so crucial to be moderate these days. And realize that you're not just addressing other feminists—you're addressing everyone. To be so radical and militant, I just think it's so harmful. You have to appeal to the people who are undecided. And you are not going to do that by painting your body blue and running up to people and screaming, 'Take a brochure!' "

Women of all ages and backgrounds want concrete, effective measures for change. They don't want to feel they are wasting energy in meaningless actions or putting off the very people the movement needs to reach. Living paycheck to paycheck and raising children at the same time, most women have precious little time for activism to begin with—they want it to count. As Sarah says, "I'd rather take my concerns with women's rights somewhere like a clinic, where I'm doing work, and not just acting like a lunatic."

The paralyzing outsider stance isn't confined to women's organizations. Women's studies classes, feminist magazines, newsletters, and books also offer little in terms of concrete, effective suggestions for pursuing equality. Instead, popular feminist literature paints such unrelenting portraits of female oppression that fighting back seems impossible and passivity inevitable. When feminists do offer a call to arms, it's often reduced to an unrealistic Band-Aid solution (censor pornography), or, even more commonly, inflated into the meaningless battle cry of the utopian vision (Overthrow the Patriarchy!).

For example, in her 1991 best-seller, *Backlash*, author Susan Faludi claims the eighties were nothing more than "one long, painful, and un-remitting campaign to thwart women's progress," but she neglects to give any specific prescription for curing this supposed societal ill. And how could she? From plastic surgery (men operate on women not be-cause they make bucco bucks but because they like the fact that women "under anesthesia don't talk back"), to jean ads featuring female butts (part of an effort on the part of fashion designers to control women through "the threat of discipline" by posing them "as if ready for a spanking"), to an article titled "Koko the Gorilla Tells Keeper She Would Like to Have a Baby" (Koko the ape is part of an insidious, sub-tle media campaign trying to "induce" women to give up their jobs and have babies), Faludi finds evidence of this "unremitting" conspiracy against women everywhere. But after four hundred and fifty pages crammed with such selective interpretations of pop culture, she doesn't offer one specific suggestion for what women can do to fight this am-biguous "backlash." Instead, she offers lurid, meaningless prose: "To re-move the backlash wall rather than to thrash continuously against it, women need to be armed with more than their privately held grievances and goals." More what, she doesn't explain. Even if Faludi wanted to present a course of action, what could she say? Stop buying all maga-zines and newspapers, throw the television out the window, never go to the movies, don't get pregnant, condemn women with nose jobs, and make sure to dress in baggy clothes? Overthrow the backlash? Get real.

Backlash isn't simply a study in paralyzing paranoia. It's replete with misinformation. Faludi's driving thesis—that women's progress was thwarted and stalled in the eighties—is largely untrue: Women gained more economic ground in the 1980s than in the entire postwar era be-fore that. The wage gap rose to seventy-two cents on the dollar from sixty cents, and for women of my generation, it rose to eighty cents.[20] And what Faludi blames for her theoretically thwarted progress—a pop-culture backlash—is also based on questionable claims. One of her most cited proofs is that in the eighties Hollywood put out more feminist-bashing movies than in the previous decade. But one study analyzing top-grossing films from 1946 to the present found that there has been a significant *profeminist* shift in women's roles since the early eighties.[21] Women were successful businesswomen (*When Harry Met Sally*), independent and smart police officers (Officer Lewis in my fa-vorite blow-'em-up movie, *Robocop*, which Faludi, amazingly, cites as an example of women as "mute and incidental" characters), and, of course, gun-toting rebels (*Thelma and Louise*). But that's the problem with using popular culture to examine society: Anyone can play pick and choose from movies, advertising, and dumb articles on apes to find the conclusion they're expecting. Looking for a "backlash" against feminism? Sure, there're plenty of demeaning images of women around. Then again, there're an awful lot of movies that portray men as sex-obsessed dolls, weirdo drug dealers, and ax-wielding criminals. But no one is arguing there is a conspiracy afoot to thwart male progress.

Yet *Backlash* was eagerly adopted by many women's studies classes. At the University of Wisconsin in Madison, for example, excerpts from Faludi's book are assigned in a section on the "future" of feminism.

And other recent feminist books leave a similar void when it comes to concrete action. Marilyn French's 1992 *The War Against Women* takes the backlash to a global scale, portraying men as the ultimate oppressors throughout history and across cultures. Like Faludi, French ends her book with combative but meaningless rhetoric: "After millennia of male war against them, women are fighting back on every front." How? French cites anecdotal examples but doesn't spell out specific strategies.

Women turning to feminist literature to learn how to fight inequality find grim, hopeless stories of male oppression, overarching conspiracies set against a helplessly besieged womankind, a truly bleak future. Overblown with rhetoric, the feminist battle cry is one of war, rage, combat, and confrontation.

Devoid of any specific programs, this cry is curiously empty, devastatingly passive.

From their lofty vantage point somewhere above society's real-life battles, feminists have launched a debilitating purity crusade. The very women the movement should be heralding as role models—from successful movie producers to female politicians—have become the subjects of feminist attacks. Not content to take an outsider stance themselves, many current feminists demand that other women in power stop working with the "boys" in so-called male institutions. The woman who dares break this command is derided as an assimilationist. And in feminist terminology, that is no compliment.

By imposing strict standards upon women—while ignoring the behavior of men in similar situations—current feminists have created a purity standard. This standard has turned the emphasis away from empowering women's advance in society to a self-defeating effort on the part of the movement to dictate personal beliefs and moral behavior. It is a double standard, and like traditional sexism's double standards, it hurts women far more than it ever helps.

"It's not that surprising that the few women who make it big in Hollywood reflect the male perspective or point of view," Susan Faludi said in the June 2, 1993, *New York Times*, in an article on feminist criticism of female movie producers. "To one degree or another they were assimilationists or collaborationists." Faludi's usage of *collaborationists* is repelling. Connotations of the word evoke the newly liberated France of 1944, when women accused of sleeping with Germans were denounced as collaborators and paraded with shaved heads as an act of public humiliation. In response, Hollywood agent Elaine Goldsmith said she feels it is unfair of feminists to criticize female-produced movies while ignoring ultraviolent films in which women are portrayed as mindless bimbos. "After we look at those pictures, which are made by men," she said to the *New York Times*, "call me and we'll talk about what women should be doing."

These exacting feminist standards reached an apex in the 1992 elections, when unprecedented numbers of women were running for office, and feminist commentators had a heyday demanding each behave with the utmost ethical and moral purity.

The idea that women must rise above politics-as-usual came with a hefty price tag. "[I]t's important for women candidates who regard themselves as part of a movement for change to establish a higher standard of campaigning. To be held to it and to hold men to it," wrote syndicated columnist Ellen Goodman in September of 1992, attacking Elizabeth Holtzman's hardball tactics against Ferraro. "This may add another burden to women's political quest. But unless we raise such a standard, women could become partners in a political system that's in full, cynical collapse."[22]

The message was clear: Women don't have a *right* to be judged as individuals in politics. We have a *duty* to change the system, an extra burden we should carry willingly in the name of feminine martyrdom.

The feminist party campaign has reached ugly heights in demanding that women candidates subscribe to every feminist tenet in the book—and then viciously attacking them if they don't. Take the case of Texas senator Kay Hutchison's 1993 campaign. Hutchison favors abortion rights, tougher rape laws, and equal credit opportunities for women. But for several feminist leaders, none of this mattered: Hutchison is a Republican. Gloria Steinem tore into Hutchison, denouncing her as a "female impersonator" and saying that "having someone who looks like us [in office] but thinks like them is worse than having no one."[23] Leading feminists may support some male Republicans—Steinem even wrote a letter supporting Oregon senator Bob Packwood, stating that he is a "courageous champion for legislation that the female half of this country desperately needs" *after* allegations of the senator's sexual misconduct arose[24]—but they obviously apply a very different standard to women. Despite attacks from feminists during her campaign, Hutchison won the election. Perhaps people in Texas supported her in part because they found it offensive that, in columnist Stephen Chapman's words, "an ambitious career woman who has the nerve to run for the U.S. Senate against a white male can expect to encounter vicious comments that no man would ever have to endure."[25]

Feminists say they want equal political representation for women, but for many this applies only to women who toe the feminist line. Supporting pro-equality candidates and pushing for parity in politics is necessary, but expecting women candidates to espouse every current feminist cause—from lesbian rights, to pacifism, to even such a core issue as Medicaid funding for abortions—simply *because* they are women is ludicrous. And it is vicious snobbery to condemn women who don't buy the entire feminist agenda as "female impersonators." As columnist Chapman notes, "Such a gratuitous malice for women who march to their own drummer is doubtless one reason so many females who endorse many of the goals of the women's movement have no use for the movement itself."

Ironically, after the 1992 elections—when exacting feminist standards and criticisms had been implicated in damaging several women's campaigns—some of the same writers who had demanded purity began to whistle a different tune. In a December 1992 column entitled "Women Politicians Set Themselves Up for a Fall," Ellen Goodman suddenly accused *other* commentators of having placed women on a "political pedestal" where the slightest impurity destroyed a campaign. "In at least three major races," she wrote, "women suffered a precipitous slide in support when they came up short of the high standards—whether they were tardy on taxes or too quick with negative ads."[26] Goodman didn't mention which races she was referring to, but it's likely the one regarding "negative ads" was the Holtzman campaign. She neglected to mention that she herself had torn into Holtzman two months prior as part of her demands to hold women to higher standards.

In fact, it seems that any woman involved in politics had better subscribe to very noble principles—and never, ever play hardball. In

1992, Emily's List, a funding-raising organization for female Democratic candidates, came under feminist attack. The group had raised a stunning $6.2 million that year and helped see women gain office in unprecedented numbers. The key to their success was keeping ideological requirements to a minimum (the candidate had only to be Democratic and pro-choice), carefully selecting those candidates who stood a chance of winning, and then showering them with money at the beginning of their campaigns. For example, in 1990, Emily's List played a key role in the election of Texas governor Ann Richards by giving her more than $400,000. Compare this with NOW, which donates a maximum of five thousand dollars, and it's obvious why Emily's List has been more effective getting women elected.[27]

But this effectiveness seemed to win Emily's List the enmity of NOW and other feminists. According to a May 2, 1993, *New York Times* article, some feminists criticized the group for not funding more women candidates across the board, instead of selecting only viable candidates. Patricia Ireland pointed to Senator Carol Moseley-Braun of Illinois, saying that NOW had the foresight to contribute to Braun's long-shot campaign early, unlike Emily's List, which didn't kick in until Braun had gained ground. Ellen Malcom, the president of Emily's List, has also been attacked for trying to exempt the group from campaign spending reforms that would prohibit nonlobbying groups from bundling. Bundling is the practice of combining individual contributors' dollars into far more influential sums, and without it Emily's List wouldn't exist. That they would oppose such legislation is understandable. It's silly to expect them to cut their own throats for the sake of a high-minded agenda. But some apparently thought they should, and they found it reprehensible that Malcom would dare work with the "good old boys" by hiring a prestigious Washington lobbying firm to work on her behalf. In the *New York Times*, Malcom defended her action: "They know how to get the job done. What the hell difference would it have made if I'd hired Bipsy and Pooh?"

Probably not much. The truth is, Emily's List isn't ever going to win the approval of many feminists. Malcom says she wants women "to be powerful players in the middle, not just a fringe element," which is why she feels NOW's third party is "a mistake." She also frankly sums up her group as "political venture capitalists" and states, "You'll rarely hear me give the typical 'we're-mad-at-the-world' feminist dogma." Her political realism doesn't toot many feminists' horns.

All this feminist nit-picking over women in politics has caused many feminist-thinking women to rebel. "We don't need feminist thought police, demanding that female thinkers and legislators toe a special-interest line," asserted a January 1992 *Glamour* editorial. "What we need are women of all opinions, a lot of them, in positions to affect the context, the background, the dialogue of decision making. They may be black or white, Republican or Democrat, easterners or westerners, feminists or traditionalists—each woman will bring aspects other than her gender to the caucus room."

For feminist writer Karen Lehrman, the constant demand that women in politics be nurturing Goody Two-shoes has a dangerous edge. "By cultivating old stereotypes, could women be creating their own political glass ceiling?" she writes. "How will these innately pacific women be able to defend a woman's right to serve in combat, let alone lead the country into war? Moreover, if women are so naturally maternal—I can hear the hard far right strategizing—why not send them back to the home, where so many troubles today lie?"[28] Feminists do create their own glass ceiling when they claim women lack many of the traits, such as an ability to take necessary aggressive action, needed to govern. They also create their own glass ceiling when they say that the only reason women should be in office is as change-makers, a notion that implies short-term action (presumably, we leave it to the boys after doing the good work), instead of long-term individuals with a right to represent concerns beyond gender.

Much of the impetus for higher standards seems to be rooted in a nostalgic longing for the early days of the movement, when women first united to fight for economic equality and political representation. There was a euphoric feeling that, given a little power, women could change the world. But as women have entered higher-paying fields and political office, many feminists seem shocked to find equality often means that women can be just as ambitious, self-oriented, and diverse in their beliefs as men. "I fear, too, that women may be losing the idealistic vision that helped inspire feminism in the first place," feminist author Barbara Ehrenreich wrote for an article titled "Sorry, Sisters, This Is Not the Revolution," in a special issue of *Time* (*Women: The Road Ahead*, Fall 1990, p. 15). Her piece sounds like a lament for the passing of the sixties: ". . . every Out group carries with it a critical perspective, forged in the painful experiences of rejection and marginalization. When that perspective is lost or forgotten, a movement stands in danger of degenerating into a scramble for personal advancement." If all Out groups carry a perspective forged in oppression, then of course the end of that oppression would mean the end of their unique perspective—and the freedom to "degenerate" into individuals. Isn't that what we want for women?

Looking at the women's movement today, the answer would have to be no. The expectation that all women should have the same ideals, morals, and political beliefs—just as confining Victorian ideals and traditional sexism did—turn individual differences into a crime against sisterhood rather than a positive sign that progress is being made. It undercuts the advancement of equality and promotes passivity. When Gloria Steinem says that "having someone who looks like us but thinks like them is worse than having no one," the message is that if taking action means acknowledging diversity, feminists would rather women do nothing at all. If equality means women thinking like men (whatever *that* means), then feminist leaders would just as soon it not happen. Women of my generation have taken feminism to heart: We believe that women and men should be judged as individual humans and not "us" and "them." But by current feminist purity standards, we become traitors, collaborators, female impersonators. The sad irony, of course, is that current feminists constantly portray themselves as not only accepting diversity but promoting it.

Yet the exact opposite is often the case. On top of offering a comforting excuse for feminist ineffectiveness in the eighties and the alienation of women from the movement, Susan Faludi's backlash theory has given feminists the perfect means to dismiss honest diversity of opinion: Just call it part of the "backlash" against feminism. For instance, the June 13, 1993, *New York Times* magazine excerpted part of young feminist author Katie Roiphe's book *The Morning After: Sex, Fear, and Feminism on Campus.* The piece was titled "Date Rape's Other Victim," and it offered an intelligent critique of the victim mentality permeating the antirape movement, as well as the inflated statistics that drive it. But Roiphe's points were often ignored in the deluge of angry letters from feminist leaders and adherents. Diane Welsh, president of New York City's NOW chapter, dismissed the piece as "a perfect example of backlash thinking."

Other women who have dared to step forward and relate their concerns about the antiporn campaign, the exclusive focus on lesbian rights, or male-bashing in today's movement have also been labeled part of the "backlash" and dismissed out of hand. I don't doubt that feminists will condemn this book as part of a so-called antifeminist "backlash." The backlash part is in a sense true: I'm fed up with repressive, extremist ideology parading itself as liberating feminism. But the antifeminist part isn't. Like other young women who feel alienated by current feminism, I deeply believe in equality, and the continuing need for a women's movement.

The feminist demands for ideological purity have seen the movement attack itself again and again. Radicals attack the more mainstream groups for being too moderate (NOW, according to Sonia Johnson, is modeled "on the patriarchal family"[29]). NOW attacks their own president for not being radical enough. Antiporn activists attack those who defend freedom of speech. Lesbian separatists attack those who would sleep with the enemy. So-called anti–sexual violence feminists attack those who question sweeping new definitions of rape. Goddess feminists attack traditionally religious feminists for being dupes of male-god beliefs. Feminist leaders attack pragmatic feminist politicians for being too, well, effective. (And, admittedly, I've contributed my share of attacks, as well.) The entire women's movement today is nothing less than a minefield. One little misstep and a would-be feminist sees her standing as an activist blow up in her face. No wonder many women want nothing to do with women's organizations and refuse to call themselves feminists. You have to be exceptionally pure to pass the feminist litmus test, and you have to have a very tough skin to deal with this kind of sisterhood.

"Where will it end?" Daphne Patai, a women's studies professor concerned about current feminist purity campaigns asked in the May 1992 *Education Digest*. "My fear is that the search—and demand—for feminist purity (of both attitudes and identity) will eventually result in a massive rejection of the very important things that feminism, broadly speaking, aims to achieve." As Patai notes, feminists "who have the temerity to criticize" feminism today "risk being automatically placed in the enemy camp."

And when you are in the enemy camp, you're obviously not welcome in women's organizations. By pursuing their stringent purity crusade, current feminists ensure that fresh ideas, differences of opinion, true diversity, and honest debate aren't welcome in their movement. In the vacuum left by their absence, all that can flourish is passivity.

Another major shift in feminist thinking occurred in the eighties, combining with the rejection of mainstream politics and the adopting of rigid purity standards for the feminist "club." Many in the movement became enamored with inner-directed examinations, from meditation to sensitivity training. This emphasis on inner change—instead of outer activism—plays a strong role in the devastating inertia of today's movement.

Much of this self-inflicted passivity comes under the guise of self-help. Gloria Steinem's 1992 best-seller, *Revolution from Within*, is a case in point. Steinem opens her book with the assertion that after working for years on women's external barriers to equality, she "had to admit there were internal ones, too." From there she launches into a mishmash of pop psychobabble and New Age claptrap—on everything from finding your inner child to a meditation guide—laced throughout with personal anecdotes on such compelling topics as her weight problem and her experience with hypnosis. In order to raise their self-esteem, women are advised to listen to their "inner voice" by "re-learning." This "re-learning" includes tapping the unconsciousness through dream recollection, meditating, and taking part in a vague cosmic "great paradigm shift." The popular appeal of Steinem's book shouldn't be surprising; after all, *Women Who Love Too Much* was a smash hit. But *Women Who Love Too Much* wasn't written by a feminist leader as a supposed answer to inequality.

The topic of sexism's effect on women's self-esteem is certainly important. If lack of self-esteem is brought on by sexism in education and the workplace, then the obvious answer is to fight sex discrimination in these realms and help women gain parity in all areas of society. But by advocating that feminism means turning one's back on external progress for a fuzzy romp through an inner-child playground, Steinem promotes passivity. In terms of effecting societal change, *Revolution from Within* is about as helpful as a mouthful of warm Elmer's glue.

While a good deal of this passive inner focus was adopted from the self-help codependency/inner child movement, some is a new twist on older forms of feminist thought. Consciousness-raising is experiencing a major revival in feminist circles. One of NOW's 1991 resolutions, for example, pushed for more consciousness-raising because the "process of CR is never-ending." In NOW, a consciousness-raising session consists of a group of women sitting in a circle (no men allowed). Each takes a turn talking about personal issues while the others remain silent and nonconfrontational. A leader directs the group's focus and makes sure that there isn't any "cross talk" or criticisms.

While CR might have been helpful for women raised in eras where women didn't talk about their experiences with sexism—let alone talk about sex—my generation often finds it redundant. Unlike our mothers, we grew up in a world where issues such as sex discrimination, sexual harassment, abortion, birth control, homosexuality, and relationships are openly discussed. My friends and I have the kind of explicit talks about our sex lives and personal experiences that would give Jerry Falwell a heart attack. Talking to young women for this book, it didn't seem odd to me that women I had never met before would talk freely about their personal lives—like the group of restaurant workers who spent a good part of the interview describing their "first time" in gory detail or another young woman who offhandedly noted she was a lesbian as she poured me another cup of coffee. Yet my mother tells me such a thing would have been unthinkable in her day. And the truth is, even in the seventies, consciousness-raising was largely a fad for middle- to upper-class women. Working mothers often didn't have the time to devote hours a week to "raising their consciousness." They still don't.

But today consciousness-raising often has less to do with women sharing their feelings than with a method for feminists to indoctrinate women in current feminist ideology. Speaking in a workshop titled "NOW 101, an Intro to Consciousness-Raising" at the 1992 NOW national conference, New York chapter NOW president Diane Welsh claimed that consciousness-raising is necessary for activists to realize that "all issues are interconnected." The woman who goes to NOW because of "one burning issue" should be helped to understand that being active in feminism means adopting the entire feminist agenda. "They need to know—we need to know—that we are in it for the long haul and that everything is connected. That's one of the things I really love about NOW. It's a multi-issue organization. I think that's profoundly important for us to know. It's not one issue at a time. It's a very complicated and subtle revolution we're pursuing here, and CR does that."

What is this "complicated and subtle revolution"? For many feminists, the key to understanding "connections" between issues is something I call "transformative philosophy." "But we have seen that revolution is insufficient," Robin Morgan writes in her 1989 book, *The Demon Lover*. "*Transformation* is necessary to save ourselves, sentient life on the planet, the biosphere itself. Transformation requires that we recognize our own just anger as being so vast that mere violence could not possibly address it. . . . And transformation requires that we *act*, that we *step off the wheel, outside the prescribed boundaries altogether*."

But while Morgan says transformation requires that women "act," the actions required would not be recognizable as such to the casual observer. That's because this philosophy grew out of a grossly oversimplified interpretation of the chaos theory of physics popularized in books such as Fritjof Capra's *The Tao of Physics*. Essentially, this school of physics espouses that order and disorder are inseparable;

that the closer you look at apparent order—from a rain cloud to a subatomic particle—the more random and chaotic things become. This means that the smallest acts have an effect in large-scale structures and that because all things are interconnected, it is impossible to predetermine the precise effect of any act.

Many feminists, from Gloria Steinem, to Marilyn French, to Riane Eisler, have become enamored with transformative philosophy. In her book *The Chalice and the Blade*, for instance, Eisler expounds that "feminists and 'chaos' theories in fact have a good deal in common" because both "focus on *transformation*." Some have taken this theory in the broadest sense to mean that since all things are interconnected in some manner and that small acts have potentially vast effects, then even when their actions seem meaningless and ineffective, they're not. Meditating is deemed just as effective as gaining political office.

Since women are said to be more intuitive, sensitive, and nurturing than men, we alone are capable of stepping "outside the prescribed boundaries," as Morgan puts it, to make profound "connections" between issues. This connection making leads to enlightenment, and enlightenment in itself will automatically transform the world. As Steinem asserts in the *Revolution from Within*, which is heavily influenced by transformative philosophy, "In the short run, each self-conscious choice affects behavior, our own brain synapses, and sends out ripples of change to those around us." These ripples of change, she maintains, can be a veritable revolutionary force, capable of affecting "the environment of our generation, our descendents, our species, the adaptation of their behavior and brains, the recurrence of certain genes, and ultimately, evolution itself."

By directing our attention inward toward emotional responses such as intuitive feeling and warm, happy thoughts, feminist transformative theory promises that inner-directed small acts will have very large-scale effects. If enough of us make the choice to adopt the feminist worldview, then, presumably without any more effort on our parts, we'll usher in the foretold utopia.

The feminist infatuation with inner-directed "transformation" invokes the passive message of the Victorian age, when women were also told that true revolution would occur only from within. Told to turn to the Bible, prayer, and other internal pursuits from within the confines of her home, the Victorian woman was promised that by maintaining the moral purity of the private sphere, "the streams which flow therefrom will sweeten and purify all the rest."[30] Many middle- to upper-class women of the time did take this option—not many other paths gave them any other promise of influence, and it was one of the few realms in which society allowed women one iota of respect. Now feminists are asking us, under the guise of gaining self-esteem, to choose a similarly passive option.

Yet this mumbo-jumbo transformation notion has seen the movement scatter into areas only loosely connected—if at all—with the quest for women's rights. Feminists are making connections, and lots of them.

One of the fastest-growing transformative-based causes over the past few years is ecofeminism. Several organizations devoted to this movement have sprung up—such as the Los Angeles–based Ecofeminist Network—while feminist magazines including *New Directions for Women* and *Ms.* give gushing praise to its tenets. *Ms.*, in fact, has a section devoted to the subject in every issue. Some women's studies classes promote ecofeminism. At the University of New Hampshire, for example, students attending an introductory women's studies course find a section of the class devoted to "Ecofeminism: Our Mother Earth." It has yet to make much of a showing in national women's organizations, though in 1991, NOW did pass a distinctly ecofeminist resolution titled "Women and the Global Environment," and the inclusion of environmental issues into their third-party platform shows a definite influence.

A booklet entitled "What is Ecofeminism Anyway?"—put out by the New York City group Ecofeminist Visions Emerging—explains the basic theory behind this cause. "Although there is no one 'correct' ecofeminism, most ecofeminists would agree that the domination of women and the domination of nature is fundamentally connected. In other words, the violence against Mother Earth is directly linked to violence against women."

The idea is that oppression of women won't end until people stop exploiting the environment—in all ways, whether driving cars or using hair spray—and vice versa. This makes environmental activism fundamental to the women's movement. "It is our belief that man's dominion over nature parallels the subjugation of women in many societies, denying them sovereignty over their lives and bodies," asserts a declaration from the Women's Foreign Policy Council, cochaired by former congresswoman turned environmental activist Bella Abzug. "Until all societies truly value women and the environment, their joint degradation will continue."[31]

Or, as Robin Morgan writes in her September/October 1991 *Ms.* editorial: "The environment is a feminist issue not only because all issues are women's issues, and not only for the economic survival of most of us and the literal survival of all of us, but because women everywhere *have been* the background—the environment—against which patriarchy plays its deadly games. Isn't it time to revive the wildness in ourselves, to hiss and growl our anger, shriek and snarl it?"

Shrieking and snarling aside, ecofeminists have accomplished little. In Germany, they have taken leadership positions in the Green party, but in the United States ecofeminist activism is fragmented at best, confined to writings and workshops. This lack of effective action is understandable under ecofeminist theory, which takes feminist dictates against hierarchical thinking and political activism to extremes. As leader Karen J. Warren explained in an interview printed in the Spring 1991 issue of *Woman of Power* magazine, "what will *not* be part of that emerging ecofeminist quilt are patriarchal thoughts and practices, even if we do not know beforehand, so to speak, which thoughts and practices those are."

In step with the transformative notion that all issues are interconnected, some feminists have eagerly adopted the fight for animal rights, claiming that "animal oppression" and women's oppression are also linked. The group Feminists for Animal Rights, dedicated to ending all forms of "animal abuse," claims to have chapters in both the United States and Canada. "Violence against animals is born of the same mindset, accepted and perpetrated in all facets of our culture, from the food on our plate, to the clothing we wear, to the products we use," feminist animal-rights activist Hilary L. Martinson wrote in the March/April 1993 *New Directions for Women*. "Chilling, indeed, are the similarities between the exploitation of animals and our experiences as women in this sexist society." Martinson wrote the article from prison, where she was serving time—she had refused to post bail—for unsuccessfully attempting to free birds at a pigeon shoot.

Carol Adams, author of *The Sexual Politics of Meat: A Feminist-Vegetarian Critical Theory* and a leader of this cause, gives her proof of just how meat eating and oppression against women are linked. "I looked at records of women battered by men, and I found that over and over again women were battered right after serving a meal in which there was no meat."[32] Without a steak to chew on, she seems to say, men will turn on their wives.

But by denouncing the killing of any living creatures—whether for food or medical research—feminist animal-rights activists have found themselves facing an ironic internal contradiction regarding abortion rights. After all, if pigeons, cows, and presumably rats all have a right to live, then by logic feminists should condemn abortion. Adams tried to sneak around this one in an article promoting animal rights for the May/June 1991 Ms. "Some feminists fear that animal rights would set a precedent for the rights of fetuses. . . . But it is disingenuous to compare a fetus with a living, breathing animal. A fetus has potential interests; an animal has actual interests."

Of course, an anti-abortionist would argue that a fetus does have actual interests, the first being to stay alive. The right to abortion is extremely important, but protecting and advancing these rights doesn't mean we should ignore the experiences of many women who have undergone abortions—and who might tell Adams that their abortions were far more traumatic than stepping on a bug or eating barbecued chicken. To dismiss the grief, guilt, confusion, and other emotions that women often feel regarding abortion doesn't help abortion-rights arguments. It only gives anti-abortionists fodder for their famous claim that feminists and liberals care more about animals than people, and it turns off women who adamantly support abortion rights but want the movement to recognize that an abortion is not something women have and then forget about the next day.

While the majority of feminist leaders condone ecofeminism and animal rights—whether vocally or through silent acquiescence—there have been a few dissenting voices in the wilderness. "Equating ecology with feminism is something that irritates me," stated Simone de Beauvoir, author of The Second Sex. "They are not automatically one and the same thing at all." As de Beauvoir pointed out, the idea of "women and her rapport with nature" is the age-old formula for pinning women into traditional roles. "[W]omen are being defined in terms of 'the other,' " she claimed, "once again they are being made into the 'second sex.' "[33]

And as feminist Betty Roszack noted in a speech to the Swedish Green party, "By acknowledging a special relationship between women and nature, do we not reinforce the projection of male responsibility onto women as saviors of the world?"[34]

The answer is yes. "For although feminists do indeed want women to become part of the structure," writes Marilyn French, ". . . they do not want women to assimilate to society as it presently exists but to change it."[35] Meanwhile, many feminists are busy trying to gain equality with the ecosystem and animals in particular while ignoring the political landscape. Congratulating themselves for making grand connections among issues but accomplishing little, their voices are raised in a distracted cacophony: ignored, unheard, passive.

*　　*　　*

Not surprisingly, many of the causes endorsed by feminists today—the antiporn campaign, the promotion of lesbianism as a political action, sweeping new definitions of rape, and goddess worship—are noteworthy for avoiding or only peripherally addressing the subjects of economic and political equality. Instead of combating inequality in public realms, which would require working with the "patriarchal" system, current feminists blame societal mores, sexual literature, pop culture, and religion for women's problems and then offer little more than the promise of transformation to solve them.

The fact that current feminist causes have accomplished little and have left most women cold hasn't hurt their popularity in the movement. If anything, it has helped. Instead of critically examining the goals and methods of a cause when it proves unappealing and irrelevant (Do most women really want to see all men as potential rapists? Does it make sense to push antiporn legislation that will only be struck down as unconstitutional?), feminists point the finger of blame at the "patriarchy" or the "backlash" when their cries fall on deaf ears. Since feminists think the world is obviously out to thwart their efforts, this means that they must be on the right track, alone, fighting the good fight.

The more a cause fails in today's movement, the more it is heralded as truly revolutionary, truly feminist. The losing cause becomes the noble cause; the winning one, a sign of co-optation.

There is a growing suspicion among women that current feminists *don't want to win.* They have picked fights that are surefire bets for failure. And from women's studies directors to women's organization presidents, it isn't in many professional feminists' interests to declare victory. They'd be out of a job. The more gains the movement has made, the more it seems feminists feel they have to create new enemies and bigger battles in order to justify their existence. The closer women have come to gaining equality, the more feminists try to uncover and invent new ways in which they're oppressed. Thus, women's studies programs are no longer defended because other curriculums neglect women's history and works (which can and is being remedied), but because no matter how inclusive academia becomes, it will always be "phallocentric" by virtue of objective thinking, "male" language, and hierarchical structure. As the National Women's Studies Association puts it: "We in women's studies know, and we try always to teach our students, that feminism cannot occupy a central position in established academic inquiry." Why? Because "its very existence is predicated on de-centering that tradition."[36] In other words, the day we no longer need women's studies is the day when colleges teach nothing but feminist theory—which, of course, will be the day pigs fly. And women's organizations have largely abandoned the role of putting women in full partnership with men, dedicating themselves to working outside the system, espousing extremist causes, and pushing a "complicated and subtle revolution" through consciousness-raising and transformation.

The truly sad thing about this is that it is so unnecessary. Women still name the old issues as their concerns; we still want a movement to remedy these problems. And the devastating thing about it is that *achievable* goals such as an affordable and trustworthy child-care system have been swept aside for hopeless causes and sweeping theories exalting oppression and victimization.

The majority of women, unlike current feminists, do want to win. We don't want the "battle between the sexes" to last forever, painted in hopeless tones, perpetuated through male bashing and differing standards for women and men. We want a women's movement that promises to do something concrete to help improve our lives. We want a movement that *listens to us* and then works on the issues we care about.

And we want a movement that can offer the most empowering idea of all: that one day soon the movement will no longer be needed. That someday organized feminism will be something our daughters will read about in history books, like the abolitionist movement—not because it degenerated into extremist malarkey, but because it achieved its goal: equality between the sexes.

While women move ahead in their lives—with the tenets of equality entrenched firmly in their hearts—the women's movement itself has stalled. Trapped in a stagnant, alienating ideology, the only thing most of the feminist movement is heading toward is complete irrelevance.

We still need a women's movement: a movement to achieve complete equality between the sexes. Feminists of the second wave did a tremendous service for women, especially for women of my generation. We need to acknowledge their gains and identify the specifics of what still needs to be done, from advancements in birth control (many young women I talk to identify this as very important; we're tired of choosing between unhealthy and ineffective birth-control options), to the pressing issue of child care, to finally seeing true parity in politics.

What we don't need is what feminism stands for today.

Part III

THE NEW VICTORIANS

Chapter 7

REPEATING HISTORY: THE FEMINIST DESCENT INTO VICTORIAN MORALITY

"I fear that the women's movement is repeating the worst errors of a century ago. The nineteenth century feminist movement began as a radical critique of women's role and status. But it became increasingly conservative and similarly shifted the burden of its argument onto a reconstituted femininity in the form of alleged female moral superiority. Much of the nineteenth century movement degenerated into a variety of morality crusades, with conservative feminists pursuing what they took to be women's agenda in anti-prostitution, anti-masturbation, anti-obscenity, and anti-vice campaigns. It will be a historical tragedy of almost unthinkable dimensions if the revived feminist movement dissipates into a series of campaigns against recreational sex, popular music, and sexually explicit materials. But this appears to be the direction in which feminism is moving."
                        —GAYLE RUBIN, feminist writer, 1981.[1]

Yes, it would be a tragedy. And tragically, that is exactly what's happening.

Today's women's movement is retreating into the protective womb of Victorian values. Not every feminist, of course, conforms with each of the causes discussed in this book, and even among adherents there is often disagreement over theory and activism. But many do—Gloria Steinem, for example, advocates nearly every trend I've examined, from the prioritization of lesbian issues, to the antiporn campaign, to goddess worship—and where young women encounter the feminist movement, this vision is powerful, strident, and overwhelming.

From antisex campaigns to the development of a passive voice, running consistently through major feminist trends are disturbing similarities to Victorian messages: popular Victorian marriage manuals decrying intercourse as invasive and sullying; nineteenth-century portrayals of men as lust-filled predators and women as their helpless victims; the Victorian war against dirty pictures; the argument that women's involvement in politics would only destroy their "milder, gentler nature"; literature promising a utopian future based on the womanly ideals of nurturance, sensitivity, and maternal instinct, and, drilled into women from childhood on, an exaltation of martyred passivity masquerading as feminine superiority. Together, these movements and beliefs defined women's role in Victorian society.

Separately and together, many of today's feminist trends and causes are recreating that role.

Like their nineteenth-century sisters who gave birth to the first wave of feminism—and saw their movement stagnate and strangle—today's feminists are sowing the seeds of their own destruction. As feminist writer Gayle Rubin observes, Victorian-era feminists started out fighting for the vote, marriage reform, and equality in divorce and education. But in time, the suffragist agenda came to reflect the most repressive antifemale mores of the time, projecting an image of women as helpless victims in need of protection, not rights. Their antisex campaigns fit neatly into their view of women as more spiritual, ethical, moral, and nurturing than men. As a result, by the late 1800s, the suffragist movement was known as a "Puritan" revolt against "intemperance" and "impurity," promoting laws used to deny lower-class women autonomy and rights and reflecting the elitist concerns of privileged white women. By the late 1920s, largely due to the widespread alienation of young and working-class women from the cause, the first wave of feminism was dead.

The same thing is happening to the second wave of feminism. A movement that began in the 1960s with a fierce fight for economic, social, and political parity has degenerated into a series of repressive moral crusades that have little to do with most women's lives. The movement that once stood for equality for all women has come to stand instead for extremist and often irrelevant academic theories and the patronizing views held by an elitist group of largely privileged women. And a feminist label that began as a critique of the feminine mystique has revived all the confining ideals of that mystique. This isn't feminism. It's *femininity*—the exaltation of a single standard of belief and behavior for all women—and it has turned the movement away from inclusive equality to a strict Victorian orthodoxy. As a result, the movement today lacks support, especially from young and working-class women.

Without new energy to carry it forward, the second wave of feminism—like the first—will crest, leaving a whole generation stranded on the shore.

Feminism of the 1800s was a response to the incredibly confined, powerless, and exploited role of women in the Victorian era. For an example of a real patriarchy, the Victorian age stands as a shining symbol.

Let's examine the life of a woman born in 1837, the year Queen Victoria took the throne—and the popularly understood birth of Victorianism. Say this fictional woman was English, born into a well-to-do middle-class London family. The industrial revolution and commercial capitalism were making England, much of the continent, and, to an extent, the United States wealthy. This enabled the middle-class to enjoy comforts—servants, well-furnished homes, and time for entertainment and education—that had previously been restricted to the elite rich. But rapid urbanization and industrial exploitation also created terrible problems: unsanitary city slums packed with the bitterly poor, hazardous factory jobs, child labor, rampant disease, crime, and increasing hostility between the classes. Part of the response to these frightening developments was a strict authoritarian morality built around the ideals of industry, sobriety, chastity, and obedience. Nearly every social ill was said to come from immorality—especially female sexual immorality—and in this way, Victorians took sexual prudery and male dominance to new heights. Victorian morality shaped England, the United States, Canada, and much of Europe until the early 1900s.

This Victorian woman's training to become a proper matron would have started early. Dressed like a miniature lady—complete with immobilizing petticoats and even tightly laced corsets—she was to be quiet, obedient, and docile. "I was mute," a French Victorian-era woman summed up her childhood.[2] Our Victorian woman was reared to care for her family in what historian Pamela Horn aptly calls "a spirit of submission and self-sacrifice."[3] Her lessons as a child focused on Scripture, embroidery, and the art of good conversation. Though she would have learned how to read and write, doctors warned that serious education for girls would lead to nervous disorders, hysteria, sterility, uterine diseases, atrophied sex organs, and stillbirths in later pregnancies. Parents were warned not to let their daughters study too much, lest they turn "mannish" and disagreeable, without hope of ever finding a husband and damned to a lifetime of neuralgia and sexual aberrations.[4] Higher education was unthought of for women until the 1900s, and while some girls from upper-class families attended expensive day schools, the majority of middle-class girls got what little education they were granted at home.[5]

She would have grown up profoundly ignorant of sexuality. While boys learned about the sex act through informal schooling—one boy's school even recommended keeping dogs so young gentlemen could learn the basics of intercourse[6]—girls were kept completely in the dark. Her reading was expunged of even a kiss. Many families read Thomas Bowdler's *Family Shakespeare*—truncated versions of the plays, which became known as Bowdlerized, for that moralist's peculiar and prissy censorship. Diaries of girls in her time illustrate that many had no knowledge of sex or of male genitalia, even up until their wedding night.[7] Only after marriage was she to learn about sex, and even then, she was expected to regard it as an unnatural and repugnant act. British physician William Acton—widely read in the United States, as well—succinctly captured the Victorian sentiment on how decent ladies should view sexual desire. "I should say that the majority of women (happily for society) are not very much troubled with sexual feeling of any kind," Acton declared in 1857. "What men are habitually, women are only exceptionally."[8]

For middle-class Victorians, the notion that women were free of sexual desire became the locus of femininity, the pure center out of which spiritual refinement, morality, and caretaking grew. It was the defining characteristic of the good Victorian woman, and only through a lack of physical passion would she achieve her true calling as mother and spiritual adviser. "The higher a woman rises in moral and intellectual culture," asserted a nineteenth-century American author, "the more is the sensual refined away from her nature, and the more pure and perfect and predominating becomes her motherhood." As a result, by the 1870s, marriage manuals were applauding female frigidity "as a virtue to be cultivated, and sexual coldness as a condition to be desired."[9]

Coupled with the endorsement of sexual frigidity were dire warnings about what would happen should a woman slip. "Spasmodic convulsions" and "voluptuous spasms" in intercourse were said to make women barren, and sexual pleasure was often linked to uterine disease. Even sexual *thoughts* were linked to uterine disease. In the United States in the late 1800s, for example, mothers were warned not to let their daughters read "vulgar" works such as Chaucer, partake of hot drinks, indulge in waltzes, or dream of puppy love, all of which would inflame their senses and thus lead to diseased organs.[10]

It does seem odd that at the same time Victorians were adamantly insisting women had no natural sexual desire, numerous tracts were published decrying voluptuous orgasms, passion-inflaming erotica, and masturbation—implicitly admitting that women did indeed have sex drives. Dominating Victorian prudery was the unspoken belief that women were actually quite impure: that hidden under the veneer of angelic chastity, the sinful Eve still lurked. Victorians were deeply afraid that given a chance, female desire would once again expel them from the Garden. "[W]hen wicked, she is the most successful minister of ruin," declared American Victorian William G. Eliot in his *Lectures to Young Men*. "The best things perverted, become the worst. . . . Take from woman's character her love and practice of virtue, and her presence becomes death to the soul."[11]

This made it crucial to convince women that their sexuality was abnormal, if not physically dangerous. As society moved toward the 1900s, notions of female purity went hand in hand with increasing restrictions against birth control, masturbation, premarital sex, and sexual literature. If Victorians couldn't keep women from feeling sexual desire, at least they could keep them silent, ignorant, and deeply ashamed about it through a campaign of censorship and threats of unwanted pregnancy and disease, and especially threats of social ostracization. "In the past, as long as she repented, the woman who once sinned—like a male transgressor—could be reintegrated into the community," write John D'Emilio and Estelle B. Freedman on the Victorian period in their book *Intimate Matters: A History of Sexuality in America*. "Now, however, because woman allegedly occupied a higher moral plane than man, her fall was so great that it tainted her for life." William Acton, for instance, admitted there were "sad exceptions" of women with "sexual desires so strong that they surpass those of men, and shock public feeling by their consequences."

While there was a substantial sentiment that men should also avoid sex except for the purpose of reproduction, it was assumed that men were naturally lustful and couldn't help demanding what women were reluctant to give. By accepting all men as sexual predators and women as their chaste prey, Victorians implicitly condoned rape, especially within marriage. After all, they often believed that sex *was* rape for decent women. "It is true that the man is brutal," wrote French Victorian Auguste Debay in his best-selling 1849 marriage manual. "O Wives! Follow this advice. Submit to the demands of your husband in order to attach himself to you all the more. . . . Believe me, grant with good grace and without hesitation that which would be demanded by force. You well know, alas! that man, seized by desires, is impetuous, sometimes brutal."[12]

Assuming that our fictional Victorian woman married, Debay had some advice for her husband. Never "take roughly and by force what is refused" and "bill and coo like a lover" in order to inflame what little female desires she has, he recommended. But such advice could be ignored with little consequence. In one American case, for instance, a woman filed for divorce on the grounds that her husband raped her twice a night—despite the fact she suffered from a uterine disease brought on by childbearing that made sex extremely painful. The husband freely admitted to her charges, claiming he couldn't "control" himself. Though she originally won her freedom on grounds of cruelty, an appeals court reversed the decision because "a large proportion of married women assent [to intercourse] under exactly those conditions."[13]

Once married, Victorian women had few rights. Until the passage of the Married Women's Property Acts of 1870 and 1882, married English women were denied control over personal property and earnings.[14] Any money they took into the marriage was promptly taken from them. They were utterly reliant upon their husbands for everything.

Still, by Victorian standards, marriage would have made our woman one of the lucky ones. Spinsters were objects of pity and contempt. "Married life is a woman's profession; and to this life her training—that of dependence—is modelled," declared the English magazine *Saturday Review* in 1857. The article went on to condemn single women viciously: ". . . by not getting a husband, or losing him, she may find that she is without resources. All that can be said of her is, she has failed in business and no social reform can prevent such failures."[15] Few women of the day could financially afford such failure. The future of an "old maid" was frightening. The best many single women could hope for was the position of governess—a poorly paid, often extremely overworked job as household servant and nanny—and, at worst, sweatshop labor. The average wage for a working woman was below the subsistence level, and not every spinster was fortunate enough to have a father or brother willing to support her.[16]

If our Victorian woman's husband beat her, she had few places to turn. Wife beating was condoned. In the words of an 1840 English ruling: "The husband hath by law power and dominion over his wife and may keep her by force, within the bounds of duty, and may beat her, but not in a violent or cruel manner."[17] Divorce was almost impossible in England until 1857, and even after that it was very difficult for women to obtain. A woman had to prove her husband was guilty of incest, bestiality, or severe cruelty in *addition* to adultery. If she left him without a divorce, she automatically forfeited custody of their children as well as any claims to their property—including any money she brought into the marriage.[18] And if she was lucky enough to get a divorce and could manage to support herself and her children, she still faced ostracization. Divorce spelled social ruin for most middle-class women.

Despite the belief that sex violated and disgusted them, women's main role in life was to produce children, lots of children. Birth control was both illegal and considered against God's will, and even the finest Victorian ladies would conceive yearly. While nursemaids and governesses helped raise middle- and upper-class children, repeated pregnancies still took a sharp physical toll on many women. Diaries of the time tell of miscarriages, fevers, and other ills brought on by annual pregnancies, and many women were left invalids or died from the effects of bearing ten or more children and having many miscarriages in rapid succession. In one poignant case in 1857, a woman was warned that another child would certainly kill her—she had already had eleven children, as well as one miscarriage—but her husband was obviously not terribly concerned, as she died a few months after bearing her twelfth child at the age of forty-four.[19]

Outside of childbearing, our fictional woman's life was essentially empty by today's standards. Her role was to act, in the flowery terms of the day, as an "angel in the house."[20] This basically meant that she should be pliant, refined, passive, sweetly spiritual, and gently guide her husband's morality to a higher plane without ever contradicting his orders. Advances in the sciences, rather than liberating her, further confined her. At the age of thirty-four, she was likely accustomed to the view expressed by Charles Darwin in his 1871 *The Descent of Man*. "Man is more courageous, pugnacious and energetic than woman, and has a more inventive genius."

Medical theory also upheld inherent gender differences. It was believed that at menstruation a girl's intellectual and emotional development was halted, with all the body's energies going toward the uterus. As the controlling organ of her body, a woman's uterus determined her feminine traits, from sensitivity to intuition, and for this reason any interference with directing the body's energy to that organ was proscribed. Popular literature of the day aimed at middle-class women argued that they take to their beds during their periods, avoid spicy foods, and especially eschew any mental stimulation or intellectual pursuits. Neglecting this advice would lead to a "disordered pelvic life" and ill health.[21]

Here Victorian society employed a powerful double-edged argument against women's rights. On one hand, women's biology was said to make them too irrational and childlike to deal with such responsibilities as controlling their property or voting: "Grant suffrage to women, and you will have to build insane asylums in every county, . . ." asserted a nineteenth-century American legislator. "Women are too nervous and hysterical to enter into politics."[22] On the other hand, women were assured that their inferiority was in fact *superiority*. Only such sweet "simplicity and dignity which a perfect purity and innocence are sure to bestow," wrote a Victorian author, could result in the "angelical natures" of womanhood.[23] Women's role in life as the moral guardians of society was far too important, in fact, for them to "coarsen" it through equality.[24] Men, who were clearly the coarser sex, took it upon themselves to shoulder the demeaning burdens of political and economic power, the impure fields of medicine, sciences, arts and law, as well as the burden of property ownership and the crushing responsibility of social freedoms. And they would do it willingly enough, to protect women.

In this way, the belief that women were inherently passive, irrational, intuitive, nurturing, and sexually innocent was used both to praise and condemn them. "Woman is more pure, tender, affectionate, and patient than man," asserted an American marriage manual of the 1850s. "She is the counterpart of man—taken out of man, to comfort him like angels and to lighten his cares. She thinks less profoundly than men; sensibility is her power."[25] Rather than two contradicting beliefs, notions of female inferiority and female superiority were simply two sides of the same sexist coin. No matter how a woman tossed it, it always landed against her.

Ensconced in her parlor, our middle-class English woman would spend her days doing needlework and light housework, teaching her daughters Scripture, and entertaining guests. Exercise was unthinkable.

Her corsets prohibited more than a short walk. Laced incredibly tight—through a system of pulleys she would attach to her bedpost—corsets resulted in a variety of problems, including fractured ribs and atrophied lungs. The most hideous result was prolapsed uteruses. The pressure of the corset and lack of muscle tone often forced women's wombs to slip down their vaginas until their cervixes protruded from their bodies. As one doctor wrote in 1882, women laced their waists so tightly that it was all they could do "to keep the uterus inside the vagina."[26]

She was rewarded for illness and passivity and punished for vitality. As Barbara Ehrenreich and Deirdre English write in *Complaints and Disorders: The Sexual Politics of Sickness*, not only "were women seen as sickly—sickness was seen as feminine." The beauty standard was the martyred consumptive victim of popular literature, sweetly resigned to her deathbed in a floating white gown, with pale skin and tubercular bright red lips. Illness was fashionable, and the proper Victorian lady could expect to spend a good part of her life in bed. Elizabeth Barrett Browning, the extremely productive poet, spent six years in bed following the death of her brother in a boating accident.[27]

The cult of invalidism led to an epidemic of "hysteria" in the United States and England, with urban middle-class women throwing violent fits and fainting constantly. Ehrenreich and English point out that while hysteria was in many ways a power play—allowing women to manipulate male attention, avoid sex and thus pregnancy—as a social revolt it failed miserably. To doctors of the time, it only confirmed that women were irrational, unpredictable and controlled entirely by their uteruses. There, of course, may have been a real medical cause for at least some of Victorian women's constant fainting: extremely tight corsets. The quickest remedy for a faint was often a sharp knife, with which men would quickly cut the corset straps to allow air into collapsed lungs.[28] But this glorification of female helplessness left its mark on popular culture. Fainting into men's arms—complete with gloriously cascading hair and a palpitating, trembling chest—would become the hallmark of the romance heroine.

Chronically short of breath, suffocated, confined, and suffering from a variety of medical problems, our Victorian woman would have spent a good deal of time reclining indoors. Drawings of the time show her sisters immobilized in yards of fabric and tremendous hoop skirts, with pale skin, sunken eyes, and heavy masses of hair. Women are pictured most often at home, sitting stiffly in their parlors with a scrap of sewing or the pages of a letter in their laps, as children play quietly under the supervision of maids. When depicted on the street or at social events, women are immovable figures of impossibly massive crinolines and tiny waists, balancing precariously on men's arms and looking fashionably bored, removed, passive, and seriously ill.

It's important to note that these depictions of middle-class women were not necessarily the full truth. As Frances B. Cogan argues in *All-American Girl: The Ideal of Real Womanhood in Mid-Nineteenth-Century America*, at the same time the ideal of female helplessness reached its height, a contradicting school of thought decried it. Many doctors and writers were outspokenly opposed to the practice of wearing tight corsets and avoiding exercise. Their primary concern was fertility. Articles warned young men that marriage to the pale, sickly lady who tight-laced herself would result in a lack of children, while marriage to a healthy young woman with "ruddy cheeks" and unhampered waist would ensure a bounty of children and a happy home.

But many women remained faithful to the cult of female invalidism. Ruddy cheeks were still seen as vulgar, and some women even drank arsenic in an attempt to give their skin that fashionable pallor.[29] Paleness, lassitude, corsets, and helplessness all separated the middle-class woman from the despised working classes. They publicly illustrated her husband's ability to support a wife who was completely idle—or could at least pretend to be—and the display of status was a powerful motivation.

If our woman lived into an unusually old age for her time, she would have witnessed the growth of the first wave of feminism and the achievement of suffrage. In 1901, Queen Victoria died, and Victorian standards of morality began to subside. In 1919, at the age of eighty-two, she would have been granted the vote along with other English women over thirty. Women under thirty were denied the vote until 1928 because they were considered too "flighty."[30] But it's highly unlikely she would have lived that long. The life expectancy for people in better neighborhoods was around forty years; for the poor residing in the slums of St. Giles, only seventeen.[31]

Things would have been radically different for her had she been born into the lower class. Victorian ideals of female delicacy and moral purity didn't apply equally to working-class women. After all, someone had to do the laundry, housework, sewing, and other labor, tasks thought to be beneath proper ladies. In the late 1800s, roughly one in eight of all women and girls in England and Wales were working in domestic service.[32] Female servants—who typically entered service at age twelve or so—spent long days hauling wood and coal for the stoves, cleaning fireplaces, scouring cooking pots and dishes, boiling and then scrubbing clothes on washboards, and other heavy labor. "I am up at half past five and six every morning and do not go to bed till nearly twelve at night," one English girl servant wrote in 1870, "and I feel so tired sometimes I am obliged to have a good cry."[33] For her labor, she would be paid a measly sum, and her best hope was to slave for a decade or more until she had collected enough money for a dowry.

Factories and mills in England and the United States also relied on the cheap labor of women and children to produce clothing and other commodities. The average working woman's wage was less than half of men's, and fourteen-hour shifts in stifling, dangerous workshops were not uncommon. Lower-middle-class women worked long hours for their husband's business, while schoolteaching and nursing—though badly paid—offered some degree of respect and independence for educated single women.[34]

Unlike their "angelic" middle-class counterparts, working women were seen in barnyard terms. Considered healthy as sows and believed to enjoy vigorous constitutions, they were seen to be conveniently unaffected by ill-paid hard labor and filthy living conditions. The truth, of course, was that poor women suffered far more from reproductive problems and ill health than their supposedly daintier sisters. The Victorian lady took to bed during her periods, pregnancy, and for the slightest upset. But her maid, the factory girl, and the American black field laborer were expected to labor twelve or more hours a day, day in and day out, through pregnancies and illness, and then return home to cottages or one-room tenements to raise their families without access to clean water or adequate sanitation. In rural areas of England, village women produced cloth and other commodities, as well as labored in the fields and raised children. On the American frontier, women worked side by side with men, clearing fields, harvesting, building homes, and performing endless other labors of settling new country—in addition to cooking, canning, cleaning, sewing, and raising broods of children. Their journals tell of frantic long days spent working nonstop, and their obituaries speak clearly of their harsh lives and early deaths. Though seen as free from most middle-class female ailments, the poor and working-class woman was still viewed as tainted. In England, she was held responsible for spreading the germs of typhoid and venereal diseases. In the United States, black and immigrant women held the additional threat of undermining racial purity by populating the country with their "inferior" offspring.[35]

And life would also have been far different for our Victorian woman if she had been born into the upper class. While rich women were also constrained by the lack of rights and stifling ideals of femininity, they alone had the benefit of sometimes being financially independent enough to rebel. Victorian women who made the history books—such as Florence Nightingale—tended to come from affluent backgrounds. Much as in our time, the rich were not held to the same rules that the middle class imposed upon themselves and upon the poor. The middle class may have condemned drink and fought against saloons in poor neighborhoods, but it was implicitly acknowledged that they could continue to enjoy a little tipple on their fine estates.[36] The rich woman also had other advantages: She tended to be better-educated and had access to birth control and abortion through discreet doctors. Victorian prudery was largely a middle-class invention and obsession.

Though surrounded with flowery praise, the middle-class woman was often held in as much contempt by society as her despised lower-class counterpart. Her life may have been easier, but it was just as constrained in many ways. She inherited one of the most lasting legacies of the Victorian era—the pedestal. If she acted as a spiritual beacon, a moral voice, an angel in the house, she was then assured her rightful place in society as the better sex. This position required her complete compliance and passivity; the reward was eternal martyrdom in the name of gentle and refined womanhood. Nearly everything she was taught was skewed: Denying her an education was good for her mental health; sexual repression would make her more fertile and a better mother; being forbidden public office and property ownership were actually rewards for her superior nature; denial of voting rights protected her from insanity; and lack of contact with the public world ensured her spiritual growth.

The Victorian pedestal was not a pedestal at all. Women of the time did not occupy a higher plane than men; they occupied a prison. No amount of romanticized claptrap about female superiority diminished the contempt women suffered. Victorian women were expected to be pure: sexually, spiritually, and morally. As the better sex, they were trapped in a cage of high expectations that effectively prevented them from achieving equality with men inside of male-based institutions. Women, the Victorians preached, were above all that.

But no transparent justification that the male burdens of political and economic power were beneath the better sex could completely stave off women's rebellion against their secondary status.

It's not surprising that the repressive, patriarchal nature of Victorian society inspired the first feminist movement. "He has made her, if married, in the eyes of the law, civilly dead," the 1848 Seneca Falls declaration asserted. "He has taken from her all right to property, even to the wages she earns. . . . He has denied her the facilities for obtaining a thorough education, all colleges being closed against her. . . . He has created a false public sentiment by giving to the world a different code of morals for men and women." This seminal declaration of women's grievances was written by early feminists who had gathered at Seneca Falls, New York.[37] From the mid-1800s to the early 1900s, increasing numbers of women in Europe and North America organized to free women from legal, economic, and moral bondage. In England, feminists won battles that allowed married women to control their earnings (1878), control their property (1882), attend universities such as Oxford and Cambridge (1870), and, finally, vote (1919).[38] In the United States, early feminists fought similar campaigns, culminating, finally, in winning suffrage in 1920.[39]

While the first wave of feminism gained women many rights, the movement had become increasingly fragmented through the late 1800s. Though feminists would come together to win the vote, that victory would signal their final hour, with the first wave of feminism sliding into obscurity soon after. By the end of the 1920s in the United States and England—less than a decade after the vote was won—the movement would be nearly dead, and for young women of the time, completely irrelevent.

The reasons for the untimely demise of early feminism is complex. But a key factor was feminists' involvement in the influential social purity crusades of the day. Social purity was a euphemism for sexual prudery (Victorians were squeamish about saying things directly). This Victorian movement was concerned with enforcing strict sexual standards, from censoring birth-control information to punishing women who dared engage in premarital sex. In short, the social purity movement was an effort to force sexuality—especially female sexuality—into the narrow confine of silence, with the single goal of intercourse being reproduction within marriage. What started as a grass-roots cause in the mid-1800s had become broad-based national movements in North America and England by the 1890s, including national purity congresses and purity organizations.[40] Temperance workers, clergy, and suffragists all came together on common ground. And at the forefront of the movement—for a time—were early feminists.

As feminist historian Judith R. Walkowitz explains, suffragist involvement in social purity crusades started as an honest concern over the difficult lives of prostitutes.[41] But this concern was quickly diverted into a feminist war against male "vice" and female sexual and reproductive freedoms. And when this war was over and the smoke cleared, the damage could be assessed: The victims were women, especially lower-class women.

In England, this war started in the 1870s, when Josephine Butler and other feminists called for a repeal of the Contagious Diseases acts, a blatant piece of persecution aimed at prostitutes. Women accused of prostitution were forced to undergo medical examinations and faced heavy penalities, while male customers went free. To promote their campaign against the Contagious Diseases acts, feminists published vivid tales of prostitutes as the innocent victims of coercion, leaning heavily on references to instrumental rapes (with speculums) during forced examinations. These sensational stories, however, soon took on overblown tones of female victimization, centered on notions of female sexual purity and helplessness. Posters begging men to protect "their" women were printed, reinforcing women's position as powerless property. These early feminists argued that rather than being "fallen" women—who must be punished for their sins—prostitutes were instead the ultimate victims of men: violated by male penises, male laws, and the "steel penis," the speculum. Women, they insisted, were coerced into the trade and never chose it.[42]

It must be recognized that for many people of the time, a prostitute was any woman who had sex outside of marriage. Along with full-time prostitutes, there were occasional prostitutes (women who slipped in and out of the business when they needed money) and a substantial subculture of young working-class women who had premarital sex in return for gifts, attention, or simple pleasure. For many lower-class women, this spectrum of "prostitution" could allow options and freedoms that chastity and marriage could not. Women were able to gain semi-independence by becoming the mistresses of well-off "benefactors" and many women in the theater made their living not from performances but from liaisons. Compared to the paltry wages earned working in sweatshops or as servants, full- and part-time prostitution often offered women a decent living. And compared with stifling middle-class morality, which promised punishment for the woman who fell from grace (an unmarried female servant who got pregnant, for example, was immediately fired without a thought to her circumstances), working-class culture often wasn't as harsh toward women who had sex outside of marriage. Many prostitutes and promiscuous young women went on to live "respectable" lives within their lower-class neighborhoods.[43]

Yet for feminists steeped in middle-class morality, the prostitute was automatically a shamed victim. And because of the nature of her victimization—sullied by sexuality—she was far from an equal. This attitude did not contradict the feminist stance against viewing prostitutes as fallen women. By asserting that all prostitutes were forced into the trade, feminists reinforced notions that decent women never consent to sex without coercion. This refusal to acknowledge that prostitutes and "loose" women may have made their own choices saw feminists portraying them as pathetic, defiled victims who needed to be saved from further impurity, not as human beings entitled to respect and open communication.

In short, the prostitute became the perfect martyr: worthy of salvation but never worthy enough to enter your house. Feminist leader Josephine Butler pleaded in a speech to save those victims who were not yet "dead to shame" and still had womanly "modesty."[44] By renouncing sexuality, some women were thought to be capable of a limited rehabilitation.

The propaganda was effective. As Walkowitz writes, the campaign to repeal the Contagious Diseases acts brought thousands of women into the political arena for the first time. Public sentiment was aroused, and the acts were suspended in 1883.[45]

Instead of relaxing their moral stand after achieving this victory, however, suffragists became even more embroiled with the subject of sex trade, turning to "traffic in women" and child prostitution. Using the tactic of sensationalism in the press again, Butler and other feminists were behind the infamous "Maiden Tribute" articles of 1885. This relatively juicy and sex-laden series on prostitution—lovingly detailed with stories of virgins kidnapped and thrown into locked rooms with lustful wealthy men—was so popular that mobs rioted at the offices of London's Pall Mall Gazette after the paper ran out of copies. Walkowitz points out that while there was probably some truth in the "Maiden Tribute" articles, there were probably many distortions, as well. Most of the women involved in prostitution at the time weren't unwitting child victims of entrapment by cunning men, as much as they were adult victims of economics.[46]

But the image of the prostitute as a child victim raped by rich men played into current societal views of female helplessness as well as an underlying hatred of the upper classes. Stamping out prostitution meant saving innocent children and protecting middle-class female virtue, and it provided an acceptable way to denounce the patriarchs of society without openly challenging their power. It did not mean remedying the incredible economic inequality that put women into prostitution in the first place; such measures would have made a devoutly sexist and classist Victorian society uncomfortable. The feminist voice on prostitution thus became subverted, advocating the *protection* of women *within* traditional sexist society instead of advancing their rights. Nothing makes this clearer than the huge demonstration held at Hyde Park in 1885, where feminists joined hands with Anglican bishops. Young "virgins dressed in white" and decent ladies carried banners plaintively pleading MEN, WAR ON VICE, INNOCENTS WILL THEY BE SLAUGHTERED and SIR PITY US.[47]

Where once the suffragists fought to overturn discriminatory legislation against prostitutes, now they were forming alliances with conservative men and heralding new and even more punitive laws. The result, writes Walkowitz, was "a particularly nasty and pernicious piece of omnibus legislation," the Criminal Law Amendment Act of 1885. This gave police great power over working-class women, from prosecuting "disorderly" boardinghouses to harassing women walking alone on the streets. It also made "indecent acts" between men a crime—the legal basis for prosecuting male homosexuals in Britain until 1967.[48]

Rather than used to halt child prostitution, this legislation was mostly enforced against poor adult women. It dramatically changed the structure of prostitution, with devastating effects for the women involved. Full-time prostitution up to that time was largely a brothel industry maintained by women. While these brothels varied from squalid shacks to fancy houses, they at least offered prostitutes some degree of safety and economic autonomy: Many women were assured food and a roof over their heads as well as protection from the authorities.[49] But under this feminist-driven law, the brothels were closed, forcing prostitutes to work on the streets, where they had to rely on male pimps for protection. The industry became even more dominated by men, and prostitutes were driven out of their homes into far more degrading and dangerous circumstances. Thrown out of their communities, occasional prostitutes were now denied a chance of integrating into society, thus becoming permanently trapped in the trade. Far from eradicating prostitution, these feminists only drove them underground—and once out of sight, the prostitute suffered more.[50]

But by then, early feminists were on a roll. Convinced they had found the root of all evil—male lust—they waged an all-out assault against anything that might promote sex, including sexual literature and birth control. Josephine Butler and friends took part in the National Vigilance Association, an antiporn group. In those days, porn was even more ill-defined than today. The NVA attacked birth-control literature and advertisements for abortion pills on the grounds they led to prostitution; they burned "obscene" books and rallied against nude paintings; they successfully prosecuted the distributors of such vile works as Balzac and Rabelais. It was all done for the protection of women, of course—such "pornographic literature" only led to "undifferentiated male lust."[51] The dainty and sexless female had to be protected from such violence-causing materials.

Across the Atlantic, American suffragists also went whole hog for social purity causes. Joining forces with clergymen in 1874, American feminists succeeded in overturning a St. Louis law allowing for regulated prostitution, and on the West Coast, feminists petitioned state legislatures to close down brothels and enforce vagrancy laws against streetwalkers. By the 1880s, suffragists in the States had successfully driven many prostitutes out of their homes and communities. Their campaigns bred measures used to repress lower-class women under the guise of protecting virtuous middle-class girls, such as punitive policies against women who attended dance halls or other places of disrepute. American social purity feminists also attacked "impure" literature. The Women's Christian Temperance Union—which was the major force for suffragism in the West and Midwest—established a department to suppress porn. One of their successes was keeping the sculpture *Bacchante and Infant* (a nude woman dancing joyously with an infant) by Frederick MacMonnies from being displayed at the Boston Public Library.[52]

Following their sexual purity ideals, many feminists became firmly convinced that birth control was evil. The use of "preventive checks" would only help men have sex outside of marriage, they argued, and turn women into "instruments" of men, thus making them prostitutes. "No woman should ever hold sexual relations with any man," expounded an American feminist in 1873, "from the possible consequences of which she might desire to escape."[53] Any separation of sexuality from reproduction—whether birth control, pornography, masturbation, or prostitution—was now held by feminists to be, oddly enough, antifeminist. The feminist purity campaigns of the 1800s thus cemented one of the foundations of sexism: denying women the right and ability to chose when to conceive.

And what were the results of the early feminist purity crusades in both England and the United States? Walkowitz details how, by the late 1880s, English feminists "had lost considerable authority in the public discussion over sex to a coalition of male professional experts, conservative churchmen, and social purity advocates."[54] A number of women left the National Vigilance Association when it became apparent the group was persecuting the "poorest, most helpless and most forlorn of womankind," and, Butler publicly warned other feminists she had learned it was "fatuous" to believe "you can oblige human beings to be moral by force."[55]

And in the United States, National American Woman Suffrage Association president Elizabeth Cady Stanton became alarmed at the growing popularity of purity causes in the movement. When some of her colleagues began promoting laws *restricting* women's ability to divorce—in order to "protect" woman from immorality—Stanton blew a fuse, and she took to the podium at an 1890 national suffrage convention to denounce them to their faces. Needless to say, Stanton's condemnation of purity causes (she claimed that what "constitutes chastity changes with time and latitude"), combined with her outspoken secular stance, saw her ostracized from the movement.[56]

But by the time feminists such as Butler woke up, it was too late. The causes they had expounded were out of their control. Their organizations, such as the NVA, were co-opted by conservatives, and their crusades had bequeathed laws that were being used for distinctly antifeminist aims.

Their work spawned repressive public policies in both England and the United States, from the Criminal Law Amendment Act of 1885 to the White Slavery Act of 1910.[57] Once enacted, these policies were enforced not by the feminists who had endorsed them, of course, but by the men in power. Under the guise of protecting women from prostitution and sexual immorality, society used these laws to punish women who stepped outside its proscribed lines. Women were denied social provisions for cohabiting with a man, denied jobs if they had criminal records (ex-prostitutes), and faced harsh punishment if they sought an abortion.[58] And yet despite the clearly oppressive results of their crusades, the feminist infatuation with purity causes continued into the early 1900s, when leaders even began arguing that the age of consent for women be raised to twenty-one.[59]

Given such results, it seems odd that these early feminists would have promoted such antifemale policies. But the women involved in the first wave of feminism were overwhelmingly middle-class, and they were not free from the values so popular with their peers. Deeply embedded beliefs in gender differences were reinforced by the purity campaigns and came to be used as arguments for the vote. "I say, if you believe in chastity," feminist Susan B. Anthony declared in 1900, "if you believe in honesty and integrity, then do what your enemy wants you not to do, which is to take the necessary steps to put the ballot in the hands of women."[60] Many feminists were also extremely classist and racist. American feminists, for example, used fear of lower-class immorality and the black vote as arguments for the women's vote.[61] And the majority were as prudish and fearful of sex as the next Victorian.

Their vision deeply colored by their own middle-class values, these early feminists seldom questioned the effects their sexual purity crusades had on women. They were incredibly naïve about how law works, seeming to assume that conservatives would use feminist-driven policies on sexuality for feminist aims, which proved absurd. And sexual purity had been one of the few weapons middle-class women had: It was the requirement for the financial security of marriage and it was a tool to be used to keep sex, and thus reproduction, under women's control. The idea that women would control when to have children—even by pleading an inherent repugnance to intercourse—was in many ways a step forward.

But this step was considerably hindered by the moral basis of feminist arguments. Unable to extricate themselves from middle-class morality, suffragists found themselves using traditional anti-erotic rhetoric—"degrading," "lustful," "impure"—to advance their case for reproductive control. This inflammatory moralistic language squashed reasonable discussion, prohibited any honest appraisal of women's experience, and placed the crux of the feminist position smack in the middle of antifeminist conservatism. By relying on sensational tales of victimization to sell their campaigns, early feminists deliberately provoked a public hysteria that led, under the guise of protecting women, to even more restrictions. And by naming *sex* as the root cause of sexism, feminists found themselves advocating chastity over birth control, protection over rights, and regulation over freedom. After all, if you honestly believe that sex is degrading, then supporting laws against birth control and easily available divorce makes sense. The result was that by 1894, a woman's journal of the time would note that feminism was a "revolt that is Puritan and not Bohemian. It is an uprising against the tyranny of organized intemperance, [and] impurity . . ."[62]

This revolt played directly into separate-sphere ideals for men and women. It is important to realize that the idea that the less lustful one becomes, the closer to God one grows is an old and still powerful belief. By promoting gender differences in sexuality ("undifferentiated male lust" and female sexual abhorrence), suffragists played into gender-difference beliefs in other realms as well, invoking the very notions of angelic femininity used so successfully against women. In the United States, for example, leading suffragist Sarah M. Grimké claimed that because "the sexual passion in man is ten times stronger than in woman," women were naturally superior to men.[63] As Walkowitz writes, one of the effects of the purity campaigns was that analysis of male dominance in mainstream feminism came to rely on a separate-sphere ideology, "implying that women were moral, 'spiritual' creatures who needed to be protected from animalistic, 'carnal' men." The 1913 slogan for an English suffragist organization called the Women's Social and Political Union captured this sentiment succinctly: "Votes for Women and Chastity for Men."[64]

In a nutshell, the early feminist purity crusades saw the movement promoting the very beliefs and laws they had once fought against. Once begun, these repressive campaigns carried the movement inexorably toward an antifeminist ideology. They opened a Pandora's box of conflicting ideas: The movement had to chose between basing its position in individualism (the right of women to be judged as people and not a gender and to enjoy personal freedoms, independence, and equality with others) or in the notion of a collective good based on gender differences (the rights of women being reliant on their supposed superiority and secondary to what is considered good for society and good for them). Sadly, the feminists chose the latter position. In this way, they found themselves working *against* women's rights, from birth control to obtainable divorce, because such rights threatened the belief that women were the moral saviors of an immoral society.

By playing into traditional sexist notions of female victimization and moral purity, early feminists ensured their own arguments would be used against them. Some antisuffragists, for example, argued that women would get raped at the polls if given the vote.[65] And using the day's feminist language of victim mythology, American tracts on white slavery in the early 1900s insisted that it was unsafe for a woman to go anyplace—even an ice cream parlor—without an escort.[66] This did not help feminist arguments for women's ability to enter the public sphere.

While engaged in purity campaigns, feminists were still pursuing the vote. Women's staunch patriotism and conduct in World War I— from entering the workforce to nursing soldiers—helped sway public opinion toward the suffragists, and the vote was granted. But that victory signaled the movement's demise in both England and the United States. The death of the first wave of feminism was due to a set of factors, including the war. Many leading feminists promptly dropped their banners to focus exclusively on war work, and they never managed to quite get it back together. After winning the vote, many organizations disbanded, seeing that victory as the end-all. A few groups continued to fight for equality in divorce and child custody, but by the end of the twenties those groups were also on the wane.[67]

Yet as feminist writer Varda Burstyn notes, the feminist purity crusades "contributed much to the dissipation of the first wave of feminism."[68] This came about in several ways. Through endorsing the state regulation of sexual behavior, suffragists further cemented male dominance over women—a policy that feminists of our time suffered from as they fought restrictions against birth control, abortion, sexual expression, and homosexuality. And by fusing the feminist position into a repressive old-fashioned morality, suffragists found their movement frozen into place as history began to pass them by, unable and unwilling to welcome younger women and working women into the movement.

"Feminism also failed to take roots in the 1920s because by and large it did not appeal to the young women of that generation," writes Lois W. Banner in *Women in Modern America*. "No movement can long prosper without attracting younger members to its ranks." As Banner explains, young American women of the 1920s had other concerns. And foremost among these was a rebellion against Victorian morality and sexual taboos.

The twenties became the age of the flapper, with an emphasis on freer sexuality and a loosening of social mores and confining gender roles. Young women, thanks to the efforts of earlier feminists, were now entering college, pursuing careers, and demanding the same rights as men. Much to the horror of older women—including feminists—these demands for equal treatment included smoking cigarettes, drinking liquor, going to dance halls in short skirts, and openly advocating birth control. While today we think of birth control as a feminist issue, at that time the charge was led largely by socialists. By 1916, the birth-control movement had grown into a national cause, and public sentiment began changing from an anti–birth control stance to a pro–birth control position. But it was the younger generation and the socialists at the forefront of the movement, not the feminists.[69] The unwillingness of feminists to endorse the birth-control movement helped contribute to their own downfall.

In many ways, the youth rebellion of the twenties was shallow, focusing more on pleasure and personal freedom than on concrete societal gains. But it did have a lasting effect. Strictures against birth control began to loosen, and by the 1930s, contraception was widely supported, especially by working-class women. In 1938, the sale of birth control (such as condoms and diaphragms) was legalized in the United States.[70] But inequality remained. Had women of the 1920s been able to count on the support of the feminist movement, this young generation might have been able to give their concerns the weight they deserved. Without an organized effort to change the underlying economic, political, and social structures upholding sexism, the flapper movement of this era petered out as little more than a fad. The double standards that punished women under the guise of protecting them remained very much a part of American life. On college campuses, for example, young women were expelled for behavior allowed men—in one 1924 case, a female student was dismissed for smoking cigarettes in public, sitting on the lap of a male while riding in a car on public streets, and other "indiscretions."[71]

By the time my mother came of age in the 1950s, Victorian strictures had translated into the feminine mystique: the passively happy housewife, sexually innocent until marriage and then properly complacent about her lack of power. My mother, like many middle-class women of her time, was raised to believe that only sluts had sex before marriage; that the only path to happiness was caretaking a husband and children; and that to pursue a career or to want an equal voice in society was a sign of some weird Freudian complex like penis envy.

It would not be until the 1960s, when middle-class women began to rebel against the pedestal of the feminine mystique, that feminism would turn into the massive organized movement of the 1970s. In fact, the repressive notions of femininity fostered by the suffragists were part of the impetus for the second wave of feminism. As Ellen Carol DuBois writes in her 1981 book, *Elizabeth Cady Stanton/Susan B. Anthony*, the "suffragists' decision to rely on the biological fact of gender to unite women, rather than on more political factors, may well have helped strengthen and rebuild coercive sexual stereotypes, thus contributing to the creation of a new version of 'true womanhood' against which a future feminist movement would eventually emerge to protest."

The similarities between current feminism and the sad plight of the first wave of feminism—as well as to Victorian mores in general—are frightening.

Like the suffragists, today's feminists have embarked on a sexual purity crusade. In their campaigns against heterosexuality, pornography, and in their sweeping redefinitions of rape, feminists echo the Victorians in declaring male lust the root of all evil. And following the path of the suffragists, they rely heavily on sensational stories of female victimization to sell these campaigns. From inflated rape statistics to antiporn slide shows claiming all porn consists of women being raped and abused, these lessons revive notions of female sexual purity and helplessness. As the suffragists claimed about prostitutes, today's feminists claim about the "institution" of heterosexuality and about pornography: Women, they insist, are always coerced into sex and never choose it.

By pushing this vision of women as the eternal victims of men's lust and brutality, today's feminists have turned the crux of their position from advancing women's rights to advocating our protection *within* traditional sexist society. The suffragists ignored economic issues in their war against prostitution and "male vice," instead joining hands with conservatives to push punitive legislation; today's feminists ignore economic issues in their war against pornography and heterosexual sex, instead joining hands with conservatives to push censorship. And just as the suffragist campaigns against prostitution, sexual material, and birth control had little to do with stopping violence, the current feminist sexual purity crusade has little to do with stopping rape. What it is really about is a profoundly antisex, antifreedom, and ultimately anti–women's rights perspective—one that, just like that of the Victorians, is willing to sell our rights down the river under the guise of protecting us from men.

In returning to Victorian ideals of sexual purity, current feminists seem drawn to make other Victorian declarations of female difference, as well: that women are intuitive, magical, sensitive, pacific, nurturing. Through goddess religion, patriarchal theory, and the passive voice, feminists have simply re-created another Victorian prison masquerading as a moral pedestal. It is noteworthy that difference feminists exalt traditional maternal traits while studiously ignoring female sexuality. Like the suffragists, who argued for women's vote on the basis of female chastity, honesty, and integrity, today's feminists have found sexual purity campaigns lead to promoting a vision of women as superior in *all* realms. A perfect example of this can be found in many women's studies classes. At Dartmouth, for instance, students taking the "Sex, Gender, and Society" class begin with several works promoting a victim-centered, puritanical view of female sexuality, including an essay by Catharine MacKinnon that declares, "Men see rape as intercourse; feminists say much intercourse 'is' rape"; an antiporn essay by Alice Walker; and the feminist film *Killing Us Softly*, which claims even the most seemingly innocuous advertisements are pornographic and degrade women. Having established female purity and victimization in the realm of sexuality—much like suffragist banners pleading SIR PITY US—the class moves on to establish the same in spirituality and morality. Carol Christ's "Why Women Need the Goddess" is taught alongside other essays applauding "feminine" spirituality. Ursula LeGuin espouses a cosmic female morality and Adrienne Rich teaches a "truly womanly idea of honor" under the section titled "Women's Stories: Contemporary Feminine Voices." Carol Gilligan's writing then extols women's "ethic of care" in a section on "Women's Experience." After midterm break, the students return to a barrage of material castigating female "collaborators" in heterosexuality, including Adrienne Rich's influential essay "Compulsory Heterosexuality" and works by Marilyn Frye and Charlotte Bunch that push separatism. The pedestal is given a final polishing under a section on the "The Family," with Sara Ruddick's regressive portrayal of women as peace-loving, gentle nurturers. With few exceptions, this entire class is dedicated to feminist works advocating women's supposed superiority, whether in sex, spirituality, or ethics; and with few exceptions, it advocates, implicitly and explicitly, that this superiority means we should withdraw from the world of men.

Because now, like the Victorian woman trapped on her moral pedestal, we are held to be above the coarse, dirty nature of mankind, with its "masculine" horrors, such as competition, aggression, lust, strength, courage, and equality. Instead, our true calling is in the realm of sexual morality, prayer, and magic. We are supposed to save our culture from the immoralities of sex, male lust, and heresy (praise the goddess), save the earth from destruction, save society from war, and save animals from slaughter, and we're supposed to do it all without dirtying our fair hands with political power. We are asked, in the name of feminism, to exalt the very ideals that were used to deny our mothers and grandmothers their rights.

Together, these feminist trends form New Victorianism. They have changed the feminist agenda from fighting for equality and choice to promoting socially, sexually, and politically repressive ideals. They have created, in writer Ellen Carol DuBois's words, another version of "true womanhood," a static, confining, sexist ideal of femininity. They have seen today's feminists, like the suffragists, arriving at a devoutly antifeminist ideology, a movement based on the notion of women as the moral saviors of an immoral world. And like the descent into repression by the first wave of feminists, this New Victorianism poses a profound danger to women's rights.

Not only is New Victorianism a diversionary waste of time and effort; it has the potential to turn back the tide of women's progress. At a time when the differences between men and women's lives are less distinct than ever before—with both sexes promised equal education, working side by side in previously male-dominated fields and seeing eye-to-eye on issues such as abortion—feminists have revived antiquated notions of gender differences. At a time when women are finally free to pursue the same activities as men—from entering law school to playing in rock bands—feminists are declaring such freedom is unsafe. Date-rape brochures warn young women not to go to men's rooms unchaperoned. (Heaven forbid they would even want to.) The movement applauds legislation designed to ban sexually oriented literature. Popular feminist literature ominously reports that working within male systems corrupts feminine nature. And from women's studies classes to mainstream organizations, restrictions such as these are called necessary.

As with the outcome of the first wave of feminism, this agenda has bred repressive policies that are clearly designed to prohibit consensual sexual activity and women's personal freedoms. On some campuses, hysteria over date rape has led to rules against overnight dorm guests of the opposite sex.[72] At least two dozen universities have banned sexual relations between faculty members and students under the guise of protecting young women from "unequal" power relations. The University of Iowa sums up the feminist-supported view: "Amorous relationships between faculty members and students are wrong when the faculty member has professional responsibility for the student. . . . Voluntary consent by the student in such a relationship is suspect, given the fundamentally asymmetric nature of the relationship." In other words, an adult female student is no better than an impressionable, easily misled child, her consent "suspect," unworthy of respect, and meaningless.[73] Forget that an eighteen-year-old female student is an adult who has a right to have sex; forget that a twenty-five-year-old woman may be perfectly capable of having a relationship with a graduate teaching fellow her own age (or, for that matter, a thirty-year-old assistant professor) without being "used."

For young women today, choice, respect, and empowerment are not the feminist message. My younger sister, for example, tells of the rape information given at her college. Though the school has reported only one rape in several years and the campus is well lighted and patrolled by security guards, she, along with all the other women in her dorm, was told that if she wants to go out at night—even just to the store two blocks away—she needs to call an escort. The names on the list of escorts she was given were *all men*. Once again, women are being treated as helpless little babies in need of protection; once again, men are being presented as holding tremendous power over us—as sexual predators who rape, as knights in shining armor who chaperone. And like the Victorian tracts on white slavery that argued it was unsafe for women to go anyplace—even an ice cream parlor—without a male escort, we are told, once again, it is all for our own good. I almost shook with anger when I read that list. Here was my sister in front of me, an intelligent, strong, capable person whose judgment I trust, and here was a group of women, calling themselves feminists, who would like her to believe that she is as defenseless as a lamb without men's protection. Here was a group of women, saying they represent her interests, who want her to believe she isn't smart enough to decide when it's safe to go out alone, that she isn't strong enough to take care of herself—that, like a dainty lady of the Victorian era, she can't cross the damn street without a male escort there to hold her hand.

The similarities between current feminism and the suffragist purity campaigns have not gone unnoticed within the women's movement. Several writers, such as Walkowitz, Rubin, and DuBois, have attempted to illustrate the commonality between current feminist anti-sex causes and those of the suffragists. Others, such as Katha Pollit and Carol Tavris, have pointed out the return to Victorian ideals of femininity in feminist spirituality and difference theory; a few dissenters, such as Katie Roiphe, have criticized the return to Victorian protectionism in the hysteria over date rape.

But their voices have gone unheard or been ignored and derided. In fact, other feminists are *proud* of the similarities between themselves and the suffragist antifemale crusades. Interviewing a national NOW staff member, I asked for information on her organization's position on porn. A hefty package soon arrived in the mail, and I wasn't too surprised to find it stuffed with photocopies of Dworkin's and MacKinnon's work alongside antiporn NOW mandates and, oddly enough, examples of "porn" that included Esprit clothes ads. But I did feel a profound sense of dismay when I pulled one piece of recommended literature from the envelope. It was a photocopy excerpt from *The Spinster and Her Enemies: Feminism and Sexuality 1880–1930*, a book on the suffragist antisex crusades by leading English feminist Sheila Jeffreys. According to Jeffreys, the early feminist campaigns against nonreproductive sexuality, sexual material, and prostitutes were wonderfully feminist, truly revolutionary. The fact that current feminist crusades against porn and "compulsory heterosexuality" mirror these repressive Victorian crusades doesn't escape Jeffreys; she applauds this similarity as a sign that feminists are on the right track. It sounds unbelievable, but it's true. That I would be sent this as a recommended piece of feminist literature by NOW was shocking at first and then saddening. Confronted with their antifemale Victorian agenda, many feminists aren't uncomfortable, they're pleased.

The women involved in the first wave of feminism had an excuse for their descent into repressive antisex campaigns and confining women-are-better arguments. They came from the Victorian era. They were raised without political, economic, or social rights. The only power they were allowed was in the moral realm. It was difficult enough for them to picture the day women could vote, go to college, or obtain a divorce. That someday women would hold public office, run businesses, marry out of choice and not necessity—or not marry at all—control their reproduction, and enjoy sex without facing ostracization was probably beyond the scope of many Victorians' imaginations. And unlike feminists today, they didn't have history to warn them of the clear antifemale effects of their crusades. They couldn't look back, as we can, to see where feminist promotions of victim mythology, sexual purity, censorship, and notions of female superiority have led—not just to sexist and repressive policies but to the alienation of women from the cause.

Today's feminists don't have an excuse.

*   *   *

Discussing this book with a young woman, I was asked, *Why?* Why, she wanted to know, are current feminists engaged in such a return to what she termed old-fashioned, puritanical ideas? At the time, I really didn't have much of an answer. I still don't.

I think the rapid growth of New Victorianism may simply point to a chance meeting of factors in the early 1980s. The women's movement was incredibly vulnerable and fragmented at the time. The fight to pass the ERA was floundering by the late seventies, and in 1982, it finally failed. Mainstream women began to abandon the movement en masse. This flight was probably not only due to the failure to pass the ERA (and for many, part of the blame rested on the lack of effective feminist organizing)[74] but also to increasing conservatism since Reagan's election and growing extremism within the movement. As a result, the women's movement was left without followers and without the clearly defined goal once provided by the ERA. Lacking troops and a vision, the people who remained in the movement were eager to find excuses for their failings and desperate to regain a sense of unity and vision. This made for fertile ground to produce new leaders and new causes.

It was at this time—the early eighties—that the feminist concern over rape transformed into crusades against sexual material and generalized condemnations of men, sex, and "colluding" women. A new crop of feminist leaders, such as Catharine MacKinnon, rode the crest of this antisex crusade, pushing more politically oriented feminists out of the picture and taking on the roles of spokeswomen for the movement. Burnt out on political activism from the ERA, the movement eagerly dropped economic and political reform to push antiporn legislation, hype the date-rape scare, and blame sex for women's troubles. Thus lesbian-feminist theory denouncing the "institution" of heterosexuality as the foundation of sexism found a willing audience within the movement and was quickly adopted by women's studies programs and feminist organizations. This contributed to a strong push to give lesbian rights top priority and to emphasize the promotion of separatism. By the mid-eighties, these causes had created a feminist obsession with dictating women's sexual lives.

Meanwhile, academic feminists of the early eighties were busy exploring "difference" and constructing elaborate conspiracy theories on the "patriarchy," "phallocentricism," and other victim-centered views of society. Without troops, the movement increasingly turned toward academic feminism for guidance in defining feminist goals, making theorists—from Mary Daly to Carol Gilligan—its leaders. The emphasis on obscure and often-irrelevant theory instead of solid activism helped the goddess religion gain credence as a feminist cause, along with other New Age examinations and fanciful transformations. Along with a rapidly increasing body of "cultural," or utopian, feminism, these explorations created a powerful vision of women as the inherently superior, if perpetually martyred, sex.

As these causes gained greater currency, many moderate feminist theories and goals were pushed steadily from the picture. In fact, the growth of New Victorianism has seen much of the movement attempt to Stalinize its own history, writing out of existence once-popular causes such as the legalization of prostitution.

Many advances made by the movement, in a sad twist, have helped engender the growth of New Victorianism. Many women of my mother's generation did not come out of the seventies unscathed. They were not raised expecting to enter the workforce—especially as single parents—and often had little higher education and few job skills. My mother was not the first woman without a college degree to find herself single-handedly raising several children, only to find a legal system that didn't care about deadbeat dads who didn't pay their child support, workplaces that refused parental leave, inaccessible child care, unaffordable health insurance, unequal pay, and limited job opportunities.

Instead of recognizing these problems as proof that the women's movement needed to gain more ground, many current feminists put the blame—either explicitly or implicitly—on equal-opportunity feminism. Explicitly, this blame comes from utopian feminists, who argue that women's entrance in the public spheres corrupts their nature. Thus, equality is bad for women. Implicitly, it comes from anti-rape feminists, who argue that rape has increased dramatically since the sixties, when women started dating without chaperones and walking freely across college campuses. The only conclusion to be drawn from this is that equal treatment is leaving women vulnerable and in need of protection. And this bizarre condemnation of equal-opportunity feminism also comes from the separatists, goddess adherents, and other "women should rule the world" feminists, who would judge people by gender, not character; and who flatly condemn them if the gender is male. Unfortunately, none of these diversions have done a thing to help single parents and struggling working women, either of my mother's age or my own generation.

I also think that some of the impetus for New Victorianism came not from within the women's movement but from outside. Several leading feminist causes, such as Gloria Steinem's New Age spirituality, the eager promotion of repressed memory syndrome, twelve-step groups, transformative philosophy, and the insistence that incest and sexual abuse underlie alcoholism and eating disorders in women (but not men), were adopted straight from inner-directed self-help movements of the eighties.

And other popular feminist causes, such as the antiporn censorship crusade, were given a strong boost in the eighties, when liberalism became a dirty word. Not just Democratic liberalism but also good old-fashioned liberalism, the kind that supports freedom of expression and upholds and respects the rights of the individual as fundamental to a free society. Gaining great credence in the eighties was the belief that social problems were the fault of excessive individual rights and freedoms, not economic and social inequalities. Youth crime, for instance, was said to be the result of liberal parenting, violence on television, and popular music. Poverty, poor education, inner-city slums, high unemployment rates for youth—particularly black youth—and an inability of government to address the needs of struggling parents (such as providing decent child care and parental leave) were irrelevant to this simpleminded view. In this way, the eighties saw a war on crime turn into a war on personal freedoms. Undoubtably, feminist leaders such as Catharine MacKinnon would still have denounced the tenets of liberalism (for allowing people to read what they please) with or without this condemnation of the *L* word. But it's unlikely they would have been able to sell their crusade for censorship under the guise of remedying a social problem—rape—to the feminist mainstream if the antiliberalism of the eighties hadn't paved the road.

As a result, by the late 1980s, New Victorianism was not only entrenched in the movement; it was spinning off new causes and trends—from ecofeminism, to animal rights, to the revived backlash theory. More and more women abandoned the women's movement.

New Victorianism has taken on a life of its own, driving the movement to its present irrelevance and extremism, and driving women further away.

Chapter 8

WHY YOUNG WOMEN ARE ABANDONING THE MOVEMENT

"In a lot of polls that they do, they [young women] won't identify them-selves as feminists. But if you ask them about feminist issues, they will agree with every one of them. So I think there's that aspect of it: What does the word mean? And maybe the fact that the years we grew up in were the Reagan/Bush years, and so some young women are more conservative than they otherwise would have been. But I think also that some of the blame has to rest with the women's movement itself, the older women in it. I think there's been a reluctance to include younger perspectives. . . . It has not necessarily been an inclusive movement. Some of these issues like child care matter a lot more to us. . . . There is a resentment, a sense that there's not a lot of room for differences of opinion within the movement. And I think to a certain extent that's true. Look at the pornography debate. It's a per-fect example of how there's very limited tolerance of different points of view. And maybe that has caused the movement to stall or splinter."

—SHANNON KOKOSKA, twenty-three,
graduate student in Pennsylvania

Shannon, a well-spoken and thoughtful young woman, is dead-on. She's right that though polls show women of our generation refuse the feminist label, they also show we hold devoutly feminist beliefs. Her point is well taken that growing up during the Reagan/Bush years might have made some of us conservative, at least fiscally. And Shannon's observation that feminists are reluctant to include younger perspectives echoes the sentiments of many young women. Even though Shannon is willing to label herself a feminist, when asked what issues she feels are important, she gives the same answers that many young women give: job security, child care, health care, reproductive rights, and better and more accessible birth-control methods. Significantly, she doesn't mention the causes championed by current feminist leaders of New Victorianism.

When asked if she thinks that there's a way to get young women involved in the movement, Shannon sounds doubtful. She says it's going to take more than outreach. It is going to take current feminists "allowing younger members to develop their own directions and what they're interested in."

From the tone of her voice, Shannon doesn't think that's likely.

In July of 1992, syndicated columnist and feminist commentator Linda Ellerbee addressed younger women's relationship to feminism. The column was an exercise in condescending virulence.

Ellerbee began by describing a dinner with Sarah Weddington, the lawyer who successfully argued *Roe* v. *Wade* before the Supreme Court. Ellerbee was bemoaning the lack of "committed young female voices" in the women's movement. As if on cue, a young woman approached their table and said she would like to get involved. "In the course of making conversation," wrote Ellerbee, "we ask her what is the latest on the Supreme Court story? [Ellerbee doesn't say which case this was, but it was probably *Planned Parenthood* v. *Casey*] Sarah and I have been away from televisions and telephones for several hours now." But the young woman, who apparently hadn't been at home glued to the TV set in expectation of a spot quiz, couldn't offer any latest updates. In fact, she didn't know much about the case at all—she had just gotten back from Africa. This, Ellerbee seemed to take it, was a prime example of how women of my generation are apathetic, possibly dim-witted ingrates. "Later, after dinner, I think about that young woman, trying not to make too much of her," writes Ellerbee, "trying not to make her a symbol for so many young women who seem to know or care so little about what is basic right here. But it's hard." From there, Ellerbee descends in a patronizing series of rhetorical questions aimed at young women—just how, she wonders, can she get through to us? Ellerbee then answers herself with a final line that rings with condescension: "At this point, I'm for shouting in little ears."[1]

A patronizing tone such as this is not uncommon coming from today's women's movement. Read commentators such as Ellerbee, pick up feminist magazines, attend a feminist conference, or follow feminists' statements to the press and you'll find that when feminists bother to address young women's alienation from the movement, they indict us as grossly apathetic, little-eared morons, homophobes, or brainwashed dupes of the "backlash." In an article on the 1992 National Women's Studies Association conference, for example, author Cathy Young tells of how, during the closing forum, a professor finally raised the issue of young women's alienation from the feminist label. "No one seemed interested in pursuing this question," Young writes. "One woman declared that young women who do not consider themselves feminists have been brainwashed by 'the backlash'; another said that 'we must deconstruct the fear of feminism' to find it is rooted in 'homophobia.' "[2]

Some current feminists don't even bother to give us that much consideration. Asked by the January 1992 magazine *Working Woman* why women of my generation hesitate to call themselves feminists, Gloria Steinem flippantly replied, "I think that part of the problem is that there is a notion that younger women were feminists in the first place." Implying—despite all the contrary evidence—that we do not hold feminist beliefs, Steinem goes on to claim that "women get more radical as they get older." Steinem has been repeating this sentiment like a broken record since 1972, when she expounded it in an essay entitled "Why Young Women Are More Conservative."[3] On being refused an interview with Steinem for this book, I was amused that along with her apologies, her office sent me this more than twenty-year-old essay, as if something so out of date would apply today.

In fact, when many feminists speak of younger women abandoning the movement, they often paint a picture of feminism as it was back in the seventies. In an article on women's rejection of the feminist label for the July/August 1993 issue of *Ms.*, for instance, feminist theorist Dale Spender neglects to mention many current feminist causes, instead presenting feminism as simply "gender equity." Gender equity may be what feminism means to Spender (and what it should mean to all of us), but it seems odd that she would present this simple phrase if she had gone to any women's organization meetings, read popular feminist books, thumbed through a few women's studies syllabi, attended an Andrea Dworkin lecture on a college campus, or even glanced at the magazine she was writing for. Blazoned across the cover of that same issue of *Ms.* was their lead story, denouncing pornography—by Catharine MacKinnon. Clearly, feminists such as Spender must be aware of the changes the movement has undergone. But when pondering why young women won't call themselves feminists, the reality of today's movement is conveniently ignored. Instead, the empowering, individualism-based seventies era of feminism is resurrected—even though the movement rejected it years ago.

Women of my generation are not the only ones who realize how dramatically things have changed. Most women in their thirties and older also refuse to identify themselves as feminists. But the movement seldom addresses this fact. It seems that the chasm between the movement and young women—their natural constituency—strikes a feminist sore spot, possibly because it so starkly illustrates how feminism has moved from its original goal of achieving equality. If it's true that the movement still advocates equal rights, then why isn't the very group of women who wholeheartedly support equality more involved? Feminist leaders would say the problem is us: our supposed apathy, ingratitude, and some lurking antifeminist beliefs yet to be uncovered.

Young women might say it's the movement itself.

Are we apathetic, as Ellerbee implies? Not at all. Given a cause we can get behind, women of my generation show up in force. An estimated 60 percent of NOW's 1992 March for Women's Lives on abortion rights, for example, consisted of young women between the ages of eighteen and twenty-three.[4] This means that only a minority were women of Linda Ellerbee's age.

Or is it, as Steinem says, that we were never feminists in the first place? If the definition of feminism is New Victorianism, the answer is yes. But if the definition of a feminist is a woman (or man) who believes in equality between the sexes, then the answer is a firm no. Surveys show that people of my generation believe overwhelmingly in every feminist tenet of the seventies, from equal pay and opportunity, to reproductive rights, to the end of confining sex roles.

The Higher Education Research Institute, for example, has conducted an annual poll of roughly 300,000 college freshmen since 1966. Their questions dealing with women's rights show that more college students today support equality than at the height of the sixties and seventies. In 1967, for example, 56.6 percent of the students believed the activities of married women are best confined to the home and family. In 1992, the figure was only 25 percent. The same year, 64.1 percent of the students supported abortion rights, compared with 55.7 percent in 1977, when the question was first asked. And nearly 90 percent of the students in 1992 believed that just because a man thinks a woman has "led him on," he is not entitled to sex.[5]

The U.S. Department of Education's 1986 "High School and Beyond" national survey of over 10,000 young people is even more telling. Asked if "a woman's job should be considered as seriously as a man's in making decisions about whether to move, where to live, etc.," 94 percent of the sample answered yes. Of young adults with a bachelor's degree or higher, only 9.8 percent of the women and 23.9 percent of the men agreed that "women are happiest when they are making a home and caring for children." Although of those surveyed with a high school diploma or less, a relatively high 33.1 percent of the women and 33.9 percent of the men felt that women are indeed happier at home, regardless of education level young women and men agreed overwhelmingly that women should earn equal pay and should be taken just as seriously as men in work and politics—93.7 percent said women should be taken just as seriously as men as politicians and executives; 97.4 percent said women should get equal pay for equal work; 98.1 percent said women should have the same educational opportunities as men.[6]

In fact, if practicing feminist beliefs is the test of feminism, then young women today are more feminist than any preceding generation—thanks to the women's movement of the seventies. Over one half of college undergraduates today are women (compared with only 20 percent in the 1950s), and they go on to earn 52 percent of all master's degrees.[7] Within just two decades, the number of women receiving Ph.D.'s and professional degrees has jumped dramatically. In 1971, for example, only 7 percent of all professional degrees awarded went to women; in 1989, the figure was 36 percent.[8] Many young women are majoring in programs once exclusively male, from medicine (33 percent of graduates in 1988) to law (40 percent of graduates in 1988).[9]

As young women graduate from these programs in record numbers, many fields that were once masculine preserves are changing dramatically. The number of women employed in commercial sciences, for example, quadrupled between 1979 and 1989 (to a still-small 13 percent of the industry), and women are close to 50 percent of the workforce in many fields, from pharmacy to economics.[10] If these trends continue, it's more than possible that another decade or two will see women gaining complete parity in most fields. This is not to say that everything is peachy. We still face many roadblocks to true equality, from a lack of child-care programs to disparity in everything from medical research to political representation.

There is, for example, the much-discussed glass ceiling in the workplace. Studies have shown that women receive fewer promotions into upper-management positions than do their male counterparts.[11] While some of this is due to outright sexism, part of it is the result of other obstacles, such as unaffordable or unreliable child care. Women with children often find themselves unable to do those things necessary to advance their careers (attend an important weekend seminar, for instance) because child care isn't provided. When it comes to choosing between advancing their career and raising their children—a choice men are seldom forced to make—many women are going to choose their kids. This is not to deny that the good old boy network isn't active in many fields. But it should be recognized that the good old boys come from an older generation of men who tend to be far more sexist than their younger male counterparts. As these men retire, we are finding the glass ceiling cracking—and soon it will shatter altogether. From 1981 to 1991, for instance, the percentage of women managers increased from 27 percent to 41 percent.[12] From 1982 to 1992, according to one survey, the number of female executive vice presidents doubled (to 9 percent), and women now hold 23 percent of senior vice president positions.[13] In the meantime, we need to do as much as possible to help women gain upper-management positions, from encouraging and funding discrimination lawsuits to fighting for child-care programs and coequal parenting. There is strength in numbers as well, and if women represent 50 percent of the workforce, discrimination is going to be nearly impossible.

But feminists seem hard-pressed to admit this reality. In the March 1990 *Seventeen*, Ellerbee theorizes that it could help us accept the feminist label if we "think of progress for women as a road. My generation graded it. Now you get out there and pave it." We are already paving that road. It's younger women who are breaking down many old barriers, from flying jet fighters, to stepping assertively into some of the last bastions of male labor. Meanwhile, we get little support, credit, or even recognition from the women's movement. If anything, we're condemned as collaborators for buying into "male" patriarchal power systems.

Esther Pettibone, a twenty-five-year-old from Washington, is one of these groundbreakers. As a welder, she's in an occupation with only 4.6 percent women, according to the Federal Bureau of Labor. Yet Esther feels positive about her chosen field and the men she works with. "There're twenty welders, and the whole company employs about four hundred and fifty people—I'm the only woman. Most of the men in my department are relatively young. There're a couple of older guys. But no one batted their eyes or turned their heads when I showed up," she says. "Most of the younger men are not discriminatory. They're very supportive and encouraging, so happy to see a woman in a male-dominated field. They are really excited about it. So I was pleasantly surprised to walk into a male-dominated field and see the reactions and how open-minded everyone was, the very feminist attitudes." When asked why she feels her field remains male-dominated, Esther points out that women simply aren't applying for the jobs. Many women, she believes, are intimidated by the thought of going into such labor. "It's a fear of the unknown, something that's a man's thing. . . . Over all, our culture has made them out to be big, scary male things that women aren't supposed to do. So it becomes a mystery that's kind of forbidding."

This young women is helping break a cycle that has kept women out of well-paying jobs and professions. And yet, even though she's realizing the dream the women's movement strove for in the late sixties and the seventies, Esther hesitates to call herself a feminist. "It's a tough question, because the word *feminist* has a lot of negative connotations I don't like. If I was going to call myself a feminist, people would automatically assume that I'm not going to shave my armpits, that I'm not going to wear makeup, that I'm not going to have any positive views on men of any sort. And that's not the way I am at all," she asserts. "I consider myself a feminist in my own way. But what feminism has become—and what people think of feminism—I am not." Considering Esther's experience with her young male coworkers, it shouldn't be surprising that she refuses a feminist label that she feels forbids any positive views toward men.

Linda Ellerbee says that women of my generation seem to "know or care so little" about feminist issues. Sorry, but it's not true. Young women know and care a great deal about feminist issues; it would be hard not to be aware of reproductive rights, economic inequality, and questions of child care these days. A 1990 poll of 505 women and men age eighteen to twenty-four by the firm Yankelovich Clancy Shulman, for example, found that four out of five believe it is difficult to juggle work and family and that too much pressure is being placed on women to bear the burdens.[14] We care about inequality.

Gloria Steinem says the problem is in thinking that women of my generation were ever feminists in the first place. But if the polls, statistics, and the faces in college, the workplace, and even the military prove anything, it's that we are.

The problem is not that we are apathetic, ungrateful, stupid, or antifeminist. The problem is that the New Victorian feminists have completely lost touch with our generation.

We are living lives radically different from the ones the current feminist leadership did at our age. Unlike those of our parents' generation, many of us grew up in single-parent homes. We came of age knowing that women were capable of anything—and often in the face of extreme difficulties. Not only are we receiving an equal education and entering male-dominated fields; we enjoy other choices and opportunities previously withheld from women. For the most part, we have access to birth control and family-planning information, we are informed about our bodies and reproductive processes, we have the right to legal abortion, and we no longer face such intense condemnation for premarital sex or even homosexuality. These factors, and others, make our lives dramatically different from our parents'.

But while we are the first generation ever to be so devoutly feminist—even if we don't accept the label—our very real concerns are often ignored or dismissed by current feminists. Along with the advances made by the women's movement and the sexual revolution, myriad other changes have taken place since the late sixties and the seventies. Vast upheavals in the nature of family life and in the workforce have occurred.

But women in their thirties and older also name child care, parental leave, health care, job opportunities, and reproductive rights as feminist priorities. These are issues, unlike those espoused by New Victorians, that are going to shape our children's world. None of the issues expounded by the New Victorians—from censoring porn to overthrowing a vague patriarchy—promise to improve society concretely for future generations. They are diversions. And younger people, facing the world as it is today, understand this. We don't have the time or energy to waste on moral crusades or flights of fancy. We don't have time for New Victorianism.

Our battle is not against sex or men or abstract cultural constructs. Our battle, and the battle of many women of all ages and walks of life, is about those solid real-life concerns we face every day: our work, our children, our relationships, our health care, our reproductive choices, our economic situation.

That's it, and that's more than enough.

"I think especially with our group, where you are bombarded with so many issues, living paycheck to paycheck—I think a lot of older women have more time to do stuff and go crazy over these action groups. It's just that there are so many other things to think about, so many other concerns. So many of my friends and I, none of us are nowhere even near stable with our job incomes and our salaries."
— SARAH BECK, twenty-four, employed in a medical firm in Pennsylvania

"The youth economy is terrible," asserts Bill Strauss, coauthor of the books *Generations: The History of America's Future 1584 to 2069* and *13th Generation*. Strauss, who has extensively researched the economic status of the young, speaks in unrelenting tones. "The economy speaks to everything for your generation. And there's no quick fix for that. You have to stop the deficit, you have to reform entitlements, you have to stop bleeding youth for the benefit of the old— you have to get back to investments."

The statistics are frightening. In the 1980s, one out of every five college graduates wound up in jobs that did not require a degree, such as laborers or office workers.[15] Of men and women age twenty to twenty-four, 11.3 percent were unemployed in 1992, nearly four percentage points above the national average.[16] It is not that they are lazy or too picky; it's simply that decent jobs aren't available. With the loss of tens of thousands of unionized, high-paying, and benefit-rich blue-collar jobs such as those in the steel and auto industries, massive layoffs in white-collar corporations, and job growth confined largely to low-wage service jobs and temp work (over 60 percent of the new jobs created between January and July of 1993 alone were part-time jobs[17]), the American workplace has changed dramatically—and for the worse.

The days when a college degree assured one of a stable, well-paying job are over. At an age when their parents were starting careers and families, many people my age are working in dead-end, low-paying service jobs and putting off having children. Many others are returning to live with their parents after failing to locate work of any kind or because they can't afford high rents on paltry incomes. According to the U.S. Census Bureau, in 1993 *58 percent of all unmarried singles age twenty to twenty-four lived with their parents*, the highest number since the Great Depression.[18] Believe me, most would rather not.

A great deal of this happened in the 1980s. In the eighties alone, the median income of Americans under age twenty-five *fell* by 10.8 percent. For all other age groups, however, the median income *rose* 6.5 percent.[19] The disparity is even sharper between those under thirty and those over sixty-five. According to the U.S. Census Bureau, the average income for families headed by parents under thirty declined 16 percent from 1973 to 1990, while the average for families headed by parents over sixty-five jumped an astounding 39 percent.[20] This decline in income hasn't escaped young people's attention. In a July 16, 1990, *Time*/CNN poll of young people age eighteen to twenty-nine, 65 percent of the respondents believed it would be "much harder" for them to live as comfortably as previous generations and 69 percent said they'd have more difficulty buying a home.

As Katherine Newman, author of *Declining Fortunes: The Withering of the American Dream*, notes, "America's youth have been even more savagely affected by the declining state of the economy than the boomers." There are several factors playing into this, including skyrocketing housing prices that are keeping young people from buying their first homes (in 1973, for instance, 23.4 percent of people under age twenty-five owned a home; in 1990, the number had fallen to 15.3 percent[21]) and the sharp withdrawal of support from programs such as student financial aid and low-cost mortgages. These are the mechanisms that helped earlier generations to gain a foothold in life. Without the GI bill, for instance, many postwar parents never would have been able to afford an education or buy a home.

While assistance for young people has dwindled, the cost of living continues to rise. Since the early eighties, the average cost of college tuition plus fees has shot up by over 10 percent a year, more than double the annual inflation rate. In the 1960s, the cost of an Ivy League degree was around fifteen thousand dollars. Today, the bill comes to over $100,000—and that's just for a bachelor's.[22] Tuitions at state universities and city colleges have also grown beyond many people's means. Not surprisingly, the number of young students finishing college has dropped.[23] Many find it difficult to juggle a full-time job along with their course load, and others simply can't afford to finish their schooling. And as Strauss and coauthor Neil Howe point out in *Generations*, the younger you are, the higher your tax bill is likely to run. In 1990, a young family with one working parent, a child, and $30,000 in wage income had to pay *five times* as much in taxes (over $5,000) than the typical retired couple with exactly the same income from public and private pensions ($1,073).[24]

Many young people today are not going to have it a little rough and then with some hard work settle into comfortable middle age. The notion that education and hard work promise economic reward is, after all, dependent on there being affordable education and stable jobs. Our economic situation—about one person out of five in my generation lives below the poverty level[25]—is not likely to improve much as we enter middle age. Throughout the eighties, as Strauss and Howe put it in *Generations*, our "economic distress has moved right up the age ladder" with us, and it will probably continue to do so. We are not assured of a long-term job with benefits and a pension, or even the safety net of Social Security.[26]

I don't mean this to sound as if we're whining. Most people of my generation aren't exactly living on the streets. In general, we can put food on the table and a roof over our heads, as well as have discretionary income for some luxuries. We are not starving and this is not another Great Depression. Acknowledging economic realities doesn't mean having to descend into self-pity or refusing to take any responsibility for one's life.

What it does mean is recognizing that for my generation, with both sexes working and often struggling to get by while raising young children, issues such as affordable and reliable child care, parental leave, flextime, health care, and the future costs of our children's education are among our most pressing concerns. For many younger women and couples thinking about having children today, the foremost concern in their minds is not if they are emotionally ready, but if they can afford to take time off from work, pay for child care, pay for health insurance, and pay for their children's future schooling. The reality is that women are in the workforce to stay. It is not possible for our society to return—economically or socially—to a time when men single-handedly supported their wives and kids. "The job market's awful," says Debbie Pacik, a twenty-four-year-old acupuncturist from the East Coast. Debbie, who does consider herself a feminist, believes economic issues play a role in young women's lack of involvement in social causes. "I think when you don't have a job, you sort of fall into your own apathetic lifestyle. You can't get up in the morning; you sit in front of the TV. I think some feel like, Why bust your ass where you need to get something accomplished, because you can't. . . . It's just getting harder to make ends meet."

In a survey of women of all ages and backgrounds by the Center for Women's Policy Alternatives and the Ms. Foundation for Women in 1992, more than half said they'd fallen behind economically during the past year. Fully a quarter named "lack of flexible work hours" as their greatest concern; 26 percent named the economy and jobs as the issue that worries them the most; 14 percent listed health care as their most critical concern; a little over one-third said they worried about making ends meet. Eighty-six percent agreed on the need for universal health care and 78 percent on equal pay. A surprisingly small 7 percent believed abortion was a pressing worry.[27] There are many concerns women share, and the last thing we need to do is get into a generational spitting match over issues that affect us all.

But there are some generational differences driving young women's concerns when it comes to single-parent and two-parent working families. Roughly 40 percent of my generation grew up in single-parent and divorced families.[28] Many remember all too well painful separations, struggling single mothers, and too often deadbeat dads. I believe that as a result, many people of my generation put an emphasis on strong family lives *and* social programs to help single mothers and struggling families.

"I know a lot of men who feel very similar to the way I feel about a lot of things [feminist issues] and I think that's important. Because that's just more people who are going to feel that way, who are going to implement that in their lives and in their jobs. I think that's really important. Because if you ostracize men, they're just going to get angry. And they're going to say, 'Why are you claiming to be so special?' I've heard a lot of that. I think it's hypocritical to say men can't get involved."

　　　　　　　—JEN DURNING, twenty-one, student and day-care worker
　　　　　　　　　　　　　　　　　　　　　from Vermont

Young women today have men friends. We attended the same schools, sat in the same classes, played together in the streets as kids. Today we work side by side, discuss our problems with one another, and respect one another as individuals. And just as women of my generation believe in equality, so do the men. There are countless men today who have never raped or sexually harassed a woman, never attempted to deny a woman her rights, respect and love the women in their lives, and yet, like their sisters, wives, lovers, and friends, don't feel welcome in the women's movement. Even more than women, they have been made to feel gun-shy around the feminist label, as if convicted of a crime they didn't commit.

And they haven't committed any crime. If anything, many men today are doing everything right when it comes to women's issues.

Among my generation, men are especially noteworthy for accepting women in the workforce and politics, as well as being more than willing to share the burdens of child rearing. In a 1990 *Time* survey of young people, 86 percent of young men said they were looking for a spouse who is "ambitious and hardworking." Nearly half said they'd like to stay home and raise the kids.[29] *Time* magazine may quote this figure as "astonishing," but many women of my generation wouldn't be too shocked. We've all known men who wistfully dream of quitting their boring jobs to become househusbands. "By any statistical measure," asserts Bill Strauss, "I would think that your generation is the least sexist. The men of your generation are pretty comfortable with the idea of women coworkers and bosses."

An August 1993 Gallup poll offers a fascinating look at this generational difference. Asked if they would prefer a male boss or a female one, 52 percent of men age eighteen to twenty-nine said the gender didn't matter. Twenty-two percent said they would prefer a female boss, while only 24 percent would prefer a male. Compare this with men over the age of fifty, of whom 47 percent said they would prefer a male boss, and it becomes clear that younger men are less sexist than older ones.

In fact, young men in this poll showed themselves to be far less sexist than even older women. Of women age thirty to forty-nine, only 29 percent said it didn't matter what sex their boss was. An amazing 43 percent preferred a man over a woman. Of women over the age of fifty, a whopping 60 percent said they preferred a male boss, while only 15 percent preferred a female one. Is that what Steinem means about women getting more radical as they get older?

By refusing to tolerate men in the movement, feminism doesn't just lose many women who won't join a movement that condones separatism, it loses a huge constituency, a massive bloc of potential activists and supporters. As Elizabeth Dennis, a thirty-year-old from the state of Washington says, "If there's a man brave enough to say, 'I'm interested in these female issues; they don't scare me,' then why don't we give him a hug and encourage him? We are not getting anywhere like this."

Elizabeth is right. We're not going to get anywhere as long as men aren't included in the movement. They need to be included not as tokens but as equals. Allowing men into leadership positions within the movement may make some women (and certainly many current feminists) uncomfortable. But we must practice what we preach. If we want full equality and partnership in the future, we have got to start today.

But the New Victorians will have none of that. In fact, they tell us we must not only keep men out of the movement but we must also keep them out of our lives and out of our beds. This is not something young women are willing to do.

Thanks in large part to the women's movement of the sixties and seventies, women of my generation are better informed and more relaxed about sexuality. We know more about birth control, talk easily about our sexual experiences, and are far freer to enjoy our bodies, whether with men, women, or ourselves. Nancy Friday writes in a November 1991 *Glamour* article on masturbation: "Young women today grew up in a climate where women were talking and writing about their sexuality with exuberance and excitement. They are the first generation to grow up with a semblance of sexual acceptance, more of an ease with masturbation."

In June of 1993, *Details* and *Mademoiselle* magazines conducted a poll on young people and sex. Although this survey was self-selective and should be taken with several grains of salt, it is still revealing. Over nine thousand subscribers (the average age of men was twenty-four; of women, twenty-two) were asked almost a hundred questions. Overall, this survey shows that young people are relaxed about sex—experimenting and enjoying various acts—yet also believe that love and companionship are far more important in life. Asked what was more important than a great sex life, the largest single bloc, 44 percent, answered "finding someone to love." Only 12 percent answered "pursuing a career." Of the men, nearly half believed that marriage "is the ultimate expression of love." The overwhelming majority of both sexes lost their virginity by their nineteenth birthday; 21 percent of the women and 31 percent of the men reported they enjoyed videotapes (presumably pornographic ones) as sexual enhancements; 29 percent of the women and 43 percent of the men said they reenacted fantasies during sex; 26 percent of the women and 30 percent of the men said they'd been tied up during sex.

Growing up after the peak of the sexual revolution, people of my generation have clearly been affected by loosening social mores. But deciphering just how they've been affected is difficult. After all, people had premarital sex, masturbated, looked at dirty pictures, and played S&M games in my mother's day; they just didn't talk about it. Perhaps the biggest sexual difference between the young and older generations is that younger people are more comfortable admitting their sexual activities and far more accepting of homosexuality.

Though some commentators have been quick to assume that AIDS and other sexually transmitted diseases have turned my generation into a nation of celibates and sexual neurotics, the fact is that outside of increased condom usage and perhaps a growing reticence toward anonymous sex, our sexual behavior has not diminished. According to the Centers for Disease Control, over half of America's high school students have had sexual intercourse. By the time they reach the twelfth grade, 71.9 percent of students have had sex.[30] A Canadian study on college students found that 74.3 percent of the men and 68.9 percent of the women had engaged in intercourse. Of these, 14.3 percent of the man and 18.6 percent of the women had engaged in anal sex.[31]

Clearly, the fear of AIDS is not keeping my generation from having sex. The focus of stopping sexually transmitted diseases should be on the prevention of disease, such as practicing safe sex, not the prevention of sexual activity—because that is simply not going to work. It never has and it never will. The use of condoms requires one essential factor, and that is the ability of the person to acknowledge openly that they want to have sex and to be prepared. As long as remnants of repressive morality hang around—and are fostered by New Victorianism—to send the message that women can have sex only if they get "carried away" (or, for feminists, "coerced") and that the young woman who carries a condom in her purse at all times must be a slut (or, for feminists, a collaborator in the "institution of heterosexuality"), then we are going to have a hard time staving off unwanted pregnancies and diseases. The women's movement took a big step for women's rights when it declared, "No means no." Now it's time for feminism to acknowledge that "Yes means yes." Feminism must respect women's choices and see that those choices aren't limited through repressive social dictates, from the right wing or the left.

If there is a single attitude that would describe how many young people feel about sex, it's this: It's nobody's business but our own. Young women do not like anyone, whether archconservatives or feminists, telling them what to do in the bedroom—which, unfortunately, is exactly what many current feminists are doing. In her May/June 1993 *Ms.* editorial, for instance, Robin Morgan criticizes Madonna for enhancing the "patriarchal establishment, pornographic and otherwise." Young women reading this editorial quickly learn that any attempt to characterize Madonna as a feminist "reveals an unfortunate lack of understanding about feminism." Why? Because if "exhibitionism, pedophilia [Madonna is a pedophile?], or wearing S and M chains and a collar projects 'being in control' then Theodore Bundy was Mr. Right." The question is not whether Madonna's depictions of sexuality make her a feminist; the question is whether they prohibit her from being deemed one.

Morgan and other leading New Victorians would answer yes. Women of my generation might answer, "Who cares, and since when is it your business?"

In the past year I've watched with dismay the plight of a small independent feminist newspaper called *Blue Stocking* in my hometown. Founded by a woman in her twenties, this paper has come under feminist fire for running a cartoon written by an ex-prostitute (titled "The Adventures of Superho," the cartoon was accused of promoting rape), printing a solitary article by a self-described feminist opposed to abortion, and showing a general willingness to publish a wide diversity of opinions. That the young woman running this paper also gives equal—if not greater—space to virulently antiporn articles and the standard New Victorian perspective doesn't seem to matter. Local feminist leaders pressured her to discontinue the cartoon, and when that didn't succeed, they condemned her in another local paper. The director of a women's health clinic pulled her advertising, and the state coordinator for NOW even gave the publisher a call, insisting she had no right to call her paper feminist if she was going to run an article by a woman opposed to abortion, though apparently the NOW official hadn't even bothered to read the article in question.

As of this writing, the young woman continues to put out her paper, noting in an editorial that she finds it ironic "that groups who say there should be no limit to women's choices want to limit what we choose to say." I hope she continues to prove me wrong, but I doubt she will want to deal for very long with attacks from her own corner over such seemingly innocuous issues as cartoons or for trying to foster dialogue, especially considering that running a small newspaper is not a lucrative proposition.

For the majority of young women, becoming active on feminist issues has become an all-or-nothing proposition: either embrace New Victorianism and work on those issues current feminists have decreed are priorities or completely eschew feminist activism.

There are some young women who have chosen the first option. On some college campuses—primarily at Ivy League schools—some young women have become involved in New Victorian campaigns, especially through women's studies classes and the date-rape hysteria. Several campus rape and sexual assault groups have sprung up, such as Duke University's Date Rape and Sexual Assault Task Force. And some of their methods are revolting. In April of 1993 at the University of Maryland, for example, a group of female students from a women's studies class went through the campus directory and picked out male names at random. They then printed posters with the men's names, announcing NOTICE: THESE MEN ARE POTENTIAL RAPISTS, then liberally papered the campus. When other students noticed the flyers, they reacted angrily, tearing down several hundred of them. The incident turned into a full-blown controversy, with some male students threatening legal action and the female students responsible refusing to step forward and identify themselves. At first, the women students' professor, Josephine Withers, said she was "very satisfied" with the outcome of her anonymous students' actions. Later she refused to talk to the press, claiming the incident had been "distorted."[32]

Unfortunately, this is far from the only action of its type. On other campuses, young activists have burned copies of student newspapers for running articles they've disliked and falsely accused male students of rape. At Princeton University, for example, a woman student stood up at a 1991 Take Back the Night rally and told a horrifying story of being brutally raped by a fellow student, further claiming that when she went to the dean about it, she was told "not to press the issue." Three days later, she wrote her story for the campus paper, and although she didn't name her supposed attacker, within days the college grapevine had spread his name across the campus. But after the university began investigating her charges—the accused student filed a formal complaint—the woman admitted that she had fabricated the entire tale. In another article for the paper, entitled "Apologizing for False Accusation of Rape," she further admitted she had never in fact met or spoken to the man.[33]

But these women are no more representative of young women than current feminist leaders such as Andrea Dworkin are representative of women of their generation. Those few young women who do adhere to New Victorianism tend to become involved while attending elite colleges. It's a serious mistake to look at what a small but noisy fraction of privileged female students believe to learn what all young women believe. As one young working woman commented laughingly to me, extremism and separatism are easy enough when you're in college. Out of school, sweeping theories and antisex causes suddenly pale next to concerns such as job opportunities and paying the rent.

And it is important to remember that the majority of young women aren't even in college. They're out in the workforce, trying to make ends meet, raising young children, starting careers, and going about their lives. They're not the voices you usually hear in the press, in part because they're not as easily accessible as vocally active college students. But they do exist. And they offer one of the most powerful and yet ignored constituencies for the women's movement.

There *are* young women trying to organize with varying degrees of independence, and varying degrees of success. One group, Students Organizing Students, rallied on campuses around the issue of reproductive rights prior to Clinton's election. SOS captures a growing sentiment among younger women: that the pro-choice movement has been limited too long to just abortion rights. SOS emphasizes that true choice should include the option to have the baby, with pre- and postnatal care. "What SOS means by pro-choice is not legal abortion by itself," SOS information analyst Veena A. C. Sud told one reporter. "What we mean by the right to choose is that it's every woman's right, and if she chooses to have that baby, she has the right to clothe, feed, and house it."[34] Since Clinton's election, SOS has expanded its mission statement to address women's health issues, HIV/AIDS education, choices about sexuality and economic concerns, and it is working to expand its base from New York to other states, as well as to tap into high school students' concerns by establishing a leadership training program.

The Third Wave, a broad-based group that concerns itself with civil rights, feminism, and ecological issues, was founded by twenty-three-year-old Rebecca Walker (the daughter of feminist writer Alice Walker) and twenty-four-year-old Shannon Liss. Their major action so far was a Freedom Summer '92 cross-country bus tour registering new voters. But with their sweeping array of concerns—Rebecca Walker says feminism needs to address environmental issues, homophobia, racism, and human rights—the Third Wave already seems fragmented, and few women of my generation are even aware that it exists.[35]

Much attention has been showered on the alternative music-based "Riot Grrrl" movement, if it can be called a movement. Riot Grrrl, an amorphous collection of young women primarily involved in alternative rock bands, was the brainchild of several women musicians from Olympia, Washington. Intent on reclaiming the word *girl*, Riot Grrrls spread their pro-female message through stapled photocopied magazines and independent record label music. The flamboyance of the movement (which became known for members drawing messages on their exposed bellies, such as SLUT or RAPE) had the press falling all over its members—their first official gathering even earning a long article in the November 1992 *Spin* magazine. But most of the young women involved don't want anything to do with the press or mainstream organizing. Though it's unlikely that this eclectic movement will gain any widespread influence, it does illustrate the independent, assertive, and empowering attitude of many young women who are not only entering previously male-dominated fields (and rock music was certainly one) but are completely convinced they have every right to do so.[36]

These groups, as well as young women's participation in abortion-rights marches, show we are not apathetic. We do care. As one young woman told me, "That's one argument I get into with my mom. She says my generation is apathetic. I say, 'What did you do? You gave us Reagan. Sure, thanks a bunch.' It makes you wonder."

We're not apathetic, but we are often resistant to organizing. The same rights and freedoms feminists won for us have allowed us to develop into a very diverse generation of women, and we value our individuality. While linked through common concerns, notions of sisterhood seldom appeal to women of my generation. Efforts to unify all women under one ideology seem pointless. Women of my generation will get involved in a group or action if they feel they'll be doing something concrete on specific issues. They will not get involved if they feel the action is meaningless, if they must fit rigidly into one set idea of what women are like, or if their individuality is threatened.

Any future movement toward equality must recognize and support these characteristics if it is to thrive. What will not thrive are groups modeled according to current feminist ideology. New York City's Women's Action Coalition, created in 1992, is a perfect example. WAC's focus on direct action originally lured hundreds of women to its weekly meetings and saw the group's arrival splashed on the covers of newspapers and glowingly reported in national magazines. But their paralyzing "antihierarchical" stance, combined with employing inflamed rhetoric instead of effective action and allowing extremist factions to silence debate, saw the organization's meetings degenerate into vicious insider attacks and ineffectiveness, and their membership plummeted from a claimed eighteen hundred members to a handful of women. In less than two years of existence, as an article aptly titled "WAC Attacks Itself" in the July 20, 1993, *Village Voice* noted, WAC fell apart at the seams. At the time of this writing, it is still hanging on, but by a very thin thread.

Just as any future movement must allow room for individual differences, it must also prioritize issues. Only by working on the concerns of a broad base of women can the feminist movement again gain strength and power. If we are to have a women's movement in the future, we *must* start tackling these issues, and not through meaningless rhetoric or window-dressing actions.

There are issues that concern women of all ages and backgrounds. They address the needs of the majority of people. Their advancement would not only further our equality but would make society better for the next generation. A movement that focused on these issues would be strong and unified, with the support of millions of both women *and* men. It would be a movement that would stand for equality, not orthodoxy; action, not ideology. It would be a truly inclusive movement, addressing women's concerns while keeping its nose out of women's private lives.

Women today still want a movement to advocate their needs. "According to a 1989 *New York Times* poll, over 70 percent of women in their twenties and thirties agree that 'the United States continues to need a strong women's movement to push for changes that benefit women,' " writes Betty Friedan in the March 1990 *Glamour*. "In the nineties, the women's movement should be giving the same priority to child care that it once gave to equality and reproductive choice. If the current leadership can't or won't do that, then new leaders are needed."

Current feminist leaders won't do it. That is the reality of New Victorianism. We can no longer wait and hope that one day they will wake up to our concerns, drop the extremist and alienating causes and theories they have adopted, and actively guide the movement back to the fight for women's rights. While a few groups continue to push for equality—and deserve our support—the majority of the women's movement has simply gone too far astray. If we want to see our concerns addressed, we are going to have to be the ones to do it. And it's not impossible.

"Things have changed so dramatically, so dramatically that I'll never have any idea what it was like to be thirteen in 1961. But neither will my mom have any idea of what it was like to be thirteen in 1982," asserts Autumn Harrison, the twenty-three-year-old student and bar worker whose words opened chapter 2. With her assertive manner, independent opinions, and pragmatic outlook, Autumn sums up the views of so many young women. "I've heard this attitude: that I haven't seen enough of life; that only women in their thirties and older know how it is." Her dark eyes focused intently on me, Autumn leans forward and makes her final point in quiet, incisive words. "But the fact is," she says, "it will be women like you and me who will shape the future."

Chapter 9

THE FINAL WAVE:
RECLAIMING FEMINISM

We want action on a number of pressing issues. But we don't necessarily have to start up organizations or devote our lives to the cause in order to do something about our concerns. There are things all of us can to do advance equality.

But I do believe that for women interested in organizing, creating single-issue groups can be just as or more effective as forming broad-based umbrella organizations. Look at the effectiveness of groups such as Emily's List that concentrate on a single goal. A movement made of a wealth of single-issue organizations would allow women and men a diversity of activism on concrete issues that concern them, while avoiding the pitfalls of overextended agendas and demands for ideological purity that often come with umbrella organizations. A woman or man who is concerned about child care, for instance, could join a group devoted to that issue without worrying about having to adopt a set of beliefs or having contributions go to causes they do not support. A movement made up of such single-issue or priority-oriented groups would draw many previously uninvolved people into activism at the same time it would allow for diversity among its members.

In this chapter, I've noted several suggestions for actions we can take. My suggestions are just that: suggestions. I don't think we all have to agree on every single cause and tactic for each of us to take part in a movement for equality.

What I consider myself to be is an equality feminist. I believe women should have the same opportunities and rights as men. What they do with those opportunities and rights is their business; the point is that they have them. And I believe it should be this principle that guides the final wave of feminism.

Child Care

A battle for a child-care system that includes giving men greater responsibility for children and would allow women more options in the workplace would not only better women's lives; it would advance equality between the sexes. That makes child care a feminist issue. In discussing child care, I'm including the need for after-school care for children over age five, as well as preschools.

America's child-care system is a mess. There are more than 21 million working women with children in the United States, and many of these are continually in a struggle to find day care for their small children and after-school care for their older children.[1] In 1987, the typical yearly cost for child care for one child in a U.S. city was three thousand dollars. About 94 percent of family day-care homes are unlicensed; these are the services that most parents can afford.[2] In 1990, thanks to the perseverance of the Children's Defense Fund, the first comprehensive child-care and family-support legislation was passed by Congress. While it provided roughly $5 billion over five years to help low- and moderate-income families obtain child care, much more work on this issue is needed. Many middle-income families are left in the lurch because they don't qualify for low-income programs and yet can't afford decent child care. And we need to create an affordable and reliable system without sacrificing diversity. Some parents, for instance, are going to want religious-oriented child care for their kids, while others today are frustrated at just how many facilities are run by people who include religious teachings in the children's day. No one wants a monolithic child-care system of institutional white buildings. But at the same time we maintain home care and diversity, we also need to ensure that every child is receiving responsible, dependable care.

This is going to take a multifaceted approach. The issue of child care is too complex to do justice to in a few paragraphs; I especially recommend *Child Care: Facing the Hard Choices* by Alfred J. Kahn and Sheila B. Kamerman for a more in-depth look. With this caveat, here are a few suggestions:

•   Take advantage of our schools. We already have a public investment in school buildings that are unused afternoons, evenings, weekends, and during the summer. Others have been closed due to a lack of students but still drain money for maintenance. Using schools would avoid one of the major expenses in creating child care: building and then maintaining the facility. We can experiment, as Kahn and Kamerman suggest, with a variety of programs: parent cooperatives, community groups, preschools, after-school centers, day care, and so on. Many communities have already created programs in their schools. Organizations can push for state expenditure in start-up funds, which would be modest, along with help in creating programs. Of course, any state or federally funded child-care facility should have to meet stringent certification guidelines—parents should be able to rest assured their children are receiving quality care.

•   Encourage state investment in child care. Creating a comprehensive child-care system through incentives and funding would offer many benefits to a region. It would create jobs, boost the local economy, and act as a lure for new business. Child care, preschools, and a good educational system are big draws in bringing industry to a state, because they assure business of a stable, qualified workforce. A few states, such as North Carolina, have adopted this strategy to their benefit. While this idea certainly requires expenditures, the returns to the local economy could easily outweigh the original investment, especially in the long run.[3]

•   Improve and strengthen Head Start. Head Start is a good program to build on. It's already in existence, it offers an array of services, and it has the potential to deliver high-quality care to low-income children from birth through age five throughout the year. At this time, however, Head Start reaches only about 35 percent of eligible children. More federal funding and leadership are needed.[4]

•   Flextime. The nine-to-five workday is no longer necessary for many businesses, and flexible work hours would do much to allow parents to be available to their children and still be productive employees. Organizing together with coworkers to push for flexible work hours is something many could do to further this cause.

•   Make child care a public issue. We can demand that political candidates answer this question: What are you going to do about the child-care problem? Politicians want to get elected, and if their stance on child care is made just as important as their stance on crime or the economy, you can bet they are going to start drawing up plans. Women and men running for local, state, and national office might do well to tap into the concern over child care and make it one of their key campaign issues. We can, of course, take the good old routes of writing letters and phoning our congresspeople and senators. Handwritten letters are far more effective than photocopied postcards (in fact, they can be *very* effective). We can contribute to those groups that are lobbying and working on child-care issues, such as the Children's Defense Fund, and we can create our own groups. It is very important that we get men involved in this cause. In fact, a fight for child care that recognizes and applauds the many caring, dedicated fathers out there—whether through advertisements, articles, or simply speaking out—would do a lot more than simply bring men into the movement. It would have a tremendous social impact in promoting coequal parenting. Teaching young men that being a responsible father is worthy of respect, if not downright sexy, would send a strong message that male involvement in child care is both welcome and necessary.

Obviously, some of these suggestions are going to require both state and federal funds. While we must demand that society view child care as an essential, not an option, we are going to have to be realistic about just how much government funding can be apportioned and how people are going to react to the specter of raised taxes. We should be willing to think of creative ways to address the problem. Take Clinton's student corps, for instance. What about putting those students to work on some facet of child care and after-school care? Give the currently employed workers a much-needed pay raise and put them in charge of the students.

Federal leadership on this issue is crucial. The child-care problem is a complicated one, and we aren't going to find all the answers until we start addressing the issue. A presidential task force on child care would be a positive beginning.

Birth Control

Women's ability to control when to conceive is fundamental to equality. But the birth-control movement in the United States has stalled. The technology is there to create radically different new forms of contraception, including birth control for men, but research is nearly nonexistent. Not only are we relying on thirty-year-old technology (the few exceptions being methods brought in from Europe, such as Norplant); we deny access of even those methods to many groups of women, especially the young. The results are clear: The United States has a higher rate of teenage pregnancy and abortions than any other industrialized country.[5] According to the National Research Council, one-third to one-half of all abortions could be prevented by more birth-control options; as many as 3 million unwanted pregnancies occur each year because of contraceptive failure.[6] We need to make birth control more accessible and socially acceptable and we need to push for more research into new and more effective methods.

While fighting for better birth control, however, it's important we stand adamantly against involuntary use (such as judges mandating Norplant for female drug users), because such methods have a long history of being enforced almost exclusively with minorities and the poor. We also need to avoid falling into moralistic traps, such as condemning teenage mothers. We must respect the right of every woman, regardless of her age or class, to have children if she so chooses—the focus should be on *choice*. Here are a few suggestions on what we can do:

• Improve research. There are several factors contributing to the dearth of birth-control research in the United States, including intimidation from the religious right. But the major factor in the withdrawal of drug companies from birth-control research is rampant litigation. Unlike drugs taken for a serious illness, birth control is administered to healthy people to prevent a condition, and this has made it a common and easy target for massive lawsuits. This is not to say that women shouldn't be able to sue companies for dangerous products such as the Dalkon Shield, an IUD sold before there was any requirement for FDA approval of medical devices, which caused fatal pelvic infections. But in many liability cases, manufactors end up paying enormous sums for questionable claims. A 1986 decision, for example, awarded $4.7 million in damages to a woman who claimed her child was born with birth defects because of a spermicide she used at the time of conception, though studies don't support such a claim.[7] Such litigation—in which no amount of testing or proof of good faith can seem to protect the manufactors—has had a chilling effect on the industry. Drug companies are unwilling to invest decades of work, testing, and millions of dollars (the industry esti-mates it costs roughly $125 million for a new drug of any kind) into new products that run such a risk, and insurance companies shy from covering contraceptives. What can we do about this? We can push for laws protecting drug companies from liability suits as long as they comply with stringent FDA requirements. Such legislation has been used for vaccines, another form of preventive medicine. We can also cap damages and we can develop no-fault compensation. Until we address this problem realistically, we are simply not going to see any major advances in birth control in the United States.[8]

• Make birth control more accessible. One of the best places to start is in our high schools. Yes, there's plenty of opposition to giving teenagers birth control, as if unavailable contraceptives will stop them from having sex (it won't). The problem is not that the far right believes this is unacceptable. The problem is that they've been allowed to dominate this issue for so long. On the local level, we can look critically at what the high schools in our areas offer and demand the institution of family-planning programs that supply students with solid information and birth-control methods. Working to institute family-planning centers and programs in high schools is an achiev-able, concrete goal for local feminist groups.

• Make birth control socially acceptable. Great strides have al-ready been made in societal acceptance of birth control, but single women and young women still face mixed messages about contracep-tion. While we are warned to protect ourselves from disease and pregnancy, these warnings tend to emphasize celibacy over protec-tion, especially for teenagers. This cannot be tolerated. It sends a strong message to women that to be prepared to prevent pregnancy is somehow immoral and wrong, and it leaves young women igno-rant about birth control. There isn't much we can do in law to change societal mores, but there is plenty we can do in social ac-tions. Groups can buy their own educational commercials and adver-tisements advocating birth-control use; we can demand better sex education for the young; we can better fund and support organiza-tions such as Planned Parenthood. Just as concern over AIDS has seen the use of condoms become socially acceptable—even ap-plauded—a movement concerned with unwanted pregnancies can see birth control treated in the same way.

Abortion Rights

The women's movement made a profound—if unintentional—error after the legalization of abortion in 1973. As a nurse practitioner in a major health organization pointed out to me, instead of working to put abortion in the mainstream health-care system—where it would simply be another medical procedure—many feminists involved in the women's health movement devoted their energy to creating separate abortion clinics. This was due to the popular feminist belief of the seventies that women's health care should be "women-centered"—that is, provided by other women in female-only facilities. Because of this focus on creating clinics, hospitals and health-maintenance organizations felt little pressure to provide the service. Many who began performing abortions—such as the Kaiser Permanente health maintenance organization in Oregon—stopped by the mid-eighties, deciding it would be easier to refer patients to clinics and let the clinics deal with political opposition rather than handle it themselves. By 1985, a whopping 60 percent of all abortions were performed in abortion clinics and 23 percent in other health facilities. Only 13 percent were done in hospitals.[9]

Rather than safeguarding abortion rights, the clinics had exactly the opposite effect: Abortion has been marginalized to this day. Segregated from other health care, abortion clinics are vulnerable to attacks from religious extremists, cut off from medical funding, and often unable to find doctors willing to face death threats and harassment for what has turned into a low-paying job. Since clinics alone are often the only places that offer abortions, many women in rural areas find they must drive over a hundred miles to obtain what should be an easily accessible service. And women in all areas find getting an abortion a difficult task, requiring a trip to a clinic, where one may have to run a gauntlet of fanatics. By marginalizing abortion in this manner, feminists ensured our rights would remain fragile and unprotected in conservative times and that the public would continue to view abortion not as an essential medical right but as a highly politicized procedure—one that in many ways inadvertently reinforces shame and guilt.

But instead of attempting to put abortion back in the mainstream, many of today's feminists continue to focus on the clinics, responding to their vulnerability by trying to build a fortress of laws protecting them. For instance, in January of 1993, the Supreme Court ruled that NOW could proceed to sue antiabortion groups on behalf of abortion clinics under the Racketeering Influenced and Corrupt Organizations Act (RICO), a federal law used as a weapon against extortion by organized crime. While this may or may not help abortion clinics (successful prosecution of RICO cases is difficult), demanding special legal protections only further separates abortion from other health care, and once again the issue is turned into a political hand grenade.[10]

This politicizing and marginalizing of abortion must end. As long as only one or two facilities in a city offer the procedure, antiabortionists have an easy time targeting them with arson, bombings, and violence, and no amount of extra legal protections will ensure their safety or financial stability in times of conservative administrations or economic recession. But if abortion were available in every hospital and tied into mainstream health-care funding, fanatics would have no vulnerable targets and economic hard times would have little impact. Try to imagine antiabortionists' frustration if every hospital in a city offered abortion; it would be impossible to harass all of them at once, and hospitals are usually too large, well funded, and secure to blockade or smoke-bomb. At the time of this writing, Clinton's proposed health-care plan covers abortion. If the plan passes, it would offer an invaluable first step in putting the procedure into mainstream health care. Should abortion be taken out of the plan, we need to examine new ways to pressure providers into offering abortions. One possibility is through the courts. *Roe* v. *Wade* defined abortion rights in terms of privacy: an issue between a woman and her doctor. But, as Supreme Court Justice Ruth Bader Ginsburg has argued, abortion should also be seen as an equality issue. To deny a woman abortion is to place an unfair burden upon her. Obviously, the father of the child won't have to take unpaid leave from work and face health complications; only she will, which makes unwanted pregnancy a form of sex discrimination. A case that upholds abortion as an equality issue would give us a powerful weapon to protect our rights. Under such a definition, it's possible hospitals receiving federal funds will be forced to stop discriminating against women and start providing abortions.

The idea that abortion will be viewed by society as simply another medical procedure might sound unlikely, especially considering the plight of the clinics for the past twenty years. But one reason the issue has remained volatile is the vulnerability of the clinics. It often seems barely a month passes without the abortion question being whipped up through news stories on bombings, shootings of abortion doctors, or another response by feminist groups. This has allowed a very small minority of right-wing extremists a ton of press coverage, which exaggerates their actual support and power. The truth is the majority of Americans support abortion rights and only a tiny faction at best support the violence committed by some antiabortionists. This majority will accept abortion being available in hospitals. Abortion is not a political act, nor is it an exclusively feminist cause. It is a medical right, and we need to start treating it like one.

Political Parity

Fighting for equal representation in government presents us with a catch-22 situation. On one hand, we want women to have parity in all levels of political office. On the other hand, it is simply unreasonable to expect people to vote for a woman simply because of her gender. In fact, it's sexist. If a male candidate who represents my concerns is running against an archconservative female candidate in my community, you can bet I will vote for the man. While we work for equal representation—which is fundamental to equality—it is important that we avoid expecting women to toe a certain line simply because they are women. Perhaps the most effective way to deal with this problem is through a variety of groups, such as Emily's List (which supports only Democratic women) and Wish List (a group that funds only pro-choice Republican women). Groups can fund those candidates who meet their political requirements, while women and men can support those organizations that fit their beliefs. A wide range of these groups—even including ones supporting antiabortion female candidates—would certainly make for a lively, diverse move toward political parity.

Sexual Violence

The United States has a pretty skewed sense of justice when it comes to dealing with sexual assault. According to a 1989 survey by the Department of Justice, the median sentence in state prisons for those convicted of rape was seventy-two months, but the average time served was only twenty-nine months.[11] At the same time, the federal government is locking up low-level drug dealers for five or more years without parole. Women deserve to have sexual assault treated as a serious crime with serious consequences for the offenders, and they deserve to have a prison system that makes an attempt to treat these offenders. An effective campaign against sexual violence needs to focus on three areas: apprehending, punishing, and rehabilitating sex offenders.

• Apprehending and convicting sex offenders. Only about half of reported rapes result in the arrest or clearance of the rapist (meaning the case was dropped or for some other reason, such as the death of the perpetrator, there was a suspect but no arrest).[12] Fewer than one in five rapes reported to the police end in a conviction.[13] We can push for more police sexual-assault units (programs vary in each city and community), we can demand our police fully investigate each allegation—and are given the funds to do so—and we can make significant objections about the all-too-common failure of grand juries and trial juries to indict and convict sex offenders. The Violence Against Women Act, proposed legislation at the time of this writing, would increase funds for police training, sexual-assault units, and the development of better prosecution policies.

• Punishment. Rapists must spend more time in jail—lots more time. The Violence Against Women Act would amend sentencing guidelines, increasing prison sentences for sex offenders and giving repeat offenders up to twice the prison time. This is definitely on the right track. But simply increasing sentencing isn't going to work as long as we are short on prison space. Right now, our prisons are filled past capacity, with many of the inmates petty drug dealers. Regardless of what we think about drugs, we have to question a system that sentences persons caught with five hundred dollars' worth of crack cocaine to up to twenty years without parole in federal prisons, overcrowds state prisons, and then releases violent criminals and rapists to make more room. It simply doesn't make any sense that a man who raped a woman gets out within two and a half years, on the average, while a nonviolent drug offender can spend ten or more years in prison. Do we really believe, as a society, that possessing drugs is worse than brutally raping a woman? What kind of message are we sending to rape victims? At the same time we need to push for stiffer penalities for violent crimes, such as rape, we are going to have to reexamine our rush to overcrowd our prison system with nonviolent drug offenders. If we don't, no amount of increased sentencing is going to make much of a difference: There won't be room for rapists. Put drug users in treatment and put low-level drug dealers in work camps for a year or two. Sentence first-time rapists to at least ten years with the possibility of parole, if they complete a treatment program. On the second offense, double the sentence with no chance of parole. On the third offense, recognize that they will always pose a threat and throw away the key.

• Rehabilitation. While we should push for stiffer penalties for sex offenders, lifetime imprisonment for all of them—particularly first-time offenders—simply isn't a viable option. Since they are going to get out of jail sometime, it's important we treat them to the best of our ability. Sex offenders are disturbed, twisted people. But that doesn't mean that keeping them from assaulting again is impossible. Treatment programs using empathetic methods (such as having offenders listen to rape victims' accounts of their experiences) can be effective. We should push for more treatment programs in prison and, more importantly, mandate treatment after release for *all* offenders. Together with an improved tracking system, this would also do much to keep tabs on sex offenders.

We will never be able to rid our society of rape completely. There will always be violent, disturbed people out there. But an improved legal system could do much to take these people off the streets and reduce the likelihood of repeat offenses. Social education is important, as well; we need to continue to make it clear that sexual assault is not acceptable, no matter if it's by a date, acquaintance, husband, or stranger. But college rape-prevention seminars and other forms of feminist social activism are not going to change the behavior of someone who is already disturbed enough to rape. For the most part, such activism only reiterates what the majority of people already believe. In short, they are preaching to the converted. If we want to reduce the occurrence of rape, if we want to show that we truly believe it is a repugnant crime, we are going to have to make concrete changes in our legal system.

And then there is the question of New Victorianism. Should we ignore it or fight it?

It's my belief that, in the long run, the best tactic is to fight it. Many moderates in the women's movement made a crucial mistake in the eighties by refusing to openly confront causes such as the anti-porn fight, out of concern that to do so would damage the feminist label or be unsisterly. Others got mixed up in thinking that because these feminists are entitled to free speech, criticizing them would be wrong. This only ensured that these causes would grow unchecked and ultimately do much damage to both the movement and to progress for women's equality. To be silent when it comes to so-called feminist attempts to censor free expression, promote male bashing, or intrude upon women's personal lives is to condone those causes. It is implicit approval.

From the attempt to ban all sexual material to condemning women who work within the political system, New Victorian causes hurt the pursuit of equality and often directly infringe upon our rights as individuals. Just because New Victorian causes fly under the banner of so-called feminism doesn't mean they won't damage our rights. In the end, it doesn't matter if inequality comes from Victorians who call themselves the religious right or Victorians who call themselves feminists. It hurts women just as much either way. And that's what matters. We should not feel we have to tolerate this because New Victorians claim that criticizing their causes makes one an agent of the "backlash." This is a lie, used to squash dissent and keep the movement closed off to the majority of women.

For these reasons, I believe that standing adamantly against New Victorianism is crucial to creating a new, truly inclusive movement concerned with equality. *We need to make it clear we do not believe they speak for feminism.* We have got to make the movement more open to women, and the only way to do that is get rid of those who are driving women away. It is not enough to say, in effect, "Let them have the feminist label. We'll create our own label, our own movement." Because as long as New Victorians are allowed to own the feminist label, more and more women will be alienated from *any* organized movement for equality—the term is simply too intrinsically entwined with women's rights—and progress will continue to be stalled. We must reclaim the feminist label and return it to the majority of women. We must say adamantly that we *are* feminists, women and men together who believe in equality.

Inclusiveness doesn't mean accepting all causes and tolerating leaders who are going to make your movement exclusive. Every group and movement draws the line someplace; today's women's movement has drawn plenty. What lines should we draw? I believe that by focusing on priority issues, groups can avoid adopting too many causes and creating an ideologically narrow movement. A group dedicated to child care, for instance, can require that members check their political and moral beliefs at the door and concentrate solely on the issue at hand. Should extremist factions demand that the group also address a multitude of other concerns, such as ecological issues, it would be perfectly reasonable for that organization to say, "No. We work only on child care. If you want to work on those concerns, go find a group that addresses them." This is not to say that groups can't and shouldn't take strong stands on issues—such as being against racism and homophobia—but that doesn't mean they must make those issues priorities.

I've also noted a few suggestions on what we can do to fight the counterproductive elements of New Victorianism. From supporting those organizations that fight to retain our right to free expression to working for true equality within education, there are things all of us can do.

• Oppose censorship. While I don't believe that supporting free speech should necessarily be a priority issue for feminists, I do believe that it is important for a movement concerned with equality to take a clear stand against censorship. Free speech is necessary for outreach and communication, as well as a fundamental right of all individuals in a free society. To support censorship either through activism or silence is to support potentially repressive and antifeminist policies. It is important that we make it clear that New Victorians are not acting in our interest when they promote laws that are used to outlaw books and magazines that some may find offensive—such as pornography—because some day that law can and will be used against us. For people interested in supporting the right to free expression and ensuring that efforts to censor material do not succeed, I recommend getting involved in and supporting these organizations: the American Civil Liberties Union, the National Coalition Against Censorship, and Feminists for Free Expression. Creating our own free speech advocacy groups is another option, as are writing letters to newspapers and speaking out against censorship in our communities.

• Dump women's studies programs. Women's studies programs had a place when they were instituted in the seventies, when very little was being taught by or about women in other departments. Unfortunately, they have proven themselves extremely counterproductive.

Many students, both male and female, are missing out on learning about women because of the exclusive and often-hostile environment of these classrooms. Teaching students from a syllabus that leans heavily toward Andrea Dworkin, Catharine MacKinnon, Mary Daly, and Starhawk is not about teaching them women's history or feminism. It's about teaching New Victorian orthodoxy, and it is doing irreparable harm to the feminist cause. Young women (and men) aren't only walking away from these classes repulsed by feminism, they're walking away bereft of a wealth of knowledge about works on and by women that are virtually ignored in these programs.

Our students, male and female, deserve better. They should be learning about women in every department of their universities. As long as only one extremist program offers the majority of those classes, we are going backward, not forward. Women's studies are marginalizing the subject of women. We need to move decisively toward the inclusion of women throughout academia, from art to history. And we need to assure our students that they will be receiving a solid, credible education, not just excerpts from Andrea Dworkin.

Young women recognize the needs in their own lives and they're willing to do something about them. They're not willing, however, to waste time with the regressive agenda of the New Victorians. If there were a movement that addressed our concerns, we would join it. If this was a feminist movement, we would gladly call ourselves feminists.

NOTES

Introduction:

1. Claudia Wallis, "Onward, Women!" *Time*, December 4, 1989, p. 80. This is far from just an American phenomenon. In a 1992 survey for British *Cosmopolitan*, 60 percent of female readers replied they were not feminists. Yet an overwhelming 84 percent of respondents did not believe that women have achieved equality with men. See "Have We Achieved Equality?" British *Cosmopolitan*, March 1992, p. 14.

2. Nancy Gibbs, "The War Against Feminism," *Time*, March 9, 1992, p. 54.

3. Karen Avenoso, "Feminism's Newest Foot Soldiers," *Elle*, March 1993, p. 114. *In View* is no longer in publication; the survey results were confirmed through their offices.

4. Cathy Young, "Victimhood Is Powerful," *Reason*, October 1992, p. 18.

5. "High School and Beyond, Third Follow-up, 1986," *Digest of Education Statistics*, 1988, U.S. Department of Education, p. 334.

6. Nancy Gibbs, "The Dreams of Youth," *Time*, Special Issue; *Women: The Road Ahead*, Fall 1990, p. 11.

7. 1986 Gallup poll cited in "20 years of the U.S. Women's Movement," *Ms.*, July/August 1992, foldout. The 29 percent figure is from a 1992 *Time* survey. See Gibbs, "The War Against Feminism," p. 54.

8. David Sheff, "Playboy Interview: Betty Friedan," *Playboy*, September 1992, p. 51.

9. Robin Morgan, "On Violence and Feminist Basic Training," *Going Too Far: The Personal Chronicle of a Feminist* (Vintage Books, 1978), p. 139.

10. Andrea Dworkin, *Intercourse* (The Free Press, 1987), p. 133.

11. "Acquaintance Rape," a pamphlet published by the American College Health Association, 1992, distributed to campuses nationwide.

12. Catharine MacKinnon, "Feminism, Marxism, Method, and the State: Towards Feminist Jurisprudence," in *Feminism and Methodology*, ed. Sandra Harding (Indiana University Press, 1987), p. 142.

13. Andrea Dworkin, "Dirt/Death," *Intercourse*, p. 181.

14. Sylvia Nasar, "Women's Progress Stalled? Just Not So," *New York Times*, October 18, 1992.

Chapter 1:
The Antiphallic Campaign

1. This paper, "Obscuring Men's Power," can be found in *Women Against Violence Against Women*, ed. Dusty Rhodes and Sandra McNeill (Onlywomen Press, 1985), p. 260. This theme was echoed throughout the conference on violence. A paper titled "Sexual Pleasure and Women's Liberation" by Margaret Jackson (p. 217) asserts that there "seems to be a widespread assumption that sexual pleasure is something every woman has a 'right' to, whether with herself, with other women, or with men." Not so, according to Jackson, she doesn't see "how we can ever assume consent under male supremacy, and it is difficult to see how a philosophy of 'anything goes' can help us to work out a feminist sexual practice." Jackson concludes that "the

whole ideology of sexual liberation can to a large extent be seen as a backlash" against feminism.

2. Adrienne Rich, "Compulsory Heterosexuality and Lesbian Existence," *Signs: Journal of Women in Culture and Society*, 5, no. 4: (1980) 637.

3. Bruce Kokopeli and George Lakey, "More Power Then We Want: Masculine Sexuality and Violence," in *Race, Class, and Gender*, ed. Patricia Hill Collins (Wadsworth, Inc., 1992), p. 443.

4. Nancy Mairs, "On Not Liking Sex," *Plaintext* (University of Arizona Press, 1986) p. 83.

5. Cheryl Clarke, "Lesbianism: An Act of Resistance," in *This Bridge Called My Back: Writings By Radical Women of Color*, ed. Cherrie Moraga and Gloria Anzaldúa (Kitchen Table: Women of Color Press, 1983), pp. 128–137. This book is frequently used as a required text in women's studies classes.

6. Andrea Dworkin, "Power," *Pornography: Men Possessing Women* (Penguin Books, 1979), p. 23.

7. Sheila Jeffreys, "Sexology and Antifeminism," in *The Sexual Liberals and the Attack on Feminism*, ed. Dorchen Liedholdt and Janice G. Raymond (Pergamon Press, 1990), pp. 17, 22.

8. Ann Ferguson, "Patriarchy, Sexual Identity, and the Sexual Revolution," *Sexual Democracy: Women, Oppression, and Revolution* (Westview Press, 1991), p. 64. In another essay, Ferguson offers an insightful criticism of Andrienne Rich and other feminists' belief in an international lesbian culture. Her essay raises important questions about the tendency of some feminists to stress historical continuity (ignoring historical context in order to identify with women of the past) over historical discontinuity (recognizing that such movements as feminism and gay rights are new and that women of the past may not have viewed themselves as fighting male domination or as fitting our ideas of lesbians). See Ann Ferguson, "Is There a Lesbian Culture?" in *Lesbian Philosophies and Cultures*, ed. Jeffner Allen (State University of New York Press, 1990), p. 63.

9. Marilyn Frye, "Some Reflections on Separatism and Power," in *Women and Values*, ed. Marilyn Pearsall (Wadsworth, Inc., 1986), pp. 132–139.

10. From an interview with Gloria Steinem in Nancy Gibbs, "The War Against Feminism," *Time*, March 9, 1992, p. 57. "Q: How are men reacting to your books? Steinem: I think some feminist books should be for women only. It happens that my book [Revolution from Within] is appropriate for men and women both. . . ."

11. "NOW's Priority Issues," National Organization for Women fact sheet, 1991.

12. Rich, "Compulsory Heterosexuality and Lesbian Existence," p. 649.

13. Donna Minkowitz, "Patricia Ireland Takes the Reins: NOW's New President Talks About Her Woman Companion, Queer Nation, and NOW's Future," *The Advocate*, October 17, 1991, p. 41.

14. Donna Minkowitz, "Despite a Troubled History, the National Organization for Women Welcomes Lesbians into the Fold," *The Advocate*, March 24, 1992, p. 45. Minkowitz writes, "Between 1969 and 1971, NOW systematically purged suspected lesbians from its ranks—[Rita Mae] Brown was among the first to go."

15. See Shane Phelan, *Identity Politics: Lesbian Feminism and the Limits of Community* (Temple University Press, 1989), p. 38. According to Phelan, Rita Mae Brown "resigned from NOW in January of 1970," stating, "Lesbian is the one word that can cause the Executive Committee a collective heart attack." For more on the history of NOW and lesbianism, see Marcia Cohen, *The Sisterhood: The Inside Story of the Women's Movement and the Leaders Who Made It Happen* (Fawcett Columbine, 1988).

16. E. M. Ettorre, "A New Look at Lesbianism," in *Issues in Feminism: A First Course in Women's Studies*, ed. Sheila Ruth (Mayfield Publishing Company, 1990), p. 249.

17. Joyce Trebilcot, "Dyke Methods," in *Lesbian Philosophies and Cultures*, p. 23.

18. Amber Hollibaugh and Cherrie Moraga, "What We're Rollin' Around in Bed With: Sexual Silences in Feminism," *Powers of Desire: The Politics of Sexuality*, ed. Ann Snitow, Christine Stansell, and Sharon Thompson (Monthly Review Press, 1983), p. 394.

19. Linda Gordon, *Woman's Body, Woman's Right: A Social History of Birth Control in America* (Penguin Books, 1974), p. 184.

20. Ibid., p. 237.

21. A good illustration of this feminist condemnation of "dominance" in sex was the uproar at a 1982 Barnard conference on feminism and sexuality. The fact that some of the feminists speaking openly supported freedom of speech and the right to sexual freedoms (from heterosexual sex to consensual lesbian S&M) saw the conference protested by groups such as the Coalition for a Feminist Sexuality and Against Sadomasochism, who distributed vicious flyers accusing speakers of "lobbying for an end to laws that protect children from sexual abuse by adults." See Marcia Pally, "The Fireworks at the Sexuality Conference," *New York Native*, May 24, 1982, p. 14. For more on feminist debates surrounding the sex act, see *Coming to Power*, edited by members of SAMOIS, a lesbian/feminist S/M organization (Alyson Publications, 1987); Rosemarie Tong, "Radical Feminism on Gender and Sexuality," *Feminist Thought: A Comprehensive Introduction* (Westview Press, 1989), pp. 121–122; and Shane Phelan, "Sadomasochism and the Meaning of Feminism," *Identity Politics*, pp. 99–134.

22. Dorchen Leidholdt, "When Women Defend Pornography," in *The Sexual Liberals and the Attack on Feminism*, p. 129.

23. Sheila Jeffreys, *Anticlimax: A Feminist Perspective on the Sexual Revolution* (New York University Press, 1990), p. 2. In comparison with her flattering review of Jeffreys' book denouncing the sexual revolution in the January/February 1991 *Ms.*, Ann Jones criticizes both the content and authorship of Paula Kamen's *Feminist Fatale: Voices from the "Twentysomething" Generation Explore the Future of the "Women's Movement"* (Donald I. Fine, Inc., 1991). As Kamen notes, women of my generation often feel alienated by several aspects of current feminism. Jones dismisses our concerns as "a depressing case study in the success of backlash propaganda." For another bit of feminist Kinsey bashing, see Dworkin, *Pornography*, pp. 179–188.

24. Catharine MacKinnon, *Feminism Unmodified: Discourses on Life and Law* (Harvard University Press, 1987), p. 99. For a different slant on the abortion issue, see Elizabeth Fox-Genovese, *Feminism Without Illusions: A Critique of Individualism* (University of North Carolina Press, 1991), pp. 81–85. Fox-Genovese, a feminist theorist who argues that the "collective good" outweighs individual rights, questions abortion

rights because they are based on the individualistic idea that determining when life begins has been left up to women and their conscience. Fox-Genovese finds this distressing, seeing the potential that individual women (not herself, of course) might interpret their right to abortion as the right to "kill all those who depend upon her and drain her resources—elderly parents, terminally ill or handicapped children. Without some such argument, the right to abortion—the woman's right to sexual self-determination—can logically lead to the right to murder with impunity." In answer to this dilemma, Fox-Genovese proposes abortion rights based on a "collective decision" on when life begins. Getting people to agree on when that is seems quite unlikely.

25. Judith R. Walkowitz, *City of Dreadful Delight: Narratives of Sexual Danger in Late-Victorian London* (University of Chicago Press, 1992), p. 134.

26. Dorchen Leidholdt, introduction, *The Sexual Liberals and the Attack on Feminism*, p. xv, footnote 8.

27. Sonia Johnson, *Wildfire: Igniting the She/volution* (Wildfire Books, 1989), pp. 25–27.

28. The letter is published in Sonia Johnson, *Going Out of Our Minds: The Metaphysics of Liberation* (The Crossing Press, 1987), pp. 225–226. Johnson's account of her run for the presidency isn't too clear on many points. For example, she neglects to say how many votes—if any—she received. But she does write, seemingly in complete seriousness: "My home state of Virginia has totally outrageous ballot-access requirements for third parties that are impossible to meet, and the law prohibits write-ins. Since I could not vote for the only candidate with integrity [herself], I did not go to the polls,"(p. 356 n. 8).

29. Katherine Creag, "NYU Students for Choice Help Break 'Chain of Life,' " *The Washington Square News*, October 20, 1992, p. 1.

Chapter 2:
Victim Mythology

1. Uniform Crime Report, Federal Bureau of Investigation, 1990.

2. John D'Emilio and Estelle B. Freedman, *Intimate Matters: A History of Sexuality in America* (Harper & Row, 1988), p. 70.

3. T. Keating Holland, "Margins of Error," *Reason*, February 1992, p. 53.

4. Erna Olafson Hellerstein, Leslie Parker Hume, and Karen M. Offen, eds., *Victorian Women: A Documentary Account of Women's Lives in Nineteenth-Century England, France, and the United States* (Stanford University Press, 1981), p. 178.

5. For articles by Koss on her survey, see Mary P. Koss, Christine A. Gidycz, and Nadine Wisniewski, "The Scope of Rape: Incidence and Prevalence of Sexual Aggression and Victimization in a National Sample of Higher Education Students," *Journal of Consulting and Clinical Psychology* 55, no. 2 (1987): 162–170, and Mary P. Koss, "Hidden Rape . . ." in *Rape and Sexual Assault*, vol. 2, ed. Ann Wolbert Burgess (Garland Publishing Company, 1988), pp. 3–25. For background on her methods, see Mary P. Koss and Cheryl J. Oros, "Sexual Experiences Survey: A Research Instrument Investigating Sexual Aggression and Victimization," *Journal of Consulting and Clinical Psychology* 50, no. 3 (1982): 455–457, and Mary P. Koss and Christine A. Gidycz, "Sexual Experiences Survey: Reliability and Validity," *Journal of Consulting and Clinical Psychology* 53, no. 3 (1985): 422–423.

6. Peter Hellman, "Crying Rape: The Politics of Date Rape on Campus," *New York*, March 8, 1993, p. 32.

7. Ibid.

8. Koss et al., "Stranger and Acquaintance Rape: Are There Differences in the Victim's Experience?" *Psychology of Women Quarterly*, vol. 12 (1988), pp. 1–23, cited in Neil Gilbert, "Realities and Mythologies of Rape," *Society*, May/June 1992, p. 4. As Gilbert points out, these numbers change according to which account of Koss's study you are reading. In the July 17, 1991, *Los Angeles Daily Journal*, for instance, Koss claims that "one quarter" of the students did not feel victimized, compared with the 11 percent figure she gave in 1988.

9. *Victorian Women*, p. 416.

10. Criminal Victimization in the United States, 1990, U.S. Department of Justice, February 1992.

11. Lifetime Likelihood of Victimization, Bureau of Justice Statistics Technical Report, U.S. Department of Justice, March 1987.

12. In their survey, the NCS asked respondents if they'd been a victim of "rape, attempted rape or other type of sexual attack." Later in the survey, they were asked specifically: "Incidents involving forced or unwanted sexual acts are often difficult to talk about. (Other than any incidents already mentioned), have you been forced or coerced to engage in unwanted sexual activity by a) someone you didn't know before, b) a casual acquaintance, or c) someone you know well?"

13. Naomi Breslau, Ph.D., et al., "Traumatic Events and Posttraumatic Stress Disorder in an Urban Population of Young Adults," *Archives of General Psychiatry* 48 (March 1991): 216–222, and Fran H. Norris, "Epidemiology of Trauma: Frequency and Impact of Different Potentially Traumatic Events on Different Demographic Groups," *Journal of Consulting and Clinical Psychology* 60, no. 3 (1992): 409–418.

14. "Rape in America: A Report to the Nation," April 23, 1992, a press release prepared by the National Victim Center, Arlington, Virginia, and the Crime Victims Research Center, Department of Psychiatry and Behavioral Sciences, Medical University of South Carolina. For information, I consulted an unpublished paper by Dean G. Kilpatrick et al., titled "The Prevalence of Sexual Assault and Assault Characteristics in a National Probability Sample of Women."

15. Sharon Johnson, "Rape: The Conservative Backlash," *Ms.*, March/April 1992, p. 88. "Now these hard-won safeguards are being reexamined due to lobbying by conservatives and opponents of the women's movement. . . . The academic point man of the 'Return to the Fifties Rape Movement' is Neil Gilbert, a sociologist and professor of social welfare at the University of California at Berkeley." This article also promotes a common erroneous perception of the National Crime Survey. "The bureau [NCS] uses a narrow definition of rape that includes neither verbal threats nor psychological pressure." This is untrue. Legal definitions of rape and attempted rape do include verbal threats of force.

16. National Organization for Women mailer, October 1992.

17. "Conference Resolutions," *National NOW Times*, August 1992, p. 13.

18. Cathianne Linzalone, "Big Trouble in Glen Ridge," WAC talk,

special insert in *New Directions for Women*, January/February 1993, p. 19.

19. Dianne F. Herman, "The Rape Culture," in *Women: A Feminist Perspective*, ed. Jo Freeman (Mayfield Publishing Company, 1989), p. 20.

20. Barbara Sinclair Deckard, "Violence Against Women," in *All American Women*, ed. Johnnetta B. Cole (The Free Press, 1986), p. 384.

21. Susan Griffin, "Rape: The All-American Crime," in *Women and Values*, ed. Marilyn Pearsall (Wadsworth, Inc., 1986), p. 179.

22. Catharine A. MacKinnon, "Feminism, Marxism, Method, and the State," in *Feminism and Methodology*, ed. Sandra Harding (Indiana University Press, 1987), p. 142.

23. Andrea Dworkin, *Pornography*, p. 30.

24. *Victorian Women*, p. 178.

25. D'Elimio and Freedman, *Intimate Matters*, p. 220.

26. Robin Morgan, *Going Too Far: The Personal Chronicle of a Feminist* (Vintage Books, 1978), p. 178.

27. John S. Haller and Robin M. Haller, *The Physician and Sexuality in Victorian America* (W. W. Norton & Company, Inc., 1977), p. 112.

28. Ibid., p. 108.

29. Joanne Jacobs, "Feminists, Yes; Victims of Men, No," reprinted in the *Oregonian*, March 24, 1993.

Chapter 3:
Dirty Pictures

1. "Resolutions on Pornography" and "National NOW's Positions on Pornography and the PVCA" are from the national office of NOW. A NOW release titled "Pornography: National Organization for Women's Discussion Outline, March 1986" asserts: "While recognizing that the feminist community is divided on many issues related to pornography, the resolutions commit NOW, as the largest feminist

organization in the United States, to take a leadership position on pornography, and to serve and extend feminist analysis through a wide range of voluntary action on this subject." A NOW fact sheet titled "Thinking About Pornography," used following a NOW presentation of the feminist antiporn documentary *Not a Love Story* to students at George Washington University, is a perfect illustration of just what NOW considers a "feminist analysis" of sexual material. "What is pornography for?" the fact sheet asks. The answer is quick in coming. "The evidence indicates that pornography is used: to sexualize the objectification and subordination of women . . . to attack women's dignity, self-esteem and physical security . . . to fetishize pregnancy and promote pregnancy discrimination [!], to promote contempt, fear, and hatred of women by men, to normalize intimidation and terrorization of women, to threaten and justify acts of violence against women [and] to silence and control women."

2. This is according to Marcia Pally, a member of Feminists for Free Expression, who states, "In 1991, there was an antiporn proposal at NOW. . . . The specific proposal, if I can remember, was to launch a national advertising campaign by getting a national advertising agency to design it—an effective campaign against pornography. Now, the people who showed up against this were the sex workers. They said, 'This is not going to help us out.' I've been speaking at conventions since before 1982, and it's always the same thing. It's always the sex-industry workers who show up and say 'don't do us any favors. First of all, outlawing the pornography industry doesn't help us—it hinders us. We want that income. . . . Don't you, sitting in your academic department, tell us sanctimoniously that we shouldn't do this.' "

3. Along with Dworkin, MacKinnon, and Smeal, other participants at this conference on porn and "hate speech" included Kathleen Barry, John Stoltenberg, and NOW staff officer Twiss Butler. For more on this conference, see "Speech, Equality, and Harm," *Off Our Backs*, April 1993, p. 4.

4. John D'Emilio and Estelle B. Freedman, *Intimate Matters: A History of Sexuality in America* (Harper & Row, 1988), p. 70.

5. Ronald G. Walters, ed., *Primers for Prudery: Sexual Advice to Victorian America* (Spectrum Books, 1974), p. 54.

6. D'Emilio and Freedman, *Intimate Matters*, p. 159.

7. Donald Alexander Downs, *The New Politics of Pornography* (University of Chicago Press, 1989), pp. 97, 109–116.

8. For a detailed analysis of MacKinnon and Dworkin's ordinance, see Downs, *The New Politics of Pornography*; see also Ronald J. Berger, et al., *Feminism and Pornography* (Praeger Publishers, 1991). For an excellent analysis of what the ordinance could do compared with existing law, see Lauren Robel, "Pornography and Existing Law: What the Law Can Do," in *For Adult Users Only: The Dilemma of Violent Pornography*, ed. Susan Gubar and Joan Hoff (Indiana University Press, 1989), pp. 178–197. Robel points out that there are already laws in place for many of the problems the ordinance is designed to address. For example, the clause against "coercing" women into pornography through intimidation or force covers many already-illegal acts, such as rape, and under tort law, any photographs of the crime could result in damages as well as an injunction against their distribution.

9. Downs, *The New Politics of Pornography*, p. 140. See also Jim Mellowitz, "Bias-Based Smut Ban Faces Test," *National Law Journal*, May 14, 1984, p. 3. MacKinnon and Dworkin's ordinance has met a similar fate in other cities where they've promoted it. In Minneapolis, for example, the ordinance was vetoed by the mayor. For more on the ordinance in Minneapolis, see Downs, *The New Politics of Pornography*; Mary Kay Blakely, "Is One Woman's Sexuality Another Woman's Pornography?" Ms., April 1985, p. 37; and Lisa Duggan, Nan Hunter, and Carol S. Vance, "False Promises: Feminist Antipornography Legislation in the U.S.," in *Women Against Censorship*, ed. Varda Burstyn (Douglas & McIntrye, Ltd., 1985), pp. 130–151. An interesting aspect of the case in Minneapolis is while MacKinnon and Dworkin were presented as "consultants," the city was in fact paying them to push their own bill. See Martha S. Allen, "Porn Consultants Bill City $18,729 Extra," *Minneapolis Star and Tribune*, February 10, 1984. According to this article, MacKinnon and Dworkin were hired by the Minneapolis city council as consultants for their own ordinance for seventy dollars an hour, up to five thousand dollars total. But the two ended up billing the city $23,729.03.

10. With the exception of accusations that Father Bruce Ritter molested boys, background on Meese commissioners can be found in

Philip Nobile and Eric Nadler, *United States of America vs. Sex* (Minotaur Press, Ltd., 1986), pp. 16–22. Also see Richard Stengel, "Sex Busters," *Time*, July 21, 1986. For allegations that Father Bruce Ritter molested boys, see William Plummer, et al. "Sex Charges Pit Four Young Men Against the Revered Founder of Covenant House," *People*, February 26, 1990, p. 39.

11. Howard Kurtz, "The Pornography Panel's Controversial Last Days: Scientists Say Report Misrepresents Their Findings to Support Conclusions on Sex Violence," *Washington Post*, May 30, 1986, and Reuter, "Pornography Panel Off Base, Two Experts Say," *Washington Post*, November 25, 1986.

12. The United States Attorney General's Commission on Pornography, Final Report, July 1986, p. 769. For a full transcript of Dworkin's speech, as well as her answers to questions from the Meese Commission, see Andrea Dworkin, "Pornography is a Civil Rights Issue," *Letters from a War Zone* (E. P. Dutton, 1988), pp. 276–307. Of note is Dworkin's answer to a question from Father Bruce Ritter on whether or not she believes depictions of consensual sadomasochistic activities (bondage, role playing, etc.) should be banned. "My answer to your question is I do object to the degradation intrinsic to the acts. . . . that material would be actionable under our law, under our civil rights law; in my view it should be, it is appropriate that it be," Dworkin responded, going on to claim that the question of women consenting to S&M sex play is irrelevant. "There is simply no reality to the motion that women consent to it, because women don't."

13. According to their literature, Morality in Media is a nonprofit interfaith national organization "working to stop the traffic in pornography constitutionally." They have been in operation since 1962. Their mailings and brochures are redolent with vituperations against rock music, radio and television shows, especially that "offensive morning Donahue show." In their words, "Morality in Media is the concerned community expressing its concern in order to inhibit the flow of smut, and bring about mass media based on the principles of LOVE, TRUTH, and TASTE."

14. See "National NOW's Position on Pornography and the PVCA," from the national offices of NOW. According to this statement, NOW originally supported an earlier version of the Pornography Vic-

tims' Compensation Act but voted in 1990 that it would "neither endorse nor oppose the PVCA."

15. Tamar Lewin, "Canada Court Says Pornography Harms Women," *New York Times*, February 28, 1992; Marla Dickerson, "Canada Tests Porn vs. Civil Liberties," *Detroit News*, April 11, 1993; Michael S. Serrill, "Smut That Harms Women," *Time* (European edition), March 9, 1992; Michele Landsberg, "Canada: Antipornography Breakthrough in the Law," *Ms.*, May/June 1992, p. 14; Karen Selick, "Censorship—More Demeaning Than Pornography," *Canadian Lawyer*, May 1993, p. 46; "A Criminal Abuse of Human Rights," *Globe & Mail*, June 19, 1993; Bill Redden, "Oh, for Christ's Sake, Canada," *PDXS*, August 30, 1993, p. 3; and "The Sex Panic: Women, Censorship and 'Pornography': A Conference Report," from the National Coalition Against Censorship, 1993.

16. For a discussion of books seized, see "Books and Magazines Detained by Customs," *Globe & Mail*, May 12, 1993; Marcy Skeiner, "Canadian Crackdown Continues," *On Our Backs*, March/April, 1993, p. 12; "Canada Confiscates Feminist Books," Feminists for Free Expression newsletter, vol. 1, no. 3 (Summer 1993); and Leanne Katz, "Censors' Helpers," *New York Times*, December 4, 1993. McCormack quote cited in Bill Redden, "Oh, for Christ's Sake, Canada," p. 3.

17. Some feminist definitions of pornography include material that is not obviously sexual in nature. For example, a Women Against Pornography press release, February 24, 1983, for the group's Second Annual Advertising Awards Ceremony attacked Maidenform underwear (for showing "undressed women in public places") and Hanes Stockings (for "men ogling women's legs") as "pornographic ads" that were said to "promote violence against women." Guy Laroche was also criticized "for an ad for Fidji Perfume that depicts a female neck encircled by a snake." WAP spokeswoman Frances Patai is quoted as saying, "This ad reduces a woman to nothing more than parted lips and an exposed, vulnerable throat. It makes a threatening situation seem exotic and alluring." The idea that mainstream advertisements can be pornography has gained an incredible amount of credence in the movement. Many women's studies classes, for instance, show the feminist film *Still Killing Us Softly*, which labels everything from clothing to perfume ads as "pornographic" and responsible for rape,

and many women's organizations—from New York City's Women Action Coalition to the Seattle chapter of NOW—have letter-writing campaigns against what they see as pornographic ads.

18. Walter E. Houghton, *The Victorian Frame of Mind 1830–1870* (Yale University Press, 1957), p. 368.

19. Susan Meyers, "Pornography: Where We Stand Today," *Women in Business*, March/April 1990, p. 16. "Researcher and psychologist Diana Russell is convinced of this. 'It promotes violence against women,' says Russell, a professor at Mills College in Oakland, California. 'It undermines men's inhibitions. It encourages men not to see women as people, and makes men feel like it's OK to rape.' " The question of just why depicting our sexuality would make men not see women as people is seldom addressed by current feminists. For feminist theory on porn causing rape, see Diana E. H. Russell, "Pornography and Rape: A Causal Model" and "The Experts Cop Out," in *Making Violence Sexy: Feminist Views on Pornography*, ed. Diana E. H. Russell (Open University Press, 1993), pp. 120–167; Catharine A. MacKinnon, "Not A Moral Issue," *Feminism Unmodified: Discourses on Life and Law* (Harvard University Press, 1987), pp. 146–162; Catharine A. MacKinnon, *Only Words* (Harvard University Press, 1993); and "Research on the Effects of Pornography," *Take Back The Night: Women on Pornography*, ed. Laura Lederer (William Morrow, 1980), pp. 185–218. Many feminist writings on the subject seem to assume the proof of a causal connection, while others dismiss the need for evidence as irrelevant. As Robin Morgan puts it in *The Anatomy of Freedom: Feminism, Physics, and Global Politics* (p. 111): "Still, it is interesting that such proof of causality is demanded at all."

20. Quote by rapist in Ronald L. Scott, "Analysis of the Need Systems of Twenty Male Rapists," *Psychological Reports*, no. 51 (1982): 1124. In this study, rapists seem to be socially insecure and guilt-ridden and use aggressive control of others to compensate for their feelings of inadequacy. Scott notes, however, that his results should not be generalized beyond his sample. For more studies on rape, see John Briere and Neil M. Malamuth, "Self-Reported Likelihood of Sexually Aggressive Behavior: Attitudinal Versus Sexual Explanations," *Journal of Research in Personality*, no. 17 (1983): 315–323. This study found no link between use of pornography and likelihood to rape; the researchers note this supports the thesis that rape is "essen-

tially unrelated to sexual frustration or sexual maladjustment." In Eugene J. Kanin, "Date Rapists: Differential Sexual Socialization and Relative Deprivation," *Archives of Sexual Behavior* 14, no. 3 (1985): 219–231, Kanin reports that early "familial and other primary group influences might have affected aspects of personality development of (1) a generalized hostility toward the female world, (2) an aggressive component and (3) a hypererotic orientation." In Neil M. Malamuth, "Predictors of Naturalistic Sexual Aggression," *Journal of Personality and Social Psychology* 50, no. 5 (1986): 953–961, Malamuth found that "sexual arousal in response to aggression is one of the factors that may create an inclination to aggress against women," but that "other factors," such as hostility toward women and dominance motivation, "must be present before such an arousal pattern will lead to aggressive behavior." In Christine Adler, "An Exploration of Self-Reported Sexually Aggressive Behavior," *Crime and Delinquency* 31, no. 2 (April 1985): 306–331, Adler concludes that a "significant relationship was found between sexual aggression and attitudes that legitimize sexual aggression of women." The key factor that indicated sexually aggressive males in her study was the presence of sexually aggressive friends. See also Nicholas Groth, Ann Wolbert Burgess and Lynda Lytle Holmstrom, "Rape: Power, Anger, and Sexuality," *American Journal of Psychiatry*, November 1977, pp. 1239–1243, and Saul M. Levin and Lawrence Stava, "Personality Characteristics of Sex Offenders: A Review," *Archives of Sexual Behavior* 16, no. 1 (1987): 57–79.

21. *Donahue* transcripts, no. 03194, Multimedia Entertainment, Inc., 1984.

22. As porn and rape researcher Neil M. Malamuth pointed out to the Meese Commission, "The laboratory is a situation where we create sanction for aggression, where aggression to some degree is justified or at least given a context where it is acceptable." See Diana E. H. Russell, "The Experts Cop Out," *Making Violence Sexy*, p. 157. A study on the effects of a violent movie, for instance, might consist of exposing the subject to the material and then giving that person permission to administer electric shocks to another subject. To extrapolate any findings from the laboratory to real life, such as someone seeing that movie in a theater with a friend, is unreasonable. Not only is the laboratory an unrealistic environment, where subjects are given permission to aggress without any fear of reprisal, but people experience a variety of other influences in their lives (loved ones,

coworkers, other media, etc.) that operate to inhibit violence. You may leave a *Terminator* movie feeling pumped up and excited, but that doesn't mean you're going to attack the first person you see in the parking lot. Claims that material directly causes violence aren't only unproven; they're dangerous. The same law that censors material on the basis that it causes violence will be a legal precedent for violent criminals to use as a defense. Their lawyers will be able to point to such a law in order to argue that their client couldn't help what he did—it was the material that was at fault. If we accept that material makes people do things they otherwise wouldn't do, we are going to have to accept that many rapists and other criminals shouldn't be held responsible for their actions.

23. *Making Violence Sexy*, p. 18.

24. *Primers for Prudery*, p. 55.

25. See, for example, Edward Donnerstein, Daniel Linz, and Steven Penrod, *The Question of Pornography: Research Findings and Policy Implications* (The Free Press, 1987).

26. John Stoltenberg, *Refusing to Be A Man: Essays on Sex and Justice* (Meridian Books, 1990). This tome was heralded by Gloria Steinem as a "courageous book that gets to the heart of the problem." Chockfull of quotes from Andrea Dworkin, smacking of condescension toward other men ("I had always felt irremediably different—even when no one else noticed, I knew; I knew I wasn't really one of them"), and full of diatribes against erect and "engorged" penises, it would seem the real heart of the book is that Stoltenberg is one of the few enlightened men on the planet. His attitude toward "them" is made clear throughout the book, as in his poem titled "At issue: marital rape." "The right to rape that comes with the wedding cake./ His conjugal right./ Her connubial duty./ Whenever he gets hungry,/ he gets his piece of cake./ Lip-smacking good. . . ." Excerpts from Stoltenberg's book are taught to women's studies students at the University of Minnesota.

27. Diana E. H. Russell, *Rape in Marriage* (Indiana University Press, 1982), p. 156.

28. Marcia Pally, *Sense and Censorship: The Vanity of Bonfires* (Americans for Constitutional Freedom and the Freedom to Read Foundation, 1991), p. 60.

29. Ibid., p. 30.

30. *American Psychologist* 42, no. 10 (1987), as cited by Pally, *Sense and Censorship*, p. 24. For studies showing that porn has not grown more violent, see T. S. Palys, "Testing the Common Wisdom: The Social Content of Video Pornography," *Canadian Psychology* 27 (1986): 22–31, and Joseph E. Scott and Steven J. Cuvelier, "Sexual Violence in Playboy Magazine: A Longitudinal Content Analysis," *Journal of Sex Research* 23, no. 4 (1987): 534–539. Tracking down the validity of many commonly accepted beliefs about the pornography industry often leads to highly questionable sources. For example, Naomi Wolf makes the oft-repeated claim that the pornography industry "generates an estimated 7 *billion* dollars a year" (*The Beauty Myth*, p. 79). For her source, she cites from MacKinnon's *Feminism Unmodified* a June 4, 1984, article in *U.S. News & World Report*, which claims that porn is an "8 billion dollar a year business." The article doesn't cite any proof for this number. But it does state that porn sent through the mail accounts for $3 billion alone—that is, "according to Morality in Media."

31. Liz Kelly, *Surviving Sexual Violence* (University of Minnesota Press, 1988), p. 41.

32. See Judith Reisman, principal investigator, "Images of Children, Crime and Violence in Playboy, Penthouse and Hustler Magazines," Executive Summary, 1987, p. 10, footnote 6. In this footnote, Reisman identifies herself as Bat-Ada. This paper is the summary of a study on cartoons in porn magazines conducted by Reisman for the Meese Commission, who found it so hopelessly unscientific, they omitted it from their report. For more on Reisman's bizarre study (she found evidence of child porn in cartoons most would believe depict grown adults), see Robin Wilson, "Controversial Study of Children in Sex Magazines Shelved by U.S.," *Chronicle of Higher Education*, November 26, 1986, p. 22.

33. The video Reisman appeared in is titled *Dangerous Behavior: A Hidden Pattern of Abuse*, produced by The Report—A Righteous Perspective, n.d. This video—an amazingly hateful piece of propaganda that implies homosexuals are to blame for child sexual abuse—was used by the Oregon Citizens Alliance in their unsuccessful attempt to pass a 1992 ordinance in Oregon tying homosexuality to pedophilia and banning any teachings by gays in schools. For the NOW state-

ment defending Reisman, see "Press Treatment of Judith Reisman's Content Analysis of Images of Children . . . ," from the National Organization for Women, Inc., June 1990.

34. Audre Lorde, "Uses of the Erotic: The Erotic as Power," in *Take Back the Night*, pp. 296, 300. Despite the fact this essay is over a decade old, it is often assigned to women's studies students as an example of the current feminist position on pornography.

35. Isabel Wilkerson, "Foes of Pornography and Bigotry Join Forces," *New York Times*, March 12, 1993. NOW president Patricia Ireland is also quoted in this article supporting the feminist crusade against pornography.

36. For feminist works critical of the antiporn crusade, see *Women Against Censorship*; *Caught Looking: Feminism, Pornography, and Censorship*, Kate Ellis, Nan D. Hunter, Beth Jaker, Barbara O'Dair and Abby Tallmer, eds. (Feminism Anti-Censorship TaskForce [FACT] Book Committee, 1986); Carol S. Vance, ed. *Pleasure and Danger*, (Routledge & Kegan Paul, 1984); and Ellen Willis, "Feminism, Moralism, and Pornography," *Beginning to See the Light: Pieces of a Decade* (Alfred A. Knopf, 1981), pp. 219–227. Betty Friedan also feels the antiporn crusade is a dangerous diversion. As part of her plan to "get the women's movement moving again," Friedan asserted feminists should "Get off the pornography kick and face the real obscenity of poverty. No matter how repulsive we may find pornography, laws banning books or movies for sexually explicit content could be far more dangerous to women. The pornography issue is dividing the women's movement and giving the impression on college campuses that to be a feminist is to be against sex." See Betty Friedan, *The Second Stage*, rev. ed. (Summit Books, 1986), p. 357. Needless to say, Friedan's warning has been ignored by many feminists.

37. Barbara Sinclair Deckard, "Violence Against Women," in *All American Women*, ed. Johnnetta B. Cole (The Free Press, 1986), p. 392.

38. Andrea Dworkin, *Intercourse*, p. 122.

39. Nina Hartley, "Reflections of a Feminist Porn Star," *Blue Stocking*, December 1993, p. 6, reprinted from *Gauntlet: Exploring the Limits of Free Expression*, no. 5.

40. Miss Ivory, "Jenny Westberg Told the Truth," *Blue Stocking*, October 1993, p. 2.

Chapter 4:
The Goddess Within

1. Estimates of the number of people actively involved in goddess worship vary wildly according to the source consulted. A May 6, 1991, *Time* magazine article entitled "When God Was a Woman" (p. 73) places the number at roughly 100,000 U.S. women, while Patricia Aburdene and John Naisbitt, *Megatrends for Women* (Villard Books, 1992) estimates the number is as high as half a million active U.S. followers. One group, the Circle Network, claims 100,000 members alone. Because many goddess worshipers practice their beliefs in small groups or alone, and because of the inclusive definitions held by many of the leaders (who might recognize anyone with an interest as a believer), estimates on the number of people involved in this religion should be viewed skeptically.

2. Merlin Stone, "The Gifts from Reclaiming Goddess History," in *To Be a Woman: The Birth of the Conscious Feminine*, ed. Connie Zweig (Jeremy P. Tarcher, 1990), p. 205.

3. Many feminist writers on goddess worship follow the Jungian notion of "feminine" and "masculine" archetypes. The feminine is the basis for traits such as nurturing, intuitive thought, and interdependence, while the masculine stands for aggression, analytical thought, and independence. While Jung stated that these archetypes are attributes of both sexes (begging the question of why he named them in gender-specific terms), he also claimed they are the dominant drives in each gender. A common criticism leveled at Jungian analysis is its often complete disregard for class, cultural, and other differences among people, as well as its perpetuation of sexist stereotypes. *Women Who Run with the Wolves* (Ballantine Books, 1992), the best-seller by Jungian analyst Clarissa Pinkola Estés, is sometimes applauded by feminists (Gloria Steinem, for instance, recommends it highly in *Revolution from Within*). But Estes herself refuses the feminist label. See Dirk Johnson, "A Message for All Women: Run Free and Wild Like the Wolf," *New York Times*, February 28, 1993.

4. Mary Reinholz, "New Age Witches Get Earthy," *New York Daily News*, May 9, 1993, p. 8.

5. Christina Hoff Sommers, "Sister Soldiers," *The New Republic*, October 5, 1992, p. 29.

6. See, for example, Jennie Ruby and Carol Anne Douglas, "NWSA: Working to Survive," *Off Our Backs*, August/September 1992, p. 1. According to this article, several years of turbulent conferences filled with accusations of oppression leveled by lesbians, "fat women," women of color, the disabled, and Jewish and other caucuses have seen the organization's conference attendance drop from over two thousand to not more than four hundred people. Debates concerning the 1992 conference included whether or not feminists should become university administrators (some say no, that climbing the career ladder is too hierarchical), serving dairy products at the conference (the ecofeminist caucus is moving to eliminate all meat, fish, and dairy products served at their events), and whether or not to call the sixteenth birthday of the organization "sweet 16" (one member claimed it was "misogynistic" because "sweet 16 is when we announce that a young woman is ready to be fucked"). Participants at the conference were also notified not to wear dry-cleaned fabrics, perfumes, or hair spray (an allergy group claimed it was being oppressed). Despite the wacky nature of the National Women's Studies Association, they are supported by the Department of Education and the Ford Foundation and are considered to represent the mainstream of women's studies.

7. These time periods vary somewhat depending on the author. Marija Gimbutas, for example, places the religion as prior to 3500 B.C., predominantly in the Neolithic period, while Merlin Stone claims that goddess worship survived in altered forms through the classical periods in Greece and until roughly A.D. 500. For a few of the feminist works on the subject, see Marija Gimbutas, *The Language of the Goddess* (Harper & Row, 1989); Merlin Stone, *When God Was a Woman* (Harvest/HBJ, 1976); and Riane Eisler, *The Chalice and the Blade* (Harper & Row, 1989).

8. Starhawk [Miriam Simos], *The Spiral Dance* (Harper & Row, 1979), p. 3.

9. Sandy Fritz, "Who Was the Iceman?" *Popular Science*, February

1993, p. 46, and Leon Jaroff, "Iceman," *Time*, October 26, 1992, p. 62.

10. Stone, *When God Was a Woman*, p. 18. For a summary on the feminist theory of the Kurgan invasions, see Marija Gimbutas, "Women and Culture in Goddess-Oriented Old Europe," in *The Politics of Women's Spirituality*, ed. Charlene Spretnak (Anchor Books, 1982), pp. 22–31.

11. Jay Mathews, "Did Goddess Worship Mark Ancient Age of Peace?" *Washington Post*, January 7, 1990.

12. Essentially, many prehistorians argue that the evidence indicates that a peaceful migration occurred at the time, not the violent conquest that many feminists argue. For excellent summaries of the controversy surrounding the Kurgan theory, see Robert Suro, "New Theories on Early Europe Cite Migration, Not Conquest," *New York Times*, May 10, 1988, and Peter Steinfels, "Idyllic Theory of Goddesses Creates Storm: Was a Peaceful Matriarchal World Shattered by Patriarchal Invaders?" *New York Times*, February 13, 1990.

13. Judy Chicago, "Our Heritage is Our Power," in *The Politics of Women's Spirituality*, p. 152.

14. N. K. Sandars, *Prehistoric Art in Europe* (Penguin Books, 1968), p. 21. For a brief discussion of male and sexless figurines, see Margaret Ehrenberg, *Women in Prehistory* (University of Oklahoma Press, 1989), pp. 66–76.

15. The figure ten thousand years is from David Anthony, assistant professor of anthropology at Hartwick College in Oneonta, New York, author's interview, May 1993.

16. From William Barnett, "Language of the Goddess," *American Journal of Archeology* 96, no. 1 (January 1992): 170.

17. Marija Gimbutas, *The Goddess and Gods of Old Europe: Myths and Cult Images* (University of California Press, 1982), p. 237. Gimbutas writes, "There is no evidence that in Neolithic times mankind understood biological conception."

18. An interesting—and startling—example of why archaeologists are disturbed by the religious and political agenda driving goddess theory is the similarity between current feminist theory and the Nazi

theory on the Indo-European Kurgan invasion. Both the Nazis and the goddess feminists have relied upon distorted archaeological evidence to uphold the idea that peaceful Europe was invaded by a race of patriarchal Indo-Europeans. The difference between current feminist theory and Nazi archaeologists is that the Nazis thought this invasion was good (because the Indo-Europeans were thought to be the original Aryan race) and feminists believe the invasion was bad (because the Indo-Europeans are thought to be the original patriarchal brutes, leading to people like the Nazis). For a fascinating look at the similarities between the two reworkings of prehistory—and the question of agenda-driven archaeology—see David W. Anthony, "Nazi and Eco-Feminist Prehistories: Ideology and Empiricism in Indo-European Archeology," presented at the "Nationalism, Politics, and the Practice of Archeology" symposium, Chicago, November 1991. This paper is slated for publication in an upcoming book tentatively titled *Nationalism, Politics, and the Practice of Archeology*, ed. Dr. Phillip Kohl and Clare Fawcett (Cambridge University Press, forthcoming).

19. Riane Eisler, "The Gaia Tradition and the Partnership Future: An Ecofeminist Manifesto," in *Reweaving the World: The Emergence of Ecofeminism*, ed. Irene Diamond and Gloria Feman Orenstein (Sierra Club Books, 1990), p. 23.

20. As cited by Patricia Aburdene and John Naisbitt, *Megatrends for Women* (Villard Books, 1992), pp. 263–264.

21. Mary Lefkowitz, "The Twilight of the Goddess: Feminism, Spiritualism, and a New Craze," *The New Republic*, August 3, 1992, p. 29.

22. Merlin Stone, "The Gifts from Reclaiming Goddess History," p. 209. Stone makes it clear that the "feminine" means "characteristic of the female."

23. Mary Daly with Jane Caputi, *Wickedary* (Beacon Press, 1988), as cited in *SageWoman*, Fall 1992, p. 21.

24. John S. Haller and Robin M. Haller, *The Physician and Sexuality in Victorian America* (W. W. Norton & Company, 1977), pp. 61–68.

25. Erna Olafson Hellerstein, Leslie Parker Hume, and Karen M. Offen, eds., *Victorian Women: A Documentary Account of Women's Lives in Nineteenth-Century England, France, and the United States* (Stanford University Press, 1981), p. 94.

26. Barbara Ehrenreich and Deirdre English, *Complaints and Disorders: The Sexual Politics of Sickness* (The Feminist Press, 1973), p. 29.

27. Kathleen Sands, "From Evil to Ecstasy: Exploring the Goddess with Margot Adler," *Sojourner*, May 1993, p. 14. For more on feminist and traditional witchcraft, see Margot Adler, *Drawing Down the Moon* (Beacon Press, 1987) and Starhawk [Miriam Simos], *The Spiral Dance*.

28. Carol Christ, "Eleusinian Mysteries," in *The Goddess Celebrates: An Anthology of Women's Rituals*, ed. Diane Stein (The Crossing Press, 1991), p. 255.

29. Stone, *When God Was a Woman*, pp. 202, 219. For an interesting portrayal of Athena, see Eileen McCullough, "Becoming the Goddess Global," *SageWoman*, Spring 1993, p. 17. According to this article on Greek goddesses, Athena is "symbolic of the patriarchy's respect for women's intuition and their fear of offending that power of knowingness."

30. Zsuzsanna Budapest, "A Witch's Manifesto," *Whole Earth Review*, Spring 1992, p. 35.

31. John D'Emilio and Estelle B. Freedman, *Intimate Matters: A History of Sexuality in America* (Harper & Row, 1988), p. 160.

32. Starhawk, "Ritual as Bonding," in *Weaving the Visions: New Patterns in Feminist Spirituality*, ed. Judith Plaskow and Carol P. Christ (Harper & Row, 1989), pp. 333–334.

33. Starhawk, "Power, Authority, and Mystery: Ecofeminism and Earth-based Spirituality," in *Reweaving the World*, pp. 75–76.

34. See, for example, Heidi E. Keller Moon, "Traveling the Galaxies with Mary Daly," *Sojourner*, May 1993, p. 34 ("Mary Daly has written a bible! . . . It is impossible to imagine that anyone who has read *Outercourse* could fail to grasp what patriarchy is about. . . . This book is the work of a master teacher!"); Coral Lansbury, "What Snools These Mortals Be," *New York Times*, January 17, 1988 (a "howling funny book [that] strikes at the very source of religious authority"; "rambunctious, tickling, and tumbling"); and the review of *Outercourse: The Be-Dazzling Voyage*, *Ms.*, January/February 1993, p. 63 ("The genre-shattering, inner and outer autobiography of one of contempo-

rary U.S. feminism's most challenging thinkers. A gourmet feast for all who cannot do without their Daly bread").

35. Peter Steinfels, "Women's Group Recasts Religion in Its Own Image," *New York Times*, April 21, 1993.

36. Alan Cowell, "Pope Issues Censure of 'Nature Worship' by Some Feminists," *New York Times*, July 3, 1993.

37. For more on the feminist movement to reform traditional churches and different readings on feminist spirituality, see Richard N. Ostling, "Cut from the Wrong Cloth," *Time*, June 22, 1992, p. 64; Cullen Murphy, "Women and the Bible," *Atlantic Monthly*, August 1993, p. 39; "Bishops' Pastoral on Women: Good, Bad, or Irrelevant?" and "Women in Theology: It's No Longer a Man's World—But Catholic Constraints Siphon Many Away," both articles in the *National Catholic Reporter*, April 24, 1992, pp. 5–8; and Mary Jo Weaver, *Springs of Water in a Dry Land: Spiritual Survival for Catholic Women Today* (Beacon Press, 1993).

38. Mary Daly quote cited in Ari L. Goldman, *The Search for God at Harvard* (Random House, 1991), p. 246.

39. June 1992 Gallup poll cited in "Majority Report: Catholic Attitudes on Sex and Reproduction," from Catholics for a Free Choice, an educational organization that supports the right to legal reproductive health care, especially family planning and abortion. Polls show that American Catholics vary little from other Americans on the abortion issue, and the majority support the use of birth control.

Chapter 5:
Overthrowing the Patriarchy

1. Robin Morgan, *The Anatomy of Freedom* (Anchor Books, 1984), p. 145.

2. Alison Jaggar, *Feminist Politics and Human Nature* (Rownman and Littlefield, 1988), p. 260.

3. This idea is particularly popular in feminist antiporn theory. It is held that in today's culture, men view pregnancy as a method to control women, literally "colonizing" them. See, for example, Twiss But-

ler, "Abortion and Pornography: The Sexual Liberals 'Gotcha' Against Women's Equality," in *The Sexual Liberals and the Attack on Feminism*, ed. Dorchen Leidholdt and Janice G. Raymond (Pergamon Press, 1990), pp. 114–122, and Andrea Dworkin's discussion of pregnancy and pornography in *Pornography: Men Possessing Women* (Penguin, 1979), pp. 218–223.

4. For an example of education being considered patriarchal, see Adrienne Rich, "Toward a Woman-Centered University," *On Lies, Secrets, and Silence* (W. W. Norton, 1979), pp. 125–155. Rich argues that universities are "androcratic" because they are hierarchical. This essay is frequently assigned to women's studies classes. For capitalism, see bell hooks, *Feminist Theory from Margin to Center* (South End Press, 1984), p. 92. She (hooks) argues that as long as the United States "is an imperialist, capitalist, patriarchal society, no large female majority can enter the existing ranks of the powerful"; for this reason capitalism must be overthrown. The book is also a popular assignment in women's studies classes. For technology, see Judith Plant, "Searching for Common Ground," in *Reweaving the World: The Emergence of Ecofeminism*, ed. Irene Diamond and Gloria Feman Orenstein (Sierra Club Books, 1990), pp. 155–161. For killing animals, see Carol J. Adams, *The Sexual Politics of Meat: A Feminist-Vegetarian Critical Theory* (Continuum Publishing Company, 1990). Adams believes that meat eating is patriarchal because it embodies violence and hierarchy; thus, feminists who eat meat have bought into patriarchal thinking.

5. At George Washington University, the syllabus for "Varieties of Feminist Theory" asserts: "In order to set the stage for feminism's internal debates, we will begin with feminist challenges to the inadequacy of Eurocentric male epistemologies (ways of knowing), analytic categories and the masculinist world views which have structured the public world. . . . We will initiate our inquiry by demystifying malestream [this is not a misspelling] 'theory,' 'reason,' and 'science.' " As part of their grade, students must keep a journal, which is an extremely common assignment in women's studies classes. The professor explains that this exercise "rejects the binary dualisms of male 'science' which separates thought from feeling and reason from emotion." Many students attending women's studies classes find that not only are they supposed to reject "masculine" forms of reasoning such as objectivity but that their grade depends upon it. At Rutgers Uni-

versity, for instance, students attending the introductory women's studies course find that 40 percent of their grade is to come from keeping a journal of "personal experiences, expressions of emotion, dream accounts, poetry, doodles, etc.," performing an "outrageous" and "liberating" act of "rebellion" outside of the class and then writing a paper on it, and attending class consciousness-raising groups. Far from being unusual, this Rutgers course is offered as a "model syllabus" by the National Women's Studies Association.

6. Karen Lehrman, "Our Minds, Ourselves: Is Feminist Education Limiting Her Potential?" *Mother Jones*, September/October 1993, p. 45. In response to Lehrman's critique of women's studies programs—which she accuses of being rigidly ideological and extremist—Susan Faludi wrote a condescending reply, published in the November/December issue of the magazine. "Maybe, just maybe," Faludi wrote, "having one's intuition respected is a bit more crucial to the average young woman's educational growth than mastery of a dead language," an ironic statement coming from a writer who has criticized other feminists for promoting sexist stereotypes of women as ultrasensitive, "intuitive" beings. On the other hand, women's studies professor and author Elizabeth Fox-Genovese wrote that she read Lehrman's piece "with a sigh of recognition," and that it's time for the field to thrive as "something more than a jealous and exclusive clique."

7. Many women's studies programs would argue that they do acknowledge varying degrees of oppression, particularly the experiences of minority women. And they do. In fact, many women's studies programs have become so enamored with portraying minority women as victims of double oppression (triple if they happen to be lesbian) that it would seem the defining characteristic of being a minority woman today is martyrdom. As Hazel V. Carby wrote in the September/October 1990 issue of *Ms.*: "Feminism in the university has created an essential black female subject for its own consumption; it is a figure that can be used as an example of the most victimized of the victims of patriarchal oppression, or as an example of the most noble of noble womanhood that endured: Faulkner's Dilsey reborn." Rather than truly acknowledging diversity—including differences in how black women feel about feminism—this ultra-oppressed female subject acts, in Carby's words, as a "hair shirt with which she [white women] can beat herself over the head and can then feel self-satisfied and politically correct." And while many in women's studies point proudly to

their inclusion of works by black and other minority women, the truth is often that they teach only those writers who happen to adhere to the current feminist agenda, such as bell hooks, Cheryl Clarke, and the late Audre Lorde. In many introductory women's studies courses, for example, teachings on minority women are confined to essays and poems from the oft-assigned *This Bridge Called My Back: Writings by Radical Women of Color*, which includes Cheryl Clarke's essay "Lesbianism: An Act of Resistance." Much of the work in this book takes an adamantly revolutionary stance—as in overthrowing capitalism and destroying the "institution of heterosexuality." To say that these writers represent the views of the majority of women, minority or not, is absurd.

8. U.S. Department of Labor, Bureau of Labor Statistics, Current Population Survey, 1992 annual averages. Women also represent 41 percent of all managerial and professional specialty occupations, 33 percent of college and university teachers, and 50 percent of social scientists and urban planners. On the other hand, we represent a measly 8.9 percent of engineers, architects and surveyors, only 10 percent of police and detectives, and so few of us are judges that we don't even merit a statistical reading.

9. Sasha Soreff, "Gender of the Table," *Barnard Bulletin*, May 5, 1993, p. 17. According to other articles in this issue on the conference—held on April 24, 1993—the subject of female difference came up frequently. For example, Betty Ellerin, a judge for the New York State Supreme Court Appellate Division, made sweeping claims about women judges being more sensitive and understanding. "Women humanize the justice system . . . with more women as judges we will have less biased courts and a greater commitment to justice and values," she stated. In rebuttal, Carol Berkman, a trial judge for the New York State Supreme Court, said, "In trying to achieve equality you don't want to lose good qualities such as compassion and caring, but labeling them as specifically women's characteristics can be a trap."

10. Erna Olafson Hellerstein, Leslie Parker Hume, and Karen M. Offen, eds., *Victorian Women: A Documentary Account of Women's Lives in Nineteenth-Century England, France, and the United States* (Stanford University Press, 1981), pp. 164–165.

11. Elsa Gidlow, "The Spiritual Significance of the Self-Identified

Woman," in *Issues in Feminism: A First Course in Women's Studies*, ed. Sheila Ruth (Mayfield Publishing Company, 1990), p. 416.

12. Walter E. Houghton, *The Victorian Frame of Mind 1830–1870* (Yale University Press, 1957), p. 351, footnote 27.

13. Eleanor Flexner, *Century of Struggle: The Woman's Rights Movement in the United States* (Harvard University Press, 1959), pp. 148–149. This is an excellent account of the first women's movement in the United States.

14. There are several different strains of feminist difference theory. Some theorists, such as the highly influential Nancy Chodorow, take a psychoanalytical focus on mothering, making sweeping claims that the mother-daughter relationship makes women more empathic and nonhierarchical, while men, who separate from their mothers, are more individualistic and competitive. Others, such as Carol Gilligan, also espouse that women are more caring and ethical, but they offer little to explain why. And many, following a school of feminist thought developed by French feminists such as Luce Irigaray and Hélène Cixous, focus heavily on language (as it forms thought) as the model for gender differences. These feminists believe in celebrating supposed female difference—which is often presented as immutable—through developing a "feminine" language in writing. For an anthology of feminist writings on difference, see Hester Eisenstein and Alice Jardine, eds., *The Future of Difference* (Rutgers University Press, 1990). For examples of work by French feminists, see Robyn R. Warhol and Diane Price Herndl, eds., *Feminisms: An Anthology of Literary Theory and Criticism* (Rutgers University Press, 1991).

15. Catharine R. Stimpson, *Women's Studies in the United States* (Ford Foundation, 1986), p. 40.

16. Gilligan's book is the product of three separate studies. The first is a "college student survey" of twenty-five students chosen from a class on moral and political choice, which is not representative of all college students. The second is an "abortion decision study" of twenty-nine women referred from clinics; no effort was made to obtain a representative sample. The third is a "rights and responsibility study" of 144 people ages six through sixty, with more intensive interviews done on a subsample of 36. In all three studies, the questions were designed to uncover differences in how women and men deal with

moral conflict. Many were hypothetical. One question posed to two eight-year-old children, for example, asked them to describe a situation "in which they were not sure of what was the right thing to do." See if you can figure out which response is the girl's and which is the boy's: (1) "When I really want to go to my friends and my mother is cleaning the cellar, I think about my friends, and then I think about my mother, and then I think about the right thing to do" and (2) "I have a lot of friends, and I can't always play with all of them, so everybody's going to have to take a turn, because they're all my friends." According to Gilligan, these responses illustrate two dramatically "contrasting" moral reasonings. The first one, which is from the boy, supposedly sets up "a hierarchical ordering." The second one, which is from the girl, is said to describe "a network of relationships." Much of the book is composed of blanket interpretations of vague responses such as these, which are then reduced to sweeping claims about gender differences. Aside from the question of how people, especially children, will often tailor their answers to please the surveyor, Gilligan's work is unrepresentative as well as questionably interpreted. She herself writes that she makes no claims that her book can be applied to a "wider population, across cultures, or through time," which raises the question of just what it does apply to. See Carol Gilligan, *In a Different Voice* (Harvard University Press, 1982), esp. pp. 1–4 and 32–33.

17. According to Suzanne Fields, "No Different from the Men," *Insight*, November 16, 1992, p. 19.

18. Gary Smalley and John Trent, *The Language of Love* (Focus on the Family Publishing, 1988), as cited in Carol Tavris, *The Mismeasure of Woman* (Simon & Schuster, 1992), p. 47.

19. Le Anne Schreiber, "The Search for His and Her Brains," *Glamour*, April 1993, p. 234. For more debunking of the corpus callosum theory, see Tavris, *The Mismeasure of Woman*, pp. 43–56.

20. Tavris, *The Mismeasure of Woman*, p. 55.

21. Anne Fausto-Sterling, *Myths of Gender: Biological Theories About Women and Men* (Basic Books, 1985), p. 215.

22. Ibid., p. 214.

23. Schreiber, "The Search for His and Her Brains," p. 234.

24. John S. Haller and Robin M. Haller, *The Physician and Sexuality in Victorian America* (W. W. Norton, 1977), pp. 48–52. These pseudoscientific theories were used quite effectively against women, who were also said to have smaller brains. When scientists were confronted with the fact that women actually have slightly larger brains in proportion to body weight, they quickly changed their tactics and began arguing that the shape of women's brains is different, making them more infantile and emotional.

25. Schreiber, "The Search for His and Her Brains," p. 237.

26. Fausto-Sterling, *Myths of Gender*, pp. 158, 194–195.

27. Charlotte Bunch, *Learning Our Way*, 1983, as cited in *Issues in Feminism*, p. 3.

28. Bureau of the Census, Current Population Reports, series P-60 (annual), as cited by William Strauss and Neil Howe, *Generations: The History of America's Future 1584 to 2069* (William Morrow and Company, 1991), p. 327.

29. Hellerstein, Hume, and Offen, eds., *Victorian Women*, p. 140.

Chapter 6:
The Passive Voice

1. Jo Freeman, "Feminism vs. Family Values," *Off Our Backs*, January 1993, p. 2, Ireland quote, p. 14.

2. "Women Watch," *Off Our Backs*, August/September 1992, and Jo Freeman, "Feminism vs. Family Values," p. 11.

3. The commercial Holtzman released accused Ferraro of taking more than $300,000 in rent from a pornographer who was a tenant in a building owned by her husband and a partner—the pornographer had alleged ties to the mob. See Alison Mitchell, "Feminists Attack Holtzman on Ads in Senate Race," *New York Times*, August 27, 1992. See also Todd S. Purdum, "The Feminist Paradox," *New York Times*, August 30, 1992.

4. Jane Gross, "Does She Speak for Today's Women?" *New York Times Magazine*, March 1, 1992. See also Nadine Brozan, "Smeal and

Goldsmith Fight for Leadership of NOW," *New York Times*, June 8, 1985. One of the things Smeal was arguing for was emphasis on the recently failed ERA. Goldsmith said that pushing the ERA during the Reagan years would be an "exercise in futility," an assessment that was proven true throughout Smeal's presidency. For some history on NOW, see Winifred D. Wandersee, *On the Move: American Women in the 1970s* (Twayne Publishers, 1988), pp. 36–54; also Marcia Cohen, *The Sisterhood: The Inside Story of the Women's Movement and the Leaders Who Made it Happen* (Fawcett Columbine, 1988). For NOW's work on the ERA, see Jane J. Mansbridge, *Why We Lost the ERA* (University of Chicago Press, 1986).

5. After taking Goldsmith's office, Smeal asserted that it was "time to go back into the streets" after the political lobbying that characterized Goldsmith's presidency. See Judy Klemesrud, "New Head of NOW Prefers Activism," *New York Times*, July 22, 1985. Today, NOW's position remains the same. See, for example, Felicity Barringer, "NOW Reasserts Its Role as Outsider," *New York Times*, January 12, 1992, and Nina J. Easton, "I'm Not a Feminist But . . . ," *Los Angeles Times Magazine*, February 2, 1992.

6. Evelyn Nieves, "With Rising Voice, Acting Head of Feminist Group Assumes Mantle," *New York Times*, July 7, 1991. See also Judy Klemesrud, "NOW's President: Assessing the Election," *New York Times*, July 27, 1985. According to this article, there were some rather disturbing questions about a faulty sample ballot distributed by Smeal's campaign that saw the election stopped, the ballots thrown away, and the procedure started from scratch again. This gave Smeal's campaign several more hours to lobby, which may have helped her win. Smeal's side denied deliberately putting out the inaccurate ballot. Goldsmith said "It's not a mistake that would easily be made," and that seemed "to go beyond coincidence."

7. For Ireland on legislation, see Megan Rosenfeld, "The NOW and Future Feminist," *Washington Post*, January 11, 1992. For NOW civil disobedience, see Beth Corbin and Loretta Kane, "NOW National Conference Launches Bold Political Agenda for the '90s" and "We Won't Go Back," both in the *National NOW Times*, Summer 1991, pp. 1, 15.

8. Allison Busch, "Feminists Arrested at White House Protest of Casey Supreme Court Decision," *National NOW Times*, August 1992,

p. 1, and "Women Watch," *Off Our Backs*, August/September 1992. For another example of Ireland getting arrested, see Katharine Loos, "Elders' Surgeon General Confirmation Stalled by Republican Senators," *National NOW Times*, August 1993, p. 1. In this case, Ireland was arrested in front of the White House while protesting the non-lifting of the military ban against lesbians and gays.

9. Julianne Malveaux, "A Change in Direction for Feminists?" *Oregonian*, July 3, 1993. While NOW often proudly points to a jump in their membership following the Clarence Thomas hearings, what they seldom mention is that the previous years saw a precipitous dip in their rolls. In 1982, NOW had a membership of roughly 200,000—a number that was to plummet to 115,000 within three years. The controversy over abortion rights during the Bush years saw membership rise back up to a current 270,000, but without a strong focus on economic issues, it's difficult to tell if NOW will be able to keep even this small base of support. For NOW's membership from 1981 to 1990, see Gary Hoover, et al., ed., *Hoover's Handbook* (The Reference Press, Inc., 1990), p. 392.

10. For example, a *Time*/CNN poll conducted by the Yankelovich company on October 23–25, 1989, asked women to identify issues that are very important to them. Ninety-four percent identified equal pay; 90 percent, day care; 88 percent, rape; 84 percent, maternity leave at work; 82 percent, job discrimination; 74 percent, abortion; and 49 percent, sexual freedom. See Claudia Wallis, "Onward, Women!" *Time*, December 4, 1989, p. 82.

11. Take the Freedom of Choice Act, proposed legislation at the time of this writing. This measure would put the constitutional right to abortion into federal law and prohibit state restrictions such as waiting periods (the Casey ruling that Ireland was arrested protesting) and reporting demands imposed on doctors. It is supported by groups such as the National Abortion Rights Action League. But in July of 1993, the National Organization for Women pulled their backing from the act, and in August, it passed a resolution to fight it. Why? Amendments allowing states to refuse to fund Medicaid abortions and impose parental notification were added to the bill. Supporters of the act note that unless parental notification remains a state option, Congress may try to force a national parental involvement bill—which could very well pass—and that the Freedom of Choice Act

could not alone restore Medicaid funding for abortions; that money has to come from the appropriations process. Though lifting parental notification and obtaining funding for abortions are important issues to work for, the Freedom of Choice Act offers a constructive start toward increasing the availability of abortion and protecting our rights. But this doesn't seem to concern NOW, which would rather the act fail than pass a law not meeting their sweeping all-or-nothing demands. At the time of this writing, it appears that the bill is dead in the water. See Beth Corbin, "Braun Withdraws Support for FOCA at NOW Request" and 1993 NOW National Conference Resolutions, "Opposing the Fake Freedom of Choice Act," *National NOW Times*, August 1993, pp. 5, 12. See also Stephen Chapman, "Freedom of Choice Bill Shoved to Far Back Burner," *Oregonian*, July 21, 1993; Robin Toner, "Success Spoils Unity of Abortion Rights Groups," *New York Times*, April 20, 1993, and "Freedom of Choice Act in Peril," editorial, *New York Times*, July 17, 1993.

12. Mary Voboril, "1992: Year of Small Steps for Womankind," *Oregonian*, January 2, 1993.

13. Sara Rimer, "Ordinary Women Receive a Tribute from Feminists," *New York Times*, July 5, 1993. Ireland's supporters inside NOW actually cited the bean-counting episode as one of the major successes of her presidency so far. See Indira A. R. Lakshmanan, "For Many Feminists, It's NOW or Never," *Oregonian*, July 3, 1993.

14. Lakshmanan, "For Many Feminists, It's NOW or Never."

15. Malveaux, "A Change in Direction for Feminists?"

16. Judy Klemesrud, "New Head of NOW Prefers Activism," *New York Times*, July 22, 1985.

17. For Eleanor Smeal's reasoning for the third party, see Ellie Smeal, "Why I Support a New Party," *Ms.*, January/February 1991, p. 72. For criticisms of the third-party idea leveled at NOW from women politicians, see Barbara Vobejda, "At 25, NOW Still Defining Feminism, Deflecting Critics," *Washington Post*, January 11, 1992.

18. "The Convention You Didn't See on TV," *Off Our Backs*, November 1992, p. 6.

19. David S. Broder, "Diversity in Women's Views Joins Their Ascent to Power," *Oregonian*, July 18, 1993. The National Women's Political

Caucus is a multipartisan organization, meaning it will endorse candidates from any party provided they meet its requirements. According to its "Candidate Endorsement Policy," a candidate must meet the following requirements: (1) support passage of the ERA; (2) support abortion rights as established by *Roe* v. *Wade*; (3) support public policies that guarantee equal access to abortion and to a full range of reproductive health services, including those under public funding; (4) support increased access to child care programs; (5) have a past record indicating support for NWPC's goals and bottom-line issues if she has held other elective office; (6) be willing to make the NWPC endorsement known; (7) be someone the NWPC should support regardless of the outcome of the present race. According to an NWPC fact sheet titled "NWPC and Women Candidates in 1992," the group donated more than half a million dollars to women running for office that year.

20. Sylvia Nasar, "Women's Progress Stalled? It Just Isn't So," *New York Times*, October 18, 1992. One reason for the closing pay gap is that, unlike our mothers, women of my generation expect to enter the workforce and are more educated and better prepared to do so. For example, this article notes that while only 7 percent of all professional degrees were earned by women in 1971, today the number is up to a third. For other examples of misinformation in Faludi's book, see Gretchen Morgenson, "A Whiner's Bible," *Forbes*, March 16, 1992, p. 152. Morgenson tears into several of Faludi's claims, including that the proportion of women applying to business schools shrank in the late eighties (according to the American Assembly of Collegiate Schools of Business it has steadily increased) and that women "poured" into low-paid "female work ghettos" (Faludi's proof of this is a statistic showing an increase of three-tenths of 1 percent of women in the secretarial pool).

21. Stanley Rothman, Stephen Powers, and David Rothman, "Feminism in Films," *Society*, March/April 1993, p. 66. Coders scored each film on questions such as goals of the characters and overall treatment of the characters. The coders were primarily female college students and used a detailed codebook along with instructions. One of their findings was that women characters in nontraditional occupations rose from 49 percent to 61 percent of all female roles from 1976 to 1989; among women in starring and supporting roles, it rose to 72 percent. Another interesting finding is that professional women are

often presented in a more favorable light than men in the same occupations. For example, 73 percent of female characters portraying businesswomen in films since 1980 received a positive character rating, compared with only 30 percent of male characters portraying businessmen.

22. Ellen Goodman, "N.Y. Senate Campaign Showed Women Are Not Above the Fray," *Oregonian*, September 29, 1992.

23. Stephen Chapman, "Why Did Feminists Bash Hutchison?" *Oregonian*, June 13, 1993.

24. Gloria Steinem, "Gloria Steinem Finds Lesson for Congress in Packwood Case," statement released December 3, 1992, from Steinem's press office at *Ms.* magazine. Steinem begins her statement by asserting, "We all deserve to have our lives judged in context." She goes on to claim that Packwood "has not been hypocritical" because he admitted to offending the dignity of the women who worked for him. Packwood is pro-choice and this earned him campaign endorsements in the past from NOW, NARAL, as well as fund-raising letters from Steinem. Within a few months of releasing this statement, however, Steinem seemed to change her mind. She made a trip to Portland, Oregon, in support of the women who had accused Packwood of misconduct, and she was one of the sponsors of a September 1993 fund-raising event for the women, held, ironically, in the same house where Packwood once attended a birthday party for *Ms.* magazine. See Rose Ellen O'Connor and Dee Lane, "Packwood Retains Political Clout," *Oregonian*, September 26, 1993.

25. Chapman, "Why Did Feminists Bash Hutchison?" The following quote from Chapman is also from this column.

26. Ellen Goodman, "Women Politicians Set Themselves Up for a Fall," *Oregonian*, December 22, 1992.

27. Contribution to Ann Richards, see Charles Kaiser, "Women on the Verge," *Vogue*, March 1992, p. 404. For NOW's maximum contribution, see Alice Cohan, "NOW/PAC Elect Women for a Change a Huge Success," *National NOW Times*, January 1993, p. 2.

28. Karen Lehrman, "The Year of the Sexist Woman," *Wall Street Journal*, October 13, 1992.

29. Sonia Johnson, "Taking Our Eyes Off the Guys," in *The Sexual*

Liberals and the Attack on Feminism, ed. Dorchen Leidholdt and Janice G. Raymond (Pergamon Press 1990), p. 59.

30. John S. Haller and Robin M. Haller, *The Physician and Sexuality in Victorian America* (W. W. Norton 1974), p.79.

31. "A Women's Declaration of Interdependence," Women's Environment and Development Organization (WEDO) of the Women's Foreign Policy Council, *Woman of Power*, Spring 1991, p. 30.

32. Kim Bartlett, "Of Meat and Men: A Conversation with Carol Adams," *The Animals Agenda*, October 1990, p. 13.

33. Cited by Ynestra King, "Healing the Wounds: Feminism, Ecology, and the Nature-Culture Dualism," *Reweaving the World*, ed. Irene Diamond and Gloria Feman Orenstein (Sierra Club Books, 1990), p. 110.

34. Cited in Jennifer Sells and Helen Cordes, "New Goddess Worship Troubles Skeptics: Is There a Danger of a New Eco-orthodoxy?" *Utne Reader*, May/June 1991, p. 20.

35. Marilyn French, *Beyond Power: On Women, Men, and Morals* (Ballantine Books, 1985), p. 443.

36. "Liberal Learning and the Women's Studies Major: A Report to the Profession," National Women's Studies Association, 1991, p. 4.

Chapter 7:
Repeating History

1. Gayle Rubin, "The Leather Menace: Comments on Politics and S/M," in *Coming to Power*, edited by members of SAMOIS, a lesbian/feminist S/M organization (Alyson Publications, 1987), p. 217. Rubin's essay on the current feminist descent into antisex morality provides insights on the issue of lesbian S&M. On one side—the feminist majority—are leaders such as Susan Griffin, who attack those who engage in dominance and submission sex as having a "disease," and Diana Russell, who claims that "defending such behavior as healthy . . . is about the most contra-feminist anti-political and bourgeois stance I can imagine." On the other side—an often ostracized minority—are lesbian-feminists such as Rubin, who argue

that the feminist intrusion into people's personal lives is "stupid and regressive." *Sadomasochism* certainly is a loaded word in our culture, and, thanks to some feminists, it is shrouded in even more shame and silence than before. But the fact is that many people will engage in S&M sex at one time or another, whether playing around with silk scarves or acting out fantasies. They are not diseased or unhealthy, and neither are the women in SAMOIS.

2. The French Victorian woman was Marie LaFarge, and the full quote is: "I was mute, because I knew that a young girl ought to be concerned about others without pretending to concern them with herself, and that she ought to use her good sense to listen gracefully and hold her tongue intelligently." See Bonnie S. Anderson and Judith P. Zinsser, *A History of Their Own: Women in Europe*, vol. 2 (Harper & Row, 1988), p. 157. For the practice of dressing girls as miniature ladies, sometimes complete with corsets, see James Laver, *The Concise History of Costume and Fashion* (Harry N. Abrams Inc., n.d.), pp. 162–163.

3. Pamela Horn, *Victorian Countrywomen* (Basil Blackwell, Inc., 1991), p. 9.

4. John S. Haller and Robin M. Haller, *The Physician and Sexuality in Victorian America* (W. W. Norton & Company, 1977), pp. 76–87.

5. Horn, *Victorian Countrywomen*, p. 65.

6. W. J. Reader, *Life in Victorian England* (B.T. Batsford, Ltd., 1964), p. 142. For more on girls raised in sexual ignorance, see Anderson and Zinsser, *A History of Their Own*, pp. 160–161.

7. Bowdler's popularity is cited in Walter E. Houghton, *The Victorian Frame of Mind 1830–1870* (Yale University Press, 1957), p. 357. For diaries of Victorian girls, see Anderson and Zinsser, *A History of Their Own*, p. 161.

8. Erna Olafson Hellerstein, Leslie Parker Hume, and Karen M. Offen, eds., *Victorian Women: A Documentary Account of Women's Lives in Nineteenth-Century England, France, and the United States* (Stanford University Press, 1981), p. 177. Not all Victorian writers, however, were as strictly prudish as Acton. Many recognized that sexual desire could exist in women and were more concerned about channeling it into reproduction in marriage. For example, American

Victorian William Sanger, excerpted in the above work (pp. 415–416), claimed that desire existed in a "slumbering state" in women until "aroused by some outside influences." But no matter the influence, Sanger wrote: "the full force of sexual desire is seldom known to a virtuous woman."

9. Haller and Haller, *The Physician and Sexuality in Victorian America*, p. 100.

10. Ibid., pp. 102–105.

11. Ronald G. Walters, ed., *Primers for Prudery: Sexual Advice to Victorian America* (Spectrum Books, 1974), p. 69. It was commonly believed that should women develop the same sexual desires as men, prostitution and illegitimacy would be rife; for this reason, a woman with sexual feelings was considered debased and immoral. Many tracts discussed "nymphomania" in lurid detail, espousing that female masturbation was a sign of this illness and even advocating clitorectomies (surgical removal of the clitoris) as a cure. See Barbara Ehrenreich and Deirdre English, *Complaints and Disorders: The Sexual Politics of Sickness* (The Feminist Press, 1973), pp. 32–35.

12. Hellerstein, Hume, and Offen, eds., *Victorian Women*, p. 176.

13. John D'Emilio and Estelle B. Freedman, *Intimate Matters: A History of Sexuality in America* (Harper & Row, 1988), pp. 80–81.

14. Mary Lyndon Shanley, *Feminism, Marriage, and the Law in Victorian England* (Princeton University Press, 1989), pp. 8–14.

15. Anderson and Zinsser, *A History of Their Own*, p. 159.

16. For the economic status of single women, see Shanley, *Feminism, Marriage, and the Law in Victorian England*, pp. 9–10. The harsh lives of servants was often frankly admitted to. A somewhat defensive account of the then recently demised Victorian era by Esmé Wingfield-Stratford, *Those Earnest Victorians* (William Morrow & Company, 1930), pp. 108–109, notes chillingly: "And however much you might sentimentalise over some delicate young lady in ringlets, once let her father lose his bank balance, and her lot, as governess, might well be one of brutal and completely unsentimental exploitation."

17. Anderson and Zinsser, *A History of Their Own*, p. 150.

18. Shanley, *Feminism, Marriage, and the Law in Victorian England*, p. 9.

19. Horn, *Victorian Countrywomen*, p. 64.

20. This is from a popular poem at the time titled "The Angel in the House," written by Coventry Patmore. The poem is printed in Hellerstein, Hume, and Offen, eds., *Victorian Women*, pp. 134–140.

21. Anderson and Zinsser, *A History of Their Own*, p. 153, and Ehrenreich and English, *Complaints and Disorders*, pp. 20–21.

22. Ehrenreich and English, *Complaints and Disorders*, p. 22.

23. Houghton, *The Victorian Frame of Mind 1830–1870*, p. 355.

24. Ibid., p. 352. This is cited from an 1889 document titled "An Appeal Against Female Suffrage," signed by about one hundred women.

25. Walters, ed., *Primers for Prudery*, p. 66.

26. A particularly horrifying story related by a Victorian physician dealt with a stout woman who laced herself very tightly into a new corset and went off to church. On the way, she was stricken with intense pains and, typically ignorant of reproduction, was convinced she was about to deliver a child. After retreating home and spending a day fruitlessly trying to deliver, a doctor was called in, and the real source of cramps was easily found. She was told that if she wore that corset again, he might have to "deliver" her womb. For this story and all other information on corsets cited, see Haller and Haller, *The Physician and Sexuality in Victorian America*, pp. 146–174.

27. Ehrenreich and English, *Complaints and Disorders*, pp. 15, 21–22.

28. Haller and Haller, *The Physician and Sexuality in Victorian America*, p. 151.

29. Ibid., pp. 143–144.

30. Anderson and Zinsser, *A History of Their Own*, p. 366.

31. The discrepancy was largely due to constant outbreaks of cholera, typhus, and other epidemic diseases in the slums. Writers of the time paint pictures of the city's poor crowded into filthy tenements, the narrow streets outside their doors a fetid swamp of human waste and rotting garbage; "all the debris of the apartments, or nearly so, was

thrown from the windows into the streets . . . floating in the stream were the entrails of cats and horses, and the other putrifying animal matter." The Thames was referred to as the "Great Stink," with an estimated 250 tons of untreated fecal matter flushed into it daily by 1857. Cartoons depicted the river as a thick, bubbling black swamp carrying the rotting carcasses of pigs and other animals. The epidemic diseases resulting from this unclean water, along with prostitution, gambling, and incest, were thought to rise from pestilent "miasmas." It was generally acknowledged that filthy living conditions and poverty created these noxious gases, but the belief that moral degeneration was catching—literally rising off poor people as invisible gases to spread to the better parts of town—did not make things congenial between the classes. See A. Susan Williams, *The Rich Man and the Diseased Poor in Early Victorian Literature* (Humanities Press International, 1987), p. 14. For life expectancy, p. 4.

32. Horn, *Victorian Countrywomen*, p. 141.

33. Anderson and Zinsser, *A History of Their Own*, pp. 255–256.

34. Ibid., pp. 262–263. See also Horn, *Victorian Countrywomen*, pp. 192–209.

35. D'Emilio and Freedman, *Intimate Matters*, pp. 245, 215–221; Ehrenreich and English, *Complaints and Disorders*, pp. 45–70; and Linda Gordon, *Woman's Body, Woman's Right: Birth Control in America* (Penguin Books, 1977), pp. 274–282.

36. Reader, *Life in Victorian England*, pp. 140–142.

37. Betty Friedan, *The Feminine Mystique* (Dell Publishing Co., 1963), pp. 76–77.

38. Anderson and Zinsser, *A History of Their Own*, pp. 361–366.

39. For a history of American early feminism, see Eleanor Flexner, *Century of Struggle: The Woman's Rights Movement in the United States* (Harvard University Press, 1959) and Olivia Coolidge, *Women's Rights: The Suffrage Movement in America 1848–1920* (E. P. Dutton & Co., 1966). For writings by feminists of the time, see the National American Woman Suffrage Association, *Woman Suffrage: Arguments and Results* (Kraus Reprint Co., 1910) and Ellen Carol DuBois, ed., *Elizabeth Cady Stanton/Susan B. Anthony: Correspondence, Writings, Speeches* (Schocken Books, 1981).

40. For more on the social purity movements, see Gordon, *Woman's Body, Woman's Right*, pp. 116–126, and D'Emilio and Freedman, *Intimate Matters*, pp. 150–156.

41. I am indebted to Judith R. Walkowitz's work on social purity feminism for this section, including her books *City of Dreadful Delight: Narratives of Sexual Danger in Late-Victorian London* (University of Chicago Press, 1992) and *Prostitution and Victorian Society: Women, Class, and the State* (Cambridge University Press, 1980). Her essay "Male Vice and Female Virtue: Feminism and the Politics of Prostitution in Nineteenth-Century Britain," in *Powers of Desire: The Politics of Sexuality*, ed. Ann Snitow, Christine Stansell, and Sharon Thompson (Monthly Review Press, 1983), pp. 419–438, is an excellent summary of the English suffragist purity crusades.

42. Walkowitz, "Male Vice and Female Virtue," pp. 422–423.

43. For broad definitions and the spectrum of prostitution, see Kathy Peiss, "'Charity Girls' and City Pleasures: Historical Notes on Working Class Sexuality, 1880–1920," in *Powers of Desire*, pp. 74–87. This essay focuses on a subculture of working women known at the time as "charity girls," who had premarital sex for gifts, attention, or just pleasure (thus "giving" it away). As Peiss notes, charity girls did not necessarily face the stigma of the "fallen woman" so prevalent in the middle class. See also Lois W. Banner, *Women in Modern America: A Brief History* (Harcourt Brace Jovanovich, Inc., 1974), pp. 75–83. For another look at working class sexual morality, see Françoise Barret-Ducrocq, *Love in the Time of Victoria: Sexuality and Desire Among Working-Class Men and Women in Nineteenth-Century London*, trans. John Howe (Penguin Books, 1992).

44. Walkowitz, *City of Dreadful Delight*, p. 92.

45. Walkowitz, "Male Vice and Female Virtue," p. 425.

46. Ibid., pp. 425–427.

47. Walkowitz, *City of Dreadful Delight*, pp. 104–105. The "Maiden Tribute" articles ran in early July 1885. A month later—on August 22—a demonstration estimated at 250,000 strong was held in Hyde Park. Along with suffragists and Anglican bishops, socialists, temperance workers, and trade unionists all took part in the mass demonstration.

48. Walkowitz, "Male Vice and Female Virtue," p. 427.

49. For more on the life of prostitutes, see D'Emilio and Freedman, *Intimate Matters*, pp. 50–51, 130–138, 208–215.

50. Walkowitz, "Male Vice and Female Virtue," p. 428.

51. Ibid. At that time, England already had a strong history of anti-porn activism under conservative direction. In 1857, the Obscene Publications Act had been passed, censoring works supposedly designed to corrupt "the morals of youth," because private organizations such as the Society for the Suppression of Vice ("a sale of poison more deadly than prussic acid") had been largely unsuccessful at stamping out sexual literature. For a history of censorship and pornography in England, see Walter M. Kendrick, *The Secret Museum* (Viking Books, 1987), pp. 115–117.

52. D'Emilio and Freedman, *Intimate Matters*, pp. 149–160.

53. Feminist critique of "preventive checks," see Walkowitz, *City of Dreadful Delight*, p. 134. Quote from American suffragist cited in Gordon, *Woman's Body, Woman's Right*, p. 97.

54. Walkowitz, "Male Vice and Female Virtue," p. 432.

55. Ibid., p. 431.

56. DuBois, ed., *Elizabeth Cady Stanton/Susan B. Anthony*, pp. 184–186.

57. Walkowitz, "Male Vice and Female Virtue," pp. 427, 433. In the United States in the early 1900s, a social purity panic over white slavery led to many repressive policies, including the White Slave Traffic, or Mann, Act of 1910. Supposedly intended to prevent the illicit trafficking of women for "immoral purposes," this was used to restrict lower-class women's lives. Noting that prostitution occurred among the lower classes, reformers put the blame for this "dastardly business" right on the shoulders of immigrants and blacks, feeding into campaigns to sterilize the "unfit." Between 1907 and 1917, sixteen states passed sterilization laws designed to prevent reproduction among undesirables. See D'Emilio and Freedman, *Intimate Matters*, pp. 208–215.

58. Varda Burstyn, "Political Precedents and Moral Crusades:

Women, Sex, and the State," in *Women Against Censorship*, ed. Varda Burstyn (Douglas & McIntyre, Ltd., 1985), pp. 12–13.

59. Walkowitz, "Male Vice and Female Virtue," p. 433.

60. Mari Jo Buhle and Paul Buhle, eds., *The Concise History of Woman Suffrage* (University of Illinois Press, 1978), p. 341.

61. Ibid., pp. 30–31. See also Gordon, *Women's Body, Woman's Right*, pp. 279–282.

62. Walkowitz, "Male Vice and Female Virtue," p. 432–433.

63. Walters, ed., *Primers for Prudery*, p. 67.

64. Walkowitz quote, see Walkowitz, "Male Vice and Female Virtue," p. 433. The suffragist slogan is cited in Anderson and Zinsser, *A History of Their Own*, p. 366.

65. Banner, *Women in Modern America*, p. 90.

66. D'Emilio and Freedman, *Intimate Matters*, p. 208.

67. Anderson and Zinsser, *A History of Their Own*, pp. 367–370, and Banner, *Women in Modern America*, pp. 146–154.

68. Varda Burstyn, "Political Precedents and Moral Crusades," p. 15.

69. For the history of the American birth-control movement, see Gordon, *Women's Body, Woman's Right*. As Gordon notes (p. 237), feminists, "especially older ones, feared sexual promiscuity. . . . They clung to notions that the human race had become oversexed, that sexual intercourse ought to be for reproduction, and that too much sexual activity was physically and spiritually weakening."

70. Ibid., p. 321.

71. Nancy L. Thomas, "The New In Loco Parentis," *Change*, September/October 1991, p. 33.

72. Ibid. This well-researched article explores the trend today to revive in loco parentis—essentially, acting as the parent—on college campuses. Much of this movement to revive in loco parentis, which was largely abandoned due to student rebellion in the late sixties, has been generated through concern over date rape. At Boston University, for instance, a new policy was passed in 1988. Along with restrictions against drinking, no overnight guests of the opposite sex were to

be allowed in dorms, and curfews of 11:00 P.M. on weekdays and 1:00 A.M. on Fridays and Sundays were to be imposed. Student reaction to the alcohol policy was minimal, but reaction to parietals was heated and loud. Students charged that the policies violated their rights of freedom to associate and right to privacy; this led to postponement of the policies. But in 1989, an only slightly revised code of conduct went into effect. Students are now allowed overnight guests of the opposite sex—but only if that guest is a family member. Other universities that have adopted policies restricting overnight guests of the opposite sex are Kentucky State University and the University of South Carolina.

73. See "Policy Nixes Harassment and Faculty-Student Romance," an information sheet on policies at the University of Iowa, from the Center for Women Policy Studies; Leon Botstein, John Boswell, Joan Blythe, William Kerrigan, "New Rules About Sex on Campus: Should Professors Be Denied Admission to Student's Beds," *Harpers*, September 1993, p. 33; and Jane Gross, "Love or Harassment? Campuses Bar (and Debate) Faculty-Student Sex," *New York Times*, April 14, 1993. As the *Times* article notes, these policies "are often inspired by feminists on campus, who point to the inherent power imbalance between a professor who gives grades and writes recommendations and an impressionable young woman. . . ." It's true that there may be a "power imbalance" between, say, a forty-year-old professor and a twenty-year-old student. But many relationships women have outside of college can be said to have "power imbalances," if the man makes more money, has more power, or, heaven forbid, is her boss. To make the leap from this to saying adult women are too "impressionable" to consent is an insult to both parties in a relationship. What is amusing about the new campus policies against consensual faculty/student relationships is that quite a few of the faculty members who voted for them are married to ex-students.

74. For an excellent analysis of the failure to pass the ERA—and an honest appraisal of the lack of effective organizing and tactics on the part of feminists—see Jane L. Mansbridge, *Why We Lost the ERA* (University of Chicago Press, 1986).

Chapter 8:
Why Young Women Are Abandoning the Movement

1. Linda Ellerbee, "Changing Times Should Ring Roe vs. Wade Alarm," *Oregonian*, July 7, 1992.

2. Cathy Young, "How They Spent Their Summer Vacation," *Heterodoxy*, September 1992, p. 1. For another example, see "Let's Get Real about Feminism," a roundtable discussion with Gloria Steinem, bell hooks, Naomi Wolf, and Urvashi Vaid, in *Ms.*, September/October 1993, p. 34. Discussing why young women are alienated from the movement, hooks weighed in with the claim that "A lot of women who go for the notion of equal rights cannot go for the notion of opposing patriarchy, because that means a fundamental opposition to the culture as a whole," while Vaid claimed it's because we're "homophobic." Naomi Wolf did bravely respond that a lot of the women she speaks to "aren't homophobic. But they are resistant to feminism because the word is synonymous with lesbianism in many parts of the country" and that "there's too much sexual judgement going on." This was quickly slapped down by hooks, who said she thought Wolf's comments were "racialized." Interestingly, this roundtable discussion was splashed on the cover of *Ms.* with the headline NO, FEMINISTS DON'T THINK ALIKE (WHO SAYS WE HAVE TO?) With the exception of Wolf, the answer to this question was made abundantly clear in the piece: Here are some feminist leaders who seem to think we should.

3. A reprint of this essay is available in Gloria Steinem, *Outrageous Acts and Everyday Rebellions* (New America Library, 1983), pp. 211–218.

4. Karen Avenoso, "Feminism's Newest Foot Soldiers," *Elle*, March 1993, p. 114.

5. From the office of UCLA's Higher Education Research Institute.

6. "High School and Beyond, Third Follow-up, 1986," *Digest of Education Statistics*, 1988, U.S. Department of Education, p. 334.

7. Claudia Wallis, "Onward, Women!" *Time*, December 4, 1989, p. 80.

8. Sylvia Nasar, "Women's Progress Stalled? It Just Isn't So," *New York Times*, October 18, 1992.

9. Ibid. See also "Now for a Woman's Point of View," *Time*, April 17, 1989, p. 51.

10. For the number of women in commercial sciences, see Elizabeth Culotta, "Women Struggle to Crack the Code of Corporate Culture," *Science* 260 (April 16, 1993): 398. While the 13 percent is for scientific industry as a whole (commercial work such as engineering, chemistry, and computer science), there is a tremendous variation in the number of women in each discipline. While women represent only 8.5 percent of engineers working outside of academia, for example, they represent 34 percent of the biological and life sciences. For the percentage of women in other fields, see Current Population Survey, Bureau of Labor Statistics, 1992.

11. See "Pipelines of Progress: A Status Report on the Glass Ceiling," U.S. Department of Labor, August 1992; Amy Saltzman, "Trouble at the Top," *U.S. News & World Report*, June 17, 1991, p. 40; Bill McAllister, "Glass Ceiling: Women Held Back in Government, Too," *New Orleans Times-Picayune*, October 29, 1992; and Louis Uchitelle, "In Economics, a Subtle Exclusion," *New York Times*, January 11, 1993.

12. Dan R. Dalton and Idalene F. Kesner, "Cracks in the Glass: The Silent Competence of Women," *Business Horizons*, March/April, 1993, p. 6.

13. Elizabeth Levitan Spaid, "Glass Ceiling Remains Thick at Companies' Top Levels," *Christian Science Monitor*, July 13, 1993, p. 9.

14. Nancy Gibbs, "The Dreams of Youth," *Time*, Special Issue; *Women: The Road Ahead*, Fall 1990, p. 13.

15. Katherine S. Newman, "No Room for the Young," *New York Times*, May 16, 1993.

16. Ibid.

17. From a report by the Economic Policy Institute, a Washington research firm, August 1993, cited in Bob Herbert, "No Job, No Dream," *New York Times*, September 8, 1993.

18. "Just Fix it!" *U.S. News & World Report*, February 22, 1993.

19. Ibid.

20. William Strauss and Neil Howe, *13th Generation: Abort, Retry, Ignore, Fail?* (Vintage Books, 1993), p. 94.

21. "A Shift in Who Owns Homes," *San Francisco Chronicle*, November 29, 1991, cited in Katherine Newman, *Declining Fortunes: The Withering of the American Dream* (Basic Books, 1993), pp. 30–31. See also "Home Ownership Found to Decline," *New York Times*, October 8, 1989.

22. Strauss and Howe, *13th Generation*, p. 94. See also Kent Paterson, "Costs, Not Causes, Are Fueling Student Protests Today," *Utne Reader*, May/June, 1990, p. 58.

23. Gary Putka, "College-Completion Rates Are Said to Decline Sharply," *Wall Street Journal*, July 28, 1989.

24. Ways and Means Committee, 1990, no. 1148, as cited in William Strauss and Neil Howe, *Generations: The History of America's Future 1584 to 2069* (William Morrow and Company, 1991), p. 327.

25. Current Population Reports, Bureau of the Census, series P-60 (annual), as cited in Strauss and Howe, *Generations*, p. 327. The federal poverty threshold is $7,141 for a one-person household and $14,343 for a four-person household.

26. There will probably always be a Social Security system, but after the baby boomers—a huge generation—get through with it, just how much will be left is open to question. In 1950, for instance, there were sixteen workers supporting every recipient of Social Security. Today there are only 3.3 workers to every recipient, and when the massive boomer generation moves as a bloc into retirement, this ratio will narrow even more. In short, far less money will be going into Social Security than leaving it. See Scott Shepard, "Sheer Numbers of Baby Boomers to Threaten Social Security," *Oregonian*, October 4, 1993. As this article further notes, the "same flood of future retirees that is straining the system, however, may join forces to preserve it."

27. Beth Frerking, "Women's Issues: Does Either Political Party Really Understand?" *Oregonian*, September 6, 1992, and Julianne Malveaux, "Feminists Fail to Find Agenda That Will Bind All Women," *Oregonian*, August 26, 1993.

28. "Just Fix It!" *U.S. News & World Report*, February 22, 1993.

29. Gibbs, "The Dreams of Youth," p. 13.

30. From the Centers for Disease Control, Youth Risk Behavior Survey 1990. This survey is of over 11,000 high school students.

31. Noni E. MacDonald et al., "High Risk STD/HIV Behavior Among College Students," *JAMA*, June 20, 1990, pp. 3155–3159. For a look at American college women's sexual activity, see Barbara A. DeBuono, M.D., et al., "Sexual Behavior of College Women in 1975, 1986, and 1989," *New England Journal of Medicine*, March 22, 1990, pp. 821–825. According to this survey, young women's sexual behavior has not diminished since the height of the sexual revolution. What has changed is increased condom usage.

32. See Anita Manning, "Gender Wars on Campus," *USA Today*, September 2, 1993, and Neil Patel, "Crying Rape in a Crowded Theatre," *Heterodoxy*, Summer 1993, p. 7.

31. Peter Hellman, "Crying Rape," *New York*, March 8, 1993, p. 32 and Neil Patel, "Crying Rape in a Crowded Theatre," *Heterodoxy*, Summer 1993.

34. Hilary Selden Illick, "Pro-Choice Movement Grows on Campus," *Utne Reader*, May/June 1990, p.60. See also Karen Houppert, "Wildflowers Among the Ivy," *Ms.*, September/October 1991, p. 52, and Students Organizing Students information package, received October 1993.

35. See Rebecca Walker, "Becoming the Third Wave," *Ms.*, January/February 1992, p. 39, and Avenoso, "Feminism's Newest Foot Soldiers," p. 114.

36. See "Riot Grrrls," *Off Our Backs*, February 1993, p. 6, and Dana Nasrallah, "Teenage Riot," *Spin*, November 1992, p. 78.

Chapter 9:
The Final Wave

1. Ellie Winninghoff, "Why Business Alone Can't Solve the Child Care Crisis," *Executive Female*, November/December 1992, p. 41. For

an excellent analysis of feminist involvement in the child-care issue, see Mary Frances Berry, *The Politics of Parenthood: Child Care, Women's Rights, and the Myth of the Good Mother* (Penguin Books, 1993).

2. Margery Leveen Sher and Gary Brown, "What to Do with Jenny," *Personnel Administrator*, April 1989, p. 31.

3. For more on this, see Alfred J. Kahn and Sheila B. Kamerman, *Child Care: Facing the Hard Choices* (Auburn House Publishing Company, 1987), pp. 246–247, 259–265.

4. This idea is detailed in Helen Blank and Gina Adams, "Head Start: A Beacon for Early Childhood Services," June 23, 1993. I received this paper from the Children's Defense Fund.

5. Doug Podolsky and Marjory Roberts, "Sorry, Not Sold in the U.S.," *U.S. News & World Report*, December 24, 1990, p. 65.

6. Eloise Salholz et al., "Politics and the Pill. Why birth-control options are limited," *Newsweek*, February 26, 1990, p. 42.

7. Richard Lincoln and Lisa Kaeser, "Whatever Happened to the Contraceptive Revolution?" *International Family Planning Perspectives* 13, no. 4 (December 1987): 143.

8. See Luigi Mastroianni, Jr., et al., "Development of Contraceptives—Obstacles and Opportunities," *New England Journal of Medicine*, February 15, 1990, pp. 482–484; Carl Djerassi, "The Bitter Pill," *Science* 245 (July 1989): 356–360; *The Contraception Report* 2, no. 4: 9–11; Louise Tyrer, "Contraception in the USA—An Unfavourable Climate," *IPPF Medical Bulletin* 20, no. 4 (August 1986): 1–3; Eloise Salholz et al., "Politics and the Pill," *Newsweek*, February 26, 1990, p. 42; Richard Lincoln and Lisa Kaeser, "Whatever Happened to the Contraceptive Revolution?" *International Family Planning Perspectives* 13, no. 4 (December 1987): 141–145; and C. Wayne Bardin, "Public Sector Contraceptive Development," *Technology in Society* 9 (1987): 289–305.

9. Nadean Bishop, "Abortion: The Controversial Choice," in *Women: A Feminist Perspective*, 4th ed., ed. Jo Freeman (Mayfield Publishing Company, 1989), p. 54.

10. RICO is hard to prosecute successfully because the plaintiffs have to establish that the party in question—in the NOW case, Operation

Rescue—is guilty of a serious felony: extortion. This means proving that it conspires to put the clinics out of business. Proving a conspiracy is something prosecutors have found difficult to do even with mobsters, and the antiabortionists have the added benefit of being able to argue that their demonstrations are protected speech. Interestingly, many liberals and civil rights activists have long argued against such a noneconomic interpretation of RICO, since the law imposes triple damages and legal fees. Even if found innocent, an activist group accused of racketeering could be driven out of business just by defending their right to free speech. Act Up and Earth First! both sided with Operation Rescue against NOW in the RICO case, fearing that their methods of protest could leave them open to charges (Earth First!, for example, could be accused of racketeering in trying to shut down the timber industry). What is baffling about NOW's use of RICO is why they would concentrate on such an ineffective method when the activities they accuse Operation Rescue of—arson, bombing, and threats—are already crimes. See Laura Mansnerus, "When Is Protest Not Protest? When You Call It Extortion," *New York Times*, January 30, 1994, and Diane Minor, "After Stunning Victory, *NOW v. Scheidler* Goes Back to Investigation, Litigation," *National NOW Times*, April 1994, p. 1.

11. Evelyn Nieves, "Jail Sentences for Sex Crimes Are Rarely Very Harsh," *New York Times*, May 2, 1993.

12. Federal Bureau of Investigations, Uniform Crime Reports, 1990.

13. Alice Vachss, "We Need to Go to War," *Parade*, June 27, 1993, p. 1.

INDEX